Internet
6 in 1

by Joe Kraynak and Joe Habraken

A Division of Macmillan Computer Publishing
201 West 103rd Street, Indianapolis, Indiana 46290 USA

Joe Kraynak - To my wife, Cecie Kraynak, for doing everything else while I wrote.

Joe Habraken - To my parents Carolyn and Joe: My mom's love of the written word inspired me to write, and my dad's strong work ethic helps me get up every morning and actually do it.

International Standard Book Number: 0-7897-1338-1

Library of Congress Catalog Card Number: 97-68677

99 98 97   8 7 6 5 4 3 2

Interpretation of the printing code: the rightmost double-digit number is the year of the book's first printing; the rightmost single-digit number is the number of the book's printing. For example, a printing code of 97-1 shows that this copy of the book was printed during the first printing of the book in 1997.

Screen reproductions in this book were created by means of the program Collage Complete from Inner Media, Inc, Hollis, NH.

Printed in the United States of America

Acknowledgments

Joe Kraynak would like to thank the following hard-working people at Que for their contributions to this book: Jill Byus (Acquisitions Editor) for finding the right mix of people to make this book, Henly Wolin (Product Development Specialist) for his insightful comments and Internet expertise, Katie Purdum (Production Editor) for deftly steering the manuscript through editorial and production, and the entire production team for transforming a collection of loose pages and pictures into an attractive, bound book.

Creating a book like this requires a team effort from a number of highly skilled and dedicated professionals. **Joe Habraken** would like to thank all the professionals at Que who were involved with the production of this book. A special thanks to Jill Byus for all her hard work while organizing the project and assembling the author team. Also, hats off to Henly Wolin, the developer for the project. And finally, a very heartfelt thanks to Katie Purdum, the production editor, who put in long hours and worked extremely hard to make sure that this book would turn out to be very special.

Trademark Acknowledgments

We'd Like to Hear from You!

Que Corporation has a long-standing reputation for high-quality books and products. To ensure your continued satisfaction, we also understand the importance of customer service and support.

Tech Support

If you need assistance with the information in this book or with a CD/disk accompanying the book, please access Macmillan Computer Publishing's online Knowledge Base at **http://www.superlibrary.com/general/support**. If you do not find the answer to your questions on our Web site, you may contact Macmillan Technical Support by phone at **317/581-3833** or via e-mail at **support@mcp.com**.

Also be sure to visit Que's Web resource center for all the latest information, enhancements, errata, downloads, and more. It's located at **http://www.quecorp.com/**.

Orders, Catalogs, and Customer Service

To order other Que or Macmillan Computer Publishing books, catalogs, or products, please contact our Customer Service Department at **800/428-5331** or fax us at **800/835-3202** (International Fax: 317/228-4400). Or visit our online bookstore at **http://www.mcp.com/**.

Comments and Suggestions

We want you to let us know what you like or dislike most about this book or other Que products. Your comments will help us to continue publishing the best books available on computer topics in today's market.

Henly Wolin
Product Director
Que Corporation
201 West 103rd Street, 4B
Indianapolis, Indiana 46290 USA
Fax: 317/581-4663 E-mail: hwolin@que.mcp.com
hwolin@aol.com hwolin-AOL

Please be sure to include the book's title and author as well as your name and phone or fax number. We will carefully review your comments and share them with the author. Please note that due to the high volume of mail we receive, we may not be able to reply to every message.

Thank you for choosing Que!

Contents

Part 3 E-Mail

Part 5   Creating Web Pages

Part 6: WWW Directory

Introduction

Congratulations! You've just decided to harness the power of the Internet. The only problem now is that you need to figure out how to navigate the Internet and all its features: the World Wide Web, e-mail, newsgroups, FTP file transfers, chat, and more. Of course, you're not looking forward to having to deal with manuals and help systems that never tell you what you really need to know—at least, not without making you waste a lot of time searching. No, with a schedule as busy as yours, what you really need is a straightforward guide that teaches you what you need to know in the shortest amount of time.

Welcome to *Internet 6 in 1*, a book designed for busy people like you. Nobody has the luxury of sitting down uninterrupted for hours at a time just to learn the Internet. That's why *Internet 6 in 1* doesn't attempt to teach you everything at once. Instead, each feature of the Internet is presented in a single, self-contained lesson, designed to take only a short time to complete. Whenever you have a few minutes to spare in your busy day, you can easily complete a lesson on navigating the Web, using Web search tools, exchanging e-mail, reading and posting newsgroup messages, or even creating your own Web page.

Whom This Book Is For

Granted, *Internet 6 in 1* might not be the right book for everyone. But if you can slide your way around Windows without too much help, it is the book for you. If you know a little bit about modems and online services but you don't know anything at all about setting up an Internet connection, navigating the World Wide Web, using e-mail, reading and posting newsgroup messages, creating Web pages, and all those other funny-sounding Internet topics, this is *definitely* the book for you.

Internet 6 in 1 is perfect for people who have busy schedules, a need to get up and running quickly, and a few ten-minute time slots every day in which to learn. If this description fits you, *Internet 6 in 1* is your book.

How This Book Is Organized

Although you can skip around this book at will and flip to a lesson at random, we have structured the book to make it easy to find the information you need and to allow you to work through the book from cover to cover, if you so desire. We have divided *Internet 6 in 1* into the following six parts:

- **Part 1: Getting Connected** After a brief orientation about the Internet and the World Wide Web, this part shows you how to set up the hardware and software you need to get wired to the Internet. You will learn the basics of accessing the Internet through America Online or by using a dedicated Internet Service Provider. Additional lessons in this part explain Internet etiquette and show you how to protect your system against computer viruses and censor the unseemly side of the Internet.

- **Part 2: The World Wide Web** This part shows you how to use Internet Explorer, Netscape Navigator, and America Online's Web browser to open and navigate multimedia pages on the World Wide Web. You will learn how to download and install the most popular Web browsers, use them to open pages and jump to connected pages, and mark your favorite pages for quick return trips. These lessons also teach you how to tune in to premium Web sites using the latest channel changers, install ActiveX controls and plug-ins to play audio and video clips, subscribe to your favorite sites, and even customize your Web browser.

- **Part 3: E-Mail** In this part, you will learn how to exchange electronic mail messages with your friends, relatives, and colleagues. These lessons teach you how to set up your e-mail account in America Online, Outlook Express, and Netscape Mail, and how to use these programs to read incoming mail, reply to messages, and initiate a correspondence. After reading this part, you'll be ready to take advantage of e-mail's postage-free, same-day delivery!

- **Part 4: Newsgroups** Newsgroups are online communities where people can post messages and read and reply to publicly posted messages. In this part, you will learn how to access newsgroups from America Online or by using Outlook Express or Netscape Collabra. These lessons teach you how to connect to a news server, subscribe to your favorite newsgroups (from a list of thousands), and read and post messages in a newsgroup.

- **Part 5: Creating Web Pages** With this part and a simple text-editing program, such as Windows Notepad, you will be able to create your very own Web pages, complete with text, graphics, links, tables, forms, scrolling marquees, and much more. In addition, you will learn how to place your page on the World Wide Web and publicize it so other people can quickly find it.

- **Part 6: WWW Directory** Although the Web offers several search tools to help you track down information, the information they turn up may not be the best. This part offers a directory of the best sites on the Web, complete with a brief description of each site.

TIP **Hey, Slow Down! I'm New to This!** If you're new to the Internet and the World Wide Web, be sure to read Part 1, Lesson 1, "Finding Out About the Internet and the World Wide Web."

Each part is divided into several lessons. Because each of the lessons takes only 10 minutes or less to complete, you'll quickly master the skills you need. In addition, the straightforward, easy-to-understand explanations and numbered lists within each lesson guide you quickly and easily to your goal of mastering the most popular Internet features.

Conventions Used in This Book

The following icons are included throughout the text to help you quickly identify particular types of information.

TIP Tip icons mark shortcuts and hints for saving time and using the Internet more efficiently.

Term icons point out easy-to-follow definitions that you'll need to know in order to understand the basics of the Internet and the programs you use to access it.

Caution icons mark information that's intended to help you avoid making mistakes.

In addition to the special icons, you'll find these conventions used throughout the text:

On-screen text	On-screen text appears in bold type.
What you type	Information you need to type also appears in bold.
Items you select	Items you need to select or keys you need to press also appear in bold type.
`Computer output`	Long sections of computer text appear in a monospace font.

Onward to the Internet!

Now that the preliminaries are out of the way, dive in to the Internet. If this is your initial foray into the Internet, start with Part 1, "Getting Connected." Without an Internet connection and a basic knowledge of what the Internet has to offer, you'll be lost without Part 1. If you're already connected, and you need instructions on how to get and use the latest tools for accessing the Internet, feel free to jump ahead to Part 2, where you will learn about the latest breed of Web browsers. Enjoy!

The Internet is a constantly evolving medium. Some of the programs described in this book were in early beta form. Some of the screenshots may depict features that differ slightly from the version you have running on your machine.

Getting Connected

Finding Out About the Internet and the World Wide Web

In this lesson, you learn what the Internet is, how the World Wide Web is a part of the Internet, and why everyone wants to get online.

What Is the Internet?

If you've been a news hound lately, you've noticed all the media hoopla over the Internet. Although the Internet, in one form or another (originally ARPAnet), has been around since the late 1960s, you would think this world-wide network of computers magically became connected overnight. The Internet has been the hot topic lately, and it doesn't seem that the news hype, and occasionally the controversy, is going to cool down in the near future.

TERM   **ARPAnet**   The Internet's first incarnation. ARPA (the Advanced Research Projects Agency) built its mega-network in the United States using computers at large universities and some government agencies. And, yes, the defense department was involved.

The Internet's popularity has fueled the demand for reference material (like this book) designed to help ease you into what, at first, must seem like a technological mishmash. And while the Internet may seem overwhelming, by the time you finish this book, you'll think of yourself as an Internet expert. You'll understand Web browsers and TCP/IP stacks, as well as e-mail and newsgroups, and you will likely end up showing less-informed Internet users how to access search engines and FTP servers.

Access to the Internet provides you with an incredible wealth of information, such as information on hang gliding and inline skating (see Figure 1.1).

You can operate on a cartoon Boris Yeltsin at the Comedy Central Web site (see Figure 1.2).

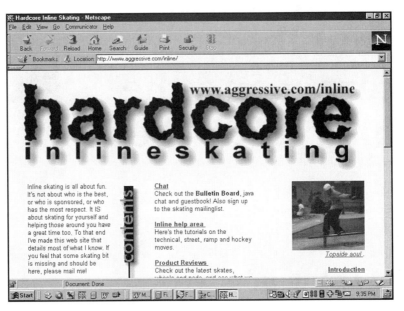

Figure 1.1   Check out inline skating on the Web.

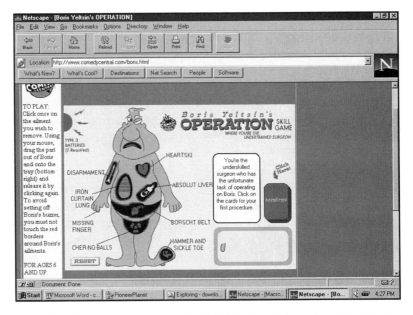

Figure 1.2   See if you can remove Boris Yeltsin's heart without making the buzzer go.

Originally designed as an academic-exchange medium, the Internet has become a favorite target of burgeoning entrepreneurs who sell everything from stocks, bonds, and mutual funds to compact discs, music boxes, and vintage wines.

The Internet's access and appeal have also naturally caught the attention of most major computer hardware and software manufacturers and vendors. They've found that the Internet, or "the Net," is an excellent way to reach their current, as well potential, customers. All the major players in the personal computer game have a presence on the Web: Intel, IBM, Compaq, Novell, Apple, and, of course, Microsoft.

Finally, you will find that the World Wide Web can be a fun place to explore. Games, puzzles, and humorous Web sites can provide a great deal of entertainment.

Pieces of the Internet: How They Fit Together

The Internet is a worldwide network of interconnected computer systems and a series of several different types of computer services. While you probably hear the most about the World Wide Web, the Internet is actually made up of several different components; there is Internet e-mail, newsgroups, FTP sites, even Internet real-time chat. The following sections outline some of the more popular services available on the Internet.

The World Wide Web

The Web is currently the most popular on-ramp to the Internet's information highway. The Web is actually a set of interconnected pages that represent specific Web sites around the world. These Web pages use special links that take the form of highlighted text or a graphic; click a link with your mouse and you are taken from your current location and whisked to a new Web page—a page that may reside on a computer on the other side of the planet. The Web does a great job of moving you seamlessly from content area to content area.

 TERM   **The World Wide Web (WWW)**   The Web went online in 1992, a creation of Tim Berners-Lee of CERN, the European Laboratory for Particle Physics in Geneva, Switzerland. By October of 1993, there were more than 200 Web servers up and running, and by June, 1995, the total number of Web servers on the Internet totaled more than 6.5 million.

In order to move around the Web, you need a Web browser. Currently, the most popular Web browsers are Netscape Navigator and Microsoft Internet Explorer. Both of these Web browsers provide you with powerful, yet easy-to-use features that allow you to take full advantage of all the content on the Web. Besides the Web's text and graphics capabilities, it also gives you access to special multimedia content that provides sounds, video, and interactive Web pages (see Figure 1.3).

 Multimedia This catch phrase often defines PC hardware capabilities as much as Internet content. In terms of the WWW, it means content that includes sound, graphics, video, and some degree of interactivity.

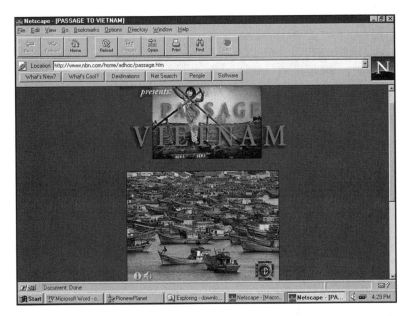

Figure 1.3 The WWW offers a huge amount of information and content; the Passage to Vietnam site offers multimedia content.

E-Mail

E-mail is the oldest Internet service, dating back to the mid '70s. Then and now, the basic concept behind e-mail is fairly simple: You log onto a computer system and write and address a text message to a user on another system. The message is then routed through the maze of interconnected computer systems until it is delivered to its intended destination (see Figure 1.4).

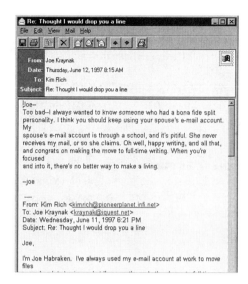

Figure 1.4   Microsoft Internet Mail is a typical e-mail program.

While the concept might be the same, the e-mail products you use now bear little resemblance to the early e-mail systems of the '70s and '80s.

Internet e-mail still provides you with the ability to send text messages, but you can also attach other types of files such as document, spreadsheets, or even sounds and graphics to your e-mail messages. Part 3 of this book gives you a lot more information on using e-mail on the Internet.

UseNet

UseNet refers to a service that's very much like a public bulletin board. UseNet allows you to post messages to a public subject area, a newsgroup, where a number of other newsgroup participants can read them. Replies (and sometimes heated rebuttals) can then be posted in the newsgroup that held your original message.

UseNet began in 1979 as a service connecting computers at Duke University and the University of North Carolina. Today, UseNet is an immensely popular Internet service that has grown to include more than 4,000 topics that users post messages and responses to; these topics range from books and movies to religion and philosophy to computers and technology. Figure 1.6 shows a screen from a typical newsreader program that can be used to access UseNet newsgroups.

Newsgroups can also be a good source of information from other users who have used certain products, have seen certain movies or shows, or have had experiences with certain companies.

If you think you might be interested in joining or participating in a newsgroup (or two or three), check out Part 4. It explains how to find them and how to join in on the discussion.

 TIP **Browser Features**   You will find that Web browsers such as Microsoft Internet Explorer and Netscape Navigator have features that allow you to send and receive e-mail, browse newsgroups, and download files from FTP sites. This all-in-one approach makes Web browsers the easiest way for you to connect to the Internet's various informational components.

FTP

FTP (File Transfer Protocol) is a way to download files from the Internet. FTP takes advantage of series of computer file servers that archive and distribute files. Many FTP sites are operated by computer hardware and software manufacturers who use their FTP sites to distribute their software and software updates. Netscape, one of the major Internet Web browser companies, uses its FTP site to distribute its Web browser, Netscape Navigator.

While FTP programs exist for the downloading of software from FTP sites, you will find that Web browsers such as Netscape Navigator and Microsoft Internet Explorer have FTP download capabilities built in. This makes it easy for you to take advantage of FTP while you are actually cruising the World Wide Web. FTP sites are also run by colleges and universities that use them to make shareware and software utilities available to a broad range of users. Part 2, Lesson 21 gives you the lowdown on accessing FTP sites.

Chat

The ability to chat on the Internet in real-time is another immensely popular Internet service. Internet Relay Chat (IRC) was the first chat system and used IRC servers as placed for users to congregate and chat via their keyboard.

A number of more sophisticated Chat clients have become available, some allowing you to chat directly on the WWW. One of the new Web chat clients is iChat (see Figure 1.5); it turns your Web browser into a chat program that allows you to view and send chat items. To learn more about iChat, check out Part 2, Lesson 22.

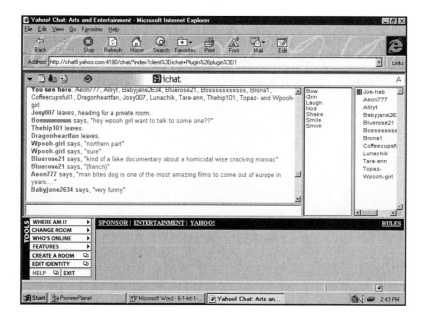

Figure 1.5 Turn your Web browser into a chat client with iChat.

In this lesson, you learned what the Internet is and why it is so popular. And you've had a brief look at the different components, World Wide Web, e-mail, newsgroups, FTP, that make up the Internet. In the next lesson, you will find an examination of the hardware and software you need to access the Internet.

Hardware and Software You Will Need to Access the Web

In this lesson, you learn about the equipment and software programs you need to get online and access the World Wide Web.

The Hardware You Need

While it is possible to access the World Wide Web with any computer that will run Windows 3.1 (which includes a 386 with as little as 2–4 megabytes of memory), you need a fairly powerful system to take full advantage of what the Web has to offer. A practical minimum configuration for using Windows 3.1 or Windows 95 is a 486/66 with 8 megabytes of memory (RAM). Unless you plan to download a tremendous volume of files, your hard disk requirements do not need to be gargantuan; a minimum hard disk of 300 megabytes is more than sufficient.

You will need VGA graphics, and while you can get by with a video card that supports only 16 colors (if you like viewing what appear to be "washed-out" graphics, or opt to use a text-only Web browser), most of the graphics you will encounter will look a lot better with a video card that supports 256 colors at least.

And last, but not least, you will need a modem to navigate the Web. The minimum speed modem you should even consider is 14,400 bps. And you probably shouldn't consider it very long unless you're getting it for free. You will find that you need a 28.8 to 33.6 modem (28,800/33,600 bps) to take advantage of some of the Web's special content.

bps   Stands for bits per second. The higher the bps, the faster a modem transfers information.

Now, if you want to get past a "minimum" configuration and start looking at a more realistic configuration, start with a Pentium processor with 16 megabytes of memory (32M would even be better), at least a gigabyte hard drive, a super VGA video card with 1 megabyte of video RAM (which will support 256 colors and more with no problem), and a 28.8-33.6 modem.

TIP   **Modems**   Modems are now available that can transmit data at 56,000 bps. Most Internet service providers (ISP) still can only handle speeds of 28.8 and 33.6, but as they upgrade their equipment, you can take advantage of high-speed data transfers that cut down lag-time on the Web.

Another item you will want to invest in is a sound card. Much of the Web now boasts multimedia content, most notably sound, and you will need a sound card, as well as speakers or a headphone set, to hear Web-based audio. If you also plan to experiment with any of the Web-based telephony products, such as Internet Phone, you will also need a microphone.

Another piece of hardware that you will want on your PC is a CD-ROM drive. While a CD-ROM drive is not essential for accessing the Web, you will find that a lot of commercial software is now being distributed on CD instead of floppy disks.

CAUTION

ISPs   You may want to establish a connection to the Internet via an Internet service provider or online service and actually spend some time on the Web before you invest in a lot of additional hardware for your system. Digital cameras, video capture cards, microphones, and other neat hardware gadgets can enhance your Web experience if you have the time to play with them. Otherwise, you may find that a typical PC hardware configuration is all you need to get what you want from the Web.

Making Your Internet Connection

After you assemble your hardware, you're ready to tackle the Internet and the World Wide Web. This book helps you access the Internet directly through an Internet service provider, not through a local area network (LAN) that has an

Internet gateway. For information on configuring an Internet connection through a LAN, talk to your local system administrator. For information about connecting to the Internet through an online service such as America Online, see Part 1, Lesson 7.

Gateway   This is a means of "passing through" or "connecting to" a system different from the one you are using. An Internet gateway for a local area network is merely a means of providing Internet access to users on a LAN.

You need an Internet account with an Internet service provider. If you don't have an Internet account yet, see Part 1, Lesson 3, which explains how to select an ISP.

You also need a means of communicating with your service provider. This book assumes that your connection is over a standard telephone line using a modem. For acceptable performance, as stated earlier, you should have a modem that is capable of communicating at a rate of at least 14,400 bits per second (bps). A 28.8 modem gives the best performance over standard phone lines.

Another communication technology that looks to have a big impact on Internet usage is ISDN. ISDN (Integrated Services Digital Network) is literally "digital telephones." Rather than convert your computer's digital signals into analog (sound waves) to be transmitted over standard telephone lines as a modem does, ISDN transmits a digital signal over digital telephone lines. The advantage is a communication connection up to 128 kilobits per second (kbps) as opposed to today's 28.8 kbps connections.

In many parts of the country, ISDN is available in roughly 70–90 percent of the local Baby Bell's service area. In addition to its lack of availability, the downsides to using ISDN lie in the difficulty of locating a knowledgeable telephone company sales office and in its cost. Many regional telephone sales offices will still respond "…ISD-what?" And when you do find service in your area, pricing is still geared more toward businesses than consumers.

Even if you do find a local Bell office knowledgeable enough about ISDN to place your order, the installation of ISDN can still be a formidable task. While the phone company might successfully run the line to your computer, getting the ISDN adapter (contrary to what you've heard, there is no such thing as an "ISDN modem") properly configured and working will still largely be your responsibility.

Another connection option that is getting lots of headlines, but that is still moving at a snail's pace, is the cable modem. Instead of getting service through your telephone company, you would connect to the Internet through your cable TV provider. Getting the proper equipment in place by the providers is still the largest roadblock.

Most of the current cable TV system is still designed as a one-way system (they provide service to you). To convert to a two-way service, fiber-optics cables need to be installed along with the necessary routing communications equipment. If Internet service demand continues at its present rate, meaning that there is still a strong profit motive in providing Internet access, cable modems in most of the country are still 18 months to two years away for most of us.

 TIP **Fast Connections** It may make more sense in the short term for you to purchase one of the new 56K modems and try to find an Internet service provider that is taking advantage of this faster modem technology. This gives you a fast connection to the World Wide Web without the anxiety and cost of an ISDN line or the long wait for good commercial cable modems and connections.

The Software You Need

Obviously, you need an operating system with a graphical user interface such as Windows 95, Windows NT, Mac System 7.5.x, or X/Windows installed on your computer to get the most out of this book and the Internet. You can connect using Windows 3.1, but there is a big push towards 32-bit software because of its improved performance, which means 95 or NT.

While a graphical user interface (GUI) is not essential for Internet access, you will probably be spending a large percentage of your time browsing the World Wide Web. And although you can view the Web in a text-only mode, the view is considerably better if you include the pictures and colors, which necessitates a GUI-based operating system.

You will also need software. Windows 95 and Windows NT provide all the software you need to connect to the Internet, as do most flavors of UNIX that support X/Windows. If you are using an Apple Macintosh, there are several good Internet access packages you can purchase rather cheaply that can get you up and running in no time. If you are currently using the new Mac OS 8 software, Internet connectivity is already available to you.

The tool you will use to access the information on the Web is a browser. Part 2, Lessons 1 and 2 show how to download and configure two of the most popular browsers: Netscape Navigator and Microsoft Internet Explorer.

Windows 95 Internet Software

If you are running Windows 95, there is a collection of preinstalled software that can aid you in connecting to the Internet. Earlier releases of Windows 95 may not provide you with much, but just as long as you have a browser you should be okay. Newer releases of the Windows 95 operating system provide everything you need to set up your computer for connecting to an Internet service provider. Lesson 5 teaches you how to configure Windows 95 for Internet access. If you're not sure if all or part of Microsoft Plus! has been installed on your computer, follow these steps to find out:

1. Select the **Start** button on the taskbar and choose **Programs**, **Windows Explorer**.

2. On your C:\ drive, locate a folder labeled **Plus!**, which is probably located in the Program Files folder. If you don't see this folder, it's likely that none of Microsoft Plus! has been installed on your PC.

3. Open the **Start** menu and choose **Programs**, **Accessories**. If your Accessories menu contains an Internet Tools option, choose **Internet Tools** to see if you have the Get on the Internet Wizard installed (see Figure 2.1).

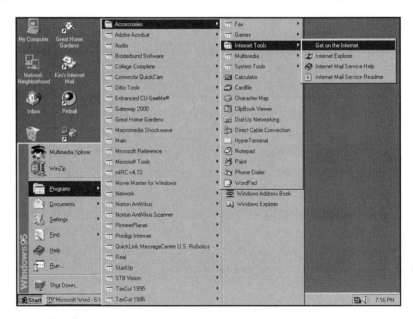

Figure 2.1   The Get on the Internet Wizard is installed.

TIP **Start Up Disks** Most Internet service providers now provide a setup disk that will help you configure Windows 95 for dial-up service through your modem.

Windows 3.1 Internet Software

A good percentage of the packaged Internet access software is designed for Windows 95, but there is still plenty to choose from that will operate on the Windows 3.1 platform. However, you can save a few dollars by checking with your service provider for it. Most Internet service providers will include software and instructions on how to set up your system at no extra charge.

UNIX and Macintosh Software

If you're operating a UNIX-based system, much of the software you will need to access the Internet through your provider comes with your operating system. If you're not sure if you have everything you need, check with your provider. There's aren't too many commercially packaged UNIX products.

As for Mac users, commercial access packages aren't quite as numerous as they are in the Windows world, but they are still fairly abundant. You can also check with your service provider for Mac utilities and setup instructions.

In this lesson, you learned about the hardware and software you need to get up and running on the Web. In the next lesson, you will learn how to select the Internet service provider that will be your on-ramp to the Internet.

Selecting an
Internet Service
Provider

In this lesson, you learn how to select an Internet service provider (ISP).

What Is an Internet Service Provider?

An Internet service provider is a company that gives you a connection to the Internet and its various components such as e-mail, the WWW, and UseNet newsgroups. Internet access comes in a variety of connection choices and account types, as you will soon see, and this depends on who provides the service and what hardware and software you use to get online. This lesson examines the service options available to users with stand-alone computers, rather than the options available to users who have Internet access through a local area network (LAN).

 Stand-Alone Computer A stand-alone computer is a computer that is not directly connected to another computer or computer system, such as a local area network. To access other computers, users with stand-alone computers usually use a modem to connect over ordinary telephone lines.

You Can Get Access Through Your Online Service

Many of the commercial online services, such as CompuServe, America Online, Prodigy, and the Microsoft Network offer Internet access. Internet access through these services is usually quick and easy to set up because it is an extension of their basic online services. The downside to using a commercial online service used to be that the "meter was constantly running" every minute you were connected. But now, most of the online services have adopted a flat-rate fee structure in order to compete head-to-head with the legion of Internet service providers who had been luring away their customer base.

Now of course, there is a new "downside" to using a commercial online service—getting access! The chief complaint many of the online services hear now is that "it is next to impossible to get through," and that users attempting to dial-in almost always get a busy signal.

Commercial online service providers counter with the argument that they offer a wide array of additional services (vendor forums, e-mail, file/program download libraries, chat rooms, and so on) that are all neatly organized and easily accessed through a familiar or easy-to-learn interface.

 TIP **Free Trial Periods** Most of the online services offer free trial periods. This is a good way to get hooked up to the Net and give it a spin while also trying out some of the special services of the particular online company. If you like the service, keep it. If not, cancel it before the trial period ends and take your search for the perfect Internet service provider elsewhere.

However, once you become familiar with the Internet, you will find that most, if not all, of these services are available at a fraction of the cost. You only need to know where to look.

The questions here are:

"What is access like in your location?"

"How much time do you plan to spend on the Internet each month?"

"What is it worth to you to have these services laid out for you in a nice, neat little package?"

About Internet Service Provider Shell Accounts

Most Internet service providers have abandoned shell accounts, but these accounts are still available—usually at rock-bottom prices. Shell accounts are cheap because they are text-only. In a world of graphical user interfaces (GUIs) and multimedia razzle-dazzle, few users are satisfied with surfing the Net with a text-only view.

On the plus side, a text-only interface does have one major advantage: speed! When you eliminate pictures and graphical fonts, you can browse the Internet very quickly. In previous lessons, you saw how you can turn off the graphics mode at times when you want to surf the Net at "warp speed" instead of cruising on "impulse power."

What Are Internet Service Provider SLIP/ PPP Accounts?

Serial Line Internet Protocol (SLIP) and Point-to-Point Protocol (PPP) are two types of Internet accounts most users presently turn to. SLIP is the older of the two types of Internet connections explained here. As its name implies, SLIP allows you to connect to a service provider over a serial communication line, such as a telephone line. Developed after SLIP, PPP is also serial in nature, but it provides a higher degree of error detection and compression in its connection to your service provider. When given a choice, choose PPP.

Still relatively inexpensive in most areas (especially compared to commercial networks), these accounts offer you Internet access through graphical interfaces and allow you to experience the full depth of the Internet and its services.

Error Detection A feature that detects errors between the source and recipient and tells the source to resend the communications signal. Error detection is built into PPP connections, but SLIP connections get error detection from an outside source—often hardware. Today's higher speed modems assist by providing extra error detection, too.

Compression The encoding of communication signals so they can be sent as shorter signals, taking less time to send.

Selecting an Internet Service Provider

Now that you know something about the types of Internet accounts available, you need to know how to go about selecting an Internet service provider. Don't attempt to make the determination solely on the basis of price. Read through the following questions, consider which of the service options are important to you, and discuss them with potential service providers.

- Is the call to your ISP a local call? The whole idea is to keep your costs to a minimum, which means avoiding long distance or toll telephone charges.

- Do you charge by the minute/hour or a flat rate? Flat-rate providers are becoming more common, but many providers keep the meter running and charge you by the hour. Some hourly rate providers give you a minimum number of hours before the meter starts. Some give you as few as 3 hours per day, while others give you as many as 100 hours per month.

- Do you offer shell, SLIP, or PPP accounts? PPP is the best type of connectivity for your money.

- How many telephone lines do you make available? The least expensive provider is not a bargain if all you get when you dial in is a busy signal.

- What communication speeds do you offer? You set your modem to this speed to communicate with your provider's modems. Hardly any service providers offer speeds less than 14,400 bits per second (bps). If you're using a modem with a top speed of 28,800bps, make sure your provider has phone lines that talk to your modem at this speed. If you think you might upgrade to ISDN connections sometime in the future, inquire as to whether your provider can support these connections. With the rapid increase in modem technology most ISPs support 14,400 to 33,600.

- Do you offer e-mail, newsgroups, and an online chat service? Can you browse the World Wide Web and send and receive files through FTP? These are all basic Internet services that your service provider should offer.

CAUTION

Buyer Beware As with any potential purchase, the phrase "Buyer Beware" is applicable for your search for a good Internet service provider. In many metropolitan areas, free computer-related news magazines are published that can give you good information on the local providers. Also don't be afraid to phone interview more than one potential provider if you truly want to get a hassle-free service.

ISDN Stands for Integrated Services Digital Network. The modems you use now communicate by converting the digital signal from your computer to an analog signal. In other words, your modem converts bits and bytes to sound and then transmits this analog signal over standard telephone lines. ISDN communicates as a digital signal, which means it does not use a "standard" modem, and thus is a lot faster (because the signal doesn't have to be converted).

A service provider should offer at least those services listed in the preceding list. Some service providers go further and make shareware software and technical support available.

To find an Internet provider, look for ads in online magazines, check the yellow pages, or simply ask someone about his provider.

Also, if you want to "sample the goods," many state-run universities have started providing Internet-access terminals in student union buildings and libraries where anyone can literally walk in off the street and get on the Internet. Most colleges and universities are also providing for their students standard, dial-up Internet accounts having recognized the Internet's potential as a valuable research source.

In this lesson, you learned what questions to ask when shopping for an Internet service provider and what services your service provider should offer. In the next three lessons of this Part, you will learn how to configure your PC to access the Internet whether you are using Windows 95, Windows 3.1, or the Apple Macintosh.

Configuration for Windows 3.1 Users

In this lesson, you learn how to configure Windows 3.1 to connect to the Internet using a dial-up connection.

What You Need

There are more than a dozen Internet kits you can buy that allow you to log in to the Internet while running Windows 3.1. You can save a few dollars by picking up a few utilities and manually configuring Windows 3.1 as your Internet client.

The three utilities you will need are:

- A Winsock program
- A dialer
- An FTP utility

A Winsock, short for Windows Sockets, specification is designed to ensure compatibility between multiple TCP/IP product vendors. The Winsock for Windows 3.1, 95, and NT are implemented in winsock.dll. There are numerous ways to load your Winsock. This lesson discusses a shareware product called Trumpet Winsock.

A dialer is simply a Winsock-compliant program used to dial into your Internet service provider (ISP). In this lesson, the dialer used is also Trumpet Winsock.

While an FTP utility is not essential for connecting to the Internet, you will find it helpful to have one so that you can download other Internet programs you will need once you set up Windows 3.1.

Configuring Trumpet Winsock

Most Internet service providers will also supply you with Trumpet Winsock and an FTP utility as part of your connection package. Follow these steps to install Trumpet Winsock:

1. Create a directory for the program, using the directory name **\TRUMPET**.

2. Copy all of the files into the \TRUMPET directory.

3. Open your **AUTOEXEC.BAT** file and type **TRUMPET** at the beginning of the PATH statement. Then reboot your PC so that the newly configured PATH statement takes effect.

4. Start Windows and start **Trumpet Winsock** by double-clicking the **TCPMAN.EXE** program in the \TRUMPET directory. Figure 4.1 shows the opening screen of Trumpet Winsock and the fields for which you will supply information.

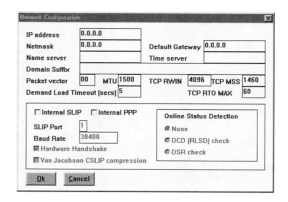

Figure 4.1   The Trumpet Winsock main screen.

5. Select **Internal SLIP** or **Internal PPP** depending on which type of connection you have with your service provider.

6. Fill in the IP addresses for your PC's IP address, netmask, name server, default gateway, and domain suffix. You can get all of this information from your service provider. Find out whether your ISP assigns you a static IP address (which means you use the same IP address every time you log in) or a dynamic IP address (which could be different each time you log in).

7. Enter the communications port (COM1, COM2, and so on) your modem is connected to, and the speed of your modem (14,400 or 28,800, for example).

8. Click **OK** to save your entries, and Trumpet Winsock displays your settings, which might look similar to those displayed in Figure 4.2.

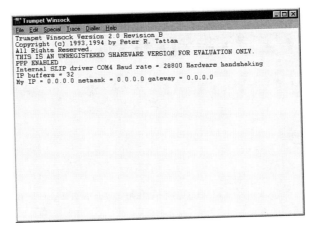

```
Trumpet Winsock
File  Edit  Special  Trace  Dialer  Help
Trumpet Winsock Version 2.0 Revision B
Copyright (c) 1993,1994 by Peter R. Tattam
All Rights Reserved.
THIS IS AN UNREGISTERED SHAREWARE VERSION FOR EVALUATION ONLY.
PPP ENABLED
Internal SLIP driver COM4 Baud rate = 28800 Hardware handshaking
IP buffers = 32
My IP = 0.0.0.0 netmask = 0.0.0.0 gateway = 0.0.0.0
```

Figure 4.2   Trumpet Winsock displays your connection parameters.

9. Open the **Dialer** menu and choose **Edit** scripts. Full instructions for editing the sample scripts are supplied in a readme file in your \TRUMPET directory.

After you finish editing the sample scripts, you are ready to test your configuration. Go back to the Dialer menu to test your connection. Follow the instructions given you by your provider for logging into your provider's system. If your connection fails, go back and check all of your entries to make sure they match the information given to you by your provider.

Once you successfully log in to your provider's system, you can use the FTP utility supplied by your service provider to start downloading additional Internet utilities you will need or want (such as a Web browser, an e-mail program, Gopher program, and so on). If you happen to be using Windows 3.1, you can use only the 16-bit software. If you are using Windows 95, you should use only the 32-bit version.

In this lesson, you learned how to configure Windows 3.1 to connect to the Internet. In the next lesson, you will learn how to configure Windows 95 so you can use it to connect to the Internet.

Configuration for Windows 95 Users

In this lesson, you learn how to set up your Windows 95 Internet connection using the Internet Wizard in Microsoft Plus!.

Installing Microsoft Plus!

Microsoft Plus! is an add-on product for Windows 95 that gives you system- and disk-maintenance tools, desktop-enhancement products, Internet support, and a really cool pinball game. Before you can use the Internet Setup Wizard, you have to install Microsoft Plus!.

 TIP You Can Also Use the Internet Jumpstart Kit! Many dealers substitute the "free" Internet Jumpstart Kit as an alternative to Microsoft Plus! for users who want access to the Internet. If the Jumpstart Kit is not included with your PC, ask your dealer or your ISP for it.

 TIP For PPP Only The Internet Setup Wizard works only for PPP (Point-to-Point Protocol) connections. But if your copy of Windows 95 came on CD, look in the /Admin/Apptools/Dscript folder for information on setting up a SLIP connection.

If you haven't installed Microsoft Plus!, go ahead and insert the CD or disk into the appropriate drive and follow the installation instructions. After you've installed it, look over Table 5.1, which lists the information you need to get from your provider so you can enter it when you run the Setup Wizard.

Table 5.1 Information Your Internet Service Provider Should Supply

Information	Definition
Domain Server or IP Address	The provider's 12-digit IP address (nnn.nnn.nnn.nnn); each segment value is in the range 0–255.
Subnet Mask	Another 12-digit address in the form nnn.nnn.nnn.nnn.
Domain Name	Your provider's domain name, in the form provider.com or provider.net.
Host Name	If used (some providers tell you to leave this blank), your provider supplies it.
Mail Server Name	Your e-mail server's domain name.
News Server Name	Your newsgroup server's domain name.
E-Mail Address	Your e-mail address in the form username@mailserver.
Commands used log in to ISP	Commands such as "Enter user name and password" to and any subsequent commands you need to follow to log in to the provider.
Type of IP address (dynamic or static)	Your provider assigns you a permanent IP address to use if it's static.
Dial-Up phone number	The phone number you dial to connect to your provider.

Running the Internet Setup Wizard

The Internet Setup Wizard is found on the Internet Tools menu under Accessories. In this lesson, you will see step-by-step how to supply the information the Setup Wizard needs to create your Internet connection. Remember, your use of the Internet Setup Wizard will differ if you use a different provider and connect from a different city.

To start the Internet Setup Wizard, follow these steps:

1. Select the Start button on the taskbar and choose Programs, Accessories, Internet Tools, and Internet Setup Wizard (see Figure 5.1).

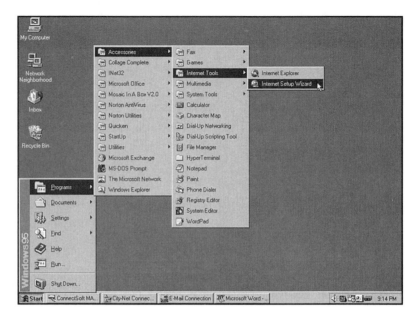

Figure 5.1   The menu path to Internet Setup Wizard.

2. At the opening screen, click the **Next>** button to begin. If your modem is not already set up, Windows 95 prompts you to set up your modem.

3. In the How to Connect dialog box, click the **I Already Have an Account with a Different Service Provider** option button as shown in Figure 5.2. Then click the **Next>** button.

Figure 5.2   Installing Internet support with your own ISP (Internet Service Provider).

4. In the Service Provider Information dialog box, enter the name of your Internet service provider. This is just a label that identifies the shortcut icon you will use to connect to your provider. It can be anything you like. Click the **Next>** button to continue.

5. In the Phone Number dialog box, enter the phone number of your provider. Even if you're dialing a local number, enter the area code and country code (select the correct code from the Country Code drop-down list). Finally, select the **Bring Up Terminal Window After Dialing** check box (see Figure 5.3). You will use the terminal window to log in to your ISP. Click the **Next>** button to continue.

6. In the User Name and Password dialog box, enter the login name (user name) and password set up for you by your provider. (Even though you enter your user name and password here, some login systems by some providers will not accept these unless you also type them in the terminal window.) Click the **Next>** button to continue.

Figure 5.3   Supply your provider's phone number.

7. In the IP Address dialog box, select how you get your user IP address. Your provider should supply you with this information (see Figure 5.4). Click the **Next>** button to continue.

8. In the DNS Server Address dialog box, enter the IP address of your DNS (Domain Name Service) server. Your provider should supply you with this information. If your provider also supplies you with an Alternate DNS server, enter that address in the second field. Select the **Next>** button to continue.

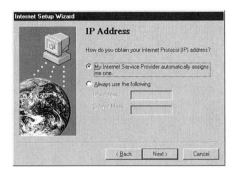

Figure 5.4   Supply your IP address information.

9. In the Internet Mail dialog box, click the Use Internet Mail check box, and then enter your e-mail address and the name of your mail server. (Your provider should supply you with this information.) Click the **Next>** button to continue.

TIP   **DNS (Domain Name Service)**   The means by which a 12-digit IP address (nnn.nnn.nnn.nnn) is converted into a recognizable name. (For example, the IP address of my service provider is 199.234.118.2; its domain name is city-net.com.)

10. In the Exchange Profile dialog box, enter the Microsoft Exchange profile name to use for Internet mail. Type the name Internet Mail Setting, as you see in Figure 5.5, which is the default profile name. Click the **Next>** button to continue.

Figure 5.5   Set the profile name for Internet mail.

11. Finally, click the Finish button to complete your wizard setup. When setup is complete, the wizard creates an Internet icon on your desktop. You can select that icon to connect to the Internet through your provider.

Connecting to the Internet

Bear in mind that what you enter to connect to your provider might be different than what you see in this lesson. The figures in this lesson show my connection to my Internet provider using a Point-to-Point Protocol (PPP) connection over a 14.4 modem. Your provider should have given you the necessary information for you to log in, such as when to enter your login name (or ID) and your password, and any additional information required.

 TIP **Check the Information from Your ISP** To double-check the information you receive from your Internet provider, compare it to the list in Table 5.1. It's possible that your ISP provided you with more information than is listed in the table, but you should not have received less.

What you see here should be enough additional information to help you connect to the Internet.

1. If you purchased and Installed Microsoft Plus!, double-click the Internet icon located on your desktop. This starts the Microsoft Internet Explorer browser. The Connect To dialog box appears (see Figure 5.6).

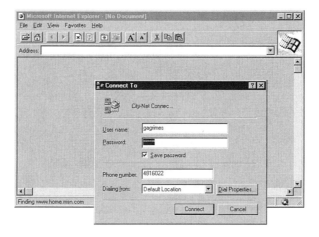

Figure 5.6 Connecting to your provider with Microsoft Internet Explorer.

If you didn't purchase Microsoft Plus!, double-click the My Computer desktop icon, and then double-click the Dial-Up Networking icon. In the Dial-Up Networking dialog box, double-click the connection you created to your provider. With or without Microsoft Plus!, you should see the connection you created and the information you supplied.

2. In the Connect To dialog box, click the Connect button to dial your provider. You'll see a dialog box like the one in Figure 5.7.

Figure 5.7 This lets you know it is dialing your provider.

CAUTION

My Connection Setup Didn't Dial! If your connection setup didn't dial, your modem might not be installed correctly. Check the manual supplied by your modem manufacturer, and check the Modems configuration utility in the Control Panel.

3. If you connect to your provider, the Post-Dial Terminal Screen window now appears and prompts you to enter the information supplied by your provider (see Figure 5.8). Enter the information: login name, password, and so on—my provider had me input PPP since I use a Point-to-Point Protocol connection. When you finish, click the Continue button or press F7.

Figure 5.8 The Post-Dial Terminal Screen window.

4. If your connection settings are correct and you enter the correct information required by your provider, in a few seconds, a message indicates that you are connected (see Figure 5.9). Notice that the connection keeps a clock running that shows you how long you are connected and the speed of your connection. You may find it convenient now to close My Computer and Dial-Up Networking. Do not close the Connect To program; minimize it instead. If you close it, you exit the program and break the connection you just established.

Figure 5.9 Your connection is complete.

Testing Your Connection

Before you get started browsing or experimenting with other Internet activities, test your connection with WinIPCfg—a testing utility supplied with Windows 95.

1. Click the **Start** button on the taskbar and choose Programs, MS-DOS Prompt to open a DOS window.

2. Type **winipcfg** and press **Enter** to run the WinIPCfg utility program. In a few seconds, the IP information you see in Figure 5.10 appears.

Figure 5.10 WinIPCfg displays IP information.

3. Click the **More Info>>** button to display Figure 5.11.

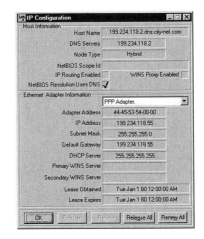

Figure 5.11 More information from WinIPCfg.

Most of the information displayed by WinIPCfg probably doesn't mean much to you, but the information should indicate whether you're connected to your provider (by showing your provider's name and IP address in the Host Name field, for example). The information in the IP Address field should either be your static IP address (if you set your own) or the dynamic IP address supplied by your provider. (If you didn't notice, back in the Post-Dial Terminal Screen window, your IP address was displayed.)

I'm Not Connected! If you are not connected, go back and recheck all the information you entered in this lesson.

CAUTION

In this lesson, you learned how to configure your Windows 95 Internet connection, connect to your Internet service provider, and test your connection. In the next lesson, you will learn how to configure an Apple Macintosh computer to connect to the Internet.

Configuration for Macintosh Users

In this lesson, you learn about the special software you need to connect to the Internet with a Macintosh computer. You also learn where to get that software and how to install and configure it.

What Your Macintosh Needs so You Can Access the Internet

In addition to your Macintosh, modem, phone line, and account with an Internet service provider (see Lesson 3, "Selecting an Internet Service Provider"), your Mac also needs some special software to help it cope with the Internet. You will need the following programs:

- MacTCP, a control panel that lets your Mac use TCP/IP (Transmission Control Protocol/Internet Protocol), the standard means of shuttling information around the Internet.
- Mac PPP, an extension (PPP) and control panel (Config PPP) set that allows your Mac to connect to a PPP account with your service provider.
- InterSLIP, an extension (InterSLIP), control panel (InterSLIP Control), and application (PSInet HOST-DCS) set that allows your Mac to connect to a SLIP account with your service provider.

Every Mac user needs MacTCP to connect to the Internet. In addition to that, you will need either Mac PPP or InterSLIP, depending on the type of account you set up with your Internet service provider (ISP). If you have a PPP account, use Mac PPP. If you have a SLIP account, use InterSLIP.

However, these three software items only allow your Mac to call and connect to the Internet through your ISP. If you actually want to do something on the Internet, you'll need a few more goodies, including the following.

- A Web browser, such as Netscape Navigator, Communicator, or Microsoft's Internet Explorer. Both of these, and many others, are available for Macintosh.
- An FTP utility for transferring files over the Internet. Anarchie and Fetch are excellent FTP utilities.
- An e-mail utility for sending and reading mail. Eudora is a powerful e-mail program.
- A compression utility that can reduce the size of the files you upload and download (which saves you time and money). Aladdin System's StuffIt is the Macintosh standard. This utility automatically comes with Netscape's Navigator and Communicator.

Where to Find Mac Software

You can find the software discussed here and other Internet software for your Mac in a number of places. The following sections discuss the different ways you can acquire such software.

Get It from Your ISP

Very often, when you sign up with an Internet service provider, it not only provides you with access to the Internet, but it also sends you an assortment of software to get you started quickly. You'll also get detailed instructions for configuring that software for use with your provider.

Although your service provider's starter kit might not contain the exact items listed in this lesson, it will have an equivalent range of software that you can use to connect. Once you're on the Internet, you can download and try the software mentioned here, or try anything else that strikes your fancy. Check out the upcoming section entitled "Find It" for tips on where to look for Mac software once you're on the Internet.

Buy It

The Internet is a hot topic, and many people want to hook into it. There are a lot of Mac-specific books and software combinations available to help you. This is the path of least resistance and doesn't involve much more than a trip to the store or a call to your favorite mail-order company.

The two best retail packages for the Mac are *The Internet Starter Kit for Macintosh* and *The Apple Internet Connection Kit*. Either is an excellent choice for Mac users.

The Internet Starter Kit for Macintosh by Adam Engst ($35, from Hayden Books) is a big book with more than you'll probably ever want to know about the Internet. It comes with a disk of all the software your Mac needs, plus more. The Starter Kit also includes customized files for more than 50 ISPs, so you won't have to configure anything.

The Apple Internet Connection Kit (approximately $50) is a complete set of software for your Mac that includes Netscape Navigator (which would cost you about $50 if you purchased it by itself). It comes with offers from a number of ISPs. If you select one of the providers from the kit, all of your Mac software is automatically configured for you.

Find It

A lot of the software you need is available on commercial online services such as America Online and CompuServe. If you have an account with either service, you can find and download all of the software listed earlier except for Netscape and Microsoft Internet Explorer. However, MacWeb is an excellent alternative to those, and it is available online.

On America Online, use the Keyword: **Net Software**, and you'll be taken to the Internet Connection's software library. There you can look for and download any of the items listed earlier in the chapter.

 TIP **Using AOL Keywords** Press **Ctrl+K** on your keyboard, and the Keyword dialog box appears. Type in the Keyword (in this case, **Net Software**) and press **Enter**.

On CompuServe, GO: **FILEFINDER**. In the list of file libraries, double-click the Macintosh entry. Then use File Finder to search for and download each of the items listed earlier.

TIP **GO on CompuServe** Press **Ctrl+G** on your keyboard. A GO dialog box will appear. Type in the GO word (in this case, **FILEFINDER**) and press **Enter**.

Both America Online and CompuServe also offer Internet access. If your account is set up to access the Internet, you can go to the Web sites listed here to get copies of the necessary software:

- Mac PPP and MacTCP: **http://www.apple.com**
- Netscape Navigator: **http://www.netscape.com**
- Microsoft Internet Explorer: **http//www.msn.com**
- For just about anything else in Macintosh software: **ftp://ftp.tidbits.com**
- Any browser available on the Net see: **www.browsers.com**
- For any other software you need, go to: **http://www.shareware.com**

Installing the Connection Software

Once the Macintosh software that's essential for you to connect to the Internet (MacTCP and either Mac PPP or InterSLIP, but not both) are all added to your System folder, you need to install them.

TIP **Internet Connection** These installation instructions are for those who located and downloaded the individual pieces of software from an online service or the Internet. If you bought *The Internet Starter Kit for Macintosh* or Apple's *Internet Connection Kit*, or if you received software directly from your ISP, follow the installation and configuration instructions that came with the product.

InterSLIP comes with an Installer that automatically places everything where it needs to be. Double-click the InterSLIP installer icon, and follow the directions that appear on your screen. The installer will restart your Mac when it's done, so be prepared.

For each component of MacTCP and Mac PPP, perform the following steps:

1. Open the icon for your hard drive. Make sure you can see the System folder.

2. Open the folder that contains the item(s) you are installing. Position the window so you can still see your System folder.

3. Click and drag the Internet software from its window, and drop it on your closed System folder. (MacTCP is one control panel. Mac PPP uses an extension and control panel. InterSLIP uses an extension and a small application.)

4. Your Mac will ask if it's okay to put each item where it belongs (in the Extensions folder or the Control Panels folder). Click **OK**.

5. Restart your Mac (open the **Special** menu and select **Restart**) so your Mac can use the software you've installed.

If you're using Mac PPP, the .PPP extension will be in your Extensions folder, and Config PPP will appear in your Control Panels folder. If you're using InterSLIP, the InterSLIP extension will be in your Extensions folder, and InterSLIP Control will be in your Control Panels folder. The InterSLIP Setup application (for some reason named PSInet HOST-DCS) and an InterSLIP manual will land on your desktop.

Any of the other software you may have acquired (Netscape, Eudora, or anything else along those lines) will either be ready to run or will come with an Installer. If there's an Installer, double-click its icon and follow the on-screen instructions.

Configuring Your Software

You need to provide your newly installed software with information about your Internet service provider. You get that from your ISP, usually in a manual or on an information sheet. Don't try to configure anything until you have that information in your hands.

MacTCP

To configure MacTCP, follow these steps:

1. Select the **Control Panels** folder and double-click the **MacTCP** icon. The MacTCP control panel opens; it will look something like Figure 6.1.

Figure 6.1 The MacTCP Control Panel.

2. Click the **PPP** icon at the top of the control panel to select it (refer to Figure 6.1), and then click **More**. The configuration dialog box shown in Figure 6.2 appears.

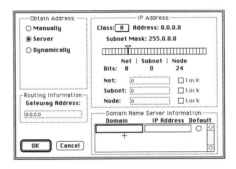

Figure 6.2 The MacTCP configuration options.

3. Carefully enter the information your ISP gave you. Generally, you'll need to select only one option in the Obtain Address box (in the upper-left corner of Figure 6.2). Then you'll fill in the first line under DOMAIN and IP ADDRESS in the Domain Name Server Information box in the lower-right corner. However, no two ISPs are alike, so carefully follow their directions.

4. When you finish entering the information, click **OK** to save it. Then close the MacTCP Control Panel.

5. Your Mac may inform you that you need to restart in order for the changes you've made to take effect. To do so, open the **Special** menu and select **Restart**.

Mac PPP

Follow these steps to configure Mac PPP:

1. Select the **Control Panels** folder (if necessary) and double-click the **Config PPP** icon. Config PPP opens; it will look something like Figure 6.3.

Figure 6.3 The Config PPP control panel.

2. Select the name of your modem from the PPP Server drop-down list at the bottom of the control panel.

3. From the Port Name drop-down list near the top of the control panel, select the port to which your modem is connected.

4. Click the **Config** button in the lower-left corner of the control panel, and the dialog box shown in Figure 6.4 appears.

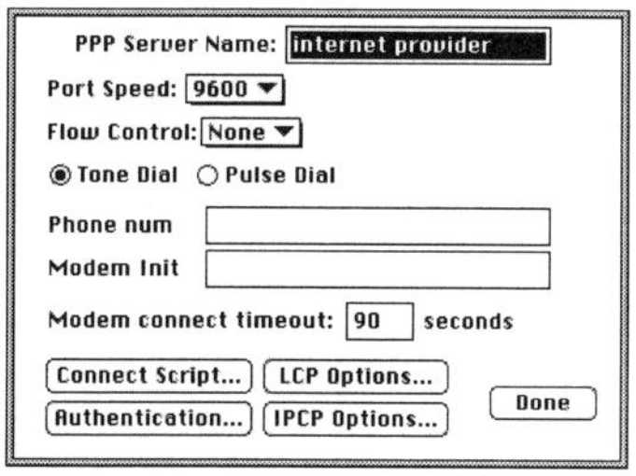

Figure 6.4 The Config PPP control panel.

5. Type the name of your ISP in the PPP Server Name text box at the top of the control panel.

6. Next, select your modem's maximum speed from the Port Speed drop-down list.

7. Then click the option button for the type of phone line you have: **Tone Dial** or **Pulse Dial**.

8. Finally, type your ISP's access telephone number in the Phone Number text box.

9. In the remaining boxes, enter any other or different information your ISP may have given you. As always, follow the instructions.

10. You may or may not need to configure the Connect Script, Authentication, LCP Options, or IPCP Options, depending on your ISP's particular needs. If you do, carefully follow their instructions.

11. When you finish, click **Done** and close the Config PPP control panel.

Notice that where you entered your modem name in the PPP Server text box, it now shows the name of your ISP.

InterSLIP

Follow these steps to configure InterSLIP:

1. Double-click the **PSInet HOST-DCS** icon on your desktop to start the InterSLIP Setup application (as I mentioned earlier, for some reason it's called PSInet HOST-DCS). The InterSLIP display shown in Figure 6.5 appears.

Figure 6.5 Setting up InterSLIP.

2. Open the **File** menu and select **New**. InterSLIP asks you to name the new configuration file.

3. Type the name of your ISP in the text box and click **OK**. The name you typed appears in the InterSLIP window.

4. Double-click the name of your ISP, and the configuration screen shown in Figure 6.6 opens.

5. Open the Serial Port drop-down list (near the top of the dialog box) and select the port to which your modem is connected.

Figure 6.6 Configuring InterSLIP for your ISP.

6. Select your modem's maximum speed from the Baud Rate drop-down list.

7. Fill in the remaining information according to the information your ISP provided.

8. When you finish, click **OK** to save the information and close the configuration dialog box.

9. To quit InterSLIP Setup, open the **File** menu and select **Quit**.

Your Other Internet Applications

Your Web browser, your e-mail utility, and any other applications you want to use on the Internet will also need information about your ISP (such as the name of the mail server, the news server, and so on). All of that information should be provided by your ISP in a manual or information sheet. The applications' Help files will explain what information needs to go where.

Connecting to Your ISP

After you configure your software, test out the configuration by connecting to your ISP. Follow these steps:

1. Open **Config PPP** or **InterSLIP** (whichever you're using) as described in the appropriate configuration section.

2. Click **Open** (in Config PPP) or Connect (in InterSLIP). A MacTCP Status window opens, telling you what it's doing as it goes through the connection process.

3. If you connect successfully, everything is fine. You can launch your Web browser and get hopping on the World Wide Web.

4. When you're done, quit your Web browser and any other Internet applications you have running.

5. Click **Close** (in Config PPP) or Disconnect (in InterSLIP) to sign off of your ISP.

If you cannot connect to your ISP, retrace your steps through the configuration process. Make sure you've entered the information from your ISP accurately (a mistake in a series of numbers is the most common problem), and try again. If you double-check your ISP information and it all looks correct, you might want to give your ISP's technical support number a call. Ask for its Macintosh person, and see if he can help you out.

In this lesson, you learned how to connect to the Internet with your Macintosh. In the next lesson, you will learn how to access the Web through Online Services.

Accessing the Web Through Online Services

In this lesson, you learn how to access the World Wide Web using two of the major online services: AOL and The Microsoft Network.

America Online

America Online (AOL) is currently the largest of the major online services with a reported user base of four million. If you've bought a computer magazine in the last six months, chances are you already have AOL software. If you haven't picked up a computer magazine lately, you can call AOL at (800) 827-3338 and order its software for free. The major online services have all been feverishly distributing their disks and CD-ROMs attached to virtually any and every computer magazine that has anything to say about the Internet. These disks and CD-ROMs usually come with a limited amount of free access. So make sure you try before you buy. During the past year, all of the major online services have added Internet access to their list of services.

Installing and Setting Up AOL

AOL is only available on the Windows and Mac platforms. In this lesson, you will be using AOL on a Windows 95 platform. AOL is not particular about running on either Windows 3.1, 95, or NT, and none of the three flavors of Windows has an advantage when running AOL.

To install AOL, follow these steps:

1. Place your AOL disk into your drive (floppy disk or CD) and select the **File**, **Run**.

2. At the Run prompt, type **x:\setup**, where **x** is the drive you placed the disk in.

3. Follow the prompts to complete the installation.

4. Double-click the **AOL** icon to start the program. When you start AOL the first time, you will have to sign up for the service. Follow the prompts to sign up for AOL. The setup will take approximately 3–5 minutes.

5. When you complete the setup, follow the prompts to the main menu shown in Figure 7.1.

Figure 7.1 AOL'S main menu.

From the main menu, click **Internet Connection** to proceed to AOL's gateway to the Internet (see Figure 7.2).

In the Internet Connection window, click the **World Wide Web** icon to start AOL's Web browser. Figure 7.3 shows the opening screen you will see.

AOL's Web browser works much the same as MS Internet Explorer. In fact, the current browser release for AOL 3.0 is an Internet Explorer Web browser. You enter the URL of the Web page or site you want to visit and in a few seconds, the page appears on your screen. For example, to visit the Smithsonian Web site, you can enter **http://www.si.edu/**, and in a few seconds, you're at the Smithsonian's Web site (see Figure 7.4).

Figure 7.2 AOL's Internet Connection.

Figure 7.3 AOL's Web browser.

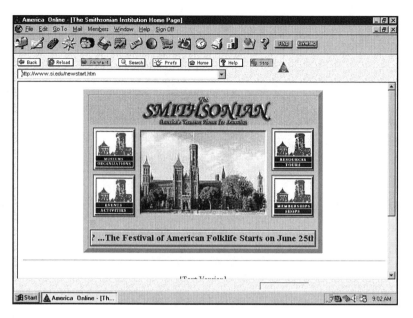

Figure 7.4   Visit the Smithsonian online.

The Microsoft Network

The inclusion of software for the Microsoft Network with Windows 95 caused a protracted legal battle between Microsoft and several of the major online service companies. They lost, Microsoft won, and your MSN software is bundled with Windows 95. This also partly explains the flurry of free software from the other services "bundled" with practically every PC Magazine in the past two years.

The upside for Microsoft with bundling MSN software in Windows 95 is that you do not have to get another disk or order a software installation package in order to install MSN. The downside for Microsoft is that MSN is only available for Windows 95. Therefore, if you're not running Windows 95, or are not thinking about switching to Windows 95, you can bypass this section.

If you are running Windows 95 and you did not install MSN when you installed Windows 95, adding MSN is a snap. Follow these steps:

1. Open the Windows 95 Control Panel and click **Add/Remove Programs**.

TIP **There Is No Listing for Microsoft Network** If you don't see MSN in the Add/Remove listing, you can still install MSN using the Internet Setup Wizard by selecting MSN as your service provider.

2. Select the Windows **Setup** tab in the Add/Remove Programs Properties dialog box. Select **The Microsoft Network** check box and click **OK**.

3. Follow the prompts to install The Microsoft Network. Make sure you have your Windows 95 installation CD or disks handy. You will be prompted to insert them so the installation program can copy the appropriate files to your PC.

4. When the installation is completed, you should see a new icon on your desktop for The Microsoft Network. Double-click the **MSN** icon to start the program.

5. Follow the initial sign-on prompts until you see the main menu pictured in Figure 7.5.

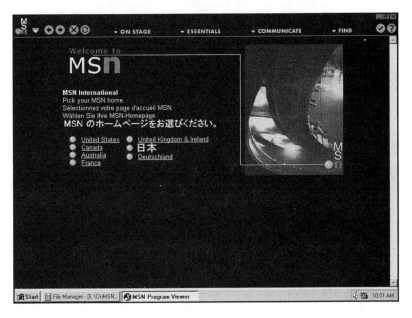

Figure 7.5 MSN's main menu.

47

6. Click **Categories** to go to the Categories Menu.

7. From the Categories menu, click **Internet Center**.

8. At the Internet Center, click **MSN on the Web**. In a few seconds, MS Internet Explorer appears, displaying the MSN home page located at **www.msn.com** (see Figure 7.6).

Figure 7.6 The MSN home page.

The Advantages and Disadvantages of Using Online Services

As you might expect, using one of the major online services to access the World Wide Web and the Internet has its pros and cons. On the plus side is the relative ease of the setup procedure. Both of the online services mentioned here have done an excellent job of making it very quick and painless to install their software and connect to the Internet in (usually) under 15 minutes. In addition, besides Internet and Web access, all of the online services mentioned here also offer a wide variety of other useful services geared toward adults and children, business and pleasure, and all in a neat package, complete with instructions on how to find and use all of their services.

Most of the major online services have adopted the flat-fee system and their charges are comparable to what most Internet service providers charge for a month of Internet access (approximately $20/month).

So does this mean that I am now advising you to take the easy road and sign up for one of the two services mentioned here? If ease of use and cost are your *only* criteria for deciding which service to use, then by all means, sign up now for either AOL or MSN (you can flip a coin to decide which one to choose).

But be aware there are some serious disadvantages to using the Online services. AOL experienced what many in the industry called "extreme growing pains" in that it apparently signed up more users than its infrastructure could reasonably handle. The result was a litany of complaints by users who got more busy signals than login prompts. AOL is still facing numerous class action lawsuits resulting from its "repricing plan."

But even after you get online, there are still some serious disadvantages in using an online service. Because you are connecting to the Internet through a carefully monitored and controlled computer environment, you are somewhat "locked" into the utility and tools the online service provides. However, many of the Online Services now let you choose your own Web browser, such as Internet Explorer and Netscape Navigator. In terms of e-mail, however, you are usually locked into the e-mail client that your online service uses.

In this lesson, you learned how to access the World Wide Web using online services such as AOL. In the next lesson, you will learn how to install AOL.

Installing America Online 3.0

In this lesson, you learn how to install the America Online 3.0 software on your computer.

Windows Setup

As with all computer software, you need to install America Online 3.0 on your computer before you can actually use it. The process is simple for all Windows variations (95, 3.1, NT).

If you received version 3.0 on a floppy disk or CD, insert the disk in the appropriate drive. If you downloaded the latest version directly from America Online, locate the folder where you placed it (it's probably inside your AOL25 folder, in the Download folder). You're now ready to begin the installation process.

AOL Installation: Windows 3.1 and NT 3.51

1. Open the **Program Manager**.
2. Select **File, Run**.
3. If you're installing from disk, type **A:\Setup** in the Run dialog text box (substitute the correct drive letter if you aren't using your A: drive, for example, E:\ for a CD-ROM drive).

   If you're installing from a downloaded copy of AOL 3.0, click **Browse and** locate the setup.exe file. Double-click **setup.exe**.
4. Click **OK**.

The AOL 3.0 setup program will start. You can skip ahead to the "Setting Up Step-by-Step" section.

AOL Installation: Windows 95 and NT 4.0

1. Click the **Start** button.
2. Click **Run** on the **Start** menu.
3. If you're installing from a disk, type **A:\Setup** in the Run dialog text box (substitute the correct drive letter if you aren't using your A: drive, for example, E:\ for a CD-ROM drive).

   If you're installing from a downloaded copy of AOL 3.0, click **Browse** and locate the setup.exe file. Double-click **setup.exe**.
4. Click **OK**.

The AOL 3.0 setup program will start.

Setting Up Step-by-Step

When the setup program launches, the first thing it does is search your hard drive for a previously installed version of America Online. If it finds one, setup will automatically copy the settings, screen names, passwords, and mail files from the previous version, so you can get right to work with AOL 3.0.

After it scans your hard drive, setup presents you with a Welcome screen. The Welcome screen gives you three options: you can continue the installation if you click **Install**; you can check or change the installation directories chosen by the setup program by clicking **Review**; or you can cancel the installation by clicking **Exit**.

To leave all the decisions to the setup program, click **Install**. It will place a copy of the new AOL software on your hard drive, and if you have a previous version of AOL, it will copy your old settings to the new version.

You can keep setup from copying information from an older version of AOL by clicking **Review**. You'll be asked to verify that you want any settings from a previous version copied to AOL 3.0 with the dialog box shown in Figure 8.1.

The Directory text box shows the location of your old version of the AOL software. To finish the installation using settings copied from the version of AOL shown in the Review dialog box, click **Continue**.

51

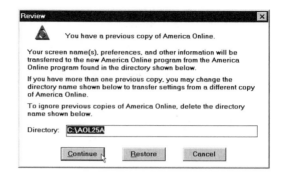

Figure 8.1 Reviewing your installation options.

If you have two or more copies of an older AOL version, and you want to copy the settings from another version shown in the Review dialog box, type the path statement to the copy with the settings you want to duplicate. Then click **Continue**.

 Path Statement This is like an abbreviated map used to note the location of a file on your hard drive. A typical path statement for your AOL folder would look like this:

C:\AOL30

To completely ignore previous versions of AOL on your hard drive, delete the path statement in the Directory box and click **Continue**. Next, setup will show you where it intends to install the AOL 3.0 software (**C:\AOL30**). If the destination is acceptable, click **Install**. If you want to install the software somewhere else, type the path statement for the new location, and then click **Install**.

Setup will install the program, add an AOL 3.0 shortcut to your Start menu's Programs submenu (Windows 95 and NT 4.0), and open the America Online 3.0 program group window on your desktop (all Windows versions) as shown in Figure 8.2.

If you're a first-time AOL user, proceed to Lesson 9 to set up your account. If you've upgraded and copied the settings from an older version, you're ready to sign on.

Figure 8.2   The America Online 3.0 program group.

Macintosh Setup

CAUTION

Macintosh Alert!   The Mac version of AOL 3.0 was not available for preview at the time this was written. The information here is based on available information and past versions of AOL. If what you see on your screen varies at all from what it says here, go with what the screen says. This book will be updated as soon as possible after the Mac version of AOL 3.0 is available.

If you received version 3.0 on floppy disk or CD, insert the disk in the appropriate drive. If you downloaded the latest version directly from America Online, you will need to find the copy on your hard drive (it's probably inside your America Online 2.5 folder, in the Download folder). You're ready to begin the installation process.

If you're installing from a downloaded copy, skip the following.

1. Double-click the **Installation Disk** icon on your desktop.
2. Double-click the **Install AOL 3.0** icon in the disk's window.

First, the installer will search your hard drive for a previously installed version of America Online. If it finds one, the installer will automatically copy the settings, screen names, passwords, and mail files from the previous version (unless you tell it otherwise). When the installer is finished searching your hard drive, it will give you a dialog box much like the one shown in Figure 8.3.

Figure 8.3 The AOL installer for Macintosh.

The dialog box gives you three options. You can continue the installation by clicking **Continue**, you can select which AOL 3.0 components are installed if you click **Custom**, or you can cancel the installation by clicking **Quit**. Unless you're very familiar with AOL, and want a custom installation, most users should click **Continue**.

Next, you'll be asked to select a hard drive on which to install the software. If you have only one, there's no choice. Then click **Install**. If you have more than one hard drive on your Mac, or if you have your hard drive divided into partitions, click **Switch disk** until the drive you want to use is selected. Then click **Install**.

The installer will place all of the necessary files on your hard drive in an America Online 3.0 folder. When it's finished, the America Online 3.0 folder window will be open on your desktop. You're ready to start AOL and set up your account. Continue on with Lesson 9.

If the installer copied your account information from a previous version of AOL, you can sign on immediately and begin exploring AOL's new features. You can start with Lesson 10 (AOL's toolbar) or any other lesson you prefer.

In this lesson, you learned how to install the America Online 3.0 software on your computer. In the next lesson, you'll set up your online account.

Setting Up Your AOL Account

In this lesson, you learn how to set up your AOL account, and how to sign onto, and off of, the service.

Launching AOL in Windows 95

You use your AOL software to establish your account with America Online. To begin, you need to launch AOL.

 Launch   A formal way to say "start an application."

If the AOL program group window (seen in Figure 8.2 in the previous lesson) is still open on your desktop, double-click the **America Online 3.0 Double-Click to Start** icon. You can also use the **Start** menu to launch AOL. Here's how:

1. Click the **Start** button.
2. Point at **Programs**.
3. Point at **America Online 3.0** on the Programs submenu.
4. Click **America Online 3.0 Double-Click to Start** on the America Online 3.0 submenu.

 TIP   **Launching Mac AOL**   Double-click the **America Online 3.0 Double Click to Start** icon in your America Online 3.0 folder.

TIP   **Launching with Windows 3.1 and NT 3.51**   Double-click the **America Online 3.0 Double-Click to Start** icon in your America Online 3.0 program group in the Program Manager.

Providing System Information

When AOL starts up, you'll see a Welcome screen like the one shown in Figure 9.1.

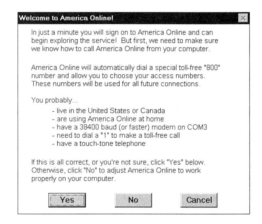

Figure 9.1   Welcome to America Online!

The account setup routine assumes some basic information about your computer, modem, and telephone line and is located on the Welcome screen. Read it over. If it's all correct, click **Yes**. If some of the information is wrong (for example, you need to dial "9" to get an outside line), click **No**. AOL will show you each bit of information and ask you to change whatever you need to change so that it's correct.

TIP   **Breaking the Connection**   While you are online, you may want to download various types of files. Some files can take several minutes to download. To ensure an uninterrupted download, you should disconnect your call waiting. This will prevent other callers from breaking your connection to AOL through the second call waiting line.

If you have no idea whether the information presented is correct, click **Cancel**, and restart the setup routine after you've had a chance to check your system and phone line information.

If you clicked **Yes**, the account setup program will remind you to have some information handy.

New members should have:

- Credit card or checking account information.
- Your America Online registration number and password (it came with the disk).

Current AOL members will need:

- Your screen name.
- The password for that screen name.

When you have the proper information, click **OK** and the account setup routine will continue.

Quick Stepping Through Account Setup

The remainder of the account setup process is basically a series of screens that ask for various information. The instructions on each are clear and simple, so a condensed version will follow.

Getting a Local Number

The first step is getting a local access number or the local telephone number your computer will dial to connect to AOL. Your AOL software will call a toll-free number to get you a local number. You won't be using the 800-number regularly.

After you connect, follow these steps:

1. The first screen will ask you to type your area code. Do so, and then click **Continue**.

2. Next, you'll be presented with a list of access numbers in and around your local calling area. Find a number that's a local call for you. Click the phone number, and then click **Select Phone Number**.

3. You'll be asked to repeat the process with a second phone number in case the first number is busy. Find a second local number, and click that phone number. Then click **Select Phone Number**. If you can't find a second number, you can choose to use your first choice for both numbers. You will get a screen asking you to confirm the phone numbers. Click **Continue**.

Entering Your Registration Number and Password

Next, you'll be asked to type in your registration number (or screen name) and your password.

- **New members** Carefully type the registration number and password in the boxes. You can get this information from the papers that came with your AOL software. Then click **Continue**.
- **AOL Members** Carefully type your Screen Name and the Password for that Screen Name in the appropriate boxes. Click **Continue**.

Entering Your Personal Information

AOL will then ask you for some personal information about yourself: Name, address, telephone numbers, and the like, which is used to establish your billing address. This information is kept confidential; no one sees it except the people at America Online. The form is a simple fill-in-the-blanks affair. Carefully type the information in the appropriate boxes. Press **Tab** to move to the next box. When you finish filling everything in, click **Continue** again.

Selecting a Method of Payment

To pay for your online usage, America Online needs to know your preferred payment method. You can pay by credit card, or you can have the monthly charges deducted automatically from a checking account. Select a payment method and click **Continue**. You'll be asked to provide additional information that will vary depending on the payment method, such as credit card or checking account numbers. Type the requested information and click **Continue**.

CAUTION

Safety Alert! This is the only time AOL will ask you to provide credit card information. Never hand out credit card, personal, or financial information online unless the transaction is done over a secure connection. Secure connections allow for safe information transactions. See Lesson 25 for other online safety tips.

Choosing a Screen Name

After you enter your payment information, you'll be asked to create a screen name for yourself. Your screen name is important: it acts as your e-mail address (see Lessons 5 and 6), and it's how you're identified in chat rooms when you speak (Lesson 11). This first one is also your master account name and cannot be changed or deleted.

A screen name must:

- Be *at least* three characters in length.
- Be *no more* than ten characters in length.
- Start with a letter.
- Not be offensive or obscene.

A screen name can be anything you like, containing any combination of numbers, letters, and spaces. If you plan to use AOL for business purposes, keep it simple and professional.

Type the screen name in the text box and select **Continue**.

If the name you've entered has already been used, AOL will let you know. You can accept its suggested variation, which is the same name with numbers added, or keep trying until you find one that hasn't been used yet. When both you and AOL are satisfied with your screen name, select **Continue**.

Choosing a Password

Finally, you'll be asked to enter a password for this account. Your password should be a word, words, numbers, or combination of numbers and words that only you will know.

Like screen names, there are a few rules that apply to passwords:

- Your password should be 4–8 characters in length.
- It should be easy to remember without writing it down.
- It should be difficult for another individual to guess what it might be.

You need to carefully type your password twice. There are two text boxes provided on the screen. When you type, you'll only see a series of asterisks (*). You will not see the letters or numbers you are typing, for security purposes. The second entry is to make sure you type the same password twice.

When you're done typing your password two times, click **Select Password**. AOL will confirm that you typed the same thing in each box. If you did, you'll continue. If not, you'll again be asked to enter your password twice.

Reading the Terms of Service

The final step in setting up your account involves reading and agreeing to America Online's Terms of Service, also referred to as TOS. These are the rules that everyone must abide by when using AOL. They are important, so read them carefully. If you accept the TOS, press **Enter**.

You're finished! You'll be disconnected from AOL so you can sign on under your newly created screen name. Try it now!

Signing On and Off

Before you begin the lessons that follow, you might want to sign onto AOL and check it out on your own. Follow these steps to successfully sign on:

1. Launch AOL, as described earlier in this lesson. The sign-on screen shown in Figure 9.2 appears.

Figure 9.2   AOL's sign-on screen.

2. Enter your password in the **Enter Password** text box. (Note that your master screen name is loaded automatically.)

3. Click **Sign On**.

Your computer will call and connect to your local access number and then connect to America Online. Explore and enjoy the service.

When you're ready to sign off, select **File**, **Exit**, or select **Go To**, **Sign Off**. The dialog box shown in Figure 9.3 appears giving you these three options:

- **Sign Off** You'll disconnect from AOL, but the software will still be running on your computer.

- **Exit** Allows you to disconnect from AOL and shut down the application.

- **Channels** You'll stay connected and go to the Channels display, or you'll see a featured area online. See Lesson 9 for more information on this topic.

Figure 9.3 AOL's Sign Off? screen.

In this lesson, you learned how to set up your AOL account and how to sign on and off the service. In the next lesson, you'll learn how to use AOL's toolbar to save you time online.

The AOL Toolbar

In this lesson, you learn what each of the buttons on the AOL toolbar is and what it does.

Work Faster, Better, Cheaper...

This is a very brief lesson, but it is also incredibly important. It will save you time and money every time you connect to America Online.

In this lesson, you learn about the handiest of all of America Online's features: the toolbar. It includes 18 buttons that give you speedy access to things you'll do almost every time you're online. Get to know it. You can see it in Figure 10.1.

Figure 10.1 The very useful AOL toolbar.

In Figure 10.1, all of the buttons are active, that is, they're ready for you to use. Sometimes (while you're not connected to AOL, for example), some of these buttons will dim. It's a visual clue to tell you that the particular tool or feature is not available.

 TIP **You Don't Have to Memorize Buttons** If you happen to forget what a toolbar button does, just point at the button with your mouse. A little reminder will pop up to explain the tool.

These are the toolbar buttons, in order, from left to right.

 Get New Mail Springs to life whenever you receive mail on America Online. To see a list of the mail you've received, click it. You'll then be able to open, read, and reply to all of your new, incoming mail. There are several lessons devoted to handling your e-mail.

 Compose Mail Always available because you might want to write a quick note at any time. When you click the Compose Mail button, AOL gives you a new, blank e-mail form. Composing mail messages is covered in Part 3, Lesson 6, also.

 Channels Previously, AOL's various subject categories were referred to as departments. Now they're called Channels (because getting around online is as easy as switching channels on a television). Click the Channels button and you'll bring up a display of all the main Channels available online.

 What's Hot Use to keep up to date on all of the new features and forums online. Not only can you find what's new, you can find out which areas are the most popular, too.

 People Connection The Channel where everybody's talking about something; it's where the Chat Rooms are. When you click the People Connection button, you'll be dropped into a general meeting room (called a Lobby) where you can settle in for a nice talk or begin your search for another chat room that better suits your mood.

 File Search Gives you instant access to powerful searching tools that will scour AOL's software libraries. You can search for a particular kind of file, a file subject, or even a specific file.

 Stocks & Portfolios Are you a Wall Street tycoon? You can keep up with all of your investments in the Stocks & Portfolios Channel.

 News Go directly to the online news center where you can read today's top stories right off the wire, see photographs, check the sports scores, and even see if it's going to rain on your parade.

 World Wide Web The fastest growing area of the Internet where graphics-based Web pages offer you all manner of information, resources, and entertainment. You'll see pages covering everything from the latest world news from CNN or *The Washington Post*, to gossip about the goings-on in the "Star Trek" universe, to a Web page that lets you watch Spam decay slowly over time.

The Marketplace   Offers a variety of online shopping.

 My AOL   The online area devoted to your preferences; how AOL looks and behaves, as well as other customizing features. They're all explained in Part 1, Lesson 11, coming up next.

 Online Clock   It's very easy to lose track of time while roaming the Channels and chatting endlessly. The Online Clock keeps track of it for you. Click the Online Clock button, and AOL will tell you the time, plus how long you've spent online so far. This is very handy.

 Print   Sends whatever document you happen to be looking at to your printer, so you can have a hard copy.

 Filing Cabinet   Opens the place where AOL stores all of the e-mail it has sent and retrieved for you via FlashSessions. It's an easy way to organize your correspondence and other online communications.

 Favorite Places   An organizing tool you can use to store all the places you visit regularly, both on AOL and in the larger world of the Internet.

 Member Services   The big question mark is a button that takes you directly to a vast (and free) online help resource. You can check your bill, change your password, read about online safety, plus all sorts of other useful tips and resources.

 Find   Like the File Search button, the Find button allows you to search through everything online. Looking for a person? Want to know what famous celebrity is appearing online tonight? Click Find. Find helps you locate Places & Things, People, and Events online.

 Keyword   Using a Keyword is the fastest way to get anywhere online. Every Channel, forum, and service on America Online has a Keyword. Click this button, type a word, click OK, and you're off.

In this lesson, you learned the function of each of the toolbar buttons, as well as references to other lessons in which you'll encounter them. In the next lesson, you'll learn how to set preferences to make AOL work the way you want it to.

Setting AOL Preferences

In this lesson, you learn how to customize the way your AOL software performs.

What Are Preferences?

You use AOL's Preferences to tell the software how you want things to look and act. You can fine-tune all of the features, from the fonts used for e-mail, to whether or not image files appear while you download them.

Depending on your computer and modem speed, some settings may improve AOL's performance, and some others may slow it down. Spend a little time exploring AOL to try various features before changing your preference settings.

Keep in mind that nothing is set in stone. If you change your settings and find they aren't to your liking, you can always change them again.

There are two ways to change your preferences: online (while connected to AOL) through My AOL, or offline (not connected to AOL) through the Preferences command on the Members menu. There is some duplication between the two preference types. All of your offline preferences are accessible from My AOL; however, My AOL includes some options that you can only adjust online.

 TIP   **Easy Does It!**   My AOL includes step-by-step instructions on setting all of your preferences. Because it holds your hand through the process, new users might be more comfortable using My AOL to set all of their preferences.

My AOL

To get to My AOL, you need to connect to America Online. After you connect, click the **My AOL** icon on the toolbar, or select **My AOL** from the **Members** menu. Either method opens the My AOL screen shown in Figure 11.1.

Master Screen Name Only   You can change many of the features of My AOL only from your Master Screen Name. That's the Screen Name you created when you first joined AOL back in Part 1, Lesson 8. Make sure that's the name you use each time you sign on to set your preferences, or you won't be able to do much.

CAUTION

Figure 11.1   Welcome to My AOL.

My AOL explains a number of customizable features for you including FlashSession, custom news delivery, AOL's Buddy List, and more. Once you set up your basic My AOL preferences, you might want to take a minute or two to explore some of these other customizable features.

To begin setting your Preferences, click **Preferences**. The Preferences window (shown in Figure 11.2) opens.

First Time AOL Users   If this is your first experience with AOL, save time: click **Set Up AOL Now**. It will walk you step-by-step through your preference options.

CAUTION

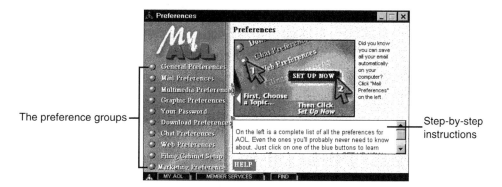

The preference groups ⎯⎯⎯ (left side annotation)

Step-by-step instructions (right side annotation)

Figure 11.2   Your Preferences start here.

The left side of the window contains buttons for the various preference groups. The right side of the window contains simple, step-by-step instructions for setting the preferences in each group. You can set these in any order.

When you click a preference group, the right side of the screen changes to display information about that preference group. Once you read it, you can set your preferences, read information about other options, or get help. Figure 11.3 shows the instructions for setting up your member profile, displaying typical instructions that you'll see for all of your preferences.

To create your own member profile, click the **Be Seen** button on the main My AOL window.

Member Profile   This is a list of basic information (Screen Name, real name, location, birthday, gender, and more) that other members can access to learn about you and your interests. You can create a member profile for each of your AOL Screen Names. If you would like to remain anonymous, you are not obligated to complete a member profile.

Click the preference group you want to work with. Read the information on the right side of the screen. If you still want to set this preference, click **SET UP NOW**, and AOL will walk you through the process. If not, click another preference group, or use **Previous** and **Next** (at the bottom of the window) to check out the rest of your customizing options.

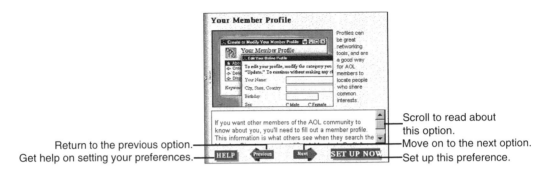

Return to the previous option. Scroll to read about this option.

Get help on setting your preferences. Move on to the next option.

Set up this preference.

Figure 11.3 Your Preferences start here.

Selecting Your Options

You set most of your preferences by clicking the items you want to activate or deactivate. Once you read an explanation of your options on the My AOL window, and once you click **SET UP NOW**, the preferences appear in a dialog box like the one shown in Figure 11.4.

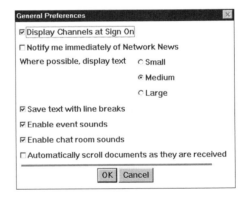

Figure 11.4 Typical General Preferences options.

Options are active when a check mark appears in front of the item (like the Display Channels at Sign On item at the top of Figure 11.4). To turn on an option that is not checked, click the check box. A check mark (✔) appears in the box.

To deactivate a checked option, click the check box a second time. The check mark will disappear, turning that particular option off.

Toggle This is any option that you can turn on when you select it, and then turn off when you click it a second time.

When you finish selecting your options, click **OK**. You return to My AOL at the same point from which you left. You can select another preference group and continue the customizing process.

Changing Preferences Later

Later on, you may discover that some of these preferences no longer meet your needs. It happens. As you get more sophisticated in your use of AOL, you'll learn better ways to do things. Or you'll find that you prefer different settings. You can easily change your preferences at any time by returning to My AOL. Repeat the processes previously described, changing only the settings you want to alter.

You can also alter some of your preferences offline (saving you money on your online charges). Here's how:

1. Launch your AOL software, but don't connect to the service. Select **Members**, **Preferences to** opens the Preferences window shown in Figure 11.5.

Figure 11.5 The preferences you can set offline.

In this window, you can press the Chat, General, Download, Graphics, Passwords, Mail, WWW, and Personal Filing Cabinet preferences buttons.

2. Click the button for the preferences you want to change, and adjust your settings as you like. Each button gives you an assortment of options such as the one shown in Figure 11.4.

69

You can change the remaining preferences, those not available here, through My AOL. Or you can change many preferences online through Member Services, which is a *free* area, so you won't incur any online charges while you change things.

In this lesson, you learned how to customize your AOL software through My AOL and the Preferences command on the Members menu. In the next lesson, you'll learn the etiquette rules for the Internet and how to behave properly online.

Internet Etiquette (Netiquette)

In this lesson, you learn netiquette: the proper Internet code of behavior to follow when interacting with other Internet users.

When Netiquette Comes into Play

Sitting alone in front of your computer surfing the Net, it may not have dawned on you that there is also an Internet protocol for interacting with other Internet users. Internet etiquette, or *netiquette*, is a set of written and unwritten rules that you are expected to learn and abide by. Depending on how you spend your time on the Internet, it is possible that you may rarely encounter other users; it is also possible to have numerous encounters each and every time you log on. The three primary areas where netiquette will most often come into play are:

- E-mail
- Newsgroups
- Chat rooms

Each of these areas has its own set of rules, and whether you follow these rules or trample all over them can mean the difference between amicable interaction and flame wars.

Flame   A very insulting and often extremely combative e-mail message you may be sent if you don't use netiquette.

Remember, too, that the information presented in this lesson is not all-inclusive. You should treat this information as a general guideline, not as the Ten Commandments for Internet Etiquette.

E-Mail and Its Code of Conduct

You may not think there is much that can go wrong using e-mail. After all, you simply write a message and then send it to someone. What could be simpler? Here is a short list of DOs and DON'Ts associated with this seemingly harmless act.

DO...

- Be considerate of others; keep your messages short and to the point. E-mail is for sending messages, not dissertations.

- Use smileys or emoticons such as :-) and :-(to express yourself in e-mail, but use them sparingly. These funny little symbols can convey the tone of a message and prevent someone from taking it in a different way than you meant it. For more information on emoticons, see the following Web page:

  http://www.jsp.umontreal.ca/~chantane/ES/internet /emoticon.txt

- Keep signature files short (no more than five or six lines). Many users have adopted the habit of adding bits of irony or witty sayings called *signatures* to the end of their e-mail messages. Many e-mail programs allow you to create a list of signature files, which they append to the end of your messages. Some examples include:

  "You can make it idiot-proof, but they'll just keep making better idiots."

  "I used to be indecisive, but now I'm not sure."

DON'T...

- USE ALL UPPERCASE LETTERS IN YOUR MESSAGES! Because e-mail messages are read and not heard, you don't have the opportunity to express yourself as you would if you were using a telephone. ALL UPPERCASE LETTERS is the e-mail equivalent of SHOUTING!

- Send junk mail! The only thing more annoying than emptying junk out of the mailbox at your front door is emptying junk mail out of your e-mail mailbox. Most users find it annoying, and it only adds to the congestion on the Internet.

- Send an e-mail message you would not want to read to your mother, or hear read on the evening news. While this may sound strange, the message here is, don't put embarrassing information in your e-mail messages.

Proper Conduct in Newsgroups

Rules of conduct on newsgroups are usually spelled out for you, and if you plan to spend much time in newsgroups, especially if you plan to post messages, you would be wise to download and read the newsgroup FAQs (Frequently Asked Questions) before you become an active participant. You can usually find rules and netiquette information in the newsgroup **news.announce.newusers**.

The **news.announce.newusers** newsgroup contains these rules (and many others) that you need to follow when you're in newsgroups:

- Insulting, degrading, and racist comments are forbidden.
- Keep your postings short and succinct, especially when quoting someone else's message or when responding to another user's posting.
- Don't post personal messages. If you need to send a personal message, use e-mail.
- Don't try to conduct business or try to solicit customers in newsgroups unless the newsgroup is used for those specific purposes.

Using Abbreviations

In trying to keep messages short and clear, a common practice you'll see in newsgroups, e-mail, and chat rooms is the use of abbreviations for commonly used terms. Using abbreviations is one place where using ALL CAPS is acceptable. Here are some you will likely encounter:

Abbreviation	Meaning
BTW	by the way
IMHO	in my humble opinion
OTOH	on the other hand
TTYL	talk to you later
ROTFL	rolling on the floor laughing
FYI	for your information

Getting Flamed

Sooner or later, you will encounter the term *flame*, especially if you spend a lot of time in newsgroups. A flame is a sharp retort or criticism to a posting or comment that users consider particularly stupid or irrelevant. You can also get flamed by committing a major breach of netiquette. As a new user, you are sometimes spared because many veteran users expect as much from *newbies*.. But not all veterans are patient, so be forewarned.

It Gets More Personal in Chat Rooms

Chat rooms are conversations in real time, so most of the same rules of protocol and behavior you would use when talking with a small group in a social setting, such as a party, usually apply in chat rooms as well.

Keep in mind, too, that some chat rooms, because of the nature of the topics (in adult rooms, for example) being discussed, may impose their own set of rules and behavior about what type of language is permitted.

In general, here are some of the basic guidelines you should follow:

- Say hello when you enter a room. It's considered polite to offer a short greeting, but don't turn this into an overture.
- Use a nickname. Chat rooms are by definition informal, so pick a nickname. Also, if you plan on doing the chat circuit on a regular basis, use the same nickname so others can become familiar with you.
- Don't use all caps. Remember, it's LIKE SHOUTING AT SOMEONE!!!
- Don't repeatedly ask the same question if it appears you are being ignored. You may think you are making a witty contribution to the conversation, but others may not.
- If you use abbreviations, don't deviate from the norm. It's very frustrating for others to see you make some relevant comment, only to have it followed up with some indecipherable jumble of letters.

CAUTION

Proper Netiquette   Sarcasm can be incredibly funny in face-to-face conversations but when you're on the Net, no one can see your face. Use sarcasm sparingly in your e-mail and chat sessions and when you do use it, employ some of the emoticons noted previously to help crystallize your sense of humor for the other Netizens that you are communicating with.

If you ever have any questions about what is proper etiquette or protocol, common sense and courtesy should get you through most situations.

In this lesson, you learned about Internet etiquette. In the next lesson, you will learn how to protect your computer from viruses.

Protecting Yourself Against Viruses

In this lesson, you learn how to download antivirus software to protect your PC from viruses.

What Are Computer Viruses?

There are more than 10,000 known computer viruses. At least six new ones are created or modified from old ones every day.

What are computer viruses? They're pieces of software that get into your machine without your knowledge or permission. Some viruses are designed to activate relatively harmless programs that just display messages or play music. Others viruses can cripple your computer by corrupting programs or erasing your hard drive.

Viruses get into a computer through a segment of software code that implants itself in an executable file or Microsoft Word document and then spreads from one file to another. You cannot get a virus simply by using the Internet or browsing the Web. You can get viruses from some types of e-mail attachments and from infected programs you download from the Net or an online service. Most online services scan their file libraries for viruses. Most Internet sites are safe, too. But you can't be too safe when it comes to viruses.

CAUTION

Virus Warning The Internet is not the only potential source of viruses. If you use a computer at work or an educational institution and then bring files home on disk, you are also creating the potential risk of introducing viruses and infected files to your PC. A number of the antivirus packages available will automatically scan a disk for viruses when you place it in your computer.

Still, only about 40 percent of computer users have antivirus programs, according to the National Computer Security Association (**http://www.ncsa.com**), a Carlisle, Pennsylvania organization that certifies antivirus software. NCSA also reports that many people install protective software only after they become infected.

You can help protect your computer before you have a problem by staying up-to-date on virus information and by downloading antivirus software from the Internet.

Finding Virus Information on the Web

Here's a sampling of sites that provide basic virus information, antivirus programs, or both:

- AntiVirus Resources: (**http://www.hitchhikers.net/av.shtml**) offers extensive news, alerts, basic information, and software. You can register for automatic e-mail notification of software upgrades.

- Symantec Antivirus Resource Center: (**http://www. symantec.com/ avcenter/index.html**) provides alerts and a virus information database (part of the site's home page is shown in Figure 13.1). You also can purchase and download copies of the popular programs Norton AntiVirus or Symantec AntiVirus for Macintosh (but you may get them cheaper from a mail-order company or software retail store).

- IBM AntiVirus: (**http://www.av.ibm.com/current/FrontPage/**) offers virus and hype alerts as well as advice for people who think their computers are infected. You also can find a large collection of detailed technical information.

TIP **Virus Hype and Hoaxes**   Sometimes, Internet pranksters spread dire warnings of impending virus plagues. These false alarms won't hurt your computer, but they can waste your time. Web resources, such as the IBM site previously mentioned, provide information that can help you debunk virus hype. Another site you may want to visit is Computer Virus Myths (**http://www. kumite.com/myths**).

Figure 13.1 Symantec offers several resources that can help you protect your computer from viruses.

- Virus:Information: (**http://csrc.ncsl.nist.gov/virus/**) provides reviews of antivirus software and miscellaneous information from the National Institute of Standards and Technology's Computer Security Research Clearinghouse.
- The Computer Virus Help Desk: (**http://www. indyweb.net/~cvhd**) offers basic information and an extensive selection of links to other virus sites.
- Stiller Research: (**http://www.stiller.com**) provides lengthy, but easy-to-understand, basic information on viruses. You also can download a shareware version of the Integrity Master antivirus program.

Shareware Software you can use and evaluate before you decide to buy it. The program will contain information on how to pay for and register it if you decide to keep it.

- McAfee: (**http://www.mcafee.com**) provides a Virus Info Library, downloadable software, and a unique feature called SecureCast. McAfee will automatically send you regular updates of antivirus technology. SecureCast is free to any McAfee customer.

- Dr. Solomon's: (**http://www.drsolomon.com**) offers Virus Alerts, a searchable Virus Encyclopedia, a full tutorial, help with virus infections, details on hoaxes, and information on several antivirus software programs.

You can find many other antivirus sites through a list of links at the NCSA site (**http://www.ncsa.com/hotlinks/virus.html**).

Downloading Antivirus Software

The Dr. Solomon's site mentioned in the previous section provides information on antivirus programs for DOS, Windows 3.x, Windows 95, Windows NT, NetWare, OS/2, Macintosh, and SCO UNIX. You can find out where to buy the programs at the site. You also can download a free evaluation version of FindVirus for DOS. Here's how:

1. Type the URL **http://www.drsolomon.com/** in your Web browser's location box and press **Enter**.

2. Scroll down Dr. Solomon's Home Page and click the **Download** icon (see Figure 13.2).

3. On the next page, choose which version suits your computer's specifications. Your choices are DOS, Windows 3.1, or Windows 95. Please note that this page also offers links to information on software products for other computer platforms, and you can download a free Virus Tutorial.

4. The next page provides basic information about FindVirus and an online registration form. After you fill out the form, click the **Submit** button near the bottom of the page.

5. The next page lets you choose either a "lite" or standard version of FindVirus. The "lite" version is a less sophisticated version than the standard, but will still fight viruses effectively. Click the name of the one you want in the appropriate geographic category for your location.

6. Your Web browser may display a dialog box asking whether you want to save the file or open it with a helper application. Choose **Save**.

7. Your browser then displays a box asking where you want to store the file. Select one of your existing folders, or create a new one.

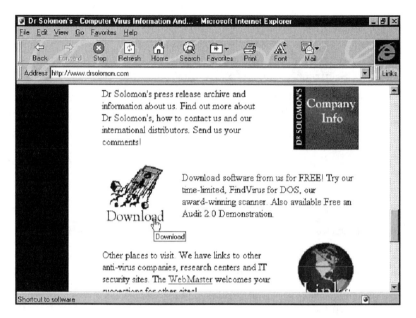

Figure 13.2   You can download a free antivirus program at Dr. Solomon's.

8. The program is delivered as a compressed file. You need to open it with file decompression software (see the following note).

9. After you decompress the FindVirus, read the text files. They will help you install, set up, and use the program.

Compressed File   A file that has been reduced in size so you can download it quickly. Some online services (America Online, for example) provide built-in programs that automatically decompress files after you download them. If the Internet software you use doesn't offer that feature, you can use decompression software, such as WinZip for PCs or Stuffit for Macs. WinZip is available at **http://www.winzip.com**; **Stuffit** and at **http://www.aladdinsys.com**.

To find out where to buy other Dr. Solomon programs, click the **Company Info** icon on the site's home page (you can return to it by using the **Back** button on your browser). On the Company Info page, scroll down and click the **Contacting Us** link. Then click **US/UK Resellers and Distributors**. When you select the link for your geographic location, you receive a list of Dr. Solomon's vendors. Click a vendor's name for more information and a link to its Web site.

Monitoring Virus Information with Online Services

Most online services include their own staff that can help you track virus information and download software. America Online, for example, offers both a PC Virus Information Center (keyword: **pc virus**) and a Macintosh Virus Information center (keyword: **mac virus**). Both offer virus news, message boards, real-time chat sessions, and libraries of antivirus programs (see Figure 13.3).

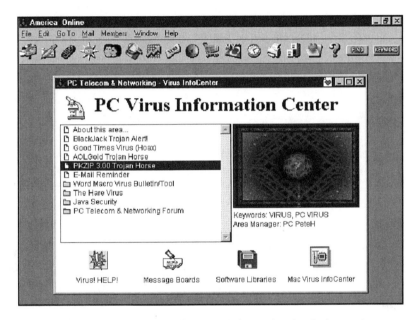

Figure 13.3 Most online services offer virus information for their members.

In this lesson, you learned how to protect your computer from viruses. In the next lesson, you'll learn how to protect your kids when they're online by screening out certain Internet content.

Protecting Your Children Online

In this lesson, you learn how to protect your children from certain kinds of Internet content.

The Internet and Your Children

While the Internet is truly an incredible information source, it also has its share of seedy back alleys; meaning there is content on the Net that is not appropriate for children. Many Web sites, chat channels, and newsgroups are G-rated, but others exist strictly for adults.

As a parent you may want to regulate the content your children view on the Net. And while a complete ban on the use of the Internet is one way to solve this content problem, you would be preventing your child from encountering some incredibly educational and fun sites on the Internet (the Web in particular).

There are two routes that you can take to regulate the sites and content areas your children visit when they're online. You can educate them to be responsible citizens of the Internet; and if this doesn't work, you can use an Internet escort, a software program that can prevent a child from accessing the dicey areas of the Internet.

Internet Escort Software   This type of software is designed to block out certain content areas on the Internet. Several programs exist that you can customize, such as SurfWatch and Cyber Patrol.

Working with Your Children

One way to guide your children to the appropriate places on the Internet is to share the experience with them. If for instance, you are familiar with the Web and know of some of the great fun and educational sites that are out there, you can steer your children toward them.

 TIP   **Site For Children**   A great site to start your children out on is Yahooligans at **http://www.yahooligans.com/**, which offers links to many appropriate Web pages and content areas.

Another way to structure use of the Net is to agree on a set of rules, for instance:

- Don't visit Web sites, newsgroups, chat groups, or FTP sites that have the word "erotica" or "sex" in their title or content listing.
- Don't "talk" to strangers or give out personal information to others on the Net.
- If you discover content that makes you uncomfortable, let's discuss it.

This approach allows you and your children to share in the responsibility. If this type of approach doesn't work for you, there is another route that you can take; use special software that blocks out content areas.

 TIP   **Monitoring Your Child**   You can check to see what Web sites your children have been visiting. Web browser's, such as Internet Explorer, have a history file that enables you to view a list of the sites visited.

Using Internet Escort Software

Internet escort software blocks out selected content areas in newsgroups, chat areas, and on the World Wide Web. One such program is Cyber Patrol. This shareware program is made available by the creators of Cyber Sentry, a program designed to prevent workers from accessing certain Internet sites during work hours.

Obviously, this type of software also will help regulate Internet access on a home computer. Parents can try the complete software package for a seven-day trial period. If you like Cyber Patrol, they ask that you register and pay the $29.95 for the product.

Another program available is SurfWatch. SurfWatch from Spyglass was also designed to regulate or filter access to the Internet, as well as a company's in-house network. Yet another Internet content blocker is Net Nanny from Net Nanny Software International.

You can get additional information on each of these content filter programs from their respective sites on the World Wide Web. Both Cyber Patrol and Net Nanny offer trial versions of the software.

Cyber Patrol	**http://www.cyberpatrol.com**
SurfWatch	**http://www.spyglass.com/products/surfwatch/**
Net Nanny	**http://www.netnanny.com/etnanny/**

Each of these software packages blocks content in generally the same way. You can set a list of keywords or content type, and then when access is attempted to a Web site or newsgroup that violates the content rules, the site will be blocked.

Installing and Using Cyber Patrol

Cyber Patrol comes with a built-in set of safeguards, such as a list of Web sites that are off limits and a list of words that it uses to block access to any sites whose name or URL suggests indecency. For example, the Playboy Web site is listed as off limits, and Cyber Patrol blocks access to any newsgroups, Web sites, chat rooms, or URLs that have "bondage" in their names. However, you can customize Cyber Patrol to prevent access to additional sites.

1. Download Cyber Patrol from **http://www.cyberpatrol.com.** (For information on downloading files from the Web see Part 2, Lessons 1 and 2.)

2. To run the installation file that you downloaded (**cp-setup.exe**); select **Start**, **Run**, or use the Windows Explorer to start the setup of the Cyber Patrol software.

After you install the software, you're ready to configure the filter settings for Cyber Patrol. Whenever you start Windows 95, Cyber Patrol automatically loads.

Setting Your Cyber Patrol Password

1. Click the **Cyber Patrol** button on the Windows taskbar. The Cyber Patrol Access Checkpoint opens (see Figure 14.1). Choose your Cyber Patrol password and configure the access constraints on certain types of Internet content.

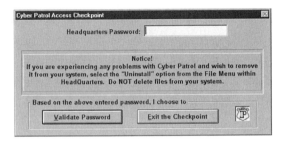

Figure 14.1 The first time you open Cyber Patrol, you select a password for the software.

CAUTION

Removing Cyber Patrol If you decide to remove Cyber Patrol from your system, switch to Cyber Patrol (by clicking its button on the taskbar). Then, select **File, Uninstall Cyber Patrol**. You will need to know the Cyber Patrol password to uninstall the software. Never try to remove the program manually or you can wreak havoc on your system.

2. Type a password into the **Headquarters Password** box and then click **Validate Password**. Make sure that you choose a password that you will remember and one that your children won't guess.

Limiting Usage Hours with Cyber Patrol

Cyber Patrol gives you the ability to set limits on the hours that the Internet can be accessed.

To prevent someone from using the Internet during certain hours:

1. Click the **Press to Set Hours of Operation** button. Red blocks mark hours during which Internet access will be blocked. Green blocks show hours where Internet access is permitted. Click a red block to turn it green, or click a green block to turn it red. You can drag over blocks to select them (see Figure 14.2).

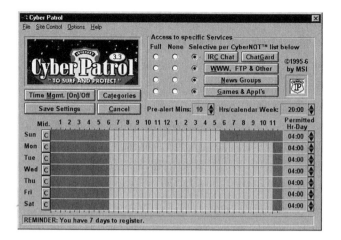

Figure 14.2 The Cyber Patrol software gives you the ability to limit the number of hours you allow your children on the Net.

TIP **Complete Access** To allow Internet access for all hours, click the **C** button for a given day. (**C** stands for Clear.)

2. To specify the number of hours per day or per week that users can access the Internet, use the scroll boxes next to **Hrs/calendar Week** and **Permitted Hr-Day** to set the allowable times.

Preventing Access to Specific Internet Services

Cyber Patrol also does a good job blocking out services and content areas on the Net. Cyber Patrol has a list of prohibited Internet services.

To prevent access to additional services or to allow access to features on Cyber Patrol's list:

1. Click a button in the **Access to Specific Services** area (see Figure 14.3).

2. If you click the **IRC - Relay Chat** button, a list of keywords appears. Cyber Patrol will prevent access to newsgroups that have these words anywhere in their names. To add a word, type it in the **Reject Wildcards** text box, and press **Enter** (see Figure 14.4).

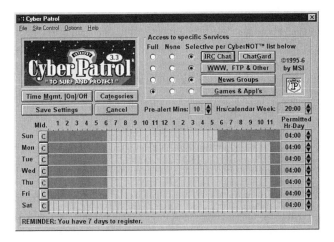

Figure 14.3 The Access to Specific Services area enables you to configure how much of a certain Internet Service is blocked by Cyber Patrol.

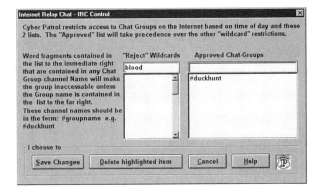

Figure 14.4 To block IRC channels that may be offensive, build a list of keywords that Cyber Patrol consults when restricting Relay Chat areas.

TIP **Monitoring Chat** To remove a word from the Reject Wildcards list, select the word, and then click **Delete Highlighted Item**.

3. To approve a specific chat room that Cyber Patrol will allow access to, type its name in the **Approved Chat-Groups** list, and press **Enter**. When you are done, click **Save Changes**.

Limiting Web and FTP Access

You can also control access to the World Wide Web and File Transfer Protocol (FTP) servers. The WWW, FTP & Other button allows you to limit access to certain sites based on their URLs.

1. To prevent access to a specific site, type its URL in the **Additional Parental Service Restrictions** text box, and press **Enter**.

2. To override Cyber Patrol's no-no list and allow access to a site that's on the list, type the site's URL in the **Additional Parental Approved Services** text box, and press **Enter** (see Figure 14.5).

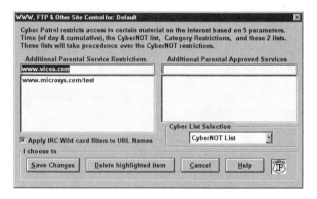

Figure 14.5 Use the Additional Parental Approved box to make your choices.

3. To prevent or allow access to certain off-beat topics, open the **Site Control** menu, and select **Category Restrictions**. The dialog box that appears allows you to block areas that you feel are inappropriate. Initially, all the topics are blocked (checked). To remove the **X** and allow access to a topic, click its name. Click **Save My Selections** when you're done.

TIP **Update Your Restrictions** The makers of Cyber Patrol are constantly updating their restriction list as more sites appear on the Internet. To update the list, open the **File** menu and select **Update CyberNOT List** (see Figure 14.6).

When Cyber Patrol is active, it will stop access to the sites and content that you specified in the program's configuration. If someone tries to access a prohibited Web site, for instance the Playboy Web site, Cyber Patrol will block it (see Figure 14.7).

Figure 14.6 Restrict sites with Category Restrictions.

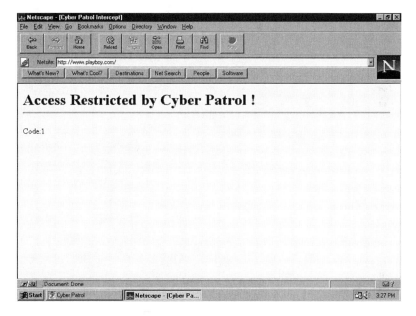

Figure 14.7 When you have your watch dog software correctly configured, Cyber Patrol blocks access to Web sites and other Internet content areas that you want blocked.

Disabling Cyber Patrol For your own Internet browsing you may want to deactivate the Cyber Patrol controls. To bypass Cyber Patrol and open access to all Internet services, open the **File** menu and select **Deputy ByPass**. This is possible because you entered Cyber Patrol via the password screen, so your children can't disarm Cyber Patrol or any of the other Internet Restriction packages available.

In this lesson, you explored some strategies for structuring your children's experience on the Internet. You learned that software watchdogs can block inappropriate content on the Internet.

89

The World Wide Web

Downloading and Installing Internet Explorer

In this lesson, you learn where to get a free copy of Microsoft Internet Explorer 4 and how to install it.

What Is Internet Explorer?

Internet Explorer 4 is actually a suite of programs, including Internet Explorer (the Web browser), Outlook Express (for e-mail and newsgroups), NetMeeting (an Internet phone program), FrontPage Express (for creating and publishing your own Web pages), and a couple of additional tools. You can download and install any or all of these components, as explained in this lesson.

The lessons in this Part focus on Internet Explorer. In these lessons, you will learn how to use Internet Explorer to open and display Web pages, which contain graphics, video clips, interactive applets (small applications), 3-D virtual worlds, and even areas where you can chat with other users! See Figure 1.1.

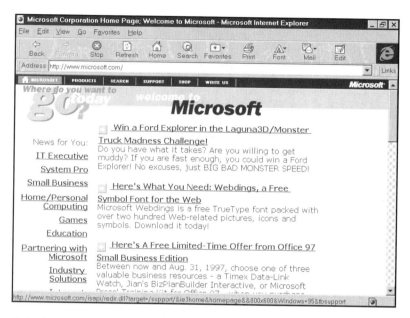

Figure 1.1 Internet Explorer displays Web pages and helps you navigate the Web.

Locating a Copy of Internet Explorer 4

Microsoft offers Internet Explorer free to the public, and has vowed that it will always be free. If you have a new computer or a copy of any new Microsoft software, you probably already have Internet Explorer 3. Check your Windows desktop for an icon called The Internet or Internet Explorer Setup. If you have such an icon, double-click it to run the installation and setup. If you don't see the icon, check your Microsoft software CDs to determine if any of them contain the Internet Explorer setup program. Internet Explorer 3 is included on the Microsoft Office 97 CD.

If you have an older version of Internet Explorer (version 3 or earlier), or a different Web browser, you can download the latest version of Internet Explorer from the Internet, as explained in the following section.

Before downloading Internet Explorer 4, keep in mind that it requires more disk space and memory than version 3. If you have an older system and it's strapped for disk space and memory, you might want to stick with Internet Explorer 3, but make sure you have the latest release of version 3.

TIP **Internet Explorer Version Number** If you have a copy of Internet Explorer, you can check its version number. Open the **Help** menu and select **About Internet Explorer**.

Downloading Internet Explorer 4 Using a Web Browser

If you have a Web browser (Mosaic, Netscape Navigator, an old version of Internet Explorer, or the Web browser you use through your online service), you can use your current browser to quickly download the latest version of Internet Explorer. If you do not have a Web browser, obtain one from your service provider.

The following steps lead you through the process of downloading Internet Explorer. However, be aware that Microsoft often changes the steps for downloading files. When performing the steps, you may need to follow a different trail of links to find the download option for Internet Explorer 4.0. Take the following steps:

1. Establish your Internet connection, as explained in Part 1.
2. Run your Web browser.
3. Look for an URL, Address, or Location text box or command. Most Web browsers display such a text box at the top of the Window, but others might require you to select the URL or Location command (usually from the File menu).
4. Drag over any text that might be in the URL or Location text box, type **http://www.microsoft.com/ie** and press **Enter**. After a moment, you should be connected to Internet Explorer's home page.
5. Click the link for Internet Explorer 4.0. During the writing of this book, Microsoft offered two versions of Internet Explorer: 3.02 and 4.0.

TERM **Link** Any highlighted text, icon, or graphic that points to another Web page or file on the Internet. You can quickly jump from page to page on the Web by clicking links.

6. Click the **Download** button. A page appears, warning you that the file you are about to download is big and may take a long time to copy.

7. Scroll down the page, and click the **Active Setup** link. You are now prompted to select the version and language you want.

8. Open the drop-down list, and select the desired language and version. For example, select **Internet Explorer 4**.

9. Click **Next**. A list of download sites appears. The links for the ie4setup.exe files point to various Internet sites from which you can download the Internet Explorer setup file, as shown in Figure 1.2.

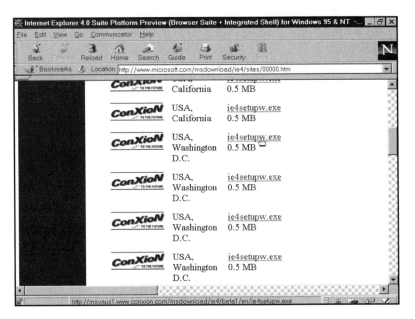

Figure 1.2 Download the **ie4setup.exe** file from a site near you.

10. Take one of the following steps to download the ie4setup.exe file using your Web browser (select the link for the site that is nearest to you):

    With an old version of Internet Explorer, right-click the link, and select the **Save Target As** option. Use the dialog boxes to save the file to the desired folder. Or, save the file to your Windows desktop for easy access.

    With Mosaic, hold down the **Shift** key while clicking the link, and then follow the dialog boxes to complete the task.

With Netscape Navigator, click the link, and use the dialog boxes to save the file.

11. Wait until the file transfer is complete.

12. Close your Web browser.

You should now have a file named ie4setupw.exe (or a similar name). Running this file initiates the setup operation, which leads you through the process of downloading the various components that make up the Internet Explorer Suite and installing them on your system. The next section explains the installation procedure.

CAUTION

Check Your Disk Space Before you download and install Internet Explorer, check the free space on your hard drive. Internet Explorer consumes as much as 20 megabytes of free space. You should have 40 to 60 megabytes free for the file you are about to download plus the files that the installation process will place on your system.

Installing Internet Explorer 4.0

Once you have the ie4setup.exe file, installation is fairly simple. You run the file, and follow the on-screen instructions. The following steps lead you through the process:

1. Double-click the **ie4setup.exe** file you downloaded in the previous section. The Internet Explorer 4.0 Setup dialog box appears, asking if you want to continue.

2. Click **Next**. Microsoft's standard license agreement appears.

3. Read the license agreement, **I accept the agreement** and click the **Next** button. (If you click **I don't accept the agreement**, you terminate the installation.) You are now presented with two download options: Install or Download Only.

4. Choose **Install** to download the installation files and then automatically install Internet Explorer. (The following steps assume you selected the Install option.) Click **Next**. The next dialog box prompts you to choose from three installation options.

5. Open the drop-down list, and select one of the following options:

> **Standard Installation** includes Internet Explorer (Web browser), Outlook Express (for e-mail), and ActiveMovie (for playing video clips on the Web).

Minimal Installation installs only Internet Explorer 4 and any components it needs to play active content, such as video clips.

Full Installation includes everything: Internet Explorer, desktop integration, Outlook Express for e-mail and newsgroups, ActiveMovie, FrontPage Express, NetMeeting (for virtual conferences), NetShow (for live video broadcasts), Microsoft Chat, Web Publishing Wizard, and Microsoft Wallet. If you want to do all the neat stuff described in this book, you will need all of the components.

6. Click the **Next** button. The installation program prompts you to select a directory for storing the Internet Explorer files.

7. To use the default drive and directory, click the **Next** button. Or, type a path to the desired drive and directory, and click **Next**. (You can use the Browse button to select a directory from the directory list.) You are now prompted to pick a download site.

8. Open the **Region** list, and select your geographical location. Then, select a download site from the **Download Location** list. Click the **Next** button. The setup program starts to download the necessary file(s) and install the Internet Explorer suite on your system (see Figure 1.3).

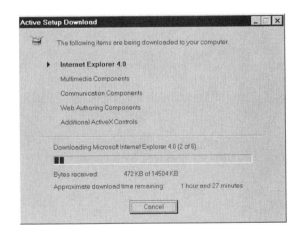

Figure 1.3   As the setup program downloads the Internet Explorer components, it displays its progress.

9. Follow the on-screen prompts to complete the operation. If you have a standard modem connection (28.8 Kbps or slower), and you selected the Full Installation, the process may take two or more hours.

When the installation is complete, you should have an icon on your desktop labeled The Internet. Click the icon.

CAUTION

What Happened to My Windows Desktop? If you installed Internet Explorer 4.0 with the desktop integration feature, your Windows desktop may now look and behave much differently. For instance, instead of double-clicking shortcut icons, you now single-click. For details on how to work with the new desktop, see Lesson 12, "Using the Internet Explorer Active Desktop."

Adding Components Later

Microsoft regularly posts updates to Internet Explorer 4 on the Web. To ensure that you have the latest version of Internet Explorer and are not missing out on any security fixes, enhancements, or additional components, you should run the Active Setup Wizard on a monthly basis. The Active Setup Wizard automatically checks Microsoft's Web site for any product updates and allows you to immediately upgrade your copy of Internet Explorer. To run the Active Setup Wizard, take the following steps:

1. Open the folder that contains the **ie4setup.exe** file, and click the file to run it. A dialog box appears, indicating that this will install Internet Explorer 4.0 on your computer.

2. Click the **Yes** button. The licensing agreement appears.

3. Read the license agreement, select **I accept the agreement**, and click the **Next** button. You are now asked to pick the type of installation desired.

4. Open the drop-down list, and select the desired installation option: **Standard**, **Minimal**, or **Full**. Click **Next**. The next dialog box asks where you want Internet Explorer installed.

5. Pick the folder in which you initially installed Internet Explorer, and click **Next**. The Reinstall All Items? dialog box appears, asking if you want to reinstall all components or upgrade only newer items.

6. Click **Upgrade only newer items**, and click **OK**. The Active Setup Wizard performs the upgrade, installing any additional components required by the installation type you chose. Click **OK**.

Running Internet Explorer 4 Applications

As mentioned earlier, Internet Explorer 4 is a suite of applications. You can run Internet Explorer (the Web browser) or any of the other applications by performing one of the following steps:

- Click **The Internet** icon on your desktop or program group. This runs the Web browser, as shown in Figure 1.4.

- Click the **Launch Mail** icon on the left end of the status bar to run the e-mail program.

- Open the Windows 95 Start menu, point to **Programs**, point to **Internet Explorer**, and click the name of the application you want to run.

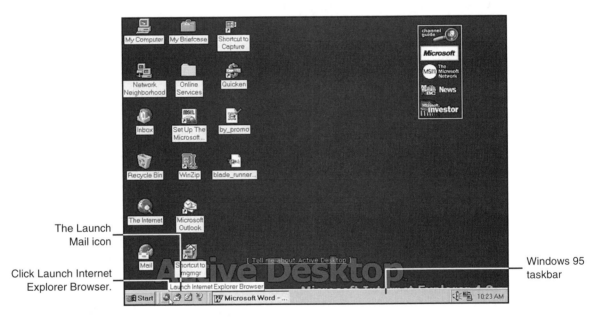

Figure 1.4   The installation program adds an icon for running Internet Explorer to the Windows 95 desktop.

In this lesson, you learned how to download and install Internet Explorer 4, and how to run its various applications. You can now skip to Lesson 5 to learn how to use Internet Explorer to start browsing the Web.

Downloading and Installing Netscape Communicator

In this lesson, you learn how to download Netscape Communicator from the Internet and install it on your computer.

What Is Netscape Communicator?

Netscape Communicator is a suite of specialized Internet programs that work together to help you take advantage of most of what the Internet has to offer. Netscape Communicator consists of the following six programs:

- **Netscape Navigator**, Netscape's award-winning Web browser, is the core program, which enables you to navigate the World Wide Web, copy files, search for specific information, display text and pictures, and much more. The lessons in this Part show you how to use Navigator to open Web pages.

- **Netscape Netcaster** allows you to subscribe to your favorite Web sites and have updated information sent directly to your computer at a scheduled time (typically during off hours when Internet traffic is light).

Push Content   Netcaster takes advantage of an Internet innovation called "push content." With push content, Web sites *push* updated pages to your computer rather than having you *pull* them with your Web browser. This speeds up Internet access by allowing sites to deliver information when you are working on something else (or sleeping).

- **Netscape Messenger** enables you to send e-mail messages postage free, with same-day delivery. It also allows you to read and respond to the messages you receive. See Part 3, "E-Mail."

- **Netscape Collabra** allows you to post messages in electronic message areas called *newsgroups*, read messages posted by other people, and respond to messages. See Part 4, "Newsgroups."

- **Netscape Conference** is a tool with which you can place voice phone calls across the Internet or on an intranet. It also enables you to hold meetings during which everyone in the group can send pictures and messages back and forth and transmit notes.

- **Netscape Composer** is a Web page desktop publishing tool. It enables you to create your own Web pages and then place them on the World Wide Web for all to see. See Part 5, "Creating Web Pages," for details.

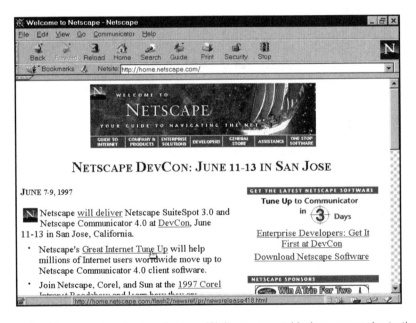

Figure 2.1   Netscape Navigator displays Web pages and helps you navigate the Web.

Downloading Netscape Communicator with Your Web Browser

If you have a Web browser—any Web browser that can display forms, you can download Netscape Communicator from Netscape's Web site. (Most Web browsers can handle this operation, including Internet Explorer, Mosaic, a previous version of Netscape Navigator, and the Web browsers used in online services, such as America Online and CompuServe.) The following steps show the basic procedure for electronically downloading products from Netscape. The procedure might differ a little when you perform the operation, because Netscape occasionally changes the procedure.

1. Connect to the Internet and run your Web browser. Most Web browsers are set up to load a home page connecting you to the company's Web site.

2. Click in the **Location** or **Address** text box (typically right above the page display area) and type **http://www.netscape.com**. Press **Enter**.

3. Your Web browser loads and displays Netscape's home page. Click the **Download Software** button in the navigation bar near the bottom of the page, and then click the link for downloading Netscape Communicator.

4. When you click the right link, your Web browser should load the form shown in Figure 2.2 (you might have to scroll down the page to see it). Use the form to specify your operating system, the desired language, and the product you want (Netscape Communicator Standard).

5. Scroll down the page, and click the **Add Components to Communicator Now** check box. This tells Netscape to send you additional Netscape components for playing media files and other file types.

6. Scroll down the page and click the **Download for Free** button. Netscape starts to download the file, and displays a dialog box, showing the progress of the download.

7. Wait until the file transfer is complete (it may take a while over a modem connection), and then close your browser and disconnect from the Internet.

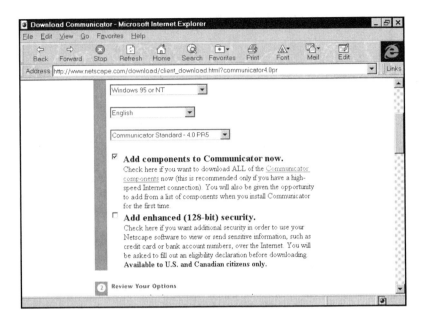

Figure 2.2   Enter the requested information.

Installing Communicator

Installing Netscape Communicator is fairly easy. You double-click the file you downloaded from Netscape's FTP site, and then you follow the on-screen instructions to complete the operation. If you have installed programs before, go ahead and install Communicator. If you need help, the following steps lead you through the process:

1. Open **File Manager** or **Windows Explorer** and double-click the Communicator file you downloaded earlier in this introduction (for example, c32e40.exe). This starts the setup program.

Windows 3.1 Setup File   In Windows 3.1, running the Netscape installation file decompresses the file. You will then have a Setup.exe file. Double-click this file to run the installation.

CAUTION

2. A dialog box appears, asking if you want to continue with setup. Click **Yes**. The InstallShield Self-extracting Exe dialog box appears, showing the progress.

3. When you see a warning telling you to close your other Windows programs, do so and click **Next**. A welcome dialog box appears.

4. Read the welcome message, and click **Next**. A license agreement appears. Read it, and click **Yes**. (If you click No, you can't use Communicator.)

5. The Setup Type dialog box (shown in Figure 2.3) appears, asking if you want to run the Typical or Custom installation. Click **Typical**. (The Custom installation allows you to install only selected components.)

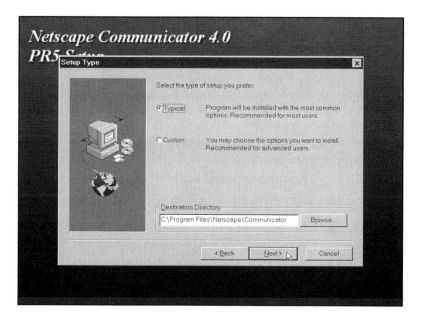

Figure 2.3   Follow the Typical installation to install all components and plug-ins.

6. The installation program displays the destination directory. If the destination directory is okay, click **Next**. If you want to change it, click **Browse**, select the desired directory, click **OK**, and then click **Next**.

What If It Doesn't Exist?   If the directory you want to use doesn't exist, you'll see a message asking if you want the setup program to create it. Click **Yes**.

CAUTION

7. The Select Program Folder dialog box appears, indicating that icons for running Communicator will be placed in the Netscape Communicator folder. Click **Next**.

8. The Start Copying Files dialog box appears, showing you all of the installation preferences you selected. Click **Install**.

9. A series of dialog boxes appear, displaying the progress of the installation. Wait until you see the Question dialog box, asking if you want to view the Readme file, which contains information about this release. (You can click **Yes** to read the file now or click **No**, and open the file later in a text editor such as WordPad.)

10. The Information dialog box appears, telling you how to run Communicator. Click **OK**.

11. The Restarting Windows dialog box appears, indicating that you must restart Windows to complete the installation. Exit any programs that are running, and click **OK**.

When you install Netscape Communicator, the installation program places a Netscape Communicator icon on the Windows 95 desktop, which you can use to run Communicator. It also creates a submenu of Communicator applications on the **Start Programs** menu.

Running Netscape Communicator for the First Time

You might think that you can run Netscape Communicator and start using it immediately. Actually, it's not quite that easy. When you first start Communicator, you'll have to answer a few questions and read the standard license agreement. The following steps show you what to expect.

1. The installation program placed the Netscape Communicator icon in several convenient locations. Look on the Windows desktop or on the Start, Programs, Netscape Communicator menu (in Windows 95), or look in the Netscape Communicator program group in Windows 3.1. Double-click the icon to run Communicator.

2. The first time you run Communicator, the Profile Setup Wizard appears, as shown in Figure 2.4. You can use profiles to enter different settings for different users, assuming you share your computer with other people or share Communicator on a network. If the Profile Setup Wizard does not appear, you can run it by selecting **Start, Programs, Netscape Communicator, Utilities, User Profile Manager**. Click the **Next** button.

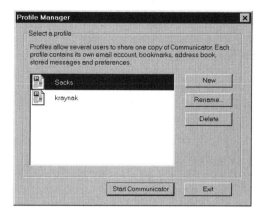

Figure 2.4 Profiles are useful if you share your computer with others or work on a network.

3. The next dialog box asks you to enter your name. Type your name.

4. Tab to the **Email Address** text box, and type your e-mail address (if you have one). If you are unsure, ask your Internet service provider. Click **Next**.

5. The next dialog box asks you to enter your profile name. Type a name that will uniquely identify your profile (such as your last name). (Optionally, you can specify the folder in which you want to save your profile and preferences.) Click **Next**.

6. The Mail and Discussions Groups Setup dialog box appears, prompting you to type information about how to connect to your service provider's e-mail and news server. Tab to the **Outgoing Mail (SMTP) Server** text box, and type the address for the outgoing mail server; for example, you might type **mail.internet.com**. Click **Next.**

7. The next dialog box asks you to specify login information for the mail server. Type your username, and enter any additional settings required to check your server for incoming mail. Click **Next**.

8. The next dialog box prompts you to enter your news server's address. Type the address specified by your service provider (for example, **news.internet.com**). (See Part 4, Lesson 3, "Setting Up a News Server in Netscape Collabra," for details on how to select a news server.)

9. Click the **Finish** button. The License Agreement may appear.

10. If the License Agreement appears, read it, and click **Accept**. If you click **Do Not Accept**, Netscape Communicator will not run.

In this lesson, you learned how to download and install Netscape Communicator. You can now skip to Part 2, Lesson 5, "Jumping to Your First Web Site," to start navigating the Web with Netscape Navigator.

Using AOL's Web Browser

*In this lesson, you learn how to access the Internet
(particularly the World Wide Web) through America Online.*

America Online Internet Access

America Online was one of the first online services to offer "free" Internet
access to its members. You'll find all of AOL's Internet related features and
services in the Internet Connection, shown in Figure 3.1. You can get there
from the Channels display by clicking Internet Connection.

TIP   **The Welcome Screen's Internet Button**   The Internet button on
the Welcome screen will also take you to the Internet Connection, but you'll
have to deal with an intermediate Welcome to the Internet screen.

AOL's Internet Connection offers you several options:

- You can click buttons to get onto the WWW.
- You can transfer files with FTP (File Transfer Protocol).
- You can read and post messages to Newsgroups, which are the
  Internet equivalent of AOL's message boards. (See Part 4, Lesson 4,
  "Accessing Newsgroups from AOL," for details.)
- You can search for information (Gopher and WAIS).
- You can read Frequently Asked Questions (FAQs) and their answers.

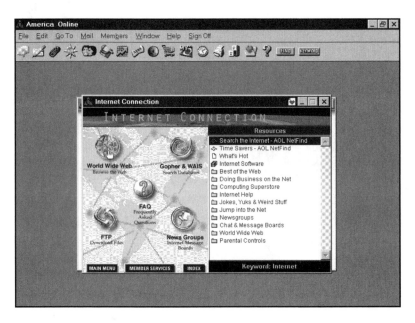

Figure 3.1   AOL's Internet Connection.

Gopher   An Internet search utility named after the University of Minnesota's Golden Gophers. Gopher allows you to navigate the Internet using a menu system.

WAIS   An Internet search utility. It stands for Wide Area Information Search, and is pronounced "ways."

This lesson will concentrate on using the World Wide Web with AOL's browser for Windows. AOL uses a modified version of Microsoft's Internet Explorer (version 3), so if you are familiar with Internet Explorer, the transition will be fairly simple. If you prefer using Netscape Navigator or some other Web browser (such as Internet Explorer 4), the next lesson explains how to use that browser over your AOL connection.

Because the WWW lets you do everything (and more) that the FTP, Gopher, and WAIS searches (mentioned in the previous bulleted list) allow, we're going to skip those features. There is abundant help available online, should you care to try them, but services on the Web have made them fairly obsolete.

Some WWW Basics

Before you plunge into the Web, you should have some basic vocabulary and concepts under your belt:

- You'll cruise the Web using a Web browser, which is a piece of software designed to handle the graphics-based information on the Web. There's one built into AOL 3.0.
- The basic unit of the World Wide Web is a Web page. A Web page is like a piece of paper. It's a single document that contains a mixture of text, pictures, and other elements.
- The place where a bunch of Web pages are stored is called a Web site.
- Most Web pages contain *links*, which appear as highlighted text, icons, or graphics. Links connect a Web page to other Web pages, helping you navigate the Web.
- You can always tell when your cursor is pointing at a link, because it turns from a standard arrow to a pointing finger. When you see the pointing finger, that means you can click whatever you're pointing at to visit another page.
- To make finding things on the Web easier, every Web page has an address. The page address is called an URL (Uniform Resource Locator and pronounced "Earl") and works just like a street address. It tells your Web browser where to look for the page you want to see.

 TIP **AOL 4.0** In its constant effort to improve, America Online is working on a new version of AOL, version 4.0, which closely integrates the Web browser with AOL's core services. In addition, this new version offers a smart update feature, which automatically installs the latest version of the Web browser.

Getting On the Web

To get on the World Wide Web, go to the Internet Connection by one of the methods described previously. When you get there, click the World Wide Web button. AOL's Web browser will launch and take you to AOL's Web page, shown in Figure 3.2.

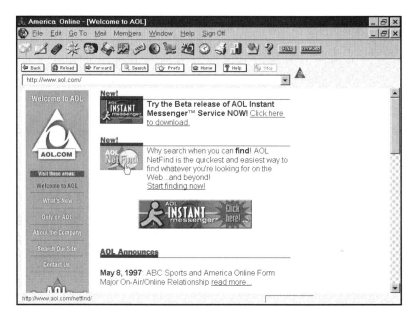

Figure 3.2 AOL's Web browser displaying a Web page.

As you can see in Figure 3.2, the toolbar just above the Web page display area contains several controls for navigating the Web. The links will vary from page to page, but the buttons on the browser toolbar are constant. Here they are in order of appearance:

Back takes you back one page in the list of pages you've visited.

Reload rereads the current page. This button is useful if the page transfer is interrupted at some point, displaying only a partial page.

Forward works only after you've used the Back button. This button takes you one page forward in the list of pages you've visited.

Search takes you to a page that will search the World Wide Web for sites that match a word or phrase you've entered.

Prefs opens a dialog box that lets you configure the Web browser.

Home takes you to AOL's Web page. You can specify another page in your WWW Preferences.

Help speaks for itself.

Stop stops whatever the browser is currently trying to do. This button is useful if a page is taking an inordinate time to load. You can click **Stop**, and then click the **Reload** button.

TIP   **Adding a Page to Your Favorites Menu**   Although AOL uses Internet Explorer as its Web browser, you won't find Internet Explorer's Favorites list in the toolbar. Instead, Internet Explorer uses the Favorite Places button in AOL's main toolbar. Refer to Lesson 10, "Creating and Organizing Internet Explorer Favorites," for details on using Favorites.

Navigating the Web

There are a few ways to get around the Web. For most beginners, your first explorations will probably start by clicking links on the AOL home page. That's a great way to start, but once you have a better idea of what you're doing, you can use faster methods to get where you're going.

As you travel around, you'll see a lot of Web addresses (URLs), both in the browser's Address box (below the toolbar), and at the lower-left corner of the window (when you point at a link). Make a note of those you like. Later, you can manually type the URL in the browser's address text box. Hit **Enter**, and you'll be taken to that specific Web page.

Moving Back and Forward

As you move around the Web, AOL's browser (and all Web browsers for that matter) keep a running list of the places you've been. If you want to return to a page you recently visited, click the **Back** arrow to move back, one page at a time, to the page you want to revisit. Once you've clicked the Back arrow, you can also use the Forward arrow to move forward through the list of pages you've visited.

Using URLs as Keywords

From anywhere on America Online, you can use a URL as a Keyword for a site you want to visit. Take the following steps:

1. Open the **Go To** menu and select **Keyword**, or press **Ctrl+K**. The Keyword dialog box appears, prompting you to enter a keyword (see Figure 3.3).

2. Instead of typing a keyword, type the address of the page you want to go to. For example, type **http://www.hollywood.com**.

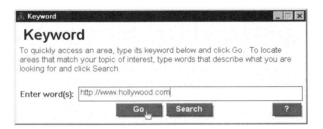

Figure 3.3   You can enter URLs as keywords.

3. Click the **Go** button or press **Enter**. AOL launches the browser and takes you to that address. If your Web browser is already running, it will open another browser window in which to display the new page.

Navigating with Links in IMs and E-Mail Messages

Friends and business associates may send you URLs in their e-mail and Instant Messages. Version 3.0 of AOL turns any such references into a Web page-type link in the message. All you have to do is click the URL, and AOL will launch the browser and take you to that address.

To find specific information on the Web, use AOL's NetFind feature. Click the **Find** button in AOL's toolbar, and double-click **Find on the Internet with AOL NetFind**, or enter the keyword **netfind**.

 TIP   **Internet Search Tools**   The Web has several search tools to help you find Web pages that interest you and to find out the addresses, phone numbers, and e-mail addresses of people you know. You can access these search tools using the AOL browser. See Lesson 7, "Tracking Down Pages and People with Search Tools," for complete instructions.

Going Back to AOL and Exiting

It's easy to get lost (or at least disoriented) on the Web. If you get lost or confused, click the **Home** button. You'll be taken back to AOL's home page (shown back in Figure 3.2) where you can get your bearings and set off again.

Once you've tired of your Web explorations, you can do two things to end your session:

- Click the browser window's **Close** button. It works like any window you've ever used, and you'll be returned to AOL.
- If you're completely finished online, simply exit AOL. Open the **File** menu and select **Exit**. Click **Sign Off and Exit** on the confirmation window, and you're done.

In this lesson, you learned about AOL's Web browser for Windows. If you prefer to use a different Web browser with AOL, the next lesson shows you what to do.

Using Your Favorite Web Browser with AOL

4

In this lesson, you learn how to use a different Web browser with the America Online service.

Why Use a Different Web Browser?

Although America Online supplies you with a fine Web browser, an adaptation of Microsoft's Internet Explorer, you may prefer a different browser, such as Netscape Navigator. For instance, Netscape Navigator is a better browser for playing Java applets, and setting up helper applications, and it may even be a little faster than Internet Explorer. Or, you may simply prefer working with Navigator's interface and controls.

Whatever the case, America Online does not force you to use its Web browser. The America Online 3.0 installation places a program file called Winsock.dll on your hard drive, which provides your system with the capability to use any Web browser or other Internet software you want to use. This lesson provides the instructions you need to download, install, and use a different browser with AOL.

CAUTION

Use Only AOL's Winsock   Don't use just any Winsock.dll with America Online. Only AOL's Winsock.dll works with America Online. Likewise, AOL's Winsock.dll will not help you use Internet applications through an Internet service provider other than AOL.

Finding and Downloading a Web Browser

You can use America Online's Web browser to download any Web browser you wish to use. However, before you download a new Web browser, you should know that, as of the writing of this book, AOL's Winsock.dll supports only 16-bit Internet applications in Windows 3.1 and 32-bit applications in Windows 95. So, when you download the browser, make sure you get the right version. (The 16-bit version may be listed as the Windows 3.1 version.)

 TIP **Winsock Help** For the latest information about AOL's Winsock.dll, press Ctrl+K, and enter the keyword **winsock**. Click the **Software Library** icon to view a list of available Internet applications that work with America Online. You can even download a new Web browser from the library.

The following list provides sites where you can go to find and download a different Web browser:

- **Netscape:** You can download Netscape Communicator at **http://www. netscape.com**. Follow the instructions in Part 2, Lesson 2, "Downloading and Installing Netscape Communicator."

- **Opera:** A relative newcomer to the browser market, Opera has gained popularity due to its speed and flexibility. Opera provides enhanced keyboard navigation, multiple windows, and a quick zoom feature that allows you to devote most of your screen to what matters most—the Web page.

- **c|net's Browser Page:** c|net is a great place to learn about the latest Internet technology. To learn about the latest, greatest Web browsers, go to c|net's browser page at **http://www.browsers.com**. c|net displays a comprehensive list of Web browsers, complete with brief reviews, comparisons, and links for downloading the browser of your choice.

- **Stroud's:** Stroud's Consummate Winsock Applications acts as an Internet software warehouse, where you will find links to many lesser-known browsers. Connect to Stroud's at **http://cws.internet.com/**, click the **16-bit Apps** button, and click the **Web Browsers link**. Stroud's displays a long list of Web browsers, as shown in Figure 4.1, complete with links to the browser's home page and links to download the various browsers.

117

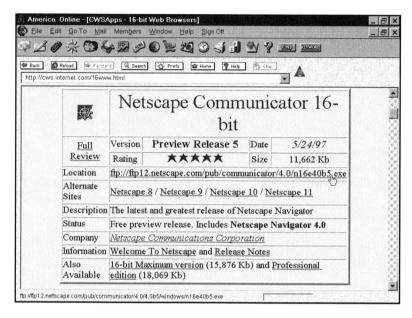

Figure 4.1 At Stroud's, you will find links to the most popular Web browsers.

When you find a link to the Web browser you want, take the following steps to download the file:

1. Click the link for the browser's installation file. The Internet Explorer dialog box appears, asking if you want to open the file or save it to disk.

2. Click the **Save to Disk** option, and click **OK**. The Save As dialog box appears, prompting you to select a drive and directory in which to store the file.

3. Select the drive and folder in which you want the file saved. (You should save the file in a separate directory that contains no other files.)

4. Click the **Save** button. Internet Explorer starts to download the file and save it to your hard drive. Depending on the size of the file, and the speed of your Internet connection, this may take several minutes or a couple of hours.

Installing Your New Web Browser

The procedure for installing the Web browser depends on which browser you downloaded. In most cases, you can simply double-click the file you downloaded. This decompresses the file, and runs the installation routine, which displays a series of dialog boxes. Respond to the dialog boxes as prompted to complete the installation.

In some cases, when you double-click the file to run it, the file merely decompresses itself, placing several files in the current directory. Look for a file called Setup.exe, Install.exe, or something similar. (This file may be in a separate directory called Disk1.) Double-click the Setup or Install file, and follow the on-screen instructions.

Using Your Web Browser with America Online

Using a different Web browser with America Online is not very difficult. Connect to America Online as you normally do; then, run your Web browser. You can run the browser just as you run any of your other applications. Double-click the browser icon or select the browser from your program menu.

The browser runs in its own separate window. You can switch back and forth between the browser window and the America Online menu whenever you wish (see Figure 4.2).

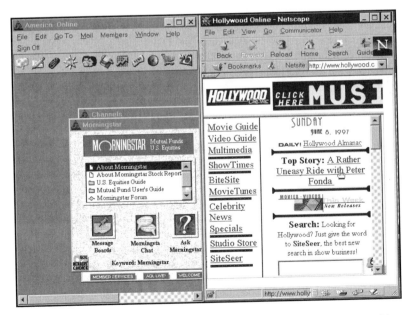

Figure 4.2 You can run America Online and a different browser side-by-side.

In this lesson, you learned how to use a browser of your choice with America Online. In the next lesson, you will learn how to open a Web page and start navigating the Web.

Jumping to Your First Web Site

In this lesson, you learn how to use your Web browser to open a Web page and skip to other pages.

Starting Your Web Browser

You start your Web browser the same way you start any of your other applications: click or double-click its icon, or select it from a menu (for instance, the Start menu in Windows 95). If you have not yet established your Internet connection, the browser typically displays a dialog box, prompting you to connect. Click the **Connect** button (or its equivalent) to give your confirmation.

If your browser does not prompt you to connect, you must establish the connection by double-clicking the icon for your Internet connection. In Windows 95, this is a Dial-Up Networking icon. In Windows 3.1, you run your Winsock application. If you are using a commercial online service, such as America Online, your Internet connection is established when you sign on.

Once you start your Web browser, it automatically loads a starting page. This is usually the home page of the company which developed the Web browser. When you start Internet Explorer, for instance, it loads Microsoft's Home Page. You can then skip to other pages on the Web by performing any of the following steps:

- Use the **File**, **Open** command to display a dialog box that allows you to type the address of the page you want to open.
- Type the address of the desired page into the Location or Address text box near the top of the browser window.
- Click links found on a Web page.

When using the File, Open command or the Location or Address text box, you need to know the address of the Web site you want to visit. Every page on the Web has an address, called an *URL* (Uniform Resource Locator). A typical URL may look like **http://www.mcp.com**. You will learn more about URLs in Lesson 6, "Navigating with Links and Page Addresses."

URL Uniform Resource Locator (most often pronounced "Earl") is the standard address that indicates the location of a page or resource on the Web or Internet universally. This location can be a computer two states or two continents away. A URL is often referred to as a *page address*.

TIP **Where Can I Find Web Addresses?** Computer magazines and Internet newsgroups are good sources for finding interesting Web addresses to visit. Check out Internet-related publications, such as *The Net*, *Net Guide*, and *Internet World*. You can also find Web pages by using a search engine, which you'll learn to do in Lesson 7, "Tracking Down Pages and People with Search Tools."

Using the File, Open Command

The standard, and most time-consuming way to open a Web page is to use the File, Open command. Take the following steps to open a page using this method:

1. Open the **File** menu and choose **Open** (the command may appear as Open Page in your browser). The Open or Open Page dialog box appears. Figure 5.1 shows Netscape Navigator's Open Page dialog box.

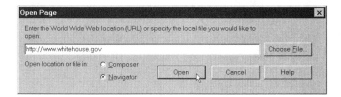

Figure 5.1 The Open Page dialog box.

2. Type the Web address you want to jump to in the text box. For example, type the following URL to go to the home page of the White House:

http://www.whitehouse.gov

TIP Skip the Prefix! You don't have to type the **http://** prefix every time you use an URL. Most newer browsers automatically examine the text you type and know whether it's a Web page address, and act accordingly.

3. Some browsers, such as Netscape Navigator give you a choice to open the page in the browser or the Web page editor (for instance, Netscape Composer). Make sure you choose to open the page in the browser.

4. Click the **Open** or **OK** button or press **Enter**. In a few seconds, the White House's home page appears on-screen (see Figure 5.2).

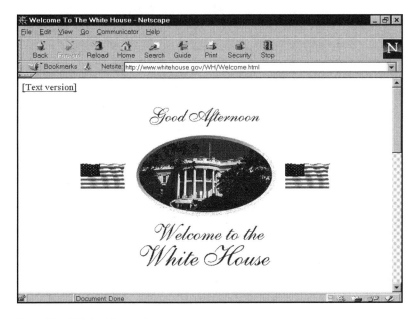

Figure 5.2 The White House home page.

Using the Location or Address Box to Jump to a Web Page

If you prefer not to use the Open Page dialog box to type Web addresses, you can easily type addresses directly into the Location or Address text box near the top of the browser window. To type directly into the Location or Address text box, follow these steps:

1. Click inside the **Location** or **Address** text box and select the text, as shown in Figure 5.3.

Type the URL here.

Figure 5.3   You can also enter Web addresses directly into the Location or Address text box.

2. Type the new URL you want to use and then press **Enter**. (When you start typing, the URL you highlighted in Step 1 is deleted.) For example, type the following URL to go to Hollywood Online:

   www.hollywood.com

3. Within moments, the new Web page downloads onto your screen.

Using Links to Jump to Other Web Pages

The third way to visit other Web sites is to click links. Links are shortcuts to other Web pages. You don't have to type an address; just click the link. Figure 5.4 shows a typical Web page link.

Links take the form of highlighted or underlined text. However, links can also be icons, graphics, and pictures. To preview where a link will take you, simply point to the link and look in the status bar to view the link's address. You will learn more about navigating with links in Lesson 6, "Navigating with Links and Page Addresses."

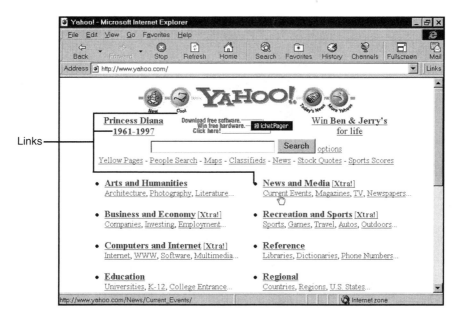

Links

Figure 5.4 You'll find links on most of the Web pages you visit.

Navigating a Web Page

Web pages are document files located on servers (computers specifically de-signed to serve up Web pages) scattered throughout the Internet. Similar to word processing files, you can scroll through Web documents by using scroll bars, view text and graphics, and select other links you want to visit. Figure 5.5 shows a typical Web page document.

Depending on the size of the document file, you may need to use the scroll bars to view different portions of the page. Click the appropriate scroll bar arrow to scroll up or down.

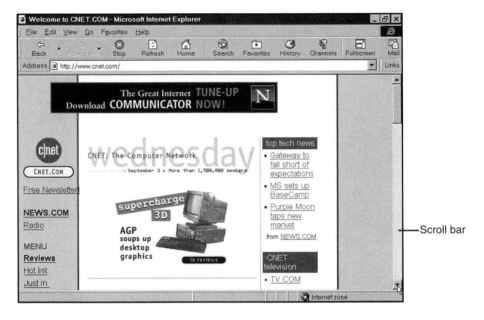

Figure 5.5 You can view more of a Web page by scrolling up or down.

Working with Frames

Some Web documents you come across may use *frames* to divide information into smaller sections within the browser window. Figure 5.6 shows an example of a Web page divided into frames. Use the scroll bars of a frame to view different portions of a document.

Frame A section within the browser window that reveals another document or part of a larger document.

For the most part, frames are fairly intuitive. In many cases, a site will display an outline or map of the site in the left frame. When you click a topic or object in the left frame, the contents are displayed in the right frame.

This frame displays the contents of the selected link.

Click a link in this frame.

Figure 5.6   Some frames are fixed where any link you click within a fixed frame appears in the larger frame.

However, frames can complicate navigation and printing. When working with frames, keep the following in mind:

- Some older browsers do not support frames. If you are using an older browser, and you connect to a site that uses frames, look for a link that points to a frameless version of the site.

- When you use the Back or Forward button to return to a page you previously visited, the browser typically steps you back through the frames, making it a little difficult to return to a previous Web site.

- Each frame displays a separate Web page; to activate a frame, click inside it.

- To print the contents of a frame, select the frame before entering the File, Print command.

- Most browsers have a separate File, Save command for frames. Use the Save Frame command instead of the standard Save As command.

- In some cases, you can resize the frames by dragging the divider line that separates the frames. However, some browsers and some Web sites do not support this feature.

Working with Forms

Another type of Web page is one with a *form*. A form is a built-in dialog box on a Web page. If you've worked with computers and their programs for any time, you are probably familiar with the purpose of dialog boxes—to extract further information from the user before completing a task. A Web page form is used to accomplish the same purpose.

A Web page form can be used to find out more information, conduct an online search, or register your thoughts and opinions. Figure 5.7 shows an example of a Web page containing a form.

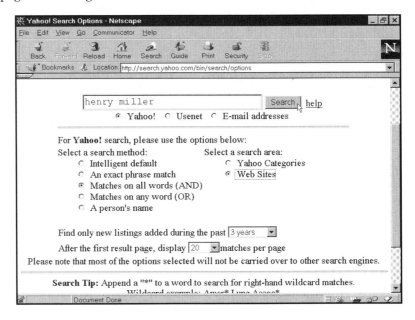

Figure 5.7 A Web page form often looks like a large dialog box.

Most forms use a standard text box for entering data. Click inside the box and start typing the requested information. With some forms, you must click the drop-down arrows to display a select list (drop-down arrows may vary, considering the type of operating system you're using). Forms also have command buttons that initiate action when pressed, such as conducting a search for online information. For example, when conducting an online search (see Lesson 7, "Tracking Down Pages and People with Search Tools"), type the text you're looking for; then click the **Search** button to start the search.

TIP **Tabbing Through Forms** To move from one text box to the next on most forms, you can use the Tab key.

CAUTION

Is It Secure? Some forms you may come across on the Web may solicit personal or confidential information. Before filling out such a form, you should first make sure the site is secure. If the site's address uses the prefix HTTPS, it's a secure Web page. Some browsers also display a security or lock icon to indicate that you are at a secure site, or a warning message indicating that you are about to send information across network lines.

Using Multiple Browser Windows

You are not limited to viewing one Web page at a time. You can open two or more browser windows and view several documents. In some cases, when you click a link, the browser automatically opens the page in a new window. In other cases, you must enter a command to open a new window. To open a window in most browsers, take one of the following steps:

- In Netscape Navigator, open the **File** menu and select **New Browser Window**. You can change windows by selecting the desired window from the Communicator menu.

- In Internet Explorer, simply run Internet Explorer again by clicking its icon.

- Right-click a link for the page you want to open, and select the command for opening the page in a new window. For example, in Internet Explorer, you right-click the link, and select **Open in New Window**.

TIP **Quick Open** In Netscape Navigator, you can quickly open a new Window by pressing **Ctrl+N**.

In this lesson, you learned how to open your first Web page and use some basic tools to work with Web pages. In the next lesson, you will learn how to navigate a Web page and use links.

Navigating with Links and Page Addresses

In this lesson, you learn how to move from one Web page to another by clicking links and entering page addresses, also referred to as URLs.

Understanding Basic Web Navigation

YourWeb browser acts as a tour bus for the Web, allowing you to travel from page to page. When you start your Web browser, it automatically loads your starting page, as you saw in Lesson 5. To view other pages, you use the following two tools:

- **Links** appear on a Web page as highlighted text, icons, or graphics that point to other pages or sections on the current page, as shown in Figure 6.1. When you click a link, your browser loads the page that the link points to. Links are excellent for wandering the Web.

- **Page Addresses (or URLs)** are addresses that point to a specific Web site or page. For example, **http://www.ibm.com** is the address for IBM's Web site. All Web browsers feature a text box into which you can type page addresses to quickly load specific pages. Figure 6.1 shows theNBA home page at **http://www.nba.com**; the address for Lycos is being entered in the Go To text box.

If you know the
address of a page,
you can enter it
here.

Click links to move
from page to page.

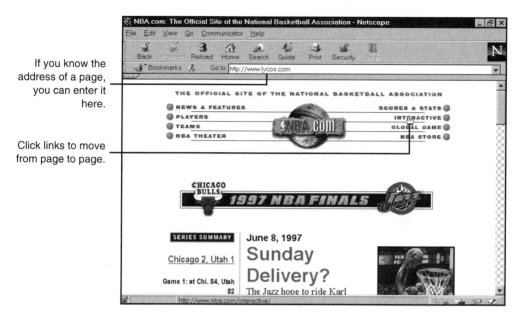

Figure 6.1 You can use links and page addresses to navigate the Web.

The following sections show you how to use links and page addresses to move from page to page on the Web.

Moving Around with Links

A link often appears as a bit of highlighted, underlined text or as a graphic or icon with a highlighted box around it. To use a link, simply click it. When you do, your browser opens the Web page that the link points to.

Before you click a link, you might want to know where it will take you. To find out, point to the link; the address of the associated Web page appears in the status bar (see Figure 6.2).

Most links appear as blue text to begin with. However, once you click a link, it changes color. Most Web browser display visited links in a different color, to indicate that you have already viewed that page. This allows you to avoid unnecessary return trips.

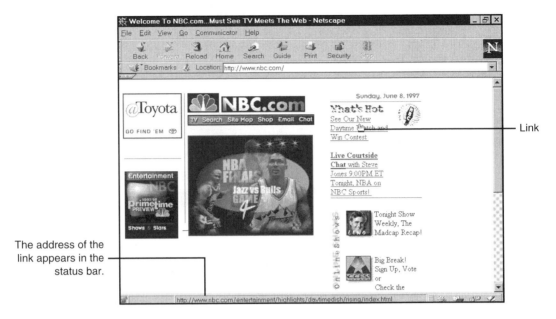

Link

The address of the link appears in the status bar.

Figure 6.2   Click a link to load the page it points to.

CAUTION

The Color of Links   Most Web browsers display unvisited links as blue, underlined text. However, sometimes the Web page contains codes that specify different colors. If you are unsure whether a chunk of text or a graphic is a link, rest the mouse pointer on it. The mouse pointer should change shape (for instance, it may appear as a hand), and the status bar should display the URL of the page that the link points to.

Using Image Maps

Many Web sites use *image maps* to help you navigate the site, as shown in Figure 6.3. An image map is typically a large graphic that has been divided into sections. Each section acts as a link, pointing to a different page.

In many cases, you can rest the mouse pointer over a particular area of the map to determine the address of the page it points to. In most Web browsers, the address is displayed in the status bar. High-end browsers, such as Netscape Navigator and Internet Explorer may display a tooltip providing additional information about the link.

In any case, you can click the various areas of the image map, just as if they were individual links.

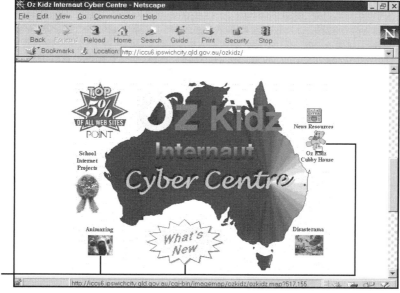

Each area of
the image map
acts as a link.

Figure 6.3 Many Web sites offer image maps, which function as navigational tools.

Playing and Saving Files

Although most links point to other Web pages, many links point to files, video clips, audio recordings, programs, and other objects stored at those sites. Many Web browsers have the capability to display pictures, and play most sound and video files.

However, if you click a link for a file type that your browser cannot play, you may be confronted by a dialog box prompting you to save the file to disk or select a player for the file type. In such cases, simply click **Cancel**. In Lessons 14 to 20, you will learn how to set up players for file types that the browser itself cannot handle.

Going to a Page When You Know Its Address

Each Web page has its own address, orURL (Uniform Resource Locator). A typical URL looks something like this:

http://www.mcp.com/frommers/newsletters/today/contents.html

If you know the address for a particular page you want to see, you can type it in theLocation orAddress text box in your Web browser, and press **Enter.** This takes you directly to the Web page whose address you entered.

 TIP   **Where Do I Get the Address for a Page?**   If you don't know the address for a particular page or even which pages you might want to view, you can search for applicable pages using a Web search tool such as InfoSeek, Yahoo!, or Lycos. See Lesson 7, "Tracking Down Pages and People with Search Tools," for more information. You can also get addresses for hot Web sites from any of several Internet magazines such as *The Net*, *Websight*, *Net Guide*, and *Internet World*. In addition, many companies now include their Web page addresses in their advertising, commonly incorporating Web page addresses into TV commercials and magazine ads.

A Web address identifies an official Internet resource. Every URL has two parts: the *content identifier* and the *location*. Take another look at our sample address, and then we'll break it down.

http://www.mcp.com/frommers/newsletters/today/contents.html

The first part, the **http://** part in our sample, is the content identifier (or content-id for short). The content-id tells your browser which protocol or language was used to create the current page. The **http://** identifier tells the browser that this page was written using HyperText Transfer Protocol (http for short). Most browsers support other protocols as well, such as **ftp://** (for transferring files), **gopher://**, and **telnet://**. This flexibility allows you to connect to other resources through the Web. For instance, you can link to a site's FTP directory or a UseNet newsgroup just as easily as you can link to another Web page—just by clicking the link.

TIP   **How Can I Tell Which Resource a Link Will Connect Me To?**   If you want to see what type of resource you're jumping to before you click its link, point to the link but don't click. The address of the link appears in the status bar. The content-id at the beginning of the address tells you whether the link connects to a Web page (**http://**) or some other type of resource.

The second part of the sample address identifies the location of the particular Web page or resource. To understand the location better, you need to divide it into two smaller parts:

- The first part (**www.mcp.com**) is the *domain name* or *host name*. Each computer connected to the Internet has a unique name that makes it easy to identify from the thousands of other computers connected directly to the Web. Your PC doesn't have a domain name, but your service provider's does because it's connected to the Web. (You connect to the Web through your service provider's domain.)

- The second part of the location (**/frommers/newsletters/today/contents. html**) is the name of a particular Web resource. This name looks very much like a directory path because that's exactly what it is. You see, every Web page is actually just a document file that exists on some computer connected to the Web. These directory paths follow the UNIX format, which means that they use forward slashes (/) in place of the backslashes (\) you're used to seeing in DOS and Windows. So the address in the sample will connect you to a document called *contents.html*, located in the /*frommers/newsletters/today/* directory of the *mcp* computer.

No Document Name?   Some addresses don't provide an actual document name. For example, you might be given the address **http://www.weather.com**, which connects you to the Weather Channel's computer. When you connect, CAUTION   that system automatically displays the Weather Channel's home page (a document file located on that computer). You'll see a lot of systems set up this way, so don't worry when you encounter an address that doesn't end in a document name.

Using Addresses to Jump to a Page

Once you have the address of a Web resource you'd like to visit, it's easy to jump to that page. Just follow these steps:

1. Click in the **Location** or **Address** text box. The address of the current page becomes selected so that you can replace it with something else. If the current address is not highlighted, double-click in the text box, or drag over the existing entry.

2. Type the address you want to go to, as shown in Figure 6.4. Make sure that you use forward slashes (/) to separate the parts of the address, and that you use the proper case.

Enter a URL here. —

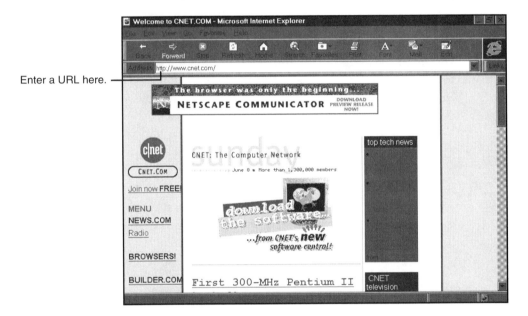

Figure 6.4 Enter a URL in the Location or Address text box.

CAUTION

Case Is Important Note that the address **http://www.weather.com/twc/homepage.html** (for example) is different from **http://www.weather.com/TWC/homepage.html**. The use of upper- and lowercase letters is very important if you're connecting to a UNIX server, especially when you are typing the path to a directory. Make sure that you write down addresses correctly and that you enter them accurately.

3. Press **Enter**, and you're taken to the Web resource at the address you entered.

If theLocation or Address text box contains an URL that's similar to the page you want to go to, you can edit the URL instead of completely replacing it. Click in the URL text box two times, so the insertion point appears inside it. Then use the Delete or Backspace key to remove text, and you can type your desired changes.

TIP

Save Yourself Some Keystrokes   If you're entering the URL of a Web page, you can usually omit the **http://** at the beginning of the URL. For example, you might enter **www.yahoo.com** in the Location or Address text box. Better yet, if the URL starts with **www** and ends with **com**, just type the in-between part—entering **yahoo** will take you to Yahoo!'s home page. Try it! The latest breed of browser features AutoComplete. As you start typing the URL of a page you previously visited, AutoComplete inserts the rest of the address for you. If the address is correct, just press **Enter**. If it is incorrect, keep typing.

What to Do When an Address Fails

Don't be surprised if you encounter several error messages as you wander the Web. By nature, the Web is always changing, and Web developers are constantly moving their Web sites and pages. Following is a list of common error messages:

File not found: If the link you click, or the address you enter, points to a Web page that has moved, you'll get an error message saying **File not found.** If that happens, you can try deleting the last part of the address (in the Location or Address text box) and pressing **Enter** again to retry it. For example, if you clicked a link that pointed to the address **http://www. movies.com/actors/gibson.html**, and it didn't work, try erasing **gibson.html**. If that doesn't work, try deleting **actors/**, too. If you can connect to **www.movies.com**, you may be able to pick up the trail to your favorite actor's Web page.

Document contains no data: If you get this error message, it's usually because the address to which the link refers is incomplete or has a typo. For example, a normal link will look something like **http://www.news. com/current/headlines/clinton.html**. If the link's address is **http://www. news.com/current/headlines/**, there's no document to which your browser can connect. Try connecting to just **http://www.news.com**. From there, you can probably find a link with the complete address of the page you want.

CAUTION

Sometimes a Page Just Won't Load   One way to know if your browser is stuck is to watch the status bar; most browsers display the page loading progress there. If nothing happens, or if it just plain takes too long, you may want to try reloading the page. To do so, click the **Stop** button, and then click the **Reload** or **Refresh** button.

Unable to locate server: You might click a link and get the error message **Browser is unable to locate the server: xxxx. The server does not have a DNS entry**. If so, try clicking the link again. If it still doesn't work, the server may no longer exist, it may be offline, or the connection to it may have been interrupted. This kind of error could also mean that your Internet connection has been broken or that the DNS server you use is down. Dial into your service provider again and retry the link.

TIP   **Busy Signal?**   If a page is popular, a lot of people might be trying to connect to it at the same time. In such a case, you'll probably get one of two error messages: **Connection refused by Host** or **Too many users, try again later**. Try again at a less busy time, such as early in the day or late at night. (However, if you get a **403** error or a similar number, you may be locked out of the site.)

In this lesson, you learned how to navigate the Web using links and page addresses. In the next lesson, you will learn how to find information and people on the Internet using some popular search tools.

Tracking Down Pages and People with Search Tools

In this lesson, you learn how to use the most popular Web search tools for information and people.

How Search Tools Work

Up to this point, you've probably found the information you were looking for on the Web by jumping from one link to another or by entering the URLs (addresses) for specific Web pages. Although they work, those are not the most efficient methods.

A better way to locate what you need is to use *Web search tools*. With a search tool, you fill out a form describing what you want to search for and click a **Search** button, and the search tool looks through its list of Web pages to find a match. As it searches, it makes a note of the number of *hits*, or matches, it finds for each Web page.

Hit   A match between your search criteria and something found in the description of a Web page. The more hits the tool finds within its description of a particular Web page, the more likely it is that the Web page contains the information you want.

When it finishes searching, the search tool lists the sites it thinks match your
search criteria. The list consists of a set of links pointing to various Web pages,
typically arranged so that the pages with the most hits (matches) are at the top.
You browse through this list and click the links for the Web sites you want to
visit. (Some search tools list most recently posted matches first, and some list
them by the *probability* of a match. Probability is based on how early in the page
the information matched. The highest probability would be an exact match in
the title.)

TIP   **Web Only**   The search tools you'll learn about in this lesson work mainly for
information on the World Wide Web and for tracking down people using online
"phone books." (Some Web search tools can help you find newsgroups and
other resources.)

In this lesson, I'll walk you through the specific steps for using Lycos and
Yahoo!. Table 7.1 contains a list of other tools and their URLs.

Table 7.1   Web Search Tools

Search Tool	Address
AltaVista	http://www.altavista.digital.com
Lycos	http://www.lycos.com
Excite	http://www.excite.com
InfoSeek	http://www.infoseek.com
Magellan	http://www.mckinley.com
WebCrawler	http://www.webcrawler.com
HotBot	http://www.hotbot.com
Open Text Index	http://index.opentext.net/

TIP   **Quick Seek**   You can access one of several popular Web search tools by
clicking the **Search** button in Navigator or Internet Explorer. These Web
browsers also allow you to type your search instructions in the Address or
Location text box. Simply type two or more words, and press **Enter**. The
browser uses the default search engine and enters your search phrase for you.

Using Lycos

Lycos is popular because it's one of the best search tools. If you can't find what you're looking for by browsing the Web, chances are you'll find it with Lycos. But if that's not enough, you can also access another helpful tool through Lycos: Top 5% Web Sites. The Top 5% Web Sites feature provides direct links that *point* you to the more popular pages on the Web and provide reviews of these pages.

Like most Web search tools, Lycos provides a simple text box into which you enter the word or words you want to search for. Lycos also offers options with which you can narrow the search and improve the results. To use Lycos, follow these steps:

1. Type **www.lycos.com** in the **Location** or **Address** text box and press **Enter**. You'll find yourself at the main Lycos screen, shown in Figure 7.1.

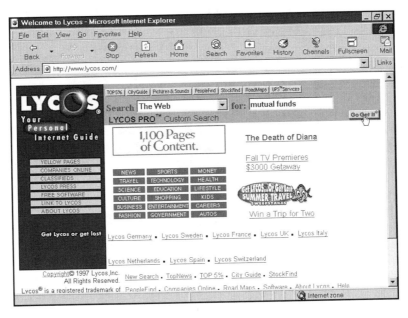

Figure 7.1 You can search the Web with Lycos.

2. Open the **Search** list and click the desired category: **The Web**, **Sounds**, **Pictures**, **Top 5% Sites**, or **UPS Tracking#**.

3. If you do not want to specify additional options for your search, type the word or words you want to search for in the **For** text box. Click **Go Get It**, and you are finished.

141

If you want to specify additional search options, do not type anything in the For text box. Instead, proceed with step 4.

4. Click the link for performing a custom search using Lycos Pro. The Lycos Search Form appears (see Figure 7.2).

5. Type the word or words you want to search for in the **Search For** text box.

6. Normally, Lycos lists Web pages that contain any of the search words. If you want Lycos to list only pages that contain *all* of the search words (providing a more narrow search), open the first **Search Options** drop-down list and click **All the words**.

Use these options to narrow your search in Lycos.

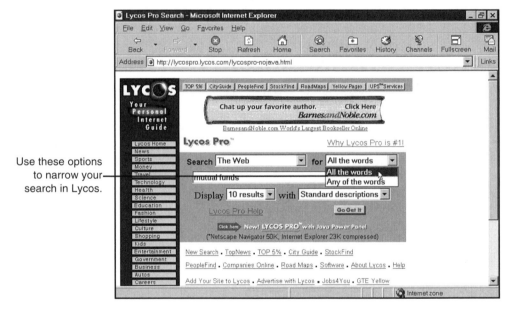

Figure 7.2 You can enter additional search options to refine your search.

7. Lycos normally displays 10 matches at a time. To display more matches per page, open the first **Display** drop-down list and select a different number.

8. Lycos also displays a brief description for each match. To control the length of this description, open the second **Display with** drop-down list (on the right) and choose **Just the links** (short), **Standard descriptions** (medium), or **Detailed descriptions** (long).

9. When you're ready to start the search, click the **Go Get It** button.

Lycos performs the search and displays a list of items that match your search criteria. Click any item to jump to the associated Web page. Remember that the pages with the most hits (the ones which come closest to matching your search criteria) appear at the beginning of the list. If the list fills more than one page, scroll down to the bottom of the page and click the link that advances you to the next page of search results. If necessary, you can return to a previous search results page by clicking the **Back** button.

 TIP **Internet Explorer's Search Bar** When you click the **Search** button in Internet Explorer, a Search bar appears on the left. You type your search instructions and choose your search tool from this bar. The results of the search appear right inside the Search bar. You can then click links in the Search bar to display the contents of the selected page in the right pane. This allows you to browse pages without having to back up to your page of found links. To turn off the Search bar, click the **Search** button again.

Searching with Yahoo!

Yahoo!, like Lycos, enables you to search its listing of Web pages by entering a few keywords. However, it also provides you with another way of searching. In Yahoo!, you can browse for what you're looking for by selecting a category that interests you from the Yahoo! Web page. From there, you can select another category and another, until you've narrowed your search sufficiently. At the bottom of the screen, you'll see a number of sites that fit the category you selected. So by using Yahoo!'s category method, you can even find a Web page without entering any keywords at all.

In addition, Yahoo! lets you combine the two methods. You can select a few categories first and then enter a keyword to search for. This enables you to limit your search to a smaller portion of the Web.

 TIP **Another Way** You can access Yahoo! with the Search button in Navigator or Internet Explorer. As you learned earlier, when you click the **Search** button, the browser connects you to one of several search tools. Click the **Yahoo** button at the top of the page or choose **Yahoo** from the **Select Provider** drop-down list.

To select a category in Yahoo! that interests you, follow these steps:

   1. Type **www.yahoo.com** in the **Location** or **Address** text box and press **Enter.** You'll see the Yahoo! opening screen, shown in Figure 7.3.

143

2. Click a category that interests you. For example, click **Arts**.

3. Yahoo! presents a list of subcategories. Continue clicking links until you find a category you like.

4. Click a link to jump to that Web page.

Alternatively, you can search for a keyword within a category. Simply enter a keyword or two into the text box, and click the **Search** button. Yahoo! searches for the requested topic and displays a list of links that match your entry. Click an entry to change to that Web page.

Categories ——

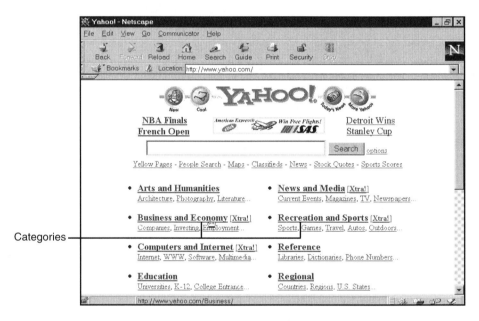

Figure 7.3   With Yahoo!, you can browse through categories to find a Web page.

 TIP   **Search Twice**   If your search results were pretty skimpy, Yahoo! allows you to search the Web again using a different Web search tool. At the end of the list of found items, Yahoo! provides links to other search tools. Click one, and the other search tool automatically performs a search using the same search criteria.

Finding People Using Web Tools

Several companies (mostly phone companies) have transformed their paper telephone directories into electronic versions and placed them on the Web. You can search for a person by last name if you know the city or state in which he or she lives. This is sort of like dialing the person's area code followed by 555-1212 and asking the operator. The following list provides the URLs for some of these search tools.

> **http://www.four11.com/**
> **http://www.bigfoot.com**
> **http://www.whowhere.com/**
> **http://www.switchboard.com/**
> **http://www.yahoo.com/search/people/**
> **http://www.tollfree.att.net/**

Follow these steps to see one of these search tools in action.

1. Run your browser, type **www.four11.com** in the **Location** or **Address** text box, and press **Enter**. Your browser loads the Four11 White Pages.

2. On the left, click the directory you want to search: E-Mail, Telephone, Netphone, Government, or Celebrity (see Figure 7.4).

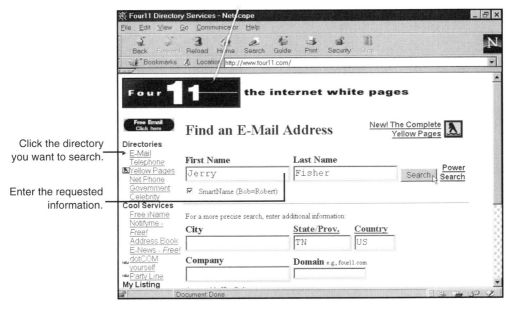

Click the directory you want to search.

Enter the requested information.

Figure 7.4 You can search for people in electronic phone books.

145

3. Complete the form to specify as much information as possible about the person you're looking for. For example, type the person's last name and the city in which that person lives in the appropriate text boxes.

4. Click the **Search** button. The search tool pulls up a list of all the people that matched your specifications.

 TIP   **Find People with Navigator**   To search for people using a variety of tools, click the **Guide** button in Navigator and then click **People**. This displays a search form at Netscape that allows you to use any of several people search tools. Click the tool you want to use, complete the form, and click the button to start the search.

In this lesson, you learned how to use several different Web search tools to track down information and people. In the next lesson, you will learn how to go back to pages you visited.

Going Back to Pages You Have Visited

In this lesson, you learn how to use various tools in your Web browser to return to pages you have recently visited.

Moving Back and Forward

As you move from one Web page to another, your browser adds the page's name and address to a *history list*. You can then use various tools in the Web browser to navigate the history list and quickly return to those pages.

 History List A list of pages you have recently visited (and their corresponding addresses). Most browsers keep track of all the pages you visited for the last 5 to 10 days (you can specify the number of days). You can specify the number of days in the options dialog box: **View**, **Internet**, **Options** in Internet Explorer, or **Edit**, **Preferences** in Navigator.

The easiest way to return to pages in the history list is to use your browser's Back and Forward buttons. You can move backward as many pages as you like simply by clicking the **Back** button, as shown in Figure 8.1. After you back up, you can return to where you were by moving forward through previously viewed Web pages. Simply click the **Forward** button. If you want to return to your starting point, you can click the **Back** button until you get there, or you can click the **Home** button. Either way, you return to your starting page.

Though simple to use, the Back and Forward buttons typically have one limitation: They work only for pages loaded during the current session. If you exit your Web browser, you have to start from scratch.

TIP **Back and Forward Menus** In the latest versions of Internet Explorer and Netscape Navigator, the Back and Forward buttons double as menus. Right-click the **Back** or **Forward** button to view a list of recently visited pages. Click the name or address of the page to reopen it.

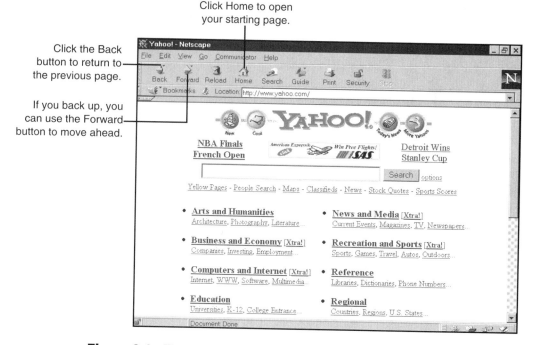

Click Home to open
your starting page.

Click the Back
button to return to
the previous page.

If you back up, you
can use the Forward
button to move ahead.

Figure 8.1 The Back and Forward buttons allow you to quickly revisit pages loaded in the current session.

Nothing Happens When I Click the Button If the Forward (or Back) button is gray, you have moved to the end (or the beginning) of the history. You can't select the button again because you've moved as far forward or backward in the history as you can.

CAUTION

Using Menu Selection to Return to Pages

Although the Back and Forward buttons offer intuitive ways to return to pages, stepping back or forward through a long list of pages is not very efficient. A more efficient way to return to pages is to select the name of the page you want to return to from one of your browser's menus:

- In Netscape Navigator, open the **Go** menu, and select the desired page from the bottom of the menu.
- In Internet Explorer, open the **File** menu, and select the desired page from the bottom of the menu, as shown in Figure 8.2.

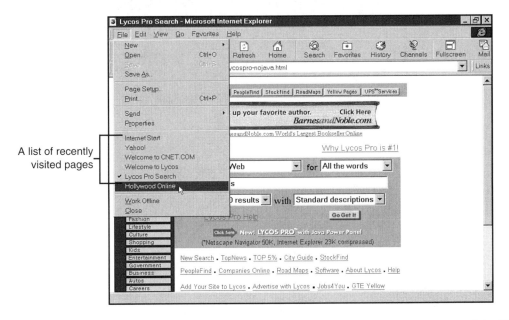

A list of recently visited pages

Figure 8.2 Internet Explorer lists recently visited pages near the bottom of the File menu.

TIP **What If I Find a Page I Like?** If you find a Web page that you plan to visit often, you can add the page's name to a menu in your Web browser. See Lesson 9, "Creating and Organizing Navigator Bookmarks," or Lesson 10, "Creating and Organizing Internet Explorer Favorites," for details.

Selecting Pages from the Location or Address List

In most Web browsers, the Address or Location text box doubles as an abbreviated history list. It keeps track of only the page addresses you typed; it does not

149

log addresses to links you click. You can quickly return to a page by selecting its address from the list. Take the following steps:

1. Click the **Location** or **Address** drop-down arrow (to the right of the text box). The list of addresses you recently entered appears, as shown in Figure 8.3.

A list of pages you've previously visited

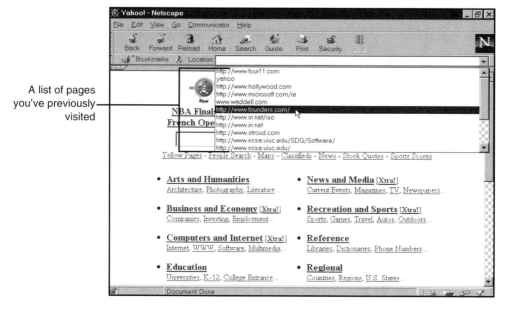

Figure 8.3   Navigator's Location list.

2. Click the address of the page you want to view. Your browser opens and displays the selected page.

If you visited the page a long time ago, you may need to select it from a more comprehensive history list, as explained in the following section.

Viewing a History of Your Journeys

Whenever you exit your Web browser, it removes the list of pages you visited from its menu system and Location or Address list. When you restart your browser, the Back and Forward buttons are both grayed out, so you can't use them to return to pages you opened in the previous session. To return to pages, you must display the comprehensive history list. Take either of the following steps to display and use the history list in Internet Explorer or Netscape Navigator:

- In Netscape Navigator, open the **Communicator** menu and select **History**, or press **Ctrl+H**. The History window appears, as shown in Figure 8.4. Double-click the name or address of a page to open it in a separate Navigator window.

- In Internet Explorer 3, open the **View** menu, select **Options**, and click the **Navigation** tab. Click the **View History** button (near the bottom of the tab). Click the name or address of the page you want to reopen.

- Internet Explorer 4 features a History bar you can view by clicking the **History** button. The History bar appears on the left side of the window. Click the day or week when you visited the page to view a list of sites visited during that week or on the selected day. Click a site to view a list of pages you visited at the site. Click the page name to load the page in the right side of the window. To close the History bar, click the **History** button again.

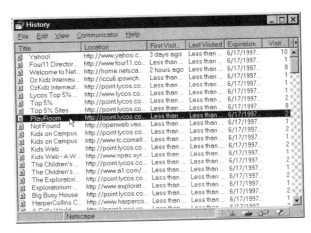

Figure 8.4 You can return to a page by selecting it from Navigator's history list.

In this lesson, you learned how to return to pages you have recently visited. In the next two lessons, you will learn how to mark your favorite pages and quickly return to them by selecting them from menus in Netscape Navigator and Internet Explorer.

Creating and Organizing Navigator Bookmarks

In this lesson, you learn various ways to mark your favorite Web pages in Navigator, so you can return to them at any time.

Going Back to Where You've Been

Navigator offers a couple of options to help you get where you're going. You can type a URL in the Location text box, or you can click a link. However, because there are so many Web pages and because URLs are so difficult to remember, Navigator offers many more options to help you return to sites you have already visited.

In Lesson 8, "Going Back to Pages You Have Visited," you learned how to use a few of these tools. You can open the Go menu and select the name of a page you visited; you can open the Location drop-down list and select a URL; you can display the history list (Communicator, History); and you can use the Back and Forward buttons. In this lesson, you will learn how to use more sophisticated tools to mark the pages you might want to revisit in the future:

- **Bookmarks** allow you to create a menu of pages and place groups of page names on submenus. For example, you could create bookmark submenus for Sports, Health, Investments, Research, Weather, and so on. To go to a page, you select it from the menu.

- **Personal toolbar** lets you create buttons for the pages you visit most often. You can then click a button to quickly load the associated page.

- **Shortcuts** allow you to create icons for pages or links and place those icons on the Windows desktop or in a folder. To load a page, you double-click its shortcut icon.

Bookmarking a Page

The best tool for flagging a page you may wish to return to is to use a bookmark. When you create a bookmark in Navigator, Navigator adds the name of the page to the Bookmarks menu or one of its submenus. Navigator offers several options for creating bookmarks, some of which are easier to use than others. Try any of the following techniques:

- Press **Ctrl+D** to bookmark the current page. The page's name is placed at the bottom of the Bookmarks menu.
- Open the page you want to mark, and then drag the **Location** icon over the Bookmarks icon, as shown in Figure 9.1. (The Location icon is just to the left of "Location.") When the mouse pointer reaches the Bookmarks icon, a submenu appears. Without dragging over any of the options on the submenu, release the mouse button.
- To create a bookmark for a link, drag the link from the current page over the Bookmarks icon, and release the mouse button.
- To create a bookmark for the current Web page, right-click a blank area of the page and select **Add Bookmark**.
- To create a bookmark for a link, right-click the link and select **Add Book-mark**.

After you create a bookmark for a page, you can return to that Web page at any time using one of following methods:

- Open the **Bookmarks** menu and select the page from the list or submenu as shown in Figure 9.2. (Your newest bookmark appears at the bottom of the list.)
- Press **Ctrl+B** to display the Bookmarks window, and then double-click the bookmark for the page you want to go to.

TIP **Trade Places** You can trade bookmark files with your coworkers. First, have your friend copy the file to a disk. Insert the disk, open the **Bookmarks** menu, and select **Edit Bookmarks**. Then, open the **File** menu and select **Import**. Select the file on the disk and click **Open**. The bookmarks are added to the bottom of your bookmark list.

Drag the Location
icon over the
Bookmarks icon.

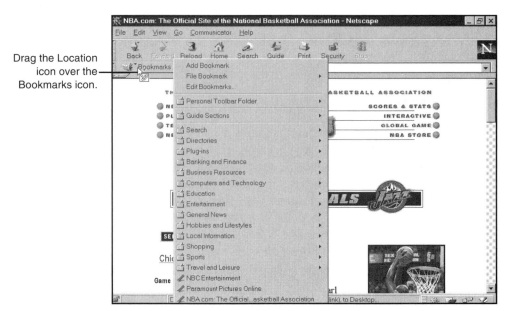

Figure 9.1 The most intuitive way to create bookmarks is to use the drag-and-drop technique.

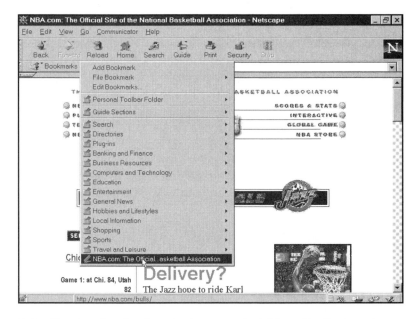

Figure 9.2 To return to a bookmarked page, select it from the Bookmarks menu or one of its submenus.

Organizing Bookmarks

Navigator enables you to sort your bookmarks, organize them in folders (to create submenus), and add comments. If you save very many bookmarks, you'll soon appreciate that you can organize them into a usable list.

You might create a folder so you can store similar bookmarks together. To create a bookmark folder, follow these steps:

1. Open the **Bookmarks** menu and select **Edit Bookmarks** (or just press **Ctrl+B**). The Bookmarks window appears.

2. In the bookmarks list, click where you want the folder to appear. The new folder appears directly below the item you select.

3. Open the **File** menu and select **New Folder**. The Bookmark Properties dialog box appears.

4. Type a name for the folder (submenu) in the **Name** text box. You can type a description in the **Description** text box, but that's optional; the description appears only if you use the Bookmark list as a Web page. Click **OK**.

5. To add an existing bookmark item to the folder, drag it to the folder as shown in Figure 9.3.

6. Click the **Close** (X) button to close the Bookmarks window.

Drag a bookmark to the new folder.

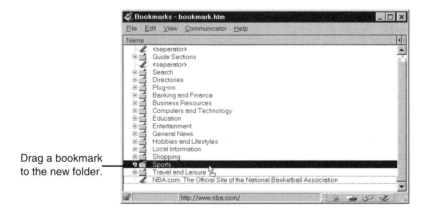

Figure 9.3   You can organize your bookmarks into folders.

155

Adding Bookmarks to Your New Folder (Submenu)

Navigator 4.0 now offers an easy way to add bookmarks, that allows you to add bookmarks on the fly. First, display the page you want to add to the Bookmarks menu. Then, open the **Bookmarks** menu, point to **File Bookmark**, and click the name of the folder to which you want to add this page. An easier way to add a bookmark to a submenu is to drag a link or the Location icon over Bookmarks, over the submenu name, and then onto that submenu.

Another way to add bookmarks to a submenu is to enter a setting that makes a specific submenu the default receptacle for any bookmarks you create. To do this, take the following steps:

1. Open the **Bookmarks** menu and click **Edit Bookmarks**.
2. Right-click the name of the folder you want to use as the default folder and click **Set As New Bookmarks Folder**.

Now, whenever you add a bookmark by selecting Add Bookmark from the Bookmarks menu or from a context menu, the bookmark will be added to the specified submenu instead of to the main Bookmarks menu. To make the main Bookmarks menu the default, right-click the main **Bookmarks** folder (at the top of the list in the Edit Bookmarks window) and select **Set As New Bookmarks Folder**.

You can also use one of your submenus as the main Bookmarks menu. Right-click the submenu you want to transform into the Bookmarks menu and select **Set As Bookmark Menu**. Then, when you open the Bookmarks menu, you will see only the bookmarks that are included in the folder you selected.

 TIP   **Let's Separate!**   One way to group bookmarks without using submenus is to use separators. To place a separator between two bookmarks, open the Edit Bookmarks window (**Bookmarks**, **Edit Bookmarks**). Click the bookmark below which you want to insert the separator line, open the **File** menu, and select **New Separator**. The next time you open the Bookmarks window, a separator line appears below the bookmark or folder you selected.

You can delete bookmarks just as easily as you can delete files on a disk; simply click the bookmark and press the **Delete** key. You can delete a bookmark folder by selecting it and pressing **Delete**. Of course, when you delete a folder, you delete all the bookmarks in it, so be careful!

When working in the Bookmarks window, you can hide the items in a folder by clicking the minus sign in front of the folder icon. To display the items in a closed folder, click the plus sign in front of the folder icon.

Updating Your Bookmarks

The Internet changes constantly, and sometimes it's a struggle to keep up. What's the best way to find out what's new?

One way is to have Navigator check your bookmarked pages and notify you of which ones contain new information. Then, you only have to visit the changed pages to get a quick update on your favorite topics. Follow these steps to set Navigator to check your bookmarked pages:

1. Open the **Bookmarks** menu and select **Edit Bookmarks**.

2. (Optional) If you want to check only a few bookmarks, select them by clicking the first bookmark and **Ctrl+**clicking on any additional bookmarks you want to check. (If you want Navigator to check all your bookmarks, skip this step.)

3. Open the **View** menu and select **Update Bookmarks**.

4. Choose whether you want Navigator to check all bookmarks or only the selected ones.

5. Click **Start Checking**. Navigator verifies each bookmark by attempting to connect to its associated Web site. (The amount of time it takes to check out your bookmarked pages will vary, depending on the number of Web sites you selected, how busy they are, and the speed of your connection.)

6. When Navigator finishes checking your bookmarks, it displays a message saying so, as shown in Figure 9.4. Click **OK**.

If you return to the Bookmarks window, you might see that some bookmark icons have changed:

- Bookmarks that point to pages whose information has changed are marked with a highlighted icon.

- Bookmarks that could not be checked are marked with a question mark icon.

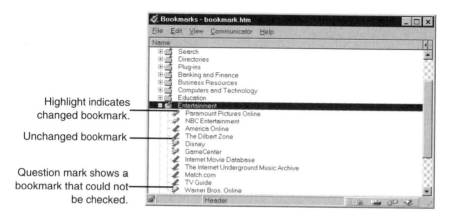

Highlight indicates changed bookmark.

Unchanged bookmark

Question mark shows a bookmark that could not be checked.

Figure 9.4   Navigator updates your bookmarks and shows you which ones have changed.

Creating a Shortcut for a Web Page

If you frequently visit a Web page when you start Navigator, but you don't want to use it as your starting page, consider making a shortcut icon for the page. When you create a shortcut, an icon for the Web page appears on the desktop. Then all you have to do is double-click the icon, and Navigator starts and automatically jumps to that Web page. (It's kind of like creating a temporary starting point that you can use whenever you want.)

Windows 95 Only   Sorry, but only Windows 95 users can create and use shortcuts.

CAUTION

Navigator offers several options for creating shortcuts. Try the following techniques to find out which one you like best:

- Right-click a link and select **Create Shortcut**. The Create Internet Shortcut dialog box prompts you to change the name of the shortcut. If desired, type a new name. Click **OK**.

- To create a shortcut for the current page, right-click a blank area of the page and select **Create Shortcut**. Click **OK** in the Create Internet Shortcut dialog box.
- Drag the **Location** icon to a blank area of the Windows desktop.
- Drag a link to the desired page over a blank area of the Windows desktop.

To use a shortcut, double-click it. If you didn't start Navigator yet, Navigator automatically runs and attempts to open the page. Shortcuts act like any Windows 95 shortcut. You can delete, copy, or move them, and you can create a separate folder for your shortcuts. Here's another trick you might try with shortcuts: Drag a shortcut into the page viewing area of the Navigator window and see what happens.

Adding Buttons to the Personal Toolbar

In addition to placing links on the Bookmarks menu and on the Windows desktop, you can place them as buttons on the Personal toolbar. To display this toolbar, click its tab. (If you hid the toolbar earlier, open the **View** menu, and select **Show Personal Toolbar**.) You can then do any of the following to add links:

- Drag a link up to the toolbar, as shown in Figure 9.5.
- Drag the **Location** icon over the toolbar to create a button that points to the current page.
- Display the page you want to add to the Personal toolbar. Open the **Bookmarks** menu, point to **File Bookmark**, and select **Personal Toolbar Folder**.
- In the Edit Bookmarks window, click the bookmark you want to add to the Personal toolbar. Open the **File** menu and click **Add Selection to Toolbar**.

In this lesson, you learned how to create and organize bookmarks. The next lesson shows how to use Internet Explorer Favorites to mark pages. If you are not using Internet Explorer, skip to Lesson 11, "Tuning In to the Web with Netscape Netcaster," to learn how to channel surf with Netscape.

Drag the Location
icon over the—
Personal toolbar.

Drag a link up to the—
Personal toolbar.

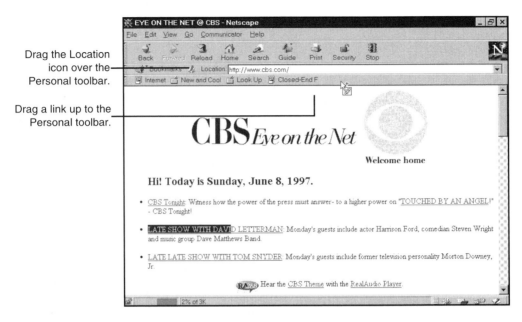

Figure 9.5   You can create buttons for your favorite pages on the Personal toolbar.

Creating and Organizing Internet Explorer Favorites

In this lesson, you learn various ways to mark your favorite Web pages in Internet Explorer, so you can return to them at any time.

Returning to Your Favorite Pages

Internet Explorer offers a couple of options to help you get where you're going. You can type a URL in the Address text box, or you can click a link. However, typing addresses and clicking links are not very efficient when you are trying to return to your favorite pages. Fortunately, Internet Explorer offers the following tools, which allow you to mark your favorite pages and quickly return to them:

- **Favorites** allow you to place the names of your favorite Web pages on the Favorites menu. To return to a page, you simply select the name of the page from the menu.
- **Quick Links toolbar** lets you create buttons for the pages you visit most often. You can then click a button to quickly load the associated page.
- **Shortcuts** allow you to create icons for pages or links and place those icons on the Windows desktop or in a folder. To load a page, you double-click its shortcut icon.

The following sections provide detailed instructions on how to use these advanced navigational tools.

Cutting Hours Off Your Trips with Shortcuts

If you've worked with Windows 95 much, you know that you can create icons for applications and documents and place them right on the Windows desktop. These icons, called *shortcuts*, allow you to bypass the menu system. Internet Explorer allows you to create shortcuts for your favorite Web pages. Take the following steps:

1. Open the page you want to mark in Internet Explorer.
2. Right-click a blank area of the page and select **Create Shortcut**. Internet Explorer places a shortcut icon on the Windows desktop.

You can also create shortcuts for links on a page. Right-click the link, and select **Copy Shortcut**, as shown in Figure 10.1. Then, right-click a blank area of the Windows desktop, and select **Paste Shortcut**.

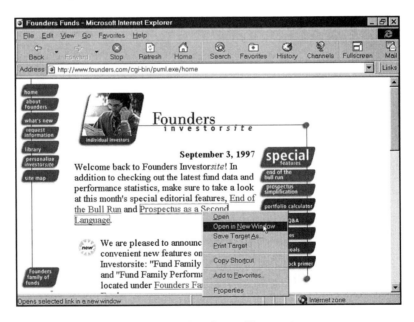

Figure 10.1 Right-click a link, and select **Copy Shortcut**.

Once you've created a shortcut to a page, you can quickly return to the page by clicking on the shortcut. If you are connected to the Internet, Internet Explorer immediately loads the page. If you are not connected, the Connect To dialog box appears, prompting you to connect. Once connected, Internet Explorer runs and loads the page.

CAUTION

One Web Browser Only If you have two Web browsers installed, only one of them can use shortcuts. You'll have to decide which Web browser you want to use as the default (only the default browser can use shortcuts). Whenever you start the browser that is *not* the default browser, a dialog box appears asking if you want to make it the default browser. Click **Yes**.

Adding Shortcuts to the Favorites Menu

Shortcuts are helpful, but when you're in Internet Explorer, you don't want to have to minimize the Explorer window and return to the Windows desktop to open a page. And, you don't have to. You can create shortcuts and place them directly on Internet Explorer's Favorites menu. Take the following steps:

1. Open the Web page you want to mark as a favorite.

2. Take one of the following steps:

   To add the current page to the Favorites menu, right-click a blank area of the page or on some normal text (not a link), and select **Add To Favorites**. Or, open the **Favorites** menu, and select **Add To Favorites**. The Add Favorite dialog box appears.

   To add a page that a link points to, right-click the link, and select **Add To Favorites**.

3. A dialog box appears, prompting you to enter additional settings for the favorite. To change the name of the page as it will appear on the Favorites menu, type a new name in the **Name** text box.

4. (Optional in Internet Explorer 4 only) Click **Yes, notify me if updates and download the page for offline viewing** to subscribe to this Web page and have updated versions of the page automatically delivered to you.

5. (Optional) To add the page to a submenu rather than to the main Favorites menu, click the **Create In** button, and select the desired submenu. (You'll learn how to create additional submenu folders later.)

6. Click the **Customize** button. This starts the Subscription Wizard, as shown in Figure 10.2, which leads you through the process of specifying subscription options.

7. Follow the on-screen instructions to subscribe to this site.

8. Click **OK** to save your new Favorite.

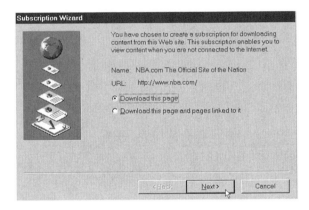

Figure 10.2 If you subscribe to a Web site, the Website Subscription Wizard prompts you to enter subscription preferences.

If you choose to subscribe to some Web sites, Internet Explorer automatically establishes your Internet connection at a predetermined time, downloads the updated page(s), and disconnects. You can then view the pages offline. See "Working with Site Subscriptions in Internet Explorer 4," later in this lesson, for more information.

 TIP **Three Favorites Menus** In case you haven't noticed, Internet Explorer 3 has two Favorites menus: one in the menu bar and one on the toolbar. In Internet Explorer 4, the Favorites button on the toolbar opens a Favorites bar on the left side of the window, displaying a list of Favorites. Internet Explorer 4 also places a Favorites menu on the Windows 95 Start menu.

What's New with My Favorite Pages?

A new feature in Internet Explorer 4, *Smart Favorites*, has taken on the responsibility of checking for page updates. If a page has changed, Internet Explorer places a red asterisk next to the page name on the Favorites menu, to show you that the page has something new. This saves you the time of having to open the page to check for updates.

Organizing Your Favorites Menu

The Favorites menu is yours to arrange and rearrange to your liking. You can delete Favorites, create new submenus, and move items from the Favorites menu to your submenus. To perform any of these management tasks, you first have to open the Organize Favorites window. Take the following steps:

1. Open the **Favorites** menu.

2. Click **Organize Favorites**. As you can see from Figure 10.3, this window is a glorified version of the My Computer window. (This figure shows the Organize Favorites window in Internet Explorer 4. If you are using Internet Explorer 3, your window will look different.) If you're accustomed to copying, moving, and deleting files in My Computer, you'll have no trouble doing it here.

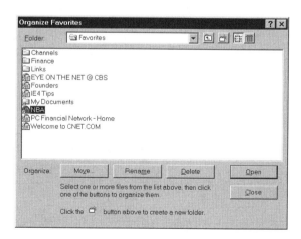

Figure 10.3 The Organize Favorites window lets you copy, move, and reorganize your Favorites menu.

TIP **Drag and Drop** Internet Explorer lets you rearrange items on the Favorites menu simply by dragging them. Open the **Favorites** menu, and then drag an item up or down on the menu. A black horizontal line appears, showing where the Favorite will be placed. Release the mouse button.

Renaming and Deleting Favorites

As with any shortcuts, you can easily rename or delete a shortcut on the Favorites menu. First, display the Organize Favorites dialog box. Then, perform one of the following steps to rename or delete the shortcut:

- To rename a shortcut, select it, and click the **Rename** button. Type the new name, and press **Enter**. (You can bypass the Rename button by selecting the shortcut and then clicking on its name.)

- To delete a shortcut, select it, and click the **Delete** button (or press the **Delete** key). Answer any warning boxes that ask whether you're really sure you want to delete the shortcut.

Do-It-Yourself Button Bar

The Quick Links bar allows you to add buttons for your favorite Web pages. To view the toolbar, double-click **Links**. You can drag **Links** down or up to make it a separate toolbar. To add buttons to the Links toolbar, drag a link or shortcut for the desired page over the Links toolbar. A vertical line appears, showing where the button will be inserted (see Figure 10.4). Release the mouse button.

In Internet Explorer 3, you cannot simply add buttons to the Links toolbar. You must replace an existing button with the button you want to use. Take the following steps:

1. Drag a link or shortcut for the desired page over an existing button on the Quick Links toolbar, and release the mouse button. The Quick Link dialog box appears, prompting you to confirm.

2. Click **Yes**. The button is renamed and now points to the desired page.

3. To rename the button, open the **View** menu, select **Options**, and click the **Navigation** tab.

4. Open the **Page** drop-down list and select the Quick Link whose name you want to change.

5. Tab to the **Name** text box, and type the desired name. Click **OK**.

Drag a link over the Links toolbar.

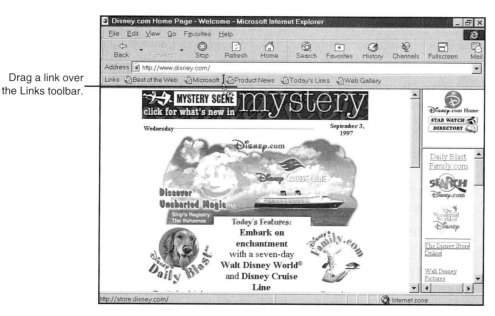

Figure 10.4   In Internet Explorer 4, you can drag links up to the Links toolbar to create buttons.

Working with Site Subscriptions in Internet Explorer 4

To subscribe to a Web page, you create a Favorite and enter settings that tell Internet Explorer how often to update the page. Internet Explorer then connects to the Web at the predetermined time(s) and downloads the updated page for you. You learned how to subscribe to sites earlier in this lesson in the section "Adding Shortcuts to the Favorites Menu." The following sections provide additional details on working with subscriptions.

CAUTION

Internet Explorer 4 Only   Internet Explorer 3 does not offer site subscriptions. If you want to subscribe to Web sites, you need to move up to Internet Explorer 4.

Setting Up a Subscription for an Existing Shortcut

Subscribing to a Web page on-the-fly as you did earlier is quick and easy, but what about all those shortcuts you created before you knew about subscriptions? You don't have to redo those shortcuts in order to subscribe. Take the following steps to enter subscription settings for an existing shortcut:

1. Find the shortcut that points to the page you want to subscribe to. The shortcut may be on the Windows desktop, in the Quick Launch toolbar on the taskbar, or in the Organize Favorites window (Favorites, Organize Favorites).

2. Right-click the shortcut and select **Properties**.

3. Click the **Subscription** tab. The Subscription tab has a message indicating that you have not subscribed to the site.

4. Click the **Subscribe Now** button. The Subscribe Favorite dialog box appears.

5. Select one of the following options:

    Only tell me when this page is updated tells Internet Explorer to display a red asterisk on the icon when the page is updated.

    Notify me of updates and download the page for offline viewing tells Internet Explorer to automatically download this page at the scheduled time. (You'll learn how to set the scheduled time later.)

6. Click the **Customize** button. This starts the Subscription Wizard, which informs you that Internet Explorer will monitor this page for changes.

    The Wizard asks if you want to be notified of page updates via e-mail. This is useful if you frequently travel or if you just want Internet Explorer to notify you, so you don't have to check for updates.

7. Click **No** or **Yes**. If you select Yes, you can click **Change Address** and specify the e-mail address to which you want updated notifications sent.

8. Click **Next**. The Wizard now asks if you need to enter a login name and password to access the site.

9. Click **No**, or click **Yes** and enter your login name and Password.

10. Click the **Finish** button, and then click **OK**.

Cancelling Subscriptions

To cancel a subscription, you first must display the Subscriptions window. Open the **Favorites** menu, and select **Manage Subscriptions**. Click the site whose subscription you want to terminate, and then click the **Delete** button or press the **Delete** key.

Entering Delivery and Notification Settings

You entered subscription settings earlier when you first marked a page as a Favorite. You indicated if and when you wanted updated pages downloaded. However, there are additional subscription settings you can enter to specify how information is delivered, and how Internet Explorer notifies you of updated pages.

To change the subscription settings for a Favorite or shortcut, right-click the shortcut, and select **Properties**. The subscription properties dialog box appears, with the Subscription tab up front. Click the **Receiving** tab and take one of the following steps:

- To be notified of updates via e-mail, click **Send an e-mail message to the following address**. You can click the Change Address button to specify the e-mail address where you want updated notices sent.

- To have Internet Explorer notify you of updates, but not download the updated page, click **Only notify me when updates occur**. (Internet Explorer notifies you of updates by displaying a red asterisk on the shortcut icon for the site.) To have Internet Explorer automatically download the page at the scheduled time, click **Notify me when updates occur, and download for offline viewing**.

If you choose Yes, download this site, Internet Explorer automatically downloads the page and all related graphics. To have additional related pages downloaded, and to automatically download sounds, videos, and other items on the page, click the **Advanced** button and select any of the following options:

> **Download linked pages within a depth of ___** allows Internet Explorer to download any pages linked to this page. Be careful with this option. Because some pages contain many links, turning this option on can cause Internet Explorer to pack your drive with a bunch of pages you may never look at. Whatever you do, don't enter a large number in the blank.

Follow links outside of this page's Web site tells Internet Explorer to trace hyperlinks to other pages not on this site. It's a good idea to keep this option off.

Images tells Internet Explorer to download any inline images contained on the page. This is on by default.

Sound and video tells Internet Explorer to download any background sounds and inline video clips on the page. (Audio and video files can be quite large.)

ActiveX Controls and Java applets is another security option. It is possible for programmers to develop destructive ActiveX Controls and Java Applets and place them on Web pages. If you download a page that has a destructive component, it can do a lot of damage while you're catching up on your sleep.

Never download more than_Kb per update allows you to limit the size of the download to prevent Internet Explorer from cluttering your disk with huge pages.

After entering the desired settings on the Receiving tab, click the **Schedule** tab, as shown in Figure 10.5, to specify when you want page updates downloaded:

Scheduled is the default setting. You can open the drop-down list and choose to have updates delivered **Daily**, **Weekly**, or **Monthly**. You can also choose **Dial as needed if connected through a modem** to have Internet Explorer automatically establish your Internet connection at the scheduled time. The **New** button allows you to create a custom schedule that will be listed in the drop-down box; you can set the day and time for downloading updates. The **Edit** button lets you change the settings for the schedule selected in the drop-down list.

Manually tells Internet Explorer not to automatically check for updates. You must manually check for updates using the **Favorites**, **Update All Subscriptions** command.

Don't update this subscription when I'm using my computer tells Internet Explorer to postpone downloading updates until you are done working in your other programs.

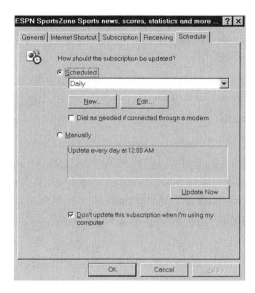

Figure 10.5 You can specify when you want Internet Explorer to check for updates or download updated pages.

Automating Your Modem Connection

If you connect to the Internet via a network connection, and you stay connected to the Internet at all times, Internet Explorer automatically downloads subscribed sites at the specified times. However, if you connect using a modem, you must enter additional connection settings. These settings allow Internet Explorer to automatically "dial" your modem and establish the Internet connection required to download subscribed sites at the scheduled times. Take the following steps:

1. Open Internet Explorer's **View** menu and select **Internet Options**.
2. Click the **Connection** tab.
3. Under Connection, click **Connect to the Internet using a modem**, and click the **Settings** button.
4. Open the **Use the following Dial-Up Networking connection** drop-down list, and select the name of your Dial-Up Networking connection.

5. Select **Connect automatically to update subscriptions** to place a check in its box. Enter your user name and password in the appropriate text boxes.

6. Enter any other desired settings to specify your dialing preferences, such as how many times Internet Explorer should dial before giving up, and how long the connection should be idle before Internet Explorer hangs up.

7. Click **OK** to return to the Options dialog box, and then click **OK** to save your settings.

If you set up Internet Explorer to automatically dial during off hours, make sure you leave your computer on during that time. If your monitor does not have a power-saving feature, turn off the monitor, but leave the system unit on, and if you have an external modem, make sure it's on, too.

In this lesson, you learned how to mark your favorite pages for quick return trips, and how to subscribe to Web sites. Skip ahead to Lesson 12, "Using the Internet Explorer Active Desktop," to learn how to work with Internet Explorer's desktop integration features.

Tuning In to the Web with Netscape Netcaster

In this lesson, you learn how to use Netscape's new product, Netcaster, to subscribe to Web sites and have updated information delivered to your desktop.

Understanding Netcaster

Netcaster is a tool that's designed to make navigating Web pages as fast and easy as flipping channels on your TV set. Netcaster enables you to subscribe to Web sites and have updated Web pages delivered to you while you are working on something else or sleeping. You can then disconnect from the Internet and view the pages offline.

Although Netcaster is a relatively small component when viewed as part of the Communicator suite, it offers two features to cut down on your connect time, and to deliver the latest Web updates (for the sites you visit most) directly to you:

- *Channels* allow you to tune in to the best sites the Web has to offer. Netcaster comes with a channel finder that allows you to select from popular sites, such as *ABC News*, *CBS SportsLine*, *CNN*, and *Wired* magazine. You can also place your favorite sites on the channel changer.
- *The Webtop* is a new concept that provides you with a desktop overlay. You can set up any Web page as an automatically updating Webtop, which displays its latest content. The Webtop allows you to stay on top of the news as it happens.

You will learn all you need to know about selecting, viewing, and subscribing to channels, and how to take control of your new Webtop.

 Site Subscriptions Although "subscribing" sounds as though this is going to cost money, you can usually subscribe to a site for free. "Subscribing" just means that you will tell Netcaster which pages you want and when to download them.

Downloading and Installing Netcaster

When you download Netscape Communicator, you do not automatically receive Netcaster. However, you can use Communicator's SmartUpdate feature to download it. Take the following steps:

1. Run Navigator.

2. Open the **Help** menu and select **Software Updates**. This connects you to Netscape's SmartUpdate page.

3. Scroll down the page, and click the **Options** button next to Netscape Netcaster.

4. Open the **Choose a download location** drop-down list, and select a download site near you, or select Netscape Communications.

5. Click the **Begin SmartUpdate** button. The SmartUpdate window appears, showing the progress of the download.

6. Wait until the download is complete and another window appears prompting you to give your okay for installing Netcaster.

7. Click the **Install** button. The installation utility automatically installs Netcaster and then displays a screen indicating that the installation was successful.

8. Exit Navigator, and restart it.

Starting Netcaster

Before you can use the Netcaster's time-saving features, you must run it. You can run Netcaster by taking one of the following steps:

- Open the **Communicator** menu and select **Netcaster** in any of the Communicator component windows (Navigator, Messenger, Collabra, or Composer), or press **Ctrl+8**.

- To have Netcaster run when you start Communicator, open Navigator's **Edit** menu, select **Preferences**, click **Appearance**, and make sure there is a check mark next to **Netcaster**. Click **OK**.

Whatever method you use to run Netcaster, it appears on the right side of your screen, as shown in Figure 11.1. On the left side of the Netcaster window is a tab with Netscape's N logo on it. Click the tab to hide the window; click the tab again to bring the window back into view. (The tab stays on top of your other windows.) To completely exit Netcaster, click **Exit** near the bottom of the window.

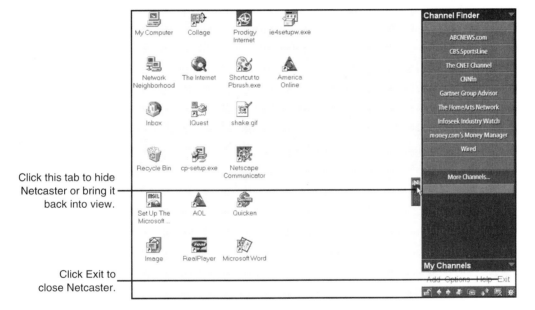

Click this tab to hide Netcaster or bring it back into view.

Click Exit to close Netcaster.

Figure 11.1 Netcaster overlays the right third of your desktop.

As you can see from Figure 11.1, the Netcaster window is divided into following four areas, listed from top to bottom:

- **Channel Finder** displays a list of popular channels that are registered with Netscape, including *ABC News* and *CNET*. You can click **More Channels** to view a list of additional channels. See "Changing Channels" later in this lesson, for details.

175

- **My Channels** is a list of channels you have chosen to tune in. Click **My Channels** to hide Channel Finder, and display a list of your favorite channels. To add channels to this list, see "Adding and Viewing Channels" later in this lesson.

- **Control Bar**, near the bottom of the window, provides options for adding a channel (to the My Channels list), configuring Netcaster (see "Controlling the Netcaster Window" later in this lesson), viewing online help, and exiting Netcaster.

- **Button Bar**, at the very bottom, allows you to use Netcaster to navigate your channels (flip forward and back, and print the current page), and to control your Webtop (hide it, move it to the front or back, or close it). You'll learn more about these buttons as you proceed through this lesson.

Changing Channels

Netcaster's main purpose is to act as a channel changer for the Web. You program in the channels you want to view, and then you can view those channels with a simple click of a button. But how do you program these channels? And what do you do if your favorite Web site isn't on Netcaster's Channel Finder list? The following sections provide answers to these questions and detailed instructions on how to "program" Netcaster.

Finding High-Profile Channels

Netcaster's Channel Finder lists over 100 popular Web sites that have registered their "stations" with Netscape. To preview these popular channels, take the following steps:

1. Click **Channel Finder** in the Netcaster window.

2. Click the name of the channel you want to preview. The channel's title and logo appear on a *card*, as shown in Figure 11.2. In the lower-left corner of the card is an Add Channel button, which you can click to view the page in Navigator and add the channel to your channel changer (see the next section for instructions).

3. If you don't see the channel you want, click **More Channels** at the bottom of the Channel Finder list. This connects you to Netscape's ChannelFinder page, which should display a list of additional channels. (At the time this book was being written, the channel offerings were slim.)

4. To view more channels, click one of the buttons on the left, such as **Coming Soon** or **Marimba Channels**. This displays a list of additional channels from registered providers.

Click a channel's name to preview it.

This card appears.

You can click Add Channel to add the channel to the My Channels list.

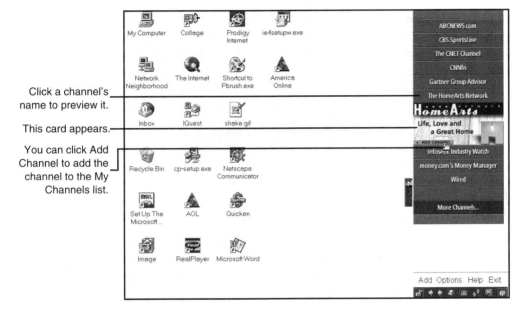

Figure 11.2 You can preview popular channels and add them to your channel changer.

TIP **Always More Channels** As Netcaster becomes a popular tool, more companies will be registering their Web sites as channels, so be sure to check Netscape regularly (by clicking **More Channels**) for additional high-profile channels.

Adding and Viewing Channels

You already have some idea of how this channel changer works, so let's go through the process of adding a channel step-by-step:

1. Click **Channel Finder** to display a list of popular channels.

2. Click the channel button for the channel you want to add to the My Channels list. The channel's card appears, letting you preview the channel.

3. Click the card. The ChannelFinder window appears, displaying the contents of the selected channel.

4. Click the **Add Channel** button in the upper-left corner of the Channel Finder window. (The first time you add a channel, you must fill out a registration form. Follow the on-screen instructions.) The Channel Properties dialog box appears, as shown in Figure 11.3, displaying the channel name and its address.

You can change the channel's name.

Specify how often you want Netcaster to request updated content.

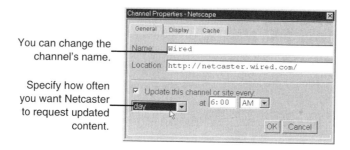

Figure 11.3 Netcaster provides several options for controlling your channels.

5. (Optional) Double-click in the **Name** text box, and type a more descriptive name for the channel. Do NOT edit the entry in the Location text box.

6. Open the **Update this channel every ___** drop-down list, and select how frequently you want Netcaster to download updates from this site. (If you choose Day or Week, specify the day or time that you want Netcaster to download the update.)

7. Click the **Display** tab, and select one of the following options:

Default Window displays the page in a standard Navigator window, providing you with Navigator's navigational tools.

Webtop Window lets the page take over all the real estate on your Windows desktop, and does not display the Navigator toolbars or menus. This makes the page nice and big but difficult to handle. See "Placing Live Content on Your Desktop" later in this lesson, for details.

8. Click the **Cache** tab, and enter the following preferences (each channel has its own default settings):

Download ___ level(s) deep in site tells Netcaster to download pages that are linked to the main channel. Be careful with this option; if a page has many links, or you select to download more than two or three levels deep, you may pack your hard drive with Web pages.

Don't store more than ___ KB of information tells Netcaster to stop downloading when it has received a certain measure of data. Again, keep this number below 1 megabyte (1000K), or you might find your hard drive full in the morning.

9. Click **OK**.

The channel is now added to the My Channels list. To view the channel, click **My Channels**. If you see a red and gray bar below your channel, Netcaster is busy downloading the latest update. When Netcaster is finished downloading, the bar disappears. You can then disconnect and view the page offline.

Adding Any Web Site as a Channel

Netcaster's Channel Finder is loads of fun and can open your eyes to popular sites you didn't know were popular (or didn't know existed). However, you probably have your own list of favorite Web pages. You can create channels for your own Web pages by taking the following steps:

1. Click the **Add** button in Netcaster's control bar. The Channel Properties dialog box appears, as shown in Figure 11.3, except the **Name** and **Location** text boxes are empty.

2. Type a name for the channel in the **Name** text box.

3. Click in the **Location** text box, and type the URL that points to the page.

4. Enter any additional options, as explained in the previous section, including how often you want Netscape to request updated content.

5. Click **OK**.

Deleting Channels

Once you've set up a couple dozen channels, your list might become a little cluttered with channels you never "watch." To clean up your list, you can delete channels by performing the following steps:

1. Click the **Options** button in the control bar. The Options dialog box appears, with the Channels tab up front.

2. Click the name of the channel you want to remove.

3. Click the **Delete** button. A warning appears, prompting you for confirmation.

4. Click the **Yes** button.

179

Placing Live Content on Your Desktop

When you first add a channel, you can choose to have its Web page displayed in a standard Navigator window or as a Webtop. You can change this window setting for any channel at any time. Take the following steps:

1. Click the **Options** button.

2. Click the name of the page that's settings you want to change.

3. Click the **Properties** button. This displays the same Properties dialog box you saw when you first set up the page as a channel.

4. Click the **Display** tab, and select **Default Window** (to display the page in a standard Navigator window) or **Webtop Window** (to make the page overlay your current desktop).

When you choose to display a channel as a Webtop, it covers your current desktop, and blocks access to any of your desktop icons, as shown in Figure 11.4.

Channel appears here.

Toolbar allows you to navigate Webtop channels and control the Webtop.

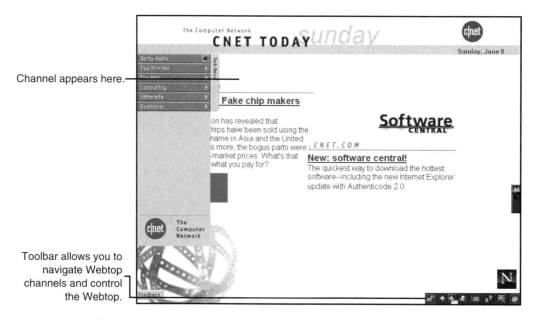

Figure 11.4   The Webtop provides the maximum viewing area for a Web page.

However, Netcaster does allow the Windows 95 taskbar to show through, and Netcaster displays the following Webtop controls:

Security is the lock icon all the way on the left. If it's locked, you're viewing a secure page.

Go to previous page on Webtop displays the previous channel that you have chosen to display as a Webtop Window. If you chose to display the channel in the Default Window, this button will not bring it into view.

Go to next page on Webtop displays the next channel that you have chosen to display as a Webtop Window.

Print the Webtop prints the Webtop.

Show or hide the Webtop turns the Webtop on or off, so you can get at your desktop icons.

Send the Webtop to the front or back moves the Webtop to the top or bottom of a stack of windows. This works only if you have other application windows open that are not maximized. Any maximized window will cover the Webtop.

Close the Webtop turns off the Webtop and returns your desktop to normal.

Open a Navigator window opens a Netscape Navigator window, which you can use to browse the Web.

 TIP **Right-Click the Webtop** Although the Webtop offers little in the way of menus, you can still right-click objects and links to display a context menu with the most common options.

Controlling the Netcaster Window

The Netcaster window is fairly large and a little difficult to manage. However, Netcaster does provide a few options to reposition and control its window. To access these options, click the **Options** button, and then click the **Layout** tab, as shown in Figure 11.5. You can then change the following settings:

- **Attach Netcaster drawer to ___** lets you move the Netcaster window to the left or right side of the screen.

- **Attach Webtop to** ___ lets you move the Webtop to the left or right side of the screen. (If you move the Netcaster window to the right, consider moving the Webtop to the left.)
- **Automatically hide Netcaster window** forces the Netcaster window to roll back whenever you select a channel. This gets it out of the way, so you can view the Web page.
- **Default Channel** allows you to pick any of your channels as the opening channel whenever you run Netcaster. Initially, Netcaster does not use a default channel. To use a channel as the default, select **Set default to**, and then pick a channel from the drop-down list.

Figure 11.5   You can reposition and configure the Netcaster window.

 TIP   **Channels as Webtops**   If a small rectangle appears to the right of a channel name, that channel is set to display in Webtop mode. No rectangle means the channel will open in a standard window. Other than the difference in modes, a Webtop is nothing more than a channel. The process for deleting, updating, and changing their properties is the same.

In this lesson, you learned how to use Netcaster to set up channels for your favorite Web pages. The next lesson shows you how to use a similar tool in Internet Explorer called the Active Desktop.

Using the Internet Explorer Active Desktop

In this lesson, you learn how to work with Internet Explorer's desktop integration features and the Active Desktop.

What's New with Your Windows Desktop?

Internet Explorer 4's desktop enhancements change the very nature of the Windows desktop. You can now single-click icons to run programs and open files. My Computer and Windows Explorer have been completely revamped. And your taskbar has many new tricks tucked up its sleeve, as shown in Figure 12.1. In this lesson, you will learn how to deal with these changes and take advantage of these improvements.

 Desktop Integration A concept whose intent is to make your desktop look and act more like the Web. With desktop integration, you can open a file or run a program by single-clicking its icon, just as if it were a link. You can also place automatically updating Web pages and other components on your desktop, making it more like an information center than a PC control panel.

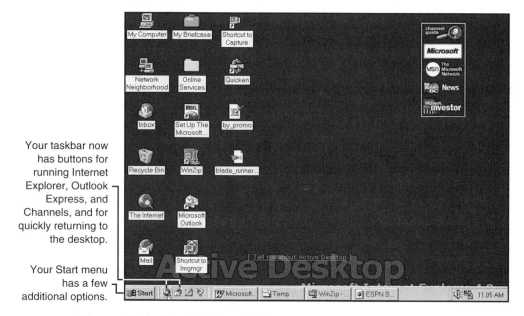

Your taskbar now has buttons for running Internet Explorer, Outlook Express, and Channels, and for quickly returning to the desktop.

Your Start menu has a few additional options.

Figure 12.1 Your Windows desktop sports a new look.

Reorienting Yourself in My Computer and Windows Explorer

The biggest changes you will have to adjust to are in My Computer and Windows Explorer. Internet Explorer has completely changed the look and behavior of these important tools, making it easier for you to access your local files. The following sections explain the most important changes to help reorient you to your Windows desktop.

What's New with My Computer?

Click the My Computer icon in the upper-left corner of the Windows desktop, and keep an eye on the screen. You now see the new, improved My Computer, a two-paned window with a pretty background. As you can see in Figure 12.2, My Computer has a new toolbar that looks more like a toolbar you might find in a Web browser; in fact, you can use this toolbar to navigate the Web. If the toolbar is not displayed, select **View**, **Toolbar**, and select the desired toolbars: **Standard Buttons**, **Address Bar**, or **Links**.

Here's what you need to know about how to access your files and folders with My Computer:

- Click a file to run an application or open a document.
- Click a folder to open it.
- Don't click a file to select it; clicking opens the file or runs it (if it is a program file). To select a file, rest the mouse pointer on the file (point to the file). My Computer highlights it.
- To select additional files, hold down the **Ctrl** key while pointing to other files you want to select.
- To select a group of neighboring files, point to the first file, and then hold down the **Shift** key while pointing to the last file in the group.
- To deselect a file, point to it.
- You can still right-click a selected file to display a shortcut menu with commands for opening, cutting, copying, and pasting files.
- To rename a file, right-click it and select **Rename**.
- You can click the **Back** button to return to the folder you previously opened. If you backed up, you can click the **Forward** button to move ahead.
- The **Up** button moves you up one level in the folder tree.
- The **File** menu keeps track of which folders (and Web pages) you have opened, so you can quickly return to a folder by selecting it from the File menu.
- The **View** menu is nearly the same as the old My Computer View menu; it contains options for arranging icons in the window.

The **Address** text box, the **Links** toolbar, the **Go** menu, and the **Favorites** menu perform the same tasks as they do in Internet Explorer. You can use these controls to navigate both the Web and your hard drive.

If My Computer opens a new window every time you open a Web page or folder, your desktop will quickly become cluttered. Open the **View** menu, select **Folder Options**, click the **Custom, based on settings you choose**, and click the **Settings** button. Make sure **Open each folder in the same window** is selected. Click **OK**.

Click Back and
Forward to
navigate your
folders.

Point to a file or
folder to select it.

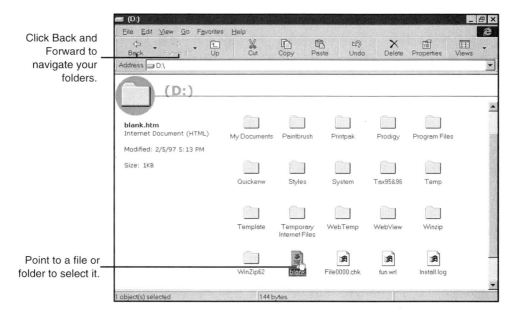

Figure 12.2   My Computer helps you navigate your File system as if it were a Web page.

TIP   **Resource Information and Help**   When you point to a disk icon in My Computer or Windows Explorer, the left pane displays the amount of total and free disk space.

Working with the New Windows Explorer

Windows Explorer has the same enhancements you find in My Computer. Windows Explorer provides one-click access to applications and files, and offers the Internet Explorer toolbar, which you can use to browse the Web or your company's intranet. To run Windows Explorer, take the following steps:

1. Open the **Start** menu, and point to **Programs**.
2. Click **Windows Explorer**.
3. If the toolbars are not displayed, select **View**, **Toolbar**, and click the desired toolbar.

You have probably worked with Windows Explorer before, and you are comfortable with its two-paned approach. The left pane displays a list of drives and folders, and the right pane displays the contents of the selected drive or folder.

 TIP   **Windows/Internet Explorer**   You can run Internet Explorer right inside the Windows Explorer window. Run Windows Explorer. In the left pane, labeled All Folders, click **The Internet**. This runs Internet Explorer in the right pane of the Windows Explorer window. You can now navigate the Web by clicking links or entering page addresses.

Returning My Computer and Windows Explorer to "Normal"

If you dislike the changes to My Computer and Windows Explorer, you can return them to the way they were. In My Computer or Windows Explorer, open the **View** menu and select **Folder Options**. Click the **General** tab, and select either of the following options under Web View:

- To make the window look and act as it did before, click **Classic style**.
- To retain the Web-like appearance but return to double-clicking, select **Custom, based on settings you choose** and click the **Settings** button. Select **Enable all web-related content on my desktop** and select **Double-click to open an item**. Click **OK**.

Working with the Active Desktop

The idea behind the Active Desktop is that it seamlessly integrates the Web, your company's network, and your local PC. The "active" part is that you can quickly and easily configure your desktop to make it look and act the way you want it to.

One of the great new features of the Active Desktop is that it allows you to place components (*desktop components*) of any size and dimensions on your desktop. Desktop components can be stock tickers, scrolling news headlines, and e-mail notification boxes. With desktop components, you have complete control of their size and position. You can even set up desktop components to receive automatic updates from the Web during the day.

The following sections provide the instructions you need to start using and configuring the Active Desktop.

What's New on the Start Menu?

Internet Explorer has placed a couple new commands on the Start menu. Open the Start menu and point to **Find** (which has always been on the Start menu). The Find submenu now has a couple additional options: **Computer** lets you search another computer on your network or intranet for files; **People** allows you to use Internet search tools to track down friends, family members, and business associates on the Web.

In addition to the new commands, you can now rearrange program icons on the Start menu simply by dragging them. To get a feel for drag-and-drop Start menu configuration, take the following steps:

1. Open the **Start** menu, point to **Programs**, and point to **Accessories**.

2. Point to **Notepad**, and drag it down to the bottom of its submenu. A black, horizontal line appears, showing where Notepad will be moved. (A button also appears at the tip of the mouse pointer.)

3. Release the mouse button. This closes the Start menu.

4. Open the **Start** menu, point to **Programs**, and point to **Accessories**. As you can see, Notepad is now at the bottom of the Accessories submenu.

Making the Most of Your Taskbar

The Windows 95 taskbar has a couple new features, as well. Just to the right of the Start button is a new toolbar that initially contains icons for running Internet Explorer, Outlook Express (for e-mail) and Channels (which you will learn about later in this lesson). This toolbar also contains a button called **Show Desktop** that you can click to quickly return to the Windows desktop when you are working in other applications.

You can take control of this new toolbar and your new taskbar in several ways:

• Drag the slider (double vertical lines) on the end of a toolbar to resize it (see Figure 12.3).

• Drag the slider to the left or right of another toolbar's slider to move the toolbar.

- Drag document icons or shortcut icons onto the new Quick Launch toolbar to create buttons for the applications you run most often.

- You can add toolbars to the taskbar. Right-click a blank area of the toolbar, point to **Toolbars**, and select any of the following options:

   Address places the Address text box on the taskbar. You can enter the address of a Web page into this text box to open a page.

   Links inserts a bar that contains buttons pointing to helpful Web pages. You can add buttons for your own favorite pages.

   Desktop displays a toolbar containing buttons for all the shortcuts on your Windows desktop.

   Quick Launch displays a toolbar that contains an icon for Internet Explorer. (This is very similar to the toolbar that appears by default.)

   New Toolbar lets you transform a folder into a toolbar. For example, you can select New Toolbar, and select Control Panel, to create a toolbar that contains icons for all the tools in the Windows Control Panel.

- To remove a toolbar, right-click a blank area of the toolbar, and select **Close**.

- To view larger icons in the toolbar, right-click a blank area of the toolbar, point to **View**, and select **Large**.

- To turn text descriptions of the toolbar buttons on or off, right-click a blank area of the toolbar, and select **Show Text**.

- To view the toolbar's name, right-click a blank area of the toolbar and choose **Show Title**.

You might also notice that the taskbar now toggles running applications. For instance, if you click the button for a running application, Windows moves the application's window to the front, so you can start working (which Windows has always done). However, when you click the button again, Windows minimizes the application window, so you can return to the previous application or to the Windows desktop.

Turning On the Active Desktop

Before you can add desktop components, first make sure the Active Desktop is on. If you see the Channel bar on your desktop, Active Desktop is on. If the bar is not there, right-click a blank area of the Windows desktop, point to **Active Desktop**, and select **View As Web Page**.

Drag a slider to
resize or move
a toolbar.

Drag the top of
the taskbar to
make it larger.

Click the Show
Desktop icon to quickly go
to the desktop.

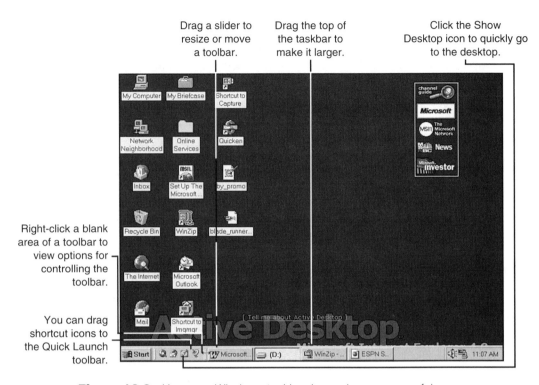

Figure 12.3   Your new Windows taskbar is much more powerful.

Right-click a blank
area of a toolbar to
view options for
controlling the
toolbar.

You can drag
shortcut icons to
the Quick Launch
toolbar.

Desktop Component   A Web page or other object that you place right on your Windows desktop. Your new desktop consists of two layers: an *HTML layer* and an *icon layer*. By using HTML to control your desktop, Internet Explorer transforms your desktop into a Web page. This allows you to place active, desktop components that are HTML-friendly right on your desktop as *frames* (independent windows).

Adding Desktop Components

To add desktop components, you must download them from the Web using Internet Explorer. Microsoft has set up a Desktop Component Gallery on the Web, where you can go to download some samples. The following steps show you how to access the gallery, download a desktop component, and place it on your Windows desktop:

1. Right-click a blank area of the Windows desktop, select **Properties**, and click the **Web** tab. A list of any installed desktop components appears.

2. Click **New**. The New Active Desktop Item dialog box appears, asking if you want to go to the Active Desktop Gallery.

3. Click **Yes**. This runs Internet Explorer and connects you to the Internet, if you are not already connected. Internet Explorer loads the Active Desktop Gallery Web page.

4. Click the link for the desktop component you want. Another page appears, describing the component and displaying a link for downloading it.

5. Click the link to download it and place it on your desktop. Internet Explorer displays a couple dialog boxes, asking for your confirmation and allowing you to specify how often you want your desktop component to update information. Enter your preferences.

Once a desktop component is on the desktop, you can move it or resize it. To move a component, point to its title bar to display a gray bar at the top of the window; drag the gray bar to move the component. To resize a component, drag one of the corners of its frame. As these desktop components become more popular, you will start to find desktop components sprinkled all over Web pages.

Removing Desktop Components

Turning off or deleting a desktop component is a little more difficult than adding one. Take the following steps:

1. Right-click a blank area of the desktop and select **Properties**. The Display Properties dialog box appears.

2. Click the **Web** tab. This tab contains a list of desktop components, as shown in Figure 12.5, including the component that replaced your Windows background.

3. To turn off a component, click its check box.

4. To completely remove a component, select it, and then click the **Delete** button.

Drag the gray bar to move the component.

Rest the mouse pointer on the title bar.

Drag a corner to resize the frame.

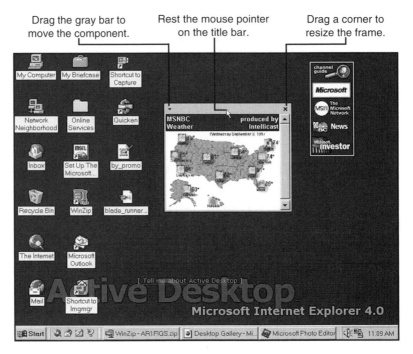

Figure 12.4 Desktop Components make your desktop and active area, where you can receive the latest news and information.

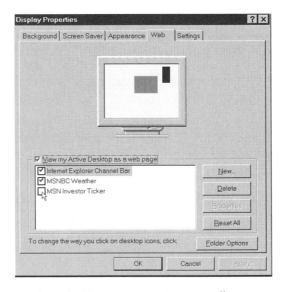

Figure 12.5 You can turn desktop components on or off.

Tuning In to the Web with Channels

With Channels, you can tune in to the best sites the Web has to offer. Channel Guide comes with a channel finder that allows you to select from popular sites and then place those sites on the channel changer. To view a site, you simply click a button on the channel changer; it's just like flipping channels on your TV set.

Accessing Channels from Internet Explorer

To channel surf, you first need to display the Channel browser bar in Internet Explorer. Click the **Channels** button in the toolbar. Initially, the bar contains one button labeled Channel Guide, which you can use to add channels to the channel changer. Take the following steps to add a channel:

1. In the Channel bar, click **Channel Guide** to connect to Microsoft's Channel Guide. This site displays a list of popular channels.

2. Click a button for the channel you want to add. The channel appears in a preview window right on the Channel Guide page, so you can decide if you want to subscribe to the channel.

3. Click the link for adding the channel to the Channels list. The Subscription dialog box appears.

4. Click the **Customize** button, and use the Subscription Wizard to enter subscription settings for this site. See Lesson 10, "Creating and Organizing Internet Explorer Favorites," for details.

5. Click **OK**. A button for this site appears in the Channels bar.

 TIP **Adding Non-Channels to the Channel Changer** You can add any Web page to the Channel bar by creating a shortcut for it in the Favorites\Channels folder. When you choose to create a Favorite, click the **Create In** button, and select the Channels folder.

Channel Surfing

Channels give Web developers more control over your subscriptions. Instead of allowing you to select the pages you want to subscribe to, the developer includes the list of pages related to the channel. To select a page, you click the button for the desired channel, and then select the desired page.

193

Navigating the Channels Window

When you click a channel in the Channel bar on the Windows desktop and select a page, the Internet Explorer opens the selected page in Full Screen view, with the Internet Explorer toolbar at the top. To return to normal view, click the **Full Screen** button in the toolbar. You can return to Full Screen view at any time by selecting **View**, **Full Screen**. To close the window, click the Close button (X) in the upper-right corner of the window.

To give the current page more room to spread out, move the mouse pointer over the page. The pane expands, hiding the Channels bar. You can click links on the page to skip to related pages, just as you do in the Internet Explorer window. To display the Channels bar, move the mouse pointer to the left side of the screen.

Tuning In on Your Windows Desktop

The Channels feature is included as a desktop component. If you turn on the Active Desktop, as explained earlier in this lesson, the Channel bar appears on the Windows desktop. If the Channel bar is not displayed, right-click the **Windows** desktop, select Properties, and click the **Web** tab. Make sure **View my Active Desktop as a Web Page** is checked, and make sure **Internet Explorer Channel Bar** is checked. Click **OK**.

To tune in to a channel, click its button, and select the desired page. This opens the page in Full Screen view, as explained in the previous section.

In this lesson, you learned how to work with your new Windows desktop and have Web sites deliver the latest information to your desktop. In the next lesson, you will learn how to save and print Web pages.

Saving and Printing Web Pages

In this lesson, you learn how to save Web pages you come across as HTML files and how to print them.

Saving a Web Page

The World Wide Web is a sprawling maze of information. As you wander from site to site, you'll come across pages you want to keep either in print or electronic form. With your Web browser, you can print out Web pages or save them as files on your computer's hard drive.

The handy part about saving a Web page onto your hard drive is you can go back and examine it later. Sure, you may choose to save the page as a bookmark and revisit it while surfing Web pages (see Lesson 9, "Creating and Organizing Navigator Bookmarks," and Lesson 10, "Creating and Organizing Internet Explorer Favorites"), but by saving the document as a file, you can open it at your leisure and take a look at its contents without tying up a phone line or incurring connection charges.

When saving a document file, you can choose to save the file in HTML format or as plain text. HTML format (which adds the extensions *.htm* or *.html* to the file name) saves the Web page with all its HTML coding. When you open the file again, you'll see it with its original Web formatting, minus the graphics. When saving Web pages, only the text and its formatting are retained. Any multimedia files or graphics must be saved separately.

HTML HTML stands for *HyperText Markup Language*, a script used when creating Web pages. HTML tags control how a document appears in your Web browser. For example, to make text bold, HTML uses the bold on and off tags, like this: **This is bold text**. Tags are also used to insert anchors that link the document to other Web pages.

When saving a file in plain text format (adds the extension *.txt* to the file name), you get a document without the HTML formatting—just plain, no-frills text.

To save a Web document, follow these steps:

1. Open the Web page you want to save.

2. Pull down the **File** menu and choose **Save As**. This opens the Save As dialog box, as shown in Figure 13.1.

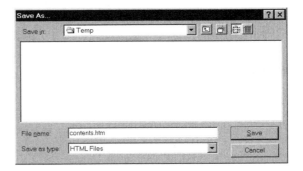

Figure 13.1 The Save As dialog box.

 TIP **Use the Shortcut Menu** If you find a link you want to save, right-click the link and choose **Save Link As** or **Save Target As** from the context menu. (Mac users must hold down the mouse button instead of clicking it.) This opens the same Save As dialog box where you can designate a storage place and file name. The command may vary depending on the Web browser you are using.

3. Select the directory or folder where you want the file saved.

4. Type in a name for the file in the **File Name** text box.

5. Open the **Save As Type** drop-down list and select the file format you want the file saved as.

6. Click the **Save** button. The Web page is saved.

196

To view the page later, simply open the **File** menu, choose **Open**. This displays a dialog box, prompting you to type the address of the page. Click the **Browse** or **Choose File** button, and use the Open dialog box to change to the drive and folder where the file is stored. Click the file's name and click **Open** or **OK**. Remember, with a saved document page, it is not necessary to connect to the Internet to view the page. You can view the file in the browser window without logging on.

TIP **Can I Save Other Types of Web Page Elements?** You can easily save pictures, sound, and audio clips onto your computer's hard drive. It's best to save such items by using the appropriate helper application or plug-in associated with the clip or picture. Use the application's **File**, **Save** command to do so. Learn more about plug-ins and helper applications in Lessons 15 to 20.

Printing a Web Page

Printing a Web page is even easier than saving it. You can print any Web page you view by using your browser's Print button or the File, Print command. Keep in mind that many Web pages are longer than what you see on your screen and can run several pages in length.

Follow these steps to print a Web page:

1. From the browser window, open the Web page you want to print.

2. Open the **File** menu and choose the **Print** command, or click the **Print** button in the browser's toolbar. This opens the Print dialog box, as shown in Figure 13.2.

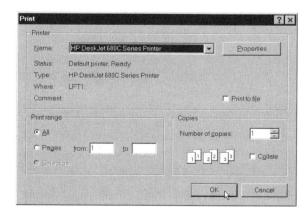

Figure 13.2 The Print dialog box.

3. Make sure the **All** option in the **Print Range** area of the dialog box is selected.

4. Click **OK** to print the page.

Changing Print Preferences

By default, the printed document appears as an 8.5×11-inch page, which typically includes a header and footer detailing the document title and URL. However, you may want to change the way a Web page is printed. To do so, you need to open your system's Page Setup dialog box. Pull down the **File** menu and choose **Print Setup** (or a similar command used by your browser).

Depending on your operating system, the Page Setup box may differ in the number and type of options available. For example, the Windows 95 Page Setup dialog box offers options for changing page margins, options for text printed in the header or footer, and options for controlling different Web page elements as printed on a page (see Figure 13.3). Mac users can find options available in drop-down lists. Unlike Windows users, the Mac Page Setup box also has print controls for paper choice and page orientation.

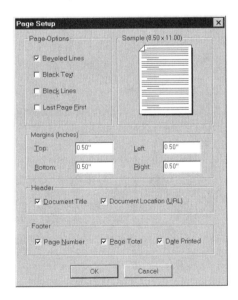

Figure 13.3 The Page Setup dialog box allows you to enter settings to control the page layout.

You may want to print a page first before making changes to the printing options. This enables you to clearly see what you want to change about the page, such as a margin. You can also preview a page before printing, which you learn to do in the next section.

When you do decide to make changes to printing preferences, simply select any options you want to change from the Page Setup dialog box, and then click **OK**. Now you can print the page using the new options you chose.

 TIP **Use Your Printer Controls** You can also control how your pages print by using your printer's setup controls. For example, if you are using Windows 95, open your printer's **Properties** window and adjust the settings for printing pages. Mac users can change printer controls in the Chooser.

Previewing Before Printing

You may want to preview how the Web page is going to look before you tell Netscape to print. It's a good idea to preview any Web page before printing, especially if you want to know if all the graphics are going to appear on the page or to check how the bulleted lists line up.

To preview your page, follow these steps:

1. Open the **File** menu and choose **Print Preview** (or a similar command in your browser). This opens the Print Preview window. Figure 13.4 shows the Print Preview window in Netscape Navigator. Your browser's Print Preview window may differ.

2. Use the **Next Page** and **Prev Page** buttons to view different pages of the Web document.

3. Click the **Two Page** button if you want to view two pages at once.

4. To get a closer look at the document, click the **Zoom In** button. To zoom out again, click the **Zoom Out** button.

5. To print the page (or pages) from the Print Preview window, click the **Print Page** button.

6. To exit the Print Preview window, click the **Close** button. This returns you to the main browser window.

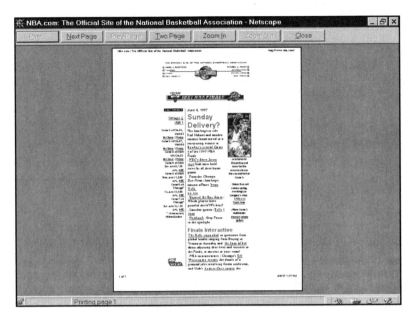

Figure 13.4   Navigator's Print Preview window.

Viewing Saved Documents

What can you do with the Web documents you save onto your computer? You can open them again in an HTML editor, such as FrontPad or Netscape Composer, and make changes to your saved documents. For example, you can save a document you found on the Web, make a few modifications, and send it to your staff as a memo.

You can also open a document to see how it is stored on the original server. By viewing a document's source script, you can learn how HTML tags are used. HTML tags are used to build Web pages and create the formatting you see when visiting a Web site. If you ever decide to create your own Web page, this information will come in handy.

To examine a document and its source script that you've downloaded from the Web, follow these steps:

1. Load the Web page that's script you want to view in your browser window.

2. Open the **View** menu and choose **Source** or **Page Source**. This opens the document into a view window where you can see all the HTML tags that make up the document, such as the page used in the print preview example (see Figure 13.5).

```
Source of: http://www.nba.com/ - Netscape
       <html>
<head>
<title>NBA.com: The Official Site of the National Basketball Associati
</head><body background="/images/til_nbahome8_short.jpg">

<center>
<MAP NAME="officialbar_alan3">
<AREA SHAPE=RECT COORDS="438,30,594,51" HREF=/score_stat/>
<AREA SHAPE=RECT COORDS="438,52,594,71" HREF=/interactive/>
<AREA SHAPE=RECT COORDS="438,72,594,94" HREF=/global/>
<AREA SHAPE=RECT COORDS="438,95,594,114" HREF=http://store.nba.com/>
<AREA SHAPE=CIRCLE COORDS="301,85,52" HREF=/masthead.html>
<AREA SHAPE=RECT COORDS="1,30,182,49" HREF=/news_feat/>
<AREA SHAPE=RECT COORDS="2,50,182,72" HREF=/playerindex.html>
<AREA SHAPE=RECT COORDS="3,73,184,92" HREF=/teamindex.html>
<AREA SHAPE=RECT COORDS="4,93,183,113" HREF=/theater/>
</MAP>  <a href="/imagemap/officialbar_alan3.map"><img src="/images/of
<p>
</center>

<center>
<TABLE border=0 width=620 cellpadding=4>
<tr><td colspan=3 height=60 align=center><center>

<MAP NAME="team_bar_home">
```

Figure 13.5 View a document's HTML tags in the View Page Source window.

3. Scroll down the page to view the various tags and how they are used.

4. To exit the View Page Source window, click the **Close (X)** button in the upper-right corner (or upper-left corner if you're using a Mac).

In this lesson, you learned how to save and print Web documents and view their HTML script. In the next lesson, you will learn how to view graphics, and play audio and video clips on the Web.

Playing Sounds, Graphics, and Video

In this lesson, you learn how to display pictures and play multimedia files, including audio and video clips.

Playing Media Files

Most Web browsers have what it takes to play media files (graphics, audio, and video). In your Web wanderings, you have probably noticed that your Web browser can display most of the graphics you encounter on the Web. When you open a page that contains graphics, the browser displays them, just as if you opened a document containing an image in your desktop publishing program or word processor.

In addition, most browsers can play standard audio files. If you open a file that contains background audio, the sounds begin to play. If you click a link for an audio file, the browser plays it, no questions asked. Likewise, if you click a link for a common video file, such as an AVI or MOV video clip, the browser starts to play it right inside the viewing area or in a separate window.

However, if you click a link to a file that the browser cannot play, and the browser displays a dialog box indicating that it cannot play the file (see Figure 14.1), you'll need to install a viewer or player for that particular file type. In this lesson, you will learn how to play files that your browser can handle. In Lessons 15 to 20, you will learn how to obtain the viewers and players you need to display and play file types that your browser is incapable of playing.

Figure 14.1   When your browser cannot play a file type, it displays a dialog box telling you so.

   Viewers and Players   Viewers and players come in various packages. In the past, browsers used helper applications exclusively to play file types that the browser could not handle. Helper applications are small, stand-alone programs designed to run quickly. Relatively recently, browsers have begun to use plug-ins and ActiveX controls to provide the browser with additional capabilities for playing media files.

Media Files that Your Browser Can Play

Your browser can play several types of media files without any outside help. It can display images in JPG and GIF formats, Java applets, most standard audio clips, and probably a couple of popular video file types. Tables 14.1 and 14.2 list the file types that Navigator and Internet Explorer can play.

Table 14.1   File Types Navigator Can Play

Program or Plug-In	Description	File Types
Netscape Navigator	Web browser	.html (Web page) .gif (graphic) .jpg, jpeg, jpe (graphic) .txt (text only) Java applets JavaScript
Cosmo Player	VRML (virtual worlds)	.wrl .wrz
Netscape Media Player	Streaming Audio Player	.lam
QuickTime	Video player	.mov

continues

Table 14.1   Continued

Program or Plug-In	Description	File Types
NPAVI32 DLL	Video player	.avi
LiveAudio	Audio player	.au
		.aif, .aiff
		.wav
		.mid, .midi
		.la, .lma

Table 14.2   File Types Internet Explorer Can Play

Program or Plug-In	Description	File Types
Internet Explorer	Web browser	.html, .htm (Web page)
		.txt (text only)
		.gif (graphic)
		.jpg, jpeg, jpe, .jfif (graphic)
		.xbm (graphic)
		.au
		.aif, .aiff, .aifc
		.snd, .wav
		.mid, .midi, .rmi
		Java applets
		JavaScriptVRML
ActiveMovie	Video Player	.avi, mpeg, .mov
ActiveX VRML	VRML Player	.wrl
		.wrz

Displaying and Working with Graphics

As you know, your browser is capable of displaying most types of graphics you encounter on the Web—GIF, JPG, and JPEG files. You simply open a Web page with graphics, and the browser displays them on the page, as shown in Figure 14.2. In Internet Explorer and Netscape Navigator, you can do even more with graphics:

- If the image is small, you can sometimes click it to display a larger version in its own window.
- To save the image, right-click it, and click the **Save Picture As** or **Save Image As** command. On a Mac, hold down the mouse button to display the menu.

- To use the image as your desktop wallpaper, right-click it and select **Set As Wallpaper**. On a Mac, hold down your mouse button to display the menu.

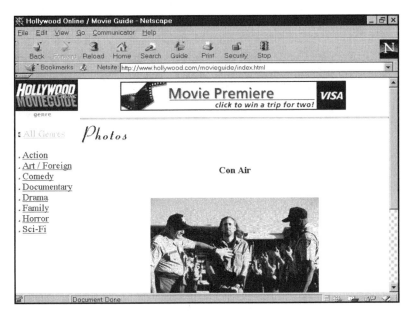

Figure 14.2 The browser displays most common graphics embedded on Web pages.

Playing Audio Clips

Not long ago, if you wanted to play audio clips on the Web, you needed a couple of special audio players to handle all the audio file formats. Now, most browsers can play those common audio file types by themselves. These file types include .AIF, .AIFF, .AU, .MID, .MIDI, .SND, and .WAV files. Sometimes, the audio clip is set up to start playing in the background as soon as you open the page. In other cases, you must click a link to play the file.

When you click a link to play an audio file, the browser typically displays its audio player as a separate window, where you can adjust the volume and balance, and replay the clip. See Figure 14.3. To check out some audio clips, use your favorite Web search tool to search for **audio clips**, or try the following sites:

- Richard Nixon Audio Archive at **http://www.webcorp.com/sounds/ nixon.htm**.

- Jammin Reggae Archives at **http://niceup.com/**.
- Star Wars: Echo Base at **http://www.azstarnet.com/~newmann/ starwars.html**.
- Sound Site at **http://www.niagara.com/~ndp/soundsite/**.

The Play, Stop, and Pause buttons

Drag the slider to adjust the volume.

Click a link to play the audio file.

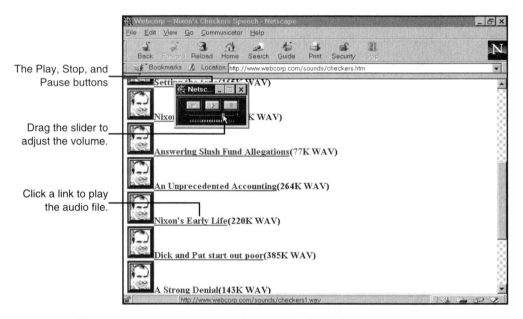

Figure 14.3 Most browsers have a built-in audio player.

 TIP **Real-Time Audio** To play most common audio files, the browser must completely download the file before it starts to play it. You can download special audio players, such as Real Audio, which play the clips as soon as they start to receive the file. This type of audio, called real-time audio, makes it seem as though you are playing a live recording. In many cases, the recording is being broadcast as you are listening to it, so it is nearly live. To play real-time audio, you need a special helper application, plug-in, or ActiveX control.

Playing Video Clips

Most of the video files you encounter on the Web come in three formats: MPEG (or MPG), MOV, and AVI. Either your browser can play the file type by itself, or your operating system has a player that can handle the file type. To play less popular video formats, such as VDO files, you need a special plug-in or helper application. For example, to play VDO files, you need to install VDOLive. RealVideo and QuickTime are two other popular video players.

To play a video file, simply click the link that points to the file. The video player typically displays the clip in its own window, as shown in Figure 14.4, but may use the browser window. You can find common video file types at the following Web sites:

- Hollywood Online at **http://www.hollywood.com**.
- Paramount at **http://www.paramount.com**.
- MGM at **http://www.mgm.com**.
- Movie Trailers at **http://www.miracles.win-uk.net/Movies.html**.
- Movies Online Film Archive Room at **http://movies-online.com.sg/Screen/index1.html**.

This video player displays the clip in its own window.

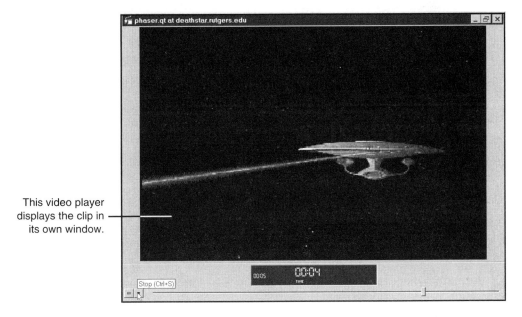

Figure 14.4   The video player starts playing the downloaded clip.

CAUTION

Large Files, Low Quality   Although video files typically come in a compressed format, video clips require a great deal of storage space for even a short, low-resolution clip. Don't be surprised if you run into a 20-second clip that fills only about a tenth of your screen and consumes 2 megabytes of storage space. Don't expect high-quality video over the Web just yet.

Playing Files that Your Browser Cannot Play

If you click a link for a file type that the browser cannot play, the browser will usually display a dialog box indicating that it cannot play the file, or display a message telling you which player you need, and offering to obtain the player for you. Take one of the following steps:

- In Netscape Navigator, you might receive a dialog box that contains a button named **Get the Plugin**. Click the button to go to Netscape's Plugin page, and obtain the required plug-in. See Lesson 15, "Going Multimedia with Navigator Plug-Ins."

- In Netscape Navigator, if you receive a dialog box with the **More Info** button, click the button to go to the Netscape Plugin page.

- In Internet Explorer, if there is an ActiveX control for playing the file, a dialog box appears, asking if you want to download and install the control. Click **Yes**.

- Many pages that contain special file types include a link that points to the player you need. Click the link, save the file to disk, and install it.

- If all else fails, save the media file to your hard drive, and then download the player you need later. You can then open and play the file from your hard drive.

In this lesson, you learned how to play media files that your browser or one of its components can play. In the next lesson, you will learn how to set up additional players in Netscape Navigator.

Going Multimedia with Navigator Plug-Ins

In this lesson, you learn how to add media playing capability to Netscape Navigator and Internet Explorer with Navigator plug-ins.

What Is a Plug-In?

A *plug-in* is a special program that extends the capabilities of Netscape Navigator. You can add plug-ins that enable you to visit virtual reality Web sites to listen to live radio broadcasts over the Net or to carry on a near-to-live "conversation." There are many plug-ins for Navigator that you can download from various sites throughout the Internet; you'll learn how to download the most popular plug-ins in upcoming lessons. Once you download a plug-in and install it, Netscape uses the plug-in's capabilities as if it were built in. Figure 15.1 shows a document Netscape can display with the help of a plug-in called Adobe Acrobat Reader.

Plug-ins can work in one of three ways: embedded in a Web page frame, expanded to fill the whole Netscape window, or hidden from view (running in the background). However, regardless of which mode a plug-in uses, its functions appear fully integrated to you, the user. In other words, you don't have to learn any special commands to use the plug-in; after you install it, the plug-in's capabilities become a part of Navigator.

This plug-in works within the Navigator window.

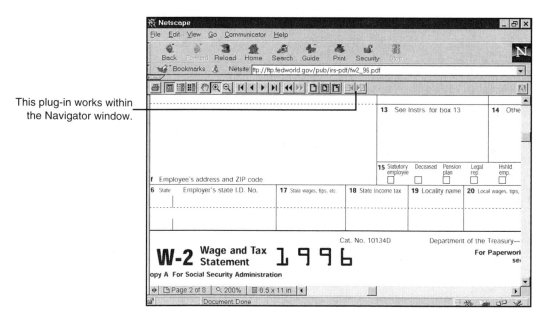

Figure 15.1   A plug-in like Adobe Acrobat Reader extends the capabilities of Netscape.

Finding Plug-Ins

The easiest way to get the plug-in you need is to try to play a file type that Navigator can't play. Navigator 4.0 is set up to notify you when you need a particular plug-in. If you click a link that Navigator cannot play, and Navigator "knows" that there is a plug-in available for that file type, Navigator displays the Plug-In Not Installed dialog box, prompting you to download the appropriate plug-in. Take the following steps to have Navigator help you find plug-ins:

1. Open a page that has a media file type that you want to play. For example, go to the RealAudio home page at **http://www.real.com**, and click links to find a page that has RealAudio recordings.

2. Click a link that points to a RealAudio file. Navigator displays either the Plugin Not Installed dialog box or the Unknown File Type dialog box (see Figure 15.2).

3. Take one of the following steps:

- In the Plugin Not Installed dialog box, click the **Get the Plugin** button.
- If the Unknown File Type dialog box appears, click the **More Info** button to display Netscape's Plug-In Finder page. Navigator opens a new browser window and displays its Plug-in Finder page.

Click More Info.━

Figure 15.2 In most cases, Navigator can help you find the plug-in you need.

4. Follow the trail of links to the page that contains the link for downloading the plug-in you want. (This trail may be very long and meandering.)

5. Click the link. The Save As dialog box appears.

6. Use the Save As dialog box to pick the drive and folder in which you want the file stored, and click the **Save** button.

In most cases, after downloading the file, you can simply double-click it to start the installation process. If the procedure is more complicated, the site from which you downloaded the file should have installation instructions. If you have problems installing the plug-in, return to its home page for instructions, or see the following section, "Installing Plug-Ins."

TIP **Visiting a Plug-In Warehouse** You can find most of the best Navigator plug-ins all in one place on the Web. Visit Stroud's at **http://www.stroud.com** or TUCOWS at **http://www.tucows.com**. Both of these sites contain lists of Web browsers, plug-ins, ActiveX controls, and helper apps, complete with reviews and links for downloading the plug-ins you need. Make sure you get the right version for your operating system: Windows 95, Windows 3.1, MacOS, or UNIX.

Installing Plug-Ins

Plug-ins are designed to work seamlessly with Netscape Navigator. Because of that, installing plug-ins is as simple as installing Navigator.

> **TIP**   **Plug-In, Helper App, or ActiveX Control?**   Many players are available as a plug-in, ActiveX control, or helper app. When selecting which format to use, keep this in mind: A plug-in usually works within the Navigator window, so it is typically easier to use. However, helper apps are more versatile because you can use them with any compatible file (outside of Navigator).
>
> Also keep in mind that if you have a plug-in (such as Live3D) and a helper app (such as WebSpace) that both handle the same file type (such as .vrml), Navigator will use the plug-in before it will use the helper app. To tell Navigator to use the helper app instead, you have to uninstall the plug-in, or save the file to disk and then open it in the helper app.

Take the following basic steps to install most plug-ins:

1. Open File Manager or Explorer and double-click the plug-in file. The installation program starts.
2. Follow the on-screen instructions.
3. When you see a message telling you that installation is complete, click **OK**.
4. Exit Navigator and restart it to make the plug-in available.

As you can see from these steps, you do not have to do anything to tell Netscape that the plug-in exists. The installation process takes care of any configuring that's necessary. So once the plug-in is installed, it's ready to use. Anytime you point Netscape to a file type that the plug-in supports, Netscape automatically calls on the plug-in's capabilities to display the file's contents.

> **TIP**   **Which Plug-Ins Are Installed?**   Navigator can supply you with a list of installed plug-ins. Open the Help menu and select **About Plug-ins**. At the top of the page is a link named **click here**. Click it to display Netscape's Inline Plug-Ins page, where you can find links to most Navigator plug-ins.

Using Plug-Ins with Internet Explorer

Internet Explorer supports plug-ins designed for Netscape Navigator. The installation utility for many plug-ins automatically searches your system for all browsers, and installs the plug-in for each installed browser.

However, if you installed another browser after installing the plug-in, you can easily copy and use the installed Navigator plug-ins in Internet Explorer. Simply copy the plug-in files from the Navigator plug-in directory (\Program Files\

Netscape\Communicator\Program\Plugins) to your Internet Explorer plug-in directory (this directory varies depending on your version of Internet Explorer). You can now use the plug-ins simply by clicking a link for a file assigned to the plug-in.

If you download a new plug-in, you can install it to run from Internet Explorer. Run the file, as explained earlier in this lesson to run the installation routine. When asked where you want to install the plug-in, select the folder you use for Internet Explorer plug-ins. You can then use the plug-in simply by clicking a link for a file that the plug-in is set up to play.

In this lesson, you learned how to expand the capabilities of your Web browser with Navigator plug-ins. In the next lesson, you will learn how to add capability with ActiveX controls.

Playing Active Content with ActiveX Controls

In this lesson, you learn how to add media playing capability to Internet Explorer and Netscape Navigator with ActiveX controls.

What Is ActiveX?

So what is ActiveX? It's a technology that lets Web page developers place all sorts of cool animations, programs, and other objects on a Web page, and lets you play them. ActiveX consists of the following five components:

- **ActiveX Controls** are sort of like plug-ins. They reside on your computer and enable Internet Explorer to play ActiveX components. For example, Internet Explorer comes with an ActiveMovie ActiveX control that plays most types of video clips.

- **ActiveX Documents** are documents that you can open and edit in any application that supports ActiveX. For example, you can open a Word document or an Excel spreadsheet right in the Internet Explorer window.

 TIP **Try It!** If you have Word or Excel and Internet Explorer 4 installed, drag the icon for a Word or Excel file into the Internet Explorer viewing area. The document appears, complete with the Word or Excel toolbar and pull-down menu, just as if you had opened the document in the application you used to create it!

- **ActiveX Scripting** is a programming language that allows Web developers to write and insert small applications on their Web pages and coordinate other ActiveX components. JavaScript and VBScript are the two ActiveX scripting languages.

- **Java VirtualMachine** allows any ActiveX-supported browser (that is, Internet Explorer) to play Java applets and allows developers to integrate Java applets with ActiveX components. See Lesson 18, "Running Java Applets," for details.

- **ActiveX Server Framework** provides several additional functions for Web servers, including enhanced security and database access. (You can pretty much ignore this one, unless you're the designated Web administrator at your company.)

Internet Explorer's Built-In ActiveX Controls

Internet Explorer comes with several built-in ActiveX controls for playing ActiveX components that are commonly embedded in Web pages. Here's a list of controls that are included:

- **ActiveMovie** plays most types of audio and video files, including AVI, QuickTime, and MPEG video and audio, WAV, AU, AIFF, and MIDI. This control comes with the Full Installation version of Internet Explorer 4.0.

- **DirectX** enables Web pages to take full advantage of the hardware on your system.

- **Sequencer** controls the timing of events on pages.

- **Structured graphics** enables the display of small, high-quality graphics that can be scaled and rotated.

- **Sprite** plays animated images.

- **Sprite buttons** displays buttons that can have two or more states (such as on and off).

- **Path** allows objects to move across a two-dimensional path.

- **Mixer** mixes two or more WAV audio files.

- **Effects** applies a graphics filter to alter images on a page.

- **Transitions** allows objects on a page, or a Web page itself to change over time.

- **Behaviors** lets developers apply high-level controls to various objects on a page.

- **Hot spot** sets regions of a Web page to act as hot spots you can click to navigate or set preferences.

Obtaining Additional ActiveX Controls

As developers start to use more ActiveX components on their Web pages, you're likely to bump into components for which you have no ActiveX control. In such cases, Internet Explorer will attempt to download the control from the page that contains the component. For security purposes, Internet Explorer checks the control to make sure it has come from a reliable source (so it doesn't introduce harmful code into your computer). Expect to see a warning dialog box, like the one shown in Figure 16.1. Click **Yes** to confirm.

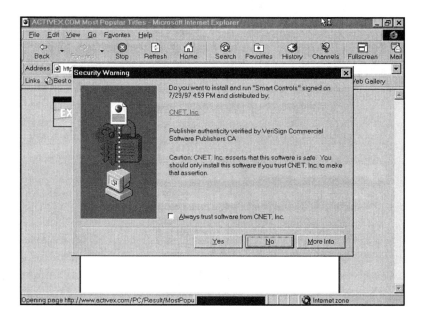

Figure 16.1 Internet Explorer asks for your confirmation before downloading and installing an ActiveX control.

CAUTION

Authenticode Security Technology   To help you verify that the ActiveX control you are downloading is from a legitimate software company, most companies electronically sign their software. When you click a link to an ActiveX control that has been signed, the Authenticode Security Technology dialog box appears, displaying a certificate verifying that the control has been signed and is safe to use. If the ActiveX control has not been signed, a dialog box without the certificate appears, warning you that the control may not come from a legitimate software company. You can cancel the transfer or give your okay.

In some cases, if Internet Explorer does not have the required ActiveX control, it may automatically load a page that does have the control, or to a page where you can search for the control. Follow the links and instructions to download and install the control.

 TIP More ActiveX Controls at Cybersource You can check out a collection of popular ActiveX controls at Cybersource's ActiveX site: **http:www.software.net/components/active.htm**.

Playing Some Sample ActiveX Content

You can also get ActiveX controls, and try them out, in clnet's ActiveX Gallery (**http://www.activex.com**). Take the following steps:

1. Go to clnet's at ActiveX page **www.activex.com**.

2. Under Control Library, click the **most popular** link. This display a list of the most popular ActiveX controls with links for downloading them. See Figure 16.2.

3. Select the desired ActiveX control to learn more about it and to download it. When you choose to download the control, Internet Explorer automatically places it in the Windows/Downloaded ActiveX Controls folder. You don't have to run an installation utility.

As of the writing of this book, Microsoft was offering 16 ActiveX controls, and had links to over 100 additional controls created by other companies. Microsoft's ActiveX controls include the following:

- **Label** displays text at any angle on the page, allowing developers to include rotated text.

- **Marquee** displays a marquee that scrolls contents horizontally or vertically on a page.

- **MCSiMenu** displays pop-up menus complete with submenus. Developers can place menus on a page, making the page act as a program window.

- **Microsoft Agent** enables Internet Explorer to play animated characters and other objects.

Figure 16.2   Visit Microsoft's ActiveX Gallery.

- **Microsoft Interactive Music** plays background audio that's embedded in Web pages.
- **Stock Ticker** lets developers place an animated ticker tape on their Web pages. The Stock Ticker updates its data at regular intervals, and displays the data on a "tape" that scrolls across the screen.

Also, visit some of the other companies that are developing ActiveX controls. Companies which develop players and viewers commonly develop them to play content at their sites. When you pull up a company's home page, look for links to demos or galleries where you can try out your new ActiveX controls.

Removing ActiveX Components

In the past, Internet Explorer placed any ActiveX controls you chose to download into the Windows/System folder, making it nearly impossible to find them, let alone remove them. Internet Explorer 4.0 now places your ActiveX controls in their own folder, so you can take inventory and quickly remove any controls you don't use (except for the controls that are integral parts of Internet Explorer, such as ActiveMovie). Take the following steps to view the controls and remove any you do not use:

1. Run your operating system's file management tool (for instance, Windows 95 My Computer).

2. Change to the **Downloaded Program Files** folder (in Windows, this folder is in the Windows folder).

3. To view information about a control, right-click it and select **Properties**.

4. To remove a control, right-click it and select **Remove Control** (see Figure 16.3).

Right-click a control.
Click Remove Control.

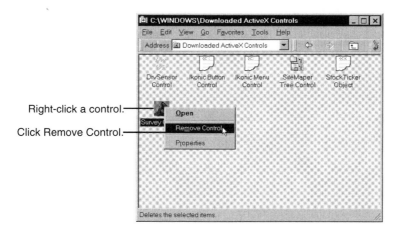

Figure 16.3 The ActiveX Control Viewer lets you determine which controls are installed and helps you remove them.

 TIP **ActiveX on Your Desktop!** If you find an ActiveX component that you like, but it is not offered as a desktop component, you can add the page it's on to your desktop. See Lesson 12, "Using the Internet Explorer Active Desktop," for details.

Using ActiveX Controls in Netscape Navigator

To play ActiveX components, Navigator needs a special plug-in, called ScriptActive, which you can obtain from NCompass. Take the following steps to download and install the plug-in:

219

1. Run Navigator.

2. Open the NCompass home page at **http://www.ncompasslabs.com**.

3. Click the **ScriptActive** link. This connects you to the ScriptActive page.

4. Follow the download and installation instructions, and the trail of links, to download and install ScriptActive.

Once ScriptActive is installed, you can download and install ActiveX components, and use them, just as if you were working with Internet Explorer. ScriptActive also includes the capabilities of DocActive, a plug-in that enables Navigator to open ActiveX documents (created in Microsoft Word, Excel, PowerPoint, and other applications that support ActiveX documents).

In this lesson, you learned how to make Internet Explorer a more powerful Web browser and media player with ActiveX controls. In the next lesson, you will learn how to add similar capabilities to Netscape Navigator with plug-ins, and use plug-ins with Internet Explorer.

Installing and Using Helper Applications

In this lesson, you learn how to configure your Web browser to use helper applications.

What Is a Helper Application?

A helper application is like a plug-in or ActiveX control, in that it extends the capabilities of your Web browser. However, a helper application goes about it in a different way.

Unlike a plug-in or ActiveX control, whose functionality interacts seamlessly with the browser, a helper application works independently of the browser. A helper application specializes in handling specific file types, such as WAV or MPEG files, for example. When your browser encounters one of these file types, it launches the appropriate helper application, and it display plays the file. The helper application then deciphers and displays the contents of the file inside its own window—*not* within the browser window (see Figure 17.1).

This helper application works in its own window.

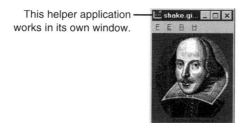

Figure 17.1   A helper application displays the contents of the file in its own window.

Because a helper application runs in its own window, it can be used separately from your Web browser. This flexibility allows you to use the helper application in other scenarios. For example, you can install LView Pro as a helper application, for displaying graphic files. You can then use LView Pro offline to open graphic files you saved to your disk, edit them, and even use those graphics in your own Web pages. However, if you just want to *view* graphics (without enhancing them or viewing them offline), leave that up to your Web browser; it's much more convenient.

TIP **Which to Choose?** If you are just looking for a way to play media files, plug-ins or ActiveX controls are the best option. Because they work alongside the Web browser, they provide for a more integrated browsing experience. However, if you plan on working with downloaded files offline, a helper application is a better choice.

Finding Helper Applications on the Web

You can find links to most of the helper applications you need, along with information and ratings by pulling up Stroud's List, a helpful Web document constructed by Forrest H. Stroud. To connect to this list, take the following steps:

1. Run your Web browser and go to **http://www.stroud.com**.

2. Scroll down the page to see the Main Menu, as shown in Figure 17.2. (If you don't see the Main Menu on the opening page, click the big graphic on the top of the page labeled **Stroud's Consummate Winsock Applications**.) This menu contains a list of Internet applications grouped by category.

3. Click the category for the type of helper application you need; for example, click **Audio Apps** for sound file players, or **Graphics Viewers** for applications that display image files. When you click a category, Stroud's displays a list of the best and most popular applications in that category.

4. When you're ready to download the file, click the link next to **Location**, and then follow the trail of links and on-screen instructions to find the link for downloading the file.

5. Right-click the link, and select the **Save** command (the command may vary depending on your browser).

6. Use the Save As dialog box to select the drive and directory where you want the file stored. Click the **Save** button.

222

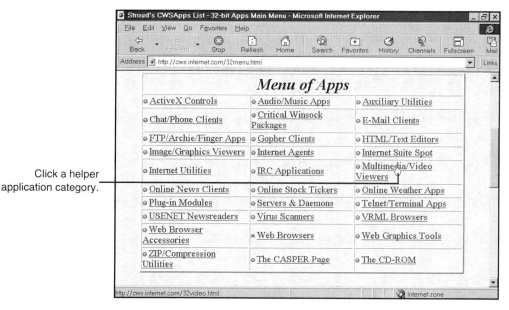

Click a helper
application category.

Figure 17.2 Stroud's Consummate Winsock Applications list provides links to the
best Internet applications.

CAUTION

Check the Version Make sure you get the right version of the helper app
(Windows 3.1, Windows 95, or Macintosh). Although Stroud's list may not
distinguish between these operating systems when listing the helper applications, the download site typically displays a form that lets you specify your
operating system, or displays links for the various versions.

TIP **Other Helper Application Sites** Although Stroud's List is the best place
to go for helper applications, there are other places that try to point you in the
right direction. Check out the following pages:

> **http://www.tucows.com**
> **http://www.shareware.com**
> **http://www.windows95.com**

Installing Helper Applications

Some helper application files you download come as self-extracting compressed
files. These files end in EXE for PCs or SEA for Macs. To decompress the file,

double-click its name. The file decompresses itself and then usually runs an installation program that installs the application.

If the file ends in ZIP or HQX, you must use a decompression utility to unzip the file. In Windows, use WinZip; you can get it at **www.winzip.com**. To install WinZip, first download the file and run it. WinZip comes as a self-extracting file that basically installs itself. To use WinZip to decompress your other files, take the following steps:

1. In Windows Explorer or File Manager, double-click the zipped file you want to decompress. This runs WinZip. The WinZip window displays the names of all the files that are packed in the zipped file.

2. Click the **Extract** button. The Extract dialog box appears, asking you to pick a folder or directory for the unzipped files.

3. Make sure **All Files** is selected, and then pick the drive and folder or directory into which you want the unzipped files placed.

4. Click the **Extract** button. WinZip decompresses the files and places them in the specified folder.

 TIP   **Install On-The-Fly**   If you display a list of compressed files in WinZip and see an install.exe or setup.exe file, you can double-click it to run the installation or setup utility. You do not need to extract the files before running the utility.

To decompress an HQX file using StuffIt Expander (for the Mac), drag the compressed file over the StuffIt Expander button, and release the mouse button. StuffIt Expander does the rest. If StuffIt Expander is properly set up, when it downloads an HQX file, it automatically converts that file into an SEA (self-extracting archive), which automatically decompresses into the installer program.

Once you've unzipped the helper application files you downloaded, read the installation instructions that came with each application for any installation steps. (The instructions are usually in a file called README.TXT or INSTALL.TXT, which you can open in Windows Notepad or WordPad. Some developers include their README files as Word, .DOC, files.)

With some applications, you can simply unzip the application, create an icon for it, and start using it. Most others require that you run a separate Setup program (in File Manager or My Computer, look for a file called SETUP.EXE or

INSTALL.EXE, and then double-click it). When you're done, you should have an icon you can double-click to run the application.

Associating File Types to Helper Applications

Your browser can display and play many file types, including HTML (the format used on most Web pages) and the graphic file types JPEG and GIF. To display the contents of other file types, your browser uses plug-ins, ActiveX controls, or helper applications.

In order to use a helper application, you must create a file association, which links files of a particular type to the right helper application. The browser then knows that when you click a link for that file type, it must call up the associate helper application to open the file. The following sections explain how to set up file associations in Navigator and Internet Explorer.

Understand MIME Types

On the Internet, each file is identified by its MIME type. MIME (Multipurpose Internet Mail Extensions) is a system that organizes various file types into groups, listing similar file types together as the same MIME type. Your browser and operating system both have a list of MIME types and file name extensions that they use to determine which applications to play when you click a link or icon for a particular file type.

When you set up file associations, you may be asked to specify the MIME type of a particular file. Table 17.1 can help you determine which MIME type to use.

Table 17.1   Common MIME Types

MIME Type	File Types
application/msword	DOC, DOT, WIZ
application/pdf	PDF
application/x-compress	ZIP
application/x-conference	NSC
audio/basic	AU
audio/x-aiff	AIF, AIFF

continues

Table 17.1   Continued

MIME Type	File Types
audio/x-mpeg	MP2, MPA, ABS, MPEGA
audio/x-pn-realaudio	RA, RAM
audio/x-wav	WAV
image/gif	GIF
image/jpeg	JPEG, JPG, JPE, JFIF, PJPEG, PJP
image/x-ms-bmp	BMP
image/x-xbitmap	XBM
midi/mid	MID
midi/rmi	RMI
text/html	HTML, HTM, HTT
text/plain	TXT, TEXT
video/mpeg	MPEG, MPG, MPE, MPV, VBS, MPEGV
video/quicktime	MOV
video/x-ms-asf	ASF, ASX
video/x-msvideo	AVI
x-world/x-vrml	WRL, WRZ

 TIP   **Unknown MIME Types**   If you don't know the MIME type for a particular file, don't worry. You can usually enter the file name's extension to associate that file type with the desired helper application.

Setting Up Helper Apps On-The-Fly

The easiest and fastest way to associate file types to helper applications is to do it on-the-fly (as long as the file type is not already associated to your Web browser or another application). The following steps show how to set up helper applications on the fly with Internet Explorer (you perform similar steps in Navigator):

1. Make sure you have installed the helper application, as explained earlier in this lesson.

2. Click a link for the special type of file you want the helper application to play. The browser displays a dialog box asking if you want to open the file or save it to disk. Click the **Open** option, and click the **OK** button. Your browser then displays a dialog box showing a list of applications (see Figure 17.3).

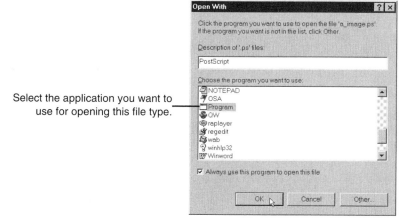

Select the application you want to use for opening this file type.

Figure 17.3 When Internet Explorer cannot play a selected file type, it displays a dialog box allowing you to select a helper application.

3. You can type a description of the file type in the text box at the top to help you remember it later (if you edit your file associations).

4. Click the application you want to use for this file. If the helper application you want to use is not in the list, click the **Other** button, and use the Open With dialog box to select the helper application.

5. Click the **Open** button.

6. If you want your browser to always use the selected application to open files of this type, click **Always use this program to open this file**.

7. Click **OK**. Now, whenever you click a link for this file type, your browser will automatically run the associated helper application and use it to play the file.

Setting Up File Associations in Netscape Navigator

If you are lucky, when you installed the helper application, its installation utility created the required file association in Navigator for you. However, in most cases, you must set up the association yourself. To associate a particular file type with a new helper application, take the following steps:

1. Install the helper application, as explained earlier in this lesson.
2. Start Navigator (you do not need to connect to the Internet).
3. Open the **Edit** menu and select **Preferences**.
4. In the **Category** box, click **Applications** under the **Navigator** category.
5. In the **Description** list, select the file type you want to associate with the helper application, and click the **Edit** button (see Figure 17.4).

CAUTION **Missing Type** If you don't see the file type you need, you can add it by clicking the **New Type** button, entering the **MIME Type** (as explained in the previous section), entering the **Application to use** (such as RealAudio or QuickTime), and clicking **OK**.

6. Click in the **Application** text box.
7. Click **Browse**, select the program's executable or .EXE file, and click **Open**.
8. Click **OK**. The next time Navigator encounters a file with the extension(s) you specified, it will pass that file to the associated helper application for viewing.

Navigator's list of helper applications

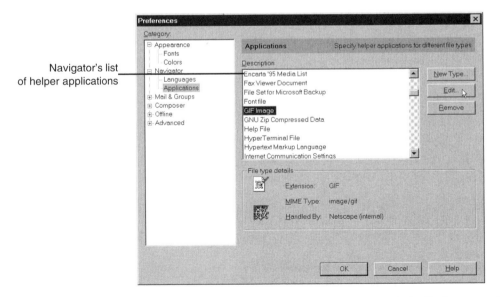

Figure 17.4 Netscape keeps track of helper applications in its Preferences dialog box.

CAUTION

Only One Helper Application Per File Type You can assign only one helper application to a particular file name extension or MIME type. If you try to assign two helper applications to the same file type, Navigator will display a warning. You must delete the existing file association or edit it to assign the file type to the new helper application.

Creating File Associations in Internet Explorer

If a file type is already associated to Internet Explorer, or you just don't want the Open With dialog box to pop up unexpectedly, you can create your file associations manually using the File Types dialog box in Windows Explorer or My Computer.

To display the File Types dialog box, first run My Computer or Windows Explorer. Open the **View** menu and select **Folder Options**. Click the **File Types** tab. You now see the page of options you can select to specify how you want Windows to handle various file types (see Figure 17.5).

Now, check to see if the file type is already associated with an application. In the Registered file types list, use the down arrow key to highlight the various file types. Keep an eye on the File types details for the following information about the highlighted file type:

- **Extension:** This displays the file name extension that is associated with a particular file type.
- **Content type (MIME):** Windows uses the MIME type to determine which helper application to run when it receives a file of a particular type. However, if you don't specify a MIME type, Windows can determine which helper application to use from the file extension you specify.
- **Opens with:** This displays the name of the application used to open files of this type. IExplore stands for Internet Explorer.

If you find a file type that matches the type to which you want to assign a helper application, click it, and then click the **Edit** button. Under Actions, click **Open**, and click the **Edit** button. Click the **Browse** button, and use the Browse dialog box to select the application you want to assign to the selected file type. Keep clicking **OK** until you've closed all the dialog boxes.

If the desired file type is not listed, you can add it to the list, and associate it with an application by creating a new file type. Take the following steps to create a new file type:

229

1. In the File Types dialog box, click the **New Type** button. The Add New File Type dialog box appears.

2. Click inside the **Description of type** text box, and type a description (for example, **MPEG Video**). See Figure 17.6.

Click a file type here.

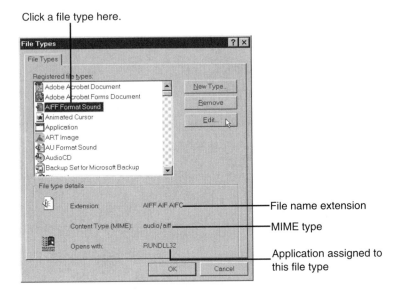

Figure 17.5   Check the File Types list to see if the file type is already associated with an application.

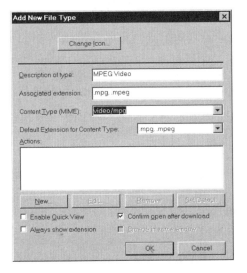

Figure 17.6   The Add New File Type dialog box.

3. Click inside the **Associated extension** text box, and type the extension for this file type (for example, **.mpg**). Windows uses this extension to assign an icon to the file type.

4. If you know the file's MIME type, open the **Content Type (MIME)** drop-down list, and choose the MIME type for this file. (If it is not listed, you can type a new MIME type in the text box; for example, type **video/mpg**.)

5. If the **Default Extension for Content Type** drop-down list is available, open it and select the extension you want to use as the default for the specified MIME type. (Some MIME types have multiple file name extensions associated to them.)

6. Under **Actions**, click the **New** button. The New Action dialog box appears.

7. In the Action text box, type **open**.

8. Click the **Browse** button, and use the Open With dialog box to select the helper application you want to use to open the new file type. Click the **Open** button. The New Action dialog box displays the **Open** command in the Actions list.

9. Click **OK**. This returns you to the New File Type dialog box.

10. Click the **OK** button. The new file association is created.

In this lesson, you learned how to configure your Web browser to use helper applications. In the next lesson, you will learn how to play Java applets, without the help of a plug-in or helper applications.

Running Java Applets

In this lesson, you learn how to find and play Java applets you encounter on Web pages.

Understanding Java

Java is a hot topic on the Internet right now—but what exactly is it? *Java* is a programming language that developers use to create mini-programs (called *applets*) that they can place right on Web pages. Java applets can run on any computer or operating system—Windows, Mac, or UNIX, so the developer does not have to create a separate application for each operating system. This allows developers to place active content on Web pages without having to worry about which operating system the visitor is using.

 Applet A small, single-purpose application such as a loan calculator or a tic-tac-toe game. Java applets cannot run by themselves; you must use a Java-enabled Web browser (such as Navigator or Internet Explorer) in order for them to work.

Java applets take many forms, including painting programs, games, and animations. Java is a quickly growing programming language. Because Java is still in developmental stages, most of the examples of Java applets you'll find out on the Internet are small, dynamic user interfaces like stock tickers or scrolling lines of text. However, Java is fast becoming a standard, and as such, it will be used more and more as an integral part of a functional Web page.

Java-Enabled Browsers In order to play Java applets, your browser must be Java-enabled. Three of the best browsers have built-in Java support: Netscape Navigator, Internet Explorer, and HotJava.

Examples of Java Applets

You'll often encounter a Java applet without even knowing it. If you see a small animation on a Web page, it's probably a Java applet. If you run into an online calculator or an interactive game, chances are that Java is at work. Figure 18.1 shows a typical Java applet in action. To play this applet, go to **www.db.erau.edu/java/pattern/**. When the applet window appears on your screen, click the **Start Sim** button in the upper-right corner of the window. The planes start circling the airport, landing, and pulling into the hangar.

Java allows developers to place active content on Web pages.

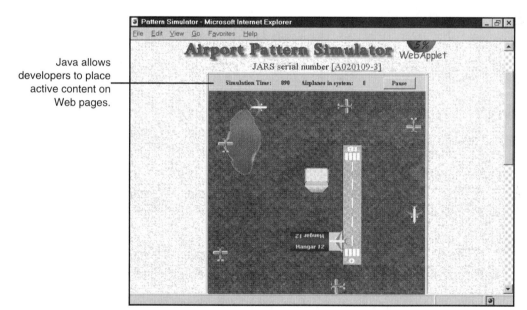

Figure 18.1 A sample Java applet in action.

The benefit of including Java applets in a Web page is live interaction with the user. For example, a Java applet might perform a calculation for you—*live*—based on information you just entered into a form. In addition, a graph embedded in the Web page might change to reflect your variable input (see Figure 18.2). You can find this Java mortgage calculator at **http://www.jeacle.ie/mortgage/**.

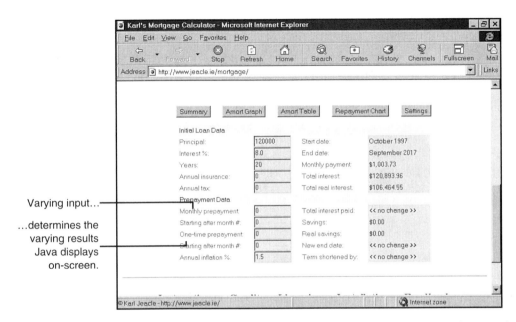

Varying input...

...determines the varying results Java displays on-screen.

Figure 18.2 A Java applet can change the display according to varying user input.

Some Java applets, such as blinking or scrolling text, draw the reader's attention to particular parts of the Web page. Other Java applets, such as a cute animation, a video that is replayed automatically, or a game, are just for fun. Go to **www. mindspring.com/~frs/kds/kdsSmall.html** to play a quick game of Planet Sisyphus (see Figure 18.3), where you get to try your hand at killing some real mean snakes. As the snake slithers around the game board, you have to use your arrow keys to move Sisyphus around and push rocks into the snake holes, in an attempt to land one on the snake's head.

You could run into a Java applet just about anywhere on the Web, but because Java is still kind of new, you might want to go to the source (Sun Microsystems) first to see some demonstrations. Its Web site is located at **http://java.sun.com**. To visit the Sun site and play one of the demos, follow these steps:

1. Connect to the Internet and start Netscape.
2. Type the address **http://www.javasoft.com/applets** into the **Location/Go to** text box and press **Enter**.
3. Click **Applets**.

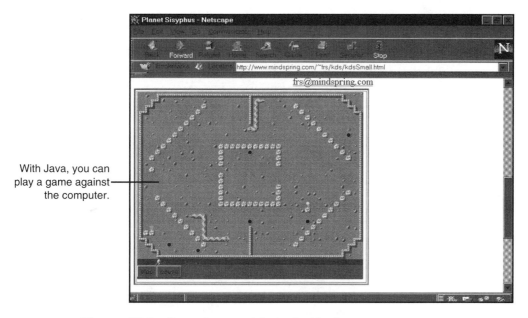

With Java, you can play a game against the computer.

Figure 18.3   Some Java applets are just for fun.

4. Scroll down to **Games and Other Diversions**.

5. Select a demo from the list. For example, click **Hangman**. The game you select appears on-screen (it may take a while to download the applet). To play Hangman, select a letter that you think belongs in the missing phrase. Continue to select letters until you uncover the phrase or you're hung.

6. When you finish playing the demo, you can click the **Back** button to return to the list of applets and select another demo if you want.

The following list names some other sites where you can find Java applets.

http://www.gamelan.com

http://www.npac.syr.edu/projects/vishuman/VisibleHuman.html

http://www.npac.syr.edu/projects/java/magic/Magic.html

http://www-md.fsl.noaa.gov/eft/internal/GFVUsersMan.html

http://www.jars.com

http://www.java.co.uk

http://www.vector.co.za/vst/java/vstj-01.htm

http://www.teamjava.com/links

Understanding JavaScript

JavaScript is a set of commands that you place within a Web page to make it more interactive. For example, you can insert a JavaScript command to create an animated control button such as a spinning wheel. With JavaScript, you can ask the user some questions on a form, and then you can respond in varying ways based on his answers. JavaScript also contains the commands needed to embed a Java applet (a program you create with the Java programming language) into a Web page.

If you don't plan to create your own Web pages, you don't need to worry about JavaScript. Like Java, JavaScript is embedded in the Web pages you view, and the JavaScript is seamlessly integrated with the rest of the page's contents.

Java Security Risks

Sun Microsystems, creator of Java, claims that Java has built-in safeguards that prevent programmers from inserting any viruses or destructive code into their applets. However, nothing in the world of computers is foolproof, and many hackers are hard at work trying to crack the latest Java security code. Although Java is relatively safe, there are ways to insert destructive code into Java applets designed to wreak havoc on your system.

Does that mean you shouldn't play Java applets? Of course not! You just need to be a little careful, play Java applets that look legitimate, and if you hear of a destructive applet, avoid it.

However, if you're concerned, you can disable Java to prevent your browser from automatically downloading Java Applets and JavaScript. To disable Java in Internet Explorer, take the following steps:

1. Open Internet Explorer's **View** menu, and click **Internet Options**.
2. Click the **Security** tab.
3. Open the **Zone** drop-down list, and select **Internet Zone**.
4. Click **Custom (for expert users)**, and click the **Settings** button. The Security Settings dialog box appears, as shown in Figure 18.4.
5. Scroll down to Java permissions, and click **Disable Java**. Now, Internet Explorer won't download or play Java Applets.
6. Click **OK** to return to the Options dialog box, and click **OK** again to save your changes.

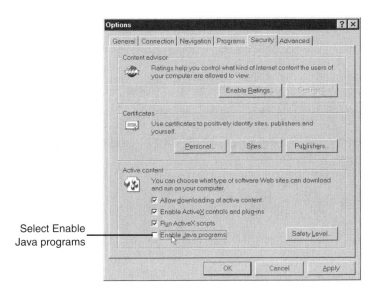

Select Enable
Java programs

Figure 18.4 For security purposes, you can prevent Internet Explorer from downloading and playing Java applets.

To disable Java in Netscape Navigator, take the following steps:

1. Open Navigator's **Edit** menu, and select **Preferences**.
2. Click **Advanced**.
3. Click **Enable Java** to remove the check from its box. This prevents Navigator from playing Java applets.
4. Click **Enable JavaScript** to remove the check from its box. This prevents
Navigator from playing embedded JavaScripts.
5. Click **OK** to save your changes.

In this lesson, you learned how to play Java applets and JavaScript with a Java-
enabled Web browser. In the next lesson, you will learn how to explore three-
dimensional, virtual worlds.

Exploring 3-D Virtual Worlds

In this lesson, you learn how to play and navigate 3-D virtual worlds with your Web browser and a VRML browser.

Understanding VRML

In Lesson 18, you learned about a programming language called Java, with which you can make your Web page interactive. VRML, *Virtual Reality Modeling Language*, is similar to Java. With the VRML programming language, developers can create three-dimensional virtual worlds, which you can enter and explore. Figure 19.1 shows a sample VRML world displayed in Navigator's Cosmo Player. In this lesson, you will learn how to access VRML worlds through Cosmo Player and through Internet Explorer's own ActiveX VRML browser.

TIP **Other VRML Browsers** Whether you use Navigator or Internet Explorer, you already have a very capable VRML browser on your system. However, other VRML browsers are available. You can check them out at Stroud's: **http://www.stroud.com**.

Finding and Playing VRML Worlds

Numerous Web sites on the Internet include VRML worlds, one of which you'll visit in a moment. Because you already have a VRML player in Navigator or Internet Explorer, playing VRML worlds is easy. You simply enter the URL for a world, and the player works along with your browser to display the world right inside the browser window. You can then use the player's controls to move around in the world.

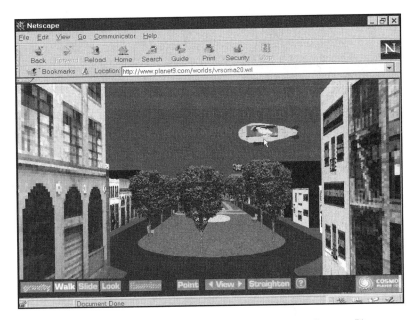

Figure 19.1 A sample VRML world displayed in Navigator's Cosmo Player.

However, before you can play a world, you need to find one. Following is a list of addresses for specific VRML worlds and places where you can find links to dozens of additional worlds:

http://www.virtus.com/vrmlsite.html

http://www.virtuocity.com

http://vrml.sgi.com/worlds

http://www.construct.net/projects/planetitaly/Spazio/
VRML/siena.wrl

http://www.tcp.ca/gsb/VRML/

http://www.sdsc.edu/vrml

http://www.meshmart.org

http://www.netscape.com/comprod/products/navigator/live3d/
cool_worlds.html

http://www.marketcentral.com/vrml

http://www.graphcomp.com/vrml

http://www.intel.com/procs/ppro/intro/vrml/nav.wrl

http://www.pointcom.com

http://www.photomodeler.com/vrml.html

http://www.clark.net/theme/worlds/ab2.wrl.gz

http://www5.zdnet.com/zdwebcat/content/vrml/

The following sections provide detailed instructions on how to use Navigator's Cosmo Player and Internet Explorer's ActiveX VRML control to display and navigate VRML worlds.

TIP **The Fast Way** Most VRML browsers are designed to support files that end with .wrl (a *world* file) or .wrl.gz (a *world* file *geometrically zipped* or compressed). If you're offered the option of viewing the same world as a .wrl or a .wrl.gz file, pick the latter because it will download faster.

Playing VRML Worlds with Navigator's Cosmo Player

Cosmo Player is Netscape's newest entry into the VRML plug-in field. Netscape teamed with Silicon Graphics to use Cosmo Player, which replaces Live 3D as Netscape's default VRML browser.

I Can't Find Cosmo Player If you're using the 16-bit version of Communicator (Windows 3.1), you will not have Cosmo Player. Instead, Live3D will be your default VRML browser.

CAUTION

Follow these steps to visit the Cosmo Player test site:

1. Connect to the Internet and start Navigator.

2. Click in the **Location** text box, type **http://vrml.sgi.com/worlds**, and press **Enter**. Click the **Gallery Index** link in the left frame.

3. Scroll down the page and click the **Virtual Skinner's Office** link. You may have to click two or three more links to eventually pull up the VRML world. After a few minutes, an image of the inside of Agent Skinner's office (yes, from the *X Files*) appears as shown in Figure 19.2. To view the office from different angles, drag the mouse pointer. For example, to "walk" closer, drag the mouse pointer (within the VRML window) toward the middle of the room.

4. **(Optional)** You can use the Dashboard to help you explore this virtual world. The Navigation Bar appears at the bottom of the VRML window. Here's a brief description of each control:

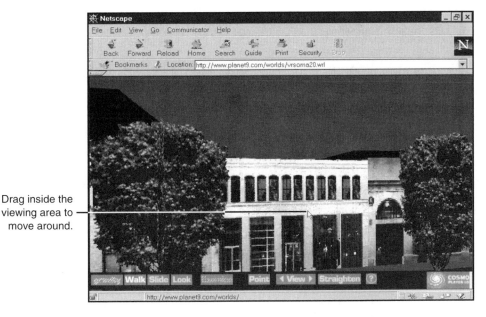

Drag inside the viewing area to move around.

Figure 19.2 Change your view by dragging the mouse pointer.

Gravity With gravity on, you can walk through the world. If you turn it off, you can fly.

Walk In Walk mode, you move in a lateral plane, as along a surface. To move, drag the mouse in the direction in which you want to "walk." For example, drag the mouse forward to move toward an object; drag backward to move away.

Slide In Slide mode, you move quickly in a single direction without spinning. To slide, drag the mouse pointer in the direction in which you want to go.

Look In Look mode, you are stationary, but the view changes as you look left, right, up, or down. To look left, drag the mouse pointer left; to look down, drag the mouse pointer downward; and so on.

Examine In Examine mode, the object in the center of the screen rotates. Drag the mouse pointer left or right to get a better view of the object you are examining. Examine mode works best when there are objects floating in space.

Point In Point mode, you move toward an object by pointing at it. When you click the object in Point mode, you move toward it.

View   Takes you back to the starting point or to one of several other viewpoints. Select the viewpoints you want with the left or right arrows.

Straighten   Takes your rotated world and returns it to a straight position.

? Opens the help page.

5. To leave the VRML world, click the **Back** button.

Navigating with Internet Explorer's VRML ActiveX Control

Internet Explorer uses an ActiveX VRML control to open and display virtual worlds. The ActiveX control opens the world right inside Internet Explorer's viewing area and displays controls you can use to navigate the world.

As of the printing of this book, Microsoft's VRML browser was not ncluded with Internet Explorer. To download it, go to **www.microsoft.com/ie/ie40** and click the **Download** link. Click the **Internet Explorer 4.0 Components** link and follow the on-screen instructions to download and install the VRML viewer.

To open a sample world using Internet Explorer and the ActiveX control, take the following steps:

1. Run Internet Explorer, type **http://www5.zdnet.com/zdwebcat/content/ vrml/outside.wrl** in the Address text box, and press **Enter**. In a few moments, ZDNet's VRML world appears. (If ZDNet moves the world, and the URL does not work, search for **terminal reality** at InfoSeek, **www. infoseek.com**.)

2. You can use the mouse along with the buttons at the bottom of the window and along the left side to control movement. Click the following buttons to specify how you want your mouse to act:

Walk moves up to or back from an object.

Pan slides you up and down or side to side.

Turn moves the viewpoint up, down, left, or right.

Roll spins the object clockwise or counterclockwise.

Go To zooms on an area of the object when you click that area.

Study rotates the object toward you or away from you, so you can see its other sides and edges. This control gives you a taste of three-dimensional space.

Zoom Out moves the object away from you, so you can see the entire object.

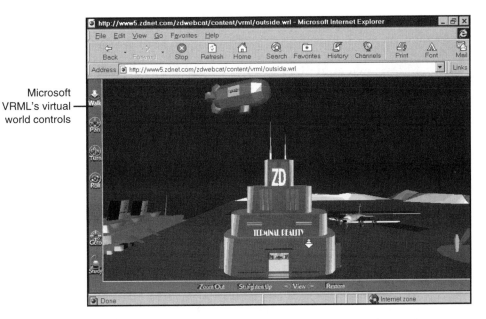

Microsoft
VRML's virtual
world controls

Figure 19.3 Microsoft VRML supplies the controls you need to explore.

Straighten Up readjusts your viewpoint so you see the object head on.

View lets you return to the previous view, or, if you backed up, lets you move forward to the next view.

Restore returns you to your original starting position.

3. Click inside the viewing area, and then drag with the left mouse button in the direction you want to move. Double-click an object in the window to quickly move closer to it.

If you have a joystick, you can use the joystick lever to explore. Movements are fairly obvious with a joystick. First, click inside the viewing area with your mouse. You can then move forward by pushing the stick forward; backward by pulling the stick toward you; and side-to-side by pushing the stick left or right. Hold down the **Shift** key to tilt while moving the stick, or hold down the **Ctrl** key to slide.

Using the Shortcut Menu

Tucked under the viewing area is a shortcut menu that offers numerous options for changing the display and speed. Right-click in the viewing area and select any of the following options to customize the viewer, or to navigate (see Figure 19.4):

Show Navigation Bar turns the toolbar that wraps around the viewing area on or off. If you turn the toolbar off, you can turn it on by right-clicking in the viewing area and selecting **Show Navigation Bar** again.

Viewpoints enables you to return to previous positions. If the VRML developer included custom viewpoints, they appear on this submenu.

Graphics contains options for controlling the display in the viewing area. You can turn a *headlight* on or off to control the illumination, select various shading options (including wire frame), and turn full color on or off. In general, the more detail you include the slower the navigation.

Speed allows you to increase or decrease the speed of movement as you drag the mouse. If you find that the object is flying off the edge of the screen with the slightest mouse movement, select a slower setting.

Movement provides most of the same options available on the toolbar. If you choose to turn the toolbar off, you can use these options instead. This submenu also contains an option for preventing collisions, which is useful if you have other objects on the screen.

Options provides several settings that enable you to control the look of the virtual world, including turning textured backgrounds on or off. You will also find options for entering default settings (for instance, turning the toolbar permanently off).

Help provides online help for using the VRML viewer.

Problems and Solutions

VRML is too cool and too new to be problem-free. Maybe the virtual world itself is buggy, or your joystick is giving you problems, or one of your settings is wrong. Whatever the case, there's surely a solution:

- **World keeps spinning?** Calibrate your joystick using the joystick control panel. If calibrating through the software doesn't work, the joystick itself probably has calibration dials that enable you to change the hardware setting.

- **Can't move?** Right-click in the viewing area, point to **Movement**, and select **Prevent Collisions**.

- **S-L-O-W?** Maybe you need more RAM, a faster CPU, or a fancy new video card. If you have all that, and the world is still slow, right-click in the viewing area, turn off some of the advanced graphics options, and crank up the speed. Right-click in the viewing area, select **Options**, turn off **Load Textures**, and turn on **Use Hardware Acceleration**.

Right-click inside the viewing area to display a context menu.

Select the desired option.

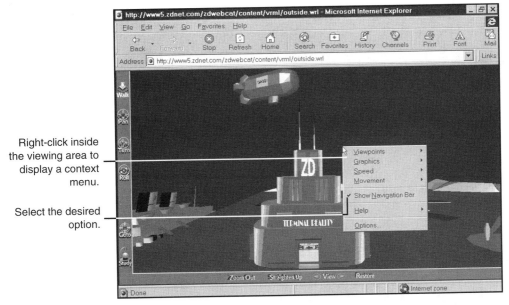

Figure 19.4 You can configure the VRML player and navigate the world with a context menu.

 TIP **Uniform VRML Controls** Unlike Java applets, NetShow presentations, and Shockwave movies, each of which comes with its own set of controls, VRML worlds have no built-in controls. The VRML browser supplies the controls, so you'll be working with the same controls no matter which world you explore.

In this lesson, you learned how to enter and navigate virtual worlds using a VRML browser. In the next lesson, you will learn how to play interactive Shockwave presentations with a special player.

Playing Interactive Shockwave Presentations

20

In this lesson, you learn how to get the Shockwave plug-in or ActiveX control and use it to view multimedia presentations over the Web.

What Is Shockwave?

Shockwave is a player created by Macromedia, whose Director program is the leading tool for putting together multimedia presentations. With Director, developers can combine still pictures, animations, and sounds, and include point-and-click interaction. If you play CD-ROM–based adventure games or use a CD-ROM reference program, odds are good that you've been using a Director presentation. Macromedia Flash is a program that puts together small and fast Shockwave multimedia. Many Web sites contain presentations created with Flash.

Shockwave lets you view Director and Flash presentations over the Web. (You *don't* need a copy of Director or Flash, unless you want to design your own presentations.) A Web site designed for use with Shockwave can present video and sound without your having to request each animation and sound file. It also allows you to interact by clicking buttons.

Downloading Shockwave

You can download Shockwave from Macromedia's Web site by following these steps:

1. Run your Web browser and use it to go to **http://www.macromedia.com/ shockwave/download/**. This takes you to the Macromedia Shockwave Web site.

2. Scroll down to the text boxes that ask for your name and e-mail address and enter the requested information.

3. The Web page automatically determines which operating system and Web browser you are using. Take one of the following steps:

   In Internet Explorer, click **AutoInstall Now**. This downloads and installs the Shockwave ActiveX control for Internet Explorer. You can skip the remaining steps.

   In Netscape Navigator, click the **Download Now** button to download the software, as shown in Figure 20.1. The Save As dialog box appears. Move on to Step 4.

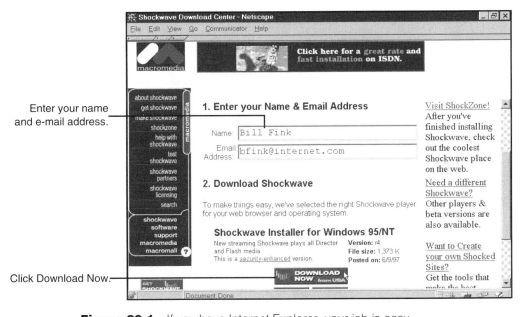

Enter your name and e-mail address.

Click Download Now.

Figure 20.1 If you have Internet Explorer, your job is easy.

4. Use the Save As dialog box to choose a directory in which to store the downloaded file (you probably have one named C:\TEMP or C:\TMP). Then click the **Save** button, and the download begins.

5. When the download is complete, you're ready to install the Shockwave. Close Navigator and disconnect from the Internet.

Installing the Shockwave Plug-In

When you finish downloading Shockwave, you will need to install it. The entire install program is contained in the single file you downloaded.

TIP **Crowded Disk?** When you need to clear some disk space, you should always look in your TEMP directories for files that have been there for some time and that you no longer need. In most cases, after you have installed the plug-in, you can remove the original file you downloaded.

Follow these steps to run the Setup program for Shockwave:

1. In Windows 95, click the **Start** button and select the **Run** command. In older versions of Windows, pull down File Manager's **File** menu and select the **Run** command.

2. Click the **Browse** button, and then locate the temporary directory to which you downloaded the Shockwave file. Select the **Shockwave_Installer.exe** file.

3. Click the **Open** button to close the Browse dialog box. Then click **OK** in the Run dialog box to run the setup program. The installation program starts.

4. First, you'll see a small dialog box asking if you want to install Shockwave. Click **Next**.

5. Next, you'll see the license agreement. Read the agreement and click **Yes** to continue the installation.

6. The installation program will ask you where you want to install Shockwave. The default location should be fine, so just click **Next**.

7. The setup program starts putting the files in place, and a meter appears, displaying the progress of the installation.

8. When the installation is complete, a dialog box appears, asking if you want to go to the Macromedia site. Leave the check box checked and click **Finish** (make sure Navigator is not open before you click the Finish button). Navigator opens and takes you to the Shockwave welcome page. After a few minutes, a movie appears, indicating that Shockwave was installed correctly.

TIP **Save on Connect Charges** Although some Shockwave presentations link to other presentations, most are self-contained. After the presentation is downloaded to your hard disk, you can disconnect from the Web and continue viewing the presentation without running up your Internet bill!

Playing Some Sample Shockwave Presentations

You can find a number of good Shockwave presentations by starting from the Macromedia Gallery page, or you can look them up in the gallery located at **http://www.macromedia.com/shockzone/**. Figure 20.2 shows a sample Shockwave presentation in action. In addition, you might want to try some of the pages listed in Table 20.1.

Unlike VRML browsers, which include their own controls, each Shockwave presentation has its own unique controls, so you'll have to figure them out for yourself.

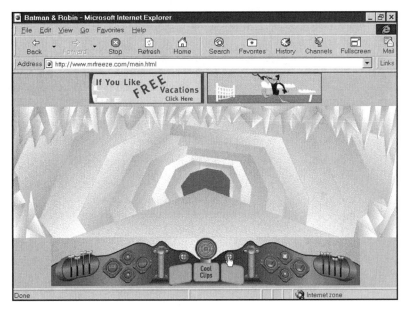

Figure 20.2   Each Shockwave presentation provides a unique interface that enables you to interact with it.

Table 20.1   Pages with Shockwave Content

Site	URL
Mudball Wall Game	**http://www.broderbund.com/studio/ activemind/mudball.html**

continues

Table 20.1 Continued

Site	URL
Daily Tortoise game	http://www.sirius.com/~jtaylor/shockwave/shockwave.html
Demolition Graphics	http://www.halcyon.com/flaherty/
Art Exhibit Educational Demos	http://www-leland.stanford.edu/~dmiller/
Etch-A-Sketch toy simulator	http://members.aol.com/dkimura/etch.html
FaceMaker	http://users.aol.com/jrbuell2/ShockFace.html
Fortune Cookie	http://www.slip.net/~maniaman/fortune.html
CleverMedia Arcade	http://clevermedia.com/arcade/
Michael's Haunted House	http://yip5.chem.wfu.edu/yip/haunted_house/mhhmain.html
Nando.net games	http://www2.nando.net/nandox/shock.html
Pop Rocket games	http://www.poprocket.com/shockwave/
Tulane University guide	http://www.bentmedia.com/bentmedia/dtulane/Shockwave.html
Velma Apparelizer	http://www.headbone.com/home.html
Virtual Drums	http://www.cybertown.com/virtdrum.html

In this lesson, you learned how to download, install, and view a presentation with Shockwave. In the next lesson, you'll learn more about downloading files with your browser.

Downloading Files from FTP Sites

21

In this lesson, you learn how to use your Web browser to access FTP servers on the Internet and transfer files.

What Is an FTP Server?

Not all sites you find on the Web are graphic-based Web servers storing hyper-documents. There are numerous FTP servers you can tap into that act as file warehouses. In the earlier days of the Internet, a system was developed to handle the transfer of files between computers; that system is FTP (File Transfer Protocol). Using FTP, people could tap into these file warehouses to obtain text files, program files, and more.

 FTP *File Transfer Protocol* is a set of rules that dictate how files are exchanged between computers.

There are plenty of FTP sites you can access to look for files. Public access archives let you log on to the site as an anonymous user to search for data. Many FTP servers enable you to use an anonymous logon to connect and access unrestricted areas on their servers. Once connected, you can search for data and download files onto your computer without leaving your Web browser.

 TIP **Anonymous Logon** Many FTP sites let you connect to their system anonymously to view or download stored files. However, you cannot make changes to the files, upload any of your files, or delete files at the site.

You may be accustomed to using an FTP program provided by your Internet Service Provider or one that you found on the Internet. With most Web browsers, you can access FTP sites without using a special FTP program. You can connect to FTP sites by using the same method used to connect to HTTP sites, but, instead of typing in the prefix **http://**, type the prefix **ftp://**.

When you log on to an FTP server, notice that the files are arranged into directories or folders, which appear as links on your browser screen. To open a directory, click the directory name (link). When you select a file, the browser attempts to display or play the file or open the appropriate plug-in or helper application to do the job. If browser or one of its players can't view the file, it will ask you if you want to download the file. You can save the file on your computer's hard disk and open it later (or run it, if it is a program file).

Finding your way to the right file on an FTP server isn't always a quick process. You usually have to dig through several layers of directories and subdirectories to find the right file. The hierarchical system is similar to how you store files on your computer. For example, if you're using Windows 95, Explorer lets you look through your folders indexed in a directory tree. Start with an index or root file; then continue to open subdirectories to find the information you want.

 TIP **You've Already Used FTP!** When you downloaded a copy of your current Web browser, you probably transferred the file from an FTP server onto your computer.

Working with FTP Files

To help you determine which files you want to view or download, you need to learn how to read the various file extensions you may come across in an FTP archive.

Text files Plain text files use the extension .TXT and are easily read from the browser window.

Executable files PC program files often use the extension .EXE. Most Mac users look for .SEA (Self Extracting Archive) files, which are also self-extracting program files. To run an EXE file, you simply double-click it after downloading it.

ZIP files PC files ending with the .ZIP extension are compressed by a program such as WinZIP or PKZIP. If you download a zipped file, you will need to unZIP (extract) it by using the same type of program.

StuffIt (SIT) files   Files ending with SIT are the Mac equivalent of ZIP files. To decompress the SIT file, you need to use StuffIt Expander.

BinHex files   Files ending with the .HQX extension are Mac files.

UNIX files   Files ending with the .tar, .tar.z, or .gnu extension are compressed UNIX archival files.

Compressed files are quite common on FTP servers. There are many programs available to compress files, thus leaving more room on your computer, and you can download them faster. Depending on your operating system, you may be accustomed to working with compressed files. For example, PC files are often compressed into a .ZIP format. To view a ZIPped file, you must use a program such as WinZIP or PKZIP to open the file. Macintosh files are often compressed into a .SIT or .HQX format. Here are a few other file types to be aware of:

.ARC	Files compressed with PKARC for DOS
.ZOO	Files compressed with Zoo210
.PIT	Files compressed with Mac's Packit program
.shar	Archived UNIX Shell files
.z	Files compressed with a UNIX compression program

Accessing an FTP Server

To jump to an FTP server by using your browser, follow these steps:

1. Start your Internet connection and run your browser.

2. In the Location or Address text box, type **ftp://ftpX.netscape.com** (where X is 2 through 20, such as ftp2 or ftp3, and so on.) and press **Enter**. This takes you to one of the Netscape FTP servers (see Figure 21.1).

 TIP   **Server Busy?**   Netscape has many FTP servers; if the first one is busy, try another. Type in **ftp://ftp2.netscape.com**, **ftp://ftp3.netscape.com**, and so on, up to 20.

3. Scroll down the page to find a directory listing.

4. Click the **pub/** directory. This opens another page listing the subdirectories found within the pub/ directory.

5. Click the **CoolTalk** directory. This opens the Cooltalk directory that lists directories where you can find the Netscape CoolTalk program file. Choose the **Mac** directory.

253

6. The next page, shown in Figure 21.2, lists the contents of the Mac directory, which happens to include program files (for a Mac) that you can download onto your computer.

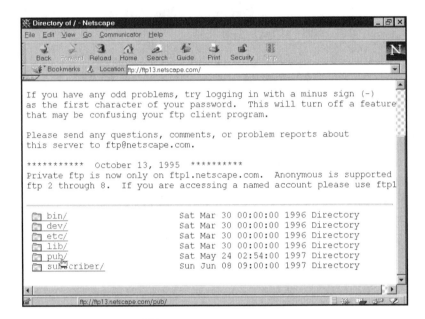

Figure 21.1 The Netscape FTP server.

TIP **What About FTP Sites that Require Passwords?** If you need to log on to a password-protected FTP site and you already have a user name and password, the URL should look similar to **ftp://gagrimes:telephone@ftp. gonzo.com**. The order is **ftp://user:password@ftp.site.com**.

Locating Files on an FTP Server

Looking through FTP sites is similar to looking for buried treasure. You never know what kinds of great files are stored on a faraway FTP server. Where do you begin to locate the files you want? There are thousands of FTP servers you can search. You'll find a monster listing of FTP sites at the following URL:

> **http://tile.net/ftp-list/**

This site enables you to browse lists of FTP servers by contents, name, or country. Scroll down the page, and click the list format you want to use. For example, you can click Contents to display an alphabetical listing of FTP servers.

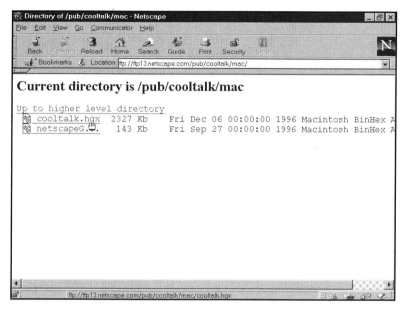

Figure 21.2 Files are listed as links on the FTP page and often indicate the size and date of creation.

You may also use a program called Archie to help you look up specific types of files on various FTP servers. Follow these steps to use Archie:

TERM **Archie**   An Internet search tool to help you locate files.

1. In your browser's Location or Address text box, type **http:// ftpsearch.ntnu.no/ftpsearch** and press **Enter**. This opens the Archie Request Form, as shown in Figure 21.3.

TIP **More Archie Sites**   A couple of other Archie sites you can use are **http:// archie.rutgers.edu/archie.html** and **http://cuiwww.unige.ch/archieplexform. html**. You'll find many more by searching for Archie under Yahoo! or Lycos.

2. Scroll down the page and fill out the Archie Request Form (see Figure 21.4). Enter the keyword(s) you want to search for, and select any other options you want to use for the search. When you're finally ready, click the **Submit** button.

255

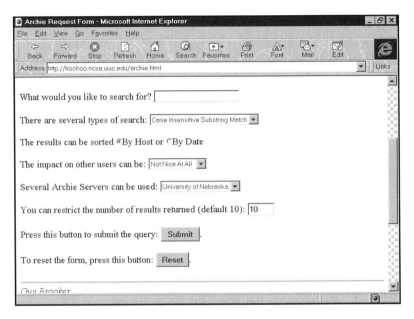

Figure 21.3   Archie can help you locate specific types of files among the many FTP sites.

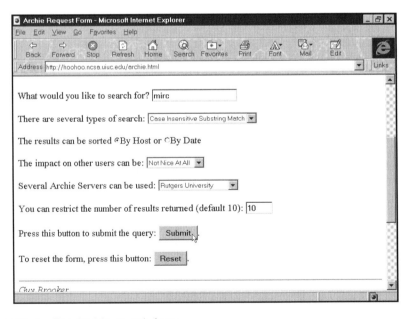

Figure 21.4   The Archie search form.

3. An Archie search can take some time, so be patient. When it's finished, a page with a list of matches appears. Click any match link to connect to the FTP server.

Downloading Files

Once you find a file you want, you can download it onto your computer. When you click a link for a file to download, your browser asks how you want to continue by presenting a dialog box or immediately opening a Save As dialog box to designate where the new file should be stored. Be sure to note the size of the file in its FTP listing. This information will help you approximate how long the download may take.

Follow these steps to transfer an FTP file onto your computer:

1. Right-click the link for the file you want to download, and select the **Save As** command from the shortcut menu. (The command varies depending on your browser.) The Save As dialog box appears. (On a Mac, you have to hold down the mouse button. In Windows 3.1, double-click the link.)

2. Select the drive and directory or folder in which you want the file stored. The file name is usually inserted in the File Name text box for you.

3. Click the **Save** or **OK** button.

4. The download starts. Depending on the size of the file, your connection speed, and the FTP traffic, the download may take a few minutes or a few hours.

5. When the download is complete, you can exit your browser and check out the file.

Uploading Files with Netscape Navigator

Want to pass on your favorite shareware program or graphic image? If you have permission, you can upload files onto an FTP server as easily as downloading them. Use these steps to transfer (upload) a file from your computer to the FTP server using Netscape Navigator:

1. Depending on your operating system, open the directory containing the file you want to upload. For example, if you're using Windows 95, open **My Computer** (or whatever similar tool you use) and select the file you want to upload.

2. From the Netscape window, open the **FTP** server and directory where you want the file stored.

3. Drag the file icon from the directory window into the Netscape window. (You may have to resize the windows to drag and drop the file.)

 TIP   **Using Navigator's Upload File Command**   If you prefer, you can also use Netscape's menu commands to upload a file. Open the **File** menu and choose **Upload File**. This opens a dialog box where you can copy the file to the FTP server.

In this lesson, you learned how to use FTP to find files on the Internet. In the next lesson, you will learn how to chat with other people on the Web.

Chatting It Up on the Web with iChat

In this lesson, you learn how to chat with other people on the Web with iChat.

Understanding Internet Chat

Internet chat allows you to "talk" with other people on the Internet by typing and sending messages back and forth. You and other people use an Internet chat program to connect to a *chat server* on the Internet. The chat server acts as host, typically offering hundreds of chat rooms (on hundreds of topics) where people can gather to chat. As you type and send messages, your messages appear on the screen of everyone in the chat room. As the other people in the room type and send messages, they appear on your screen, as shown in Figure 22.1.

The Internet offers several ways to chat. The following list provides some details:

- **Internet Relay Chat (IRC):** Internet chat started with IRC. Using a program, such as VisualIRC or PIRCH, you can connect to an IRC server and chat with users in other rooms. This is a relatively complicated way to chat on the Internet, but it does draw thousands of chatters.

- **Web Form Chat:** In an attempt to bring the simplicity of the Web to the world of chat, developers came up with Web Form Chat. To send a message, you fill out a form and click a button. The Web chat site automatically sends an updated Web page to everyone in the room, showing everybody's recent messages. This type of chat is cumbersome and not very popular.

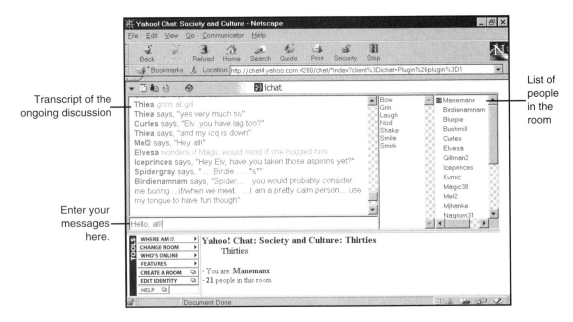

Transcript of the ongoing discussion

Enter your messages here.

List of people in the room

Figure 22.1 In chat rooms, everyone talks at once.

- **Web Client Chat:** This type of chat is currently the best way to chat on the Web. With a Web browser and the right plug-in or ActiveX control, you can chat right inside the browser window. iChat, described in this chapter, is the most popular tool for chatting on the Web.

- **Avatar and Comic Chat:** Avatar and comic chat allow you to play the role of a particular character in a chat room. You can then move the character around in the room, gesture to other chatters, and even bump into people. To use avatar or comic chat, you need a special chat program, such as Microsoft V-Chat or Worlds Away.

Downloading and Installing iChat

To start mingling in iChat chat rooms, you first need to download and install iChat. iChat (the company) allows you to download and use iChat for free. To get your free copy, take the following steps:

1. Run your Web browser and go to iChat's home page at **http://www. ichat.com**.

2. Click the **Download** link. iChat displays the download page, prompting you to fill out a form.

3. To complete the form, select **ichat plug-in/ActiveX Client** from the first drop-down list, select your operating system (for instance, Windows 95), and select your Web browser (Navigator or Internet Explorer).

4. Type your name and e-mail address in the appropriate text boxes.

5. Read the license agreement, and click **I ACCEPT the License Agreement Below**. You are now taken to a page with download instructions.

6. Scroll down the page and click the **Download Now** link. If your browser displays a message indicating that it cannot play the file, click the Save option, and click **OK**. The Save As dialog box appears.

7. Open the **Save In** drop-down list, and select **Desktop**, as shown in Figure 22.2.

8. Click the **Save** button. Your browser downloads the iChat installation file, and places it on your desktop.

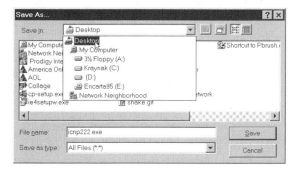

Figure 22.2 Save the installation file to your desktop, so you won't misplace it.

Installing the iChat Plug-In

If you have Netscape Navigator, you downloaded the iChat plug-in for Netscape Navigator. To install the plug-in, take the following steps:

1. Exit any programs that are currently running.

2. Return to your desktop or to the folder in which you downloaded the iChat installation file.

3. Double-click the icon for the iChat installation file you downloaded. The Welcome dialog box appears.

4. Click **Next**. A warning appears, reminding you to exit Navigator before running the installation. The Select the Installation Drive dialog box shows you where iChat will be installed.

5. Click **Next**. The installation program copies the necessary iChat files to your hard drive, and then displays a dialog box indicating that the operation is complete, and asking if you want to view the Readme file. The Readme file contains the latest information about iChat.

6. Click **Yes** or **No**. If you click Yes, the Readme file opens in your default text editor. In either case, you have successfully installed the iChat plug-in. Skip to "Connecting and Chatting in iChat Rooms," below.

 TIP   **Delete the Installation File**   After you install iChat, you can safely delete the installation file. It is no longer needed for running iChat.

Installing the iChat ActiveX Control

As with most ActiveX controls, installing the iChat ActiveX control is very easy. Take the following steps:

1. Exit any programs that are currently running.

2. Return to your desktop or to the folder in which you downloaded the iChat installation file.

3. Double-click the icon for the iChat installation file you downloaded. The installation program copies the necessary iChat files to your hard drive, and then displays a dialog box indicating that the operation is complete, and asking if you want to view the Readme file. The Readme file contains the latest information about iChat.

4. Click **Yes** or **No**. If you click Yes, the Readme file opens in your default text editor. In either case, you have successfully installed the iChat plug-in. You're ready to move to the next section and start chatting.

Connecting and Chatting in iChat Rooms

Now that you have the chat plug-in or control, you can start chatting. Let's try out the new chat toy at Yahoo! Take the following steps to connect to Yahoo!'s chat area and enter a chat room:

1. Use your browser to pull up Yahoo!'s Home Page at **http://www.yahoo. com**.

2. Scroll down to the bottom of the page, and click the **Chat** link. This opens a page describing the steps you need to take to set up Yahoo! Chat.

3. Ignore the **GET THE SOFTWARE** step. You already obtained the software you need. Scroll down the page, and click the **SIGN UP AND CHAT NOW** button. A form appears, prompting you to enter a chat name, password, and other information.

4. Complete the form. Your login name is the name that will identify you to other people in the chat room. Be sure to write down your name and password, so you can sign on later.

5. Click the **Register me now!** button. In a few moments, the Yahoo! Chat Agreement appears.

6. Read the agreement, especially the chat room rules, and click the **I Accept** button. Yahoo! returns you to the opening Chat page, which now shows your newly created chat identity.

7. Under Select Your Software, pick **Plug-in**. Although you can chat using the Java applet, the ActiveX control or plug-in works better.

8. Under Pick a Hot Topic, select the desired category you want to chat about, and then click the **Start Chatting** button. Yahoo! places you in a chat room that corresponds with the selected category. Figure 22.3 shows you what to expect.

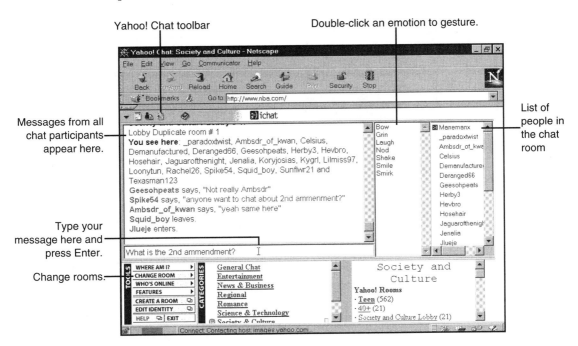

Figure 22.3 Yahoo! Chat brings chat to the Web.

Chatting It Up in a Chat Room

Once you are in a chat room, you can start chatting. The ongoing discussion is displayed in the large frame in the upper left. To send a message to the other people, click inside the small frame just below where the ongoing discussion is taking place, type your message, and press **Enter**. As other people type and send messages, those messages pop up on your screen with little delay.

In addition to sending text messages, you can "gesture" to others in the room. To gesture, click an emotion in the pane just to the right of the discussion pane, as shown in Figure 22.4. This sends a text description of your gesture.

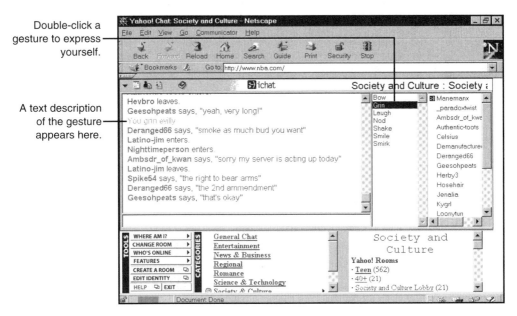

Double-click a gesture to express yourself.

A text description of the gesture appears here.

Figure 22.4   You can gesture to other people in the room.

Checking Out the Other Chatters

Click the name of someone in the room, and then right-click the person's name. This displays a context menu, which allows you to find out more about the person, send the person a private message or a file, start following the person (if the person changes rooms), or ignore the person (prevent the person's messages from appearing on your screen).

To find out more about a person in the chat room, click the person's login name, right-click the name, and select **Who is <loginname>**. If the person entered information about himself or herself, that information is displayed in the Who Is dialog box. To send a private message to the person, take the following steps:

1. Click the person's login name, right-click the name, and select **Send Private Message to <loginname>**. The Send Private Message dialog box appears, as shown in Figure 22.5.

Type your message.

Click Send.

Select this option to keep the Send Private Message dialog box on the screen.

Figure 22.5   You can send a private message that appears only on the selected person's screen.

2. Type your message in the Message area.

3. If you want the Send Private Message dialog box to remain on your screen so you can continue to converse in private, click **Always Visible**.

4. Click the **Send** button. The message pops up on the other person's screen, but there's no guarantee that the person will reply.

Changing Your User Profile

One of the most appealing features of online chat is that you can be anyone you want to be. You simply edit your profile, adding any details about yourself (fact or fiction) that you want others to see. When they check your profile, that information pops up on your screen. To edit your profile, take the following steps:

1. In the Tools list in the lower-left corner of the chat window, click **Edit Profile**. The Yahoo! Chat Identity Editor window appears, as shown in Figure 22.6.

2. Use your mouse or Tab key to move from one text box or option to the next, and enter any details that you want to include in your profile. You don't have to fill in all the blanks.

3. Scroll to the bottom of the window, and click the **Save Changes** button.

Enter details about yourself: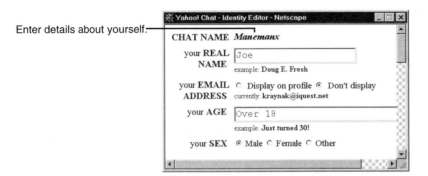

Figure 22.6 You can enter details about yourself that other chatters will see when they check your profile.

Sensitive Information Avoid adding any information to your profile that might help a less desirable individual to find you in real life. Don't enter your real name, e-mail address, or phone number. If you establish a close relationship with someone you trust, you can send that information to the person later.

CAUTION

Going to a Different Room

If you get stuck in a room that's very quiet or where you don't have much in common with many people, you can leave the room and try another. Take the following steps to change to a different Yahoo! Chat room:

1. In the Tools list in the lower-left corner of the chat window, click **Change Room**. A list of categories appears to the right of the Tools list.

2. Click the category for the desired topic. A list of rooms in the selected category appears on the right.

3. Scroll down the list, and click the link for the room you want to go to. You are immediately transported to the selected room. Start chatting!

Chatting in Private

If you hit it off with someone online, or just want to chat with a friend or relative in private, you can create a private room, whose name does not appear in the Yahoo! rooms list. To enter the room, someone who knows your chat name has to follow you into the room. To create a private room, take the following steps:

1. In the Tools list at the lower-left corner of the window, click **Create Room**. The Create Private Room window appears.

2. Drag over the entry in the Room Name text box, and type a name for your room.

3. Drag over the entry in the Describe Your Room text box, and type a brief description of your room, if desired.

4. Under **Room Rating**, select an option to specify the censor level for language in your room.

5. To ensure privacy, click **Private** under **Access**.

6. Click the **Create My Room** button. Your room is now accessible to anyone who wishes to follow you into the room.

If you are invited to a private room, here's what you do to go there: type /**follow** *chatname* (where *chatname* is the person's chat name) in the space where you typically type messages, and press **Enter**. Once all your welcomed guests have arrived, you can lock your room; type /**room secure on** in the message area, and press **Enter**. To unlock the room, type /**room secure off** and press **Enter**. Your room ceases to exist as soon as everyone leaves.

Finding Additional iChat Rooms

Although Yahoo! has plenty of chat rooms full of interesting people, it may not have the best rooms for the particular topic that interests you the most. The best place to look for specific rooms that support iChat is at the iChat Web site. Take the following steps to connect to iChat and find iChat-friendly chat rooms:

1. Go to iChat at **http://www.ichat.com**, and click the **Chat Sites** link at the top of the page. This opens a page that provides a list of chat categories, including Business, Entertainment, Sports, and Romance.

2. Click the desired category. iChat displays a list of companies that offer chat areas for the selected category.

3. Click a link for the desired chat area. Your browser connects you to that site's home page.

4. Follow the links at the current site to locate its chat rooms. The steps for connecting, picking a login name, and chatting will vary depending on the site.

TIP **Check Out the Chat Schedule** iChat also offers a list of special chat events, which looks like a TV show listing. After clicking the Chat Sites link, scan the list to see if there are any special chat events you would like to join. If something catches your eye, click its link.

Other Web Chat Tools

Although iChat is the premier chat tool for the Web, there are many other tools you can use to chat on the Web, and many sites use Java to incorporate chat areas. Check out the following sites for additional information:

- **Club Wired (http://www.talk.com/talk)** is *HotWired* magazine's chat area. Here, you can chat using either a Java applet or an ActiveX control. When you first connect, Club Wired prompts you to fill out a couple of forms and download the required software. Follow the on-screen instructions, and you'll be chatting in no time.

- **WorldVillage Chat (www.worldvillage.com/wv/chat/html/chat2.htm)** is a family oriented chat area that offers access via IRC. Instead of using a dedicated IRC program, WorldVillage Chat uses a Java applet that it runs through your Web browser. After connecting, make sure you select the **JavaChat** option. It takes about 2–3 minutes to download the required Java applet.

- **ChatBox (www.chatbox.com/)** is one of the most basic chat tools on the Web. It's a simple Java applet that's embedded in a Web page. To chat, connect to the address given here, and click the link for the chat topic in which you are interested. A chat window appears, showing the ongoing discussion and displaying a small message area where you can type your own messages.

- **ChatWeb (www.chatweb.net/)** is another forms-based chat tool, which allows you to chat right inside the browser window. You type your message and click the **Chat/Refresh** button. ChatWeb then sends an updated Web page with the most recent message postings.

- **The Coffee Shop (members.aol.com/rwneilljr/chat.htm)** allows you to chat using either forms-based chat or Java. Simply connect to The Coffee Shop using the address above, and select a room. Enter your handle, and choose Java, if you're offered the option.

In this lesson, you learned how to use iChat and a couple of other chat tools to "talk" with other people on the Internet. In the next two lessons, you will learn how to customize Internet Explorer and Netscape Navigator.

Customizing Netscape Navigator

In this lesson, you learn how to change Navigator's look and control its behavior.

Customization Basics

Although Navigator is set up to run immediately with settings that anyone can use, Navigator allows you to customize it to make it look and act the way you want it to. You can enlarge the viewing area by turning toolbars off, change the screen colors, load pages without loading graphics, and much more.

In this lesson, you will learn how to take control of Navigator's toolbars and to change some of the settings that control Navigator's look and behavior.

Controlling Navigator's Toolbars

There are a few things you can do to Navigator's interface without hunting through the menu system for customization options. For one, you can create more screen space by hiding any of the toolbars. To hide a toolbar, click its tab (see Figure 23.1). You can also drag a tab to move the toolbar up or down.

To turn a toolbar completely off so that not even the tab is showing, open the **View** menu, and click the **Hide** command for the toolbar you want to hide. To redisplay a toolbar, open the **View** menu, and select the **Show** command for the desired toolbar.

Drag a tab to move the toolbar.

Click a toolbar's tab to hide the toolbar or bring it into view.

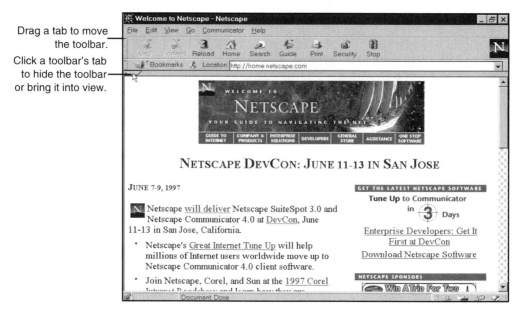

Figure 23.1 You can use the toolbar tabs to hide or display each toolbar.

Entering Appearance Preferences

The Appearance Preferences panel contains most of the options you might want to adjust. Here, you can change the background and text color for Web pages, the appearance of Navigator's toolbars, and the way in which Navigator displays images. To enter any preferences, take the following steps:

1. Open the **Edit** menu and select **Preferences**. The Preferences dialog box appears, as shown in Figure 23.2, offering categories of settings.

2. Click the category that looks as though it might contain the settings you want to change, and then enter your changes. (When you click a category, the panel on the right changes to show the available options.) The following sections explain the options for five panels that deal with Navigator.

3. When you finish entering changes, click **OK**.

Setting Your Appearance Preferences

When you open the Preferences dialog box, the Appearance category should be selected (see Figure 23.2). If the category is not selected, click it. You can then change the following options:

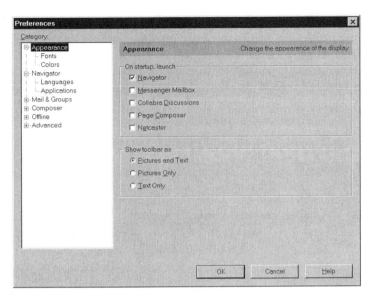

Figure 23.2 The Preferences dialog box.

On Startup, Launch This setting gives you the option of starting Navigator, Messenger Mailbox (for incoming e-mail), Collabra Discussions (for accessing newsgroups), Page Composer (for creating Web pages), and Netcaster, automatically, when you double-click the Netscape Communicator icon that's on the Windows desktop.

Show Toolbar As This option allows you to control the appearance of the buttons in the toolbar. You can choose **Pictures and Text** (for large buttons that show the button names), or **Pictures Only** (for small buttons without names), or **Text Only** (for small buttons without pictures). If you choose Pictures Only, you can still see the name of a button by resting the mouse pointer on it.

Setting Font Preferences

Web pages consist of text and codes that provide instructions to the Web browser on how to display text, insert and position images, and display the page in the correct layout. The codes typically provide general instructions that the Web browser must interpret. That's why no page looks the same when displayed in two different Web browsers.

Because Navigator is in charge of assigning fonts, you can pick the fonts you want to use to style the text. With the Preferences dialog box displayed, click the

Fonts category (directly below Appearance). If Fonts is not displayed, click the **plus sign** next to Appearance. The Fonts panel allows you to enter the following font settings:

- **Variable Width Font** A *variable width font* gives each character only the amount of space it needs. A skinny "i" gets less space than a wide "w." Variable width fonts are used for most of the text on a Web page.

- **Fixed Width Font** A *fixed width font* gives each character the same amount of room. A slender "i" gets the same space as a wide-body "W." Fixed width fonts are usually used to display file names at FTP sites, and to display other types of "computer" text.

- **Use My Default Fonts, Overriding Document-Specified Fonts** This option tells Navigator to always use the fonts you selected instead of using the fonts specified on the Web page.

- **Use Document-Specified Fonts, but Disable Dynamic Fonts** Select this option to use the fonts that are built into the Web page. If additional (dynamic) fonts will increase the download time for the page, Navigator won't use the dynamic fonts.

- **Use Document-Specified Fonts, Including Dynamic Fonts** Choose this option if you want Navigator to always use the fonts built into the Web page, even if they increase the download time for the page.

To change a font, open the drop-down list for the font you want to change, and then click the desired font. To change the size of the text, select the size from the drop-down list next to the font's name.

CAUTION

Encoding Font Leave the **For the Encoding** setting alone. Most sites in the United States and in other countries that use the Roman alphabet use codes based on Latin letters. If you try to visit sites in China or Turkey and the pages do not display properly, you can change this setting.

Changing Navigator's Colors

Unless a Web page specifies which colors to use for the page background, links, and other items on the page, Navigator uses its default color settings. To change these settings, display the Preferences dialog box and click the **Colors** category (below Appearance). You can then change the following color settings:

Text This option lets you specify the color to use to display most of the text on the page (not including links). You should probably leave this set to black; but if you're going to pick a dark background, select a lighter color for your text.

Background   Lets you pick a background color for any Web page that does not have a background color. The Default setting gives pages a gray background, which makes dark text easy to read. To pick a different color, click the **Background** button to display a dialog box that lets you change the background color.

Use Windows Colors   This option tells Navigator to use the same color settings that Windows uses.

Unvisited Links   Controls the colors of the links you haven't yet tried. If you like blue links, don't change this setting. If you would prefer some other color, click the color button next to this option. In the Color dialog box, click the desired color and click **OK**.

Visited Links   Sets the color for links that you've already tried. To change this color setting, perform the same steps you performed for the Unvisited Links setting.

Underline links   Typically, Navigator displays links in a different color and underlined. You can turn the underlining on or off.

Always Use My Colors, Overriding Document   Tells Navigator to use your colors and background setting even if the Web page you load is set to display a different color or background.

Clashing Colors   Be careful when setting the background and text colors. If you pick a light background color and then load a page that has yellow or white text, you may not be able to see that text.

CAUTION

Entering Navigator Preferences

Next in the list of preference categories are the Navigator preferences. The following list provides an overview of the options you should look at:

Navigator Starts With   This option lets you specify which page you want Navigator to load when you start it. You can select **Blank Page** (if you don't want Navigator to load a page), **Home Page** (to specify a starting page), or **Last Page Visited** (Navigator starts with the page that was opened when you last exited Navigator).

Home Page   This option lets you specify the URL of the Web page you want to use as a starting page (assuming you selected Home Page under

Browser Starts With). You can select **Use Current Page** to use the currently displayed Web page as your starting page.

History   This option lets you specify the number of days you want Navigator to keep track of pages you have visited. You can click the **Clear History** button to delete the history from your hard disk and reclaim some disk space.

Setting the Offline Preferences

Navigator lets you work offline to view pages you have already opened. This allows you to download pages during the evening and morning hours when the Internet is less busy, and then view the pages at your convenience. To set the Offline preferences, open the Preferences dialog box, and click **Offline**. You can then choose **Online Work Mode** (to always open pages when you are online), **Offline Work Mode** (to always open pages from your hard disk), or **Ask Me** (to have Navigator display a dialog box when you first start it, asking if you want to work online or offline).

The Download option (directly below Offline) allows you to set options for reading discussion groups (newsgroup messages) offline.

Increasing Performance with the Cache Settings

You can improve the speed at which Navigator loads pages by tinkering with the cache preferences. These preferences allow you to change the size of the cache (a temporary storage area) so that Navigator can use more disk space for storing pages you have already visited. Follow these steps to change the cache size:

1. Open the **Edit** menu and select **Preferences**. The Preferences dialog box appears.

2. Under Category, click the plus sign (+) next to Advanced, and then click **Cache** (see Figure 23.3).

Cache   A *cache* (pronounced "cash") is memory or disk space that Navigator (or any other program) uses to temporarily store data. In Navigator's case, the cache is used to store Web pages you've already loaded, so if you go back or forward to a page, Navigator doesn't have to reload the page from the Web site.

You can increase your cache, but don't decrease it.

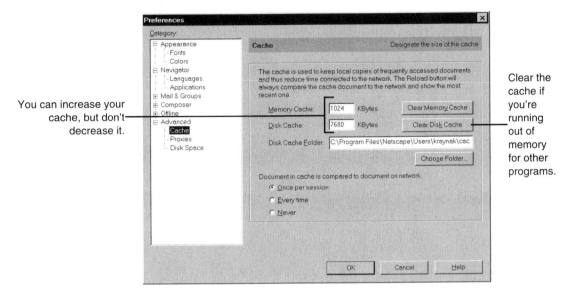

Clear the cache if you're running out of memory for other programs.

Figure 23.3 You are in control of the disk and memory caches.

3. The minimum numbers for the disk and memory cache are already entered for you; don't go any lower. If you have scads of disk space or memory, click in the **Memory Cache** or **Disk Cache** text box and type the desired amount in kilobytes. (1000 kilobytes is approximately 1 megabyte.)

4. The buttons next to the disk and memory cache settings (**Clear Memory Cache** and **Clear Disk Cache**) are useful if you have trouble running your other Windows programs because your system is low on memory. These buttons clear the cache, freeing that storage space for other use.

5. Under **Document in Cache Is Compared to Document on Network**, you can specify how often you want Navigator to check a Web document you've loaded against the original (**Once per Session**, **Every Time**, or **Never**). The less often Navigator has to verify documents, the faster it will run. The more often Navigator verifies documents, the more likely it is that Navigator will display the current page.

6. Click **OK** to save your settings.

In this lesson, you learned how to change the appearance of Navigator and the pages it displays. You also learned some strategies for improving its performance. The next lesson shows how to configure Internet Explorer.

Customizing
Internet Explorer

*In this lesson, you learn how to change Internet Explorer's look
and control its behavior.*

Customization Basics

Although Internet Explorer is set up to run immediately with settings that
anyone can use, Internet Explorer allows you to customize it to make it look and
act the way you want it to. You can enlarge the viewing area by turning toolbars
off, change the screen colors, load pages without loading graphics, and much
more.

You can change most settings by opening the **View** menu, selecting **Internet
Options**, and then clicking the tab for the set of options you want to change:
General, Security, Content, Connection, Programs, and Advanced. The following sections provide detailed instructions on how to change the most common
settings.

Going Full Screen

One of the biggest problems with any Web browser is that it occupies space that
could otherwise be used to display Web pages. Internet Explorer has a simple
solution: Full Screen View. To go full screen, open the **View** menu and select
Full Screen or click the **Fullscreen** button in the toolbar.

Your new window contains only a scroll bar and the Standard Buttons bar—all
you need to navigate the Web. To change back to normal view, click the
Fullscreen button in the toolbar.

Controlling the Toolbars

The toolbars (near the top of the Internet Explorer window) let you bypass the pull-down menus. For example, instead of opening the **Go** menu and selecting **Back**, you can return to the previous page by clicking on the **Back** button. However, if the toolbars get in your way, and Full Screen View doesn't appeal to you, you can hide various toolbars or resize them:

- To turn the entire toolbar on or off, open the **View** menu select **Toolbar**, and click a toolbar's name to turn it off. (Or, right-click any toolbar to view a context menu that offers the same options.)

- To hide or bring back the Address text box, double-click **Address**. When the Address text box is hidden, the Quick Links bar comes into view.

- To display or hide the Quick Links bar, double-click **Links**.

- To display some Links buttons without completely hiding the Address text box, drag the **Links** slider (the double vertical line) to the left.

- To rearrange the toolbars, drag **Address** or **Links** up or down. For example, you can drag **Links** down to create a new area of the toolbar displaying the Links buttons. You can drag **Address** up to move the Address text box next to the Standard Buttons bar (see Figure 24.1).

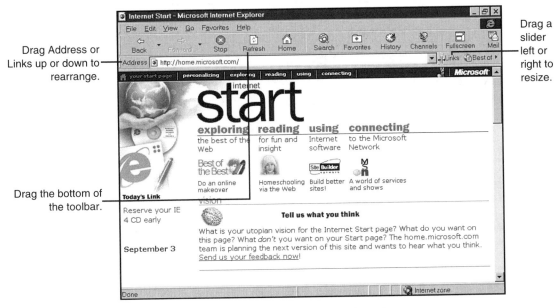

Drag Address or Links up or down to rearrange.

Drag a slider left or right to resize.

Drag the bottom of the toolbar.

Figure 24.1 You can rearrange Internet Explorer's toolbar.

TIP **Keyboard Navigation** If you turn off the Standard Buttons bar, you can quickly enter commands by tapping keystrokes. For example, you can jump back one page by pressing **Alt+Left Arrow**, or skip ahead by pressing **Alt+Right Arrow**.

Picking a Different Starting Page

Whenever you start Internet Explorer, it loads Microsoft's home page, displaying links to Microsoft's new products, technical support, software downloads, and news. If you have your own favorite place to start, however, you can specify a different starting page. Take the following steps to change the starting page:

1. Open the page you want to use as your starting page. For example, click inside the **Address** text box, type **http://www.yahoo.com**, and press **Enter**.

2. Open the **View** menu, select **Internet Options**, and click the **General** tab. The General tab lets you pick the start page you want to use.

3. Click the **Use Current** button, as shown in Figure 24.2.

4. Click **OK**.

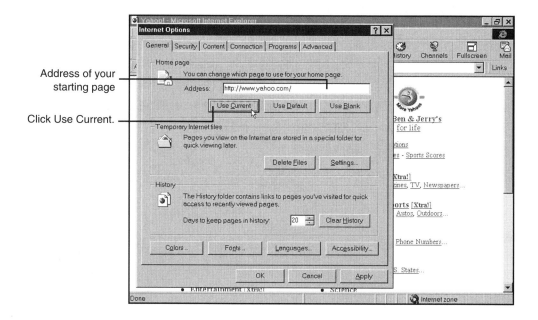

Figure 24.2 You can specify which page to load on startup.

Now, whenever you start Internet Explorer, it loads the specified Web page instead of Microsoft's home page. If you decide later that you would rather use Microsoft's home page, repeat the steps, but click **Use Default** in Step 3.

The Links bar you encountered in Lesson 10, "Creating and Organizing Internet Explorer Favorites," contains buttons for some very helpful Microsoft Web pages. You can rename those buttons and make them point to different pages. Take the following steps:

1. Open the **Favorites** menu and select **Organize Favorites**. This displays the Organize Favorites window.
2. Double-click the **Links** folder to display a list of shortcuts on the Quick Links bar.
3. To remove a button, click its name, and click the **Delete** button.
4. To rename a button, click its name, click **Rename**, type a new name for the button, and press **Enter**.
5. To change the address of the page that the link points to, right-click the link and click **Properties**. Type the new address, and click **OK**.
6. When you are done configuring your links, close the **Organize Folders** window.

You can quickly add buttons to the Quick Links toolbar by dragging links from the currently displayed Web page up to the toolbar.

Changing the Text and Background Appearance

By default, Internet Explorer gives each Web page you load the power to display its own colors. If the Web page does not specify a color scheme, Internet Explorer uses your current Windows color settings. However, Internet Explorer allows you to enter your color preferences. Take the following steps:

1. Open the **View** menu, and select **Internet Options**. The Options dialog box appears.
2. Click the **General** tab, and click the **Colors** button. The Colors dialog box appears, as shown in Figure 24.3.
3. Under Colors, click **Use Windows colors**, to remove the check from the box and turn the option off.

4. To change the text color, click the , click the desired color, and click **OK**.

5. To change the background color, click the **Background** button, click the desired color, and click **OK**.

Click a button to change the text or background color.

Remove the check mark to use your custom colors.

Use these options to change the appearance of links.

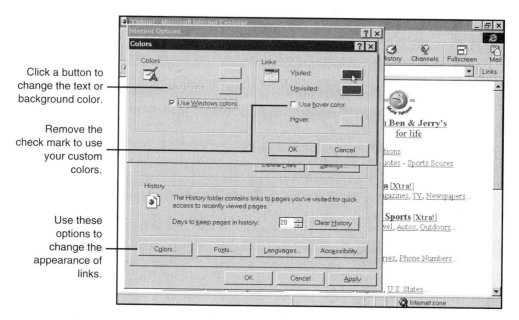

Figure 24.3   Internet Explorer lets you choose the text and background colors.

CAUTION

Color Settings   Internet Explorer uses the background and text colors you selected only for pages that do *not* have a code that specifies a background color. The background and text colors specified by a Web page override any settings you enter.

6. To change the way Internet Explorer displays links, enter your preferences for the following options:

> **Visited** lets you change the color of links that point to pages you've already visited.
>
> **Unvisited** lets you change the color of links that point to pages you haven't yet seen.
>
> **Use hover color** lets you specify the color you want displayed when your mouse pointer is over a link.

7. Click the **OK** button to save your changes.

Increasing Performance

If you are accustomed to running programs and opening files stored on your hard disk, the Internet might seem somewhat slow to you. It takes quite a while for a large Web page with many graphics to travel across Internet connections.

The easiest way to increase Internet Explorer's speed is to create shortcuts, subscribe to sites, and download content during off-hours. The following sections explain two other ways to increase the speed at which Internet Explorer downloads Web pages.

Loading Text-Only Pages

Although graphics liven up Web pages, they also increase the time it takes your Web browser to download pages. To speed up the process, you can tell Internet Explorer to load only text, no graphics. When you reach a page that has graphics you want to view, you can then click a placeholder to view that image. To turn off graphics, take the following steps:

1. Open the **View** menu, and select **Internet Options**. The Options dialog box appears.
2. Click the **Advanced** tab.
3. Under Multimedia, click **Show pictures**, **Play animations**, **Play sounds**, and/or **Play videos** to turn these options off (remove the check marks).
4. Click the **OK** button to save your settings.

With Show pictures, Play sounds, and Play videos off, Internet Explorer displays the page's text, but inserts icons in place of graphics, sounds, and video clips (see Figure 24.4). You can click an icon to display or play the file.

Using the Cache for Quick Return Trips

Because the Web is relatively slow, most Web browsers store the Web pages you visit in a temporary storage area called a *cache* (pronounced "cash"). Internet Explorer uses a disk cache and a memory cache for storing pages you have opened. When you return to a page you've already visited, Internet Explorer loads the page from the cache instead of downloading it fresh from the Web. Because Internet Explorer is loading the page from a local source, the page pops up much more quickly.

Figure 24.4 With Pictures off, Internet Explorer displays icons in place of pictures.

Cache A temporary storage area on your hard drive or in your computer's memory. Browsers use a cache system to quickly reload pages you revisit.

To increase the speed at which Internet Explorer loads the pages you've previously visited, you can change the cache settings. Take the following steps:

1. Open the **View** menu, and select **Internet Options**. The Options dialog box appears.
2. Click the **General** tab, and click the **Settings** button under Temporary Internet Files. The Settings dialog box appears, as shown in Figure 24.5.
3. Drag the slider below **Amount of disk space to use** to the right, to increase the amount of disk space reserved for the disk cache. The more space you use for the cache, the more pages Internet Explorer can store for later revisits.

Monitor Your Disk Space If you don't have much free space, lower the cache setting to prevent cluttering your drive (a cluttered drive often gives rise to Insufficient Memory messages).

CAUTION

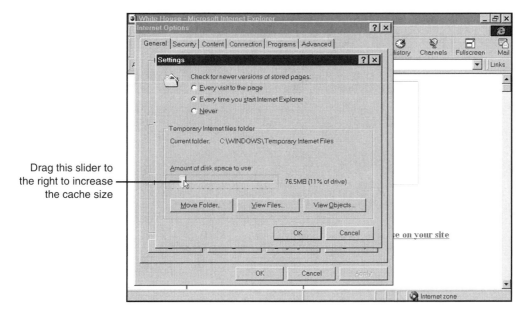

Drag this slider to the right to increase the cache size

Figure 24.5 Increasing the cache increases the speed at which pages are reloaded.

4. Under **Check for newer versions of stored pages**, specify how often you want Internet Explorer to check a cached page against the latest page on the Web:

> **Every visit to the page** is a little excessive and will slow you down.
>
> **Every time you start Internet Explorer** (the default setting) checks the page the first time you revisit it in a session.
>
> **Never** is a little risky, because you might miss page updates, but it does make for speedy revisits.

5. Click the **OK** button to save your cache settings and return to the Options dialog box. Click **OK**.

In the Options dialog box, the General Settings tab also has a button called Delete Files, which you can click to remove all cached files from your hard drive. If you're running low on disk space, this is the button to use to free up a few megabytes.

In this lesson, you learned how to change the appearance and performance of Internet Explorer. In Part 3, "E-Mail," you will learn how to send and retrieve e-mail messages over the Internet.

E-Mail

Understanding
Internet E-Mail

In this lesson, you learn about e-mail and online services. You will learn how to choose a client, how e-mail works, and how to send and recieve messages.

Electronic mail (e-mail) is a system that enables users to send messages via modem, or over a network, from one computer to another. If you have an Internet connection, you can send messages via e-mail to anyone else on the Internet. All you need to know is their e-mail address.

E-mail messages sent over the Internet take the form of text messages. You can, with the right e-mail software package, attach other files to your messages. These attached files can be just about anything—a graphic, a sound file, another document, even a software program. In this lesson, you will learn how e-mail works, and what you need to send and receive e-mail.

The Ins and Outs of E-Mail

Obtaining a sound understanding for how Internet e-mail works is really not difficult. Having a good grasp on how e-mail sends and receives messages will help you even more if you have to troubleshoot your own e-mail software and connection.

There are three things that you must have to send and receive e-mail. These include an Internet e-mail account, a connection to the Internet, and a software application that handles e-mail. This is also referred to as a client.

E-Mail Client   The software that you install on your PC to send and receive e-mail.

Your E-Mail Account

The first thing you need is an e-mail account. Sometimes you can get one through your workplace or the school you attend, but if you're like most people, you will have to sign up for an e-mail account with an Internet service provider. E-mail is one of the standard features provided with any Internet account from an Internet service provider. For information on choosing an Internet service provider, see Part 1, Lesson 3, "Selecting an Internet Service Provider."

Your service provider (or network administrator at work or school) will assign you an e-mail address; it is the e-mail address that will uniquely identify you on the Internet. It is similar to your street address, which uniquely identifies your location for your regular mail (of course, it doesn't always seem to uniquely identify you when the U.S. Post Office is concerned).

Internet e-mail addresses all look alike: *username@domain.com*. The first part of the address is the username. It is a name or nickname that you choose or that your Internet service provider assigns you. It identifies you. The @ symbol in the address is used to separate the user name from the domain name. The domain name is the name of your Internet service provider's computer. So, you can see that the combination of your username and the name of your service provider's mail server will get your Internet mail delivered to the right place.

 TERM **Domain**   Given to a specific computer on the Internet domain names are assigned by a special organization called InterNIC. Since these names are regulated, there is assurance that a particular domain name will be unique on the Internet.

 TIP **Identifying Domains**   You can identify the type of institution that a particular domain belongs to by the suffix that follows the domain name. For instance, domainname.com would be a domain registered to a commercial enterprise (.com). Some of the other suffixes that you will run into are .edu (educational), .net (an Internet server),.gov (government), or .mil (military).

When your Internet service provider assigns you your e-mail address, they will also provide you with a method of connecting to the Internet through your modem. For more information on configuring specific operating systems to connect to an Internet service provider, see Lessons 2 and 3.

E-Mail and Online Services

If you are trying to send e-mail to someone who connects to the Internet through one of the online services such as AOL, you will find that their e-mail addresses take on a particular form (particularly CompuServe e-mail addresses). The following list shows you the format of an e-mail address for each of the most popular online services.

Online Service	Sample Address
CompuServe	71354.1234@compuserve.com
America Online	joeguy@aol.com
Prodigy	joeguy@prodigy.com
The Microsoft Network	joeguy@msn.com

Choosing an E-Mail Client

Once you have an e-mail address and a connection to the Internet, all you have to do is choose an e-mail client and install it on your computer. A large number of commercial and shareware e-mail packages exist. Windows 95 comes with its own e-mail client called Microsoft Exchange. Microsoft Office 97 comes with Microsoft Outlook, a personal information manager that can also send and receive e-mail.

Full-featured e-mail clients are also available as part of the Web browser suites that Netscape Communicator and Microsoft Internet Explorer offer. You will learn how to configure and use the e-mail clients in Netscape Communicator and Internet Explorer in this section of the book. Finally, be aware that each of the online services such as America Online also provide an e-mail system for their customers. If you use AOL e-mail, check out Lessons 6 and 9. When choosing your e-mail package, you may want to keep the following in mind:

- Is the e-mail client's interface user-friendly?
- Does the e-mail package have an electronic phone book where you can keep a list of your important e-mail addresses?
- Does the e-mail package have the ability to encode and decode files attached to e-mail messages?
- Does the e-mail package have a spelling checker?

While all the items listed previously aren't vital to make an e-mail package usable, they are features that many e-mail packages offer as a matter of course.

How E-Mail Works

Once you have an e-mail address, a connection to the Internet, and an e-mail package. you're ready to start sending e-mail. The only other thing that you have to know is the person's e-mail address to whom you want to send the message.

E-Mail clients are very consistent in that there will be a New Message button or menu choice that allows you to create a new e-mail message. Once you open a window for a new message, you will need to provide certain information to make sure that the message gets to its intended destination.

- **TO:** This is where you type the e-mail address of the person you are sending the e-mail to.
- **CC:** You can copy the message to another e-mail address or addresses.
- **SUBJECT:** Keep the subject short, just type a short heading that will key the recipient to the subject of your message.

The remainder of the e-mail form is for your message. When typing your message, follow the typical conventions that you would use if you were sending someone a letter or an interoffice memo.

E-mail does have some conventions, however, that you will not find in a typical memo. One of these is *emoticons*; emoticons are images made from keyboard characters and used to impart emotion to e-mail messages. You should look at emoticons sideways. A list of some of the many emoticons follows.

Emoticon	*Expression*
:)	Smile
:(	Frown
:|	Expressionless
;(	Winking
:D	Laughing

A number of acronyms are also in common use on the Internet and can be used in e-mail messages. Just make sure that the recipient of your e-mail is savvy to them.

Acronym	Meaning
LOL	Laughing Out Loud
IMHO	In My Humble Opinion
TIA	Thanks In Advance
OTOH	On The Other Hand
ROTFL	Rolling On The Floor Laughing

Sending E-Mail

Once you've completed the message, make sure you click the Send button or choose Send from the appropriate menu. The message is placed in your Outbox.

 TIP **Creating Messages Offline**   If you have several e-mail messages to send, you can create each one while you're offline (that is, not connected to the Internet) and save it in your Outbox. Then when you're ready to send the messages, you can connect to the Internet and send all the messages in the Outbox at once.

Once your e-mail message or messages are in the Outbox, all you have to do is choose the command that actually sends your e-mail from your machine to the beginning of its journey to the recipient's computer. This is accomplished by connecting to your Internet service provider. Then your e-mail message is transmitted over the phone line by your modem. It goes to your service provider's SMTP (Simple Mail Transfer Protocol) mail server. The message is then coded with SMTP information specific to you and the person to whom you are sending the message.

It's not unlike addressing an envelope with a mailing address and a return address. Then the e-mail message is placed out on the Internet and moves from server to server until it reaches its destination—the POP (Post Office Protocol) mail server for the person you sent the message to (actually, it would be this person's Internet service provider's POP server). Then when the person you sent the e-mail to logs onto the mail server, the message is downloaded to their PC.

POP and SMTP A **Post Office Protocol** mail server receives e-mail messages; a **Simple Mail Transfer Protocol** mail server sends e-mail. One server (meaning one computer) can serve both as the POP and SMTP server. Whether or not there are separate servers to receive and send mail depends on your Internet service provider; it's their hardware.

Receiving E-Mail

To receive your e-mail , it's just a matter of logging onto your Internet service and then starting your e-mail client. Any messages awaiting you will be downloaded to your PC and appear in your Inbox. To read a particular message, double-click it. Once you've read the message, you can delete it, keep it, or reply to it.

 TIP **Automatically Checking E-Mail** You can configure your e-mail program to automatically check for mail every so often.

Replying to a Message

To reply to an e-mail message, open the message or make sure that it's selected in the Inbox and then click the Reply button or choose Reply from the appropriate menu. When you reply to a message, most e-mail programs include the text of the original message for reference. You can customize your e-mail program so that the original text is not included if you want, or you can simply delete the text if you don't want to include it in a particular reply.

If you do want to include the original message in the reply, you should place your response above the message. That way, the person who sent you the e-mail doesn't have to read their own message to find your response. Once you complete your reply, click the Send button. The response is off to the Outbox and treated like any other e-mail message that you create.

 TIP **Replying to Messages** You can reply to, forward, or redirect any message you receive. When you reply to a message, your e-mail program automatically fills in the address of the originator in your new message. All you have to do is type your reply and then send the message.

In this lesson, you learned how Internet e-mail works and what you need to send and receive e-mail. In the next lesson, you will learn how to configure Netscape Messenger, the e-mail client in the Netscape Communicator Internet suite.

Configuring Netscape E-Mail

In this lesson, you learn how to set up Netscape Messenger for the sending and receiving of Internet e-mail.

Using Netscape's Built-In E-Mail

Netscape Communicator 4.0 provides you with a full-featured Web browser as you saw in Part 2, Lesson 2, "Downloading and Installing Netscape Communicator." The Communicator suite also provides you with an excellent e-mail package—Netscape Messenger. To use Messenger as your e-mail client you must configure it.

 E-Mail Client   The software that serves as your Internet e-mail package. Your e-mail client can be a stand-alone e-mail package such as Eudora or part of an Internet suite such as Netscape Messenger.

To configure Netscape Messenger, you must provide the software with certain information. This information ranges from the very obvious (such as your name) to information that you must obtain from your Internet service provider. A list follows:

- Your Name
- Your E-Mail Address: This information is provided to you by your service provider.
- Your Organization (optional): This could be the name of your own business or the company for which you work.
- Your E-Mail User Name: This is (usually) the first part of your e-mail address, such as the *joe* in *joe@online.com*.
- Your Mail Server: This information should be provided to you by your service provider. It will typically take the form of *mailhost.service provider name.com*.

CAUTION

Messenger and most e-mail packages must be configured for both an incoming (POP) mail server and an outgoing (SMTP) mail server. In most cases this information will be the same; one server will handle incoming and outgoing mail. Make sure you have the correct server information from your Internet service provider before you attempt to configure Messenger.

Configuring Netscape Messenger

Netscape provides you with more than one avenue to configure Messenger as your e-mail client. You can access the Preferences dialog box (the place where you will enter your account information) via the Netscape Navigator menu system or the Netscape Messenger menu system.

1. Start either Netscape Navigator or Netscape Messenger via the **Start** button or an appropriate icon on the Windows Desktop.

2. Select **Edit, Preferences**. The Preferences dialog box appears, containing a tree-like Category menu that lets you select the various configuration options for the Communicator components, such as Messenger.

3. To access the Mail preferences click the **Plus Symbol** (+) to the left of the Mail and Groups panel (see Figure 2.1). This will display all the mail and newsgroup preferences.

The Mail and Newsgroup preferences are listed below with a short description of each.

Identity   Information about you such as your name, e-mail address, and signature file go here.

Messages   This box enables you to control whether or not copies of your sent e-mail messages are sent to another e-mail address or a Sent folder.

Mail Server   This is where you designate the name of your service provider's mail server.

Groups Server   This box is reserved for information about your service provider's news server.

Directory   This is where you select the search order for address resources such as your personal address book and e-mail directories on the Web such as Four11.

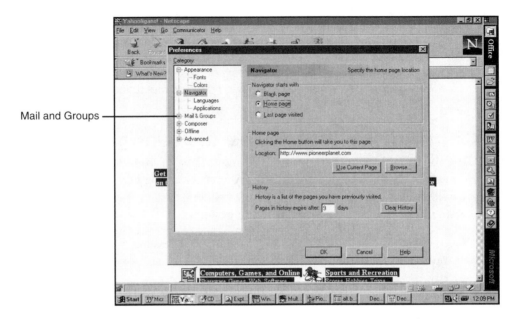

Mail and Groups

Figure 2.1 Click the Mail and Groups panel to access the parameters that you must set to configure Messenger to send and receive e-mail.

4. Click **Identity** the first of the mail preferences. Place the appropriate information in the *Your Name, Email Address, Reply to Address,* and *Organization* boxes. When you have completed the Identity information you are ready to move on to the next set of mail parameters (see Figure 2.2).

TIP **Know the Easiest Way to Move from Box to Box?** You can use the Tab key to move forward from text box to text box in a dialog box such as Preferences. To move back a box use the Shift key plus the Tab.

TIP **You can create a signature file that is attached to the end of each of your e-mail messages.** This is a great way to personalize your messages. The signature file can be created in any text program such as the Windows Notepad. Then place the file name in the Signature file box in the Identity dialog box.

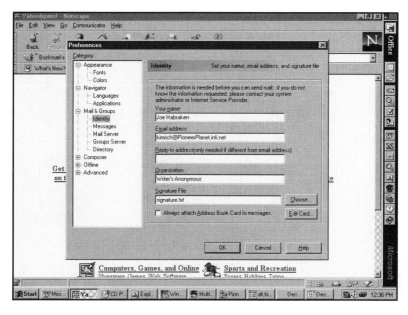

Figure 2.2   The Identity box is where you identify yourself and your e-mail address.

Specifying Mail Server Information

To complete the Netscape Messenger e-mail configuration you must provide Messenger with the appropriate mail server information. This is done in the Mail Server dialog box. Click **Mail Server** in the Category box. This Mail Server dialog box opens; this is where you specify the names of your Service Provider's incoming and outgoing mail servers.

The name of your e-mail server will be information that your Internet service provider gives you, and it will be something like *mailhost.name of service provider.com*. E-mail packages, such as Messenger, must be configured for both an incoming (POP) mail server and an outgoing (SMTP) mail server. In most cases this information will be the same; the one mail server will handle incoming and outgoing mail (see Figure 2.3).

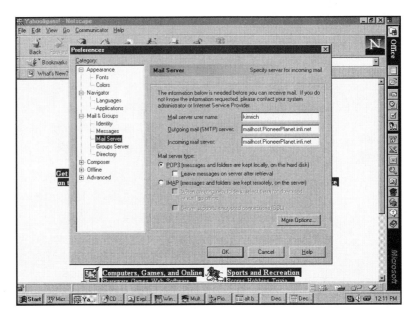

Figure 2.3 The Mail Server dialog box is where you place the names of your service provider's incoming and outgoing mail servers.

Setting Message Format

Messenger also provides you with several choices related to the actual format of your sent messages and whether or not you want to forward copies of all your outgoing e-mail messages to another e-mail address.

In the Messages Property box you can determine the format of your messages and the line length of your messages. The default format for Messenger e-mail messages is HTML—HyperText Markup Language—the same coding system used on Web documents. HTML gives your e-mail a nice formatted appearance. However, some of the people you send e-mail to may not have e-mail clients that can read HTML messages.

1. To change the message format from HTML to plain text, deselect the check box for **send HTML messages**.

2. Messenger is configured to automatically quote messages in your replies to them. To change this default deselect the check box.

TIP **Help** Remember that you can get help by clicking the Help button if you don't understand all the parameters in the various configuration boxes.

Copying Sent Messages

The Message dialog box is also where you determine whether or not you want to copy your sent messages to another e-mail address. For instance, you might want to copy e-mail messages sent from your office e-mail to your home e-mail address or vice versa. The copies of outgoing messages box is also where you decide if you would like copies of your sent e-mail messages to be placed in a Sent folder for you.

1. To designate an e-mail address that will be copied on all your sent e-mail messages make sure the Self box is checked next to Mail messages and then type an e-mail address into the Other address box.

2. You also have the option of having all your sent e-mail messages copied to a Sent folder. By default this check box is selected. To change the default click the check box.

 TIP **It's a very good idea to have your sent messages copied to a sent folder.** If you ever have to review a message it is readily available. You can also delete unneeded messages from your Sent folder whenever you wish.

Because Messenger is part of Netscape Communicator—an Internet suite product—some of the mail parameters related to Communicator's Newsgroup reader are also found in your Messages dialog box. You can reply to a newsgroup message via your e-mail package. Messenger enables you to also keep a copy of these messages when you send them (see Figure 2.4). For more about Newsgroups see Part 4 of this book.

3. To turn off the default for the copying of Newsgroup e-mail messages deselect the check box next to Groups Messages.

4. When you have completed selecting your mail preferences make sure to click the **OK** button.

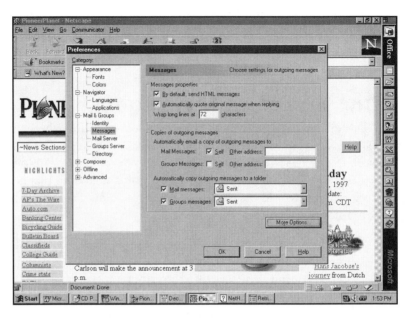

Figure 2.4 The Messages dialog box is where you determine the message format and whether or not you save a copy of sent messages.

Completing the Messenger Configuration

After you've designated the Identity information in the Identity box and the mail server information in the Mail Server box, Netscape Messenger is ready to send and receive e-mail messages. Other e-mail parameters such as those found in the Messages and Directory boxes will be things that you will want to fine-tune as you use and experiment with Messenger.

In this lesson, you learned how to configure the e-mail parameters for Netscape Messenger. In the next lesson, you will learn how to configure the e-mail client in Microsoft Internet Explorer.

Configuring Internet Explorer E-Mail

In this lesson, you learn how to configure Outlook Express, the e-mail client in the Microsoft Internet Explorer suite.

Using Outlook Express

Internet Explorer provides you with a full-featured Web browser as you saw in Part 2. The Explorer Internet suite like the Netscape Communicator suite also provides you with an excellent e-mail package—Outlook Express. To use Outlook as your e-mail client you must configure it.

Any e-mail package that you configure will need certain information like your e-mail address, your password, and the name of your Internet Service Provider's mail server.

The first time you use Outlook it starts the Internet Connection Wizard, which will work you through the creation of your Outlook e-mail account. To fully configure Outlook Express, however, you'll have to get familiar with additional mail options.

Using the Internet Connection Wizard

As soon as you start Outlook for the first time, the Internet Connection Wizard (ICW) appears. It asks a series of questions that gives it the information it needs to send and receive e-mail messages to and from your Service Provider's Internet mail server.

1. The ICW'S first screen asks you to enter a name for the mail account you are going to create. You can name it something like *Joe's Account*. Keep the name simple since it is for reference purposes only. Once you've typed the name into the textbox (see Figure 3.1), click **Next**.

Figure 3.1 The ICW asks you a series of questions as it configures your Outlook e-mail account.

Naming Your Account Name the account something that will make sense to you later. Outlook allows you to configure multiple e-mail accounts. So, if you need to reconfigure any of the information in your account you will need to

CAUTION know its name.

2. The next screen asks for your Internet e-mail display name. This is the name that will appear in the **From** box when you send e-mail. You determine the display name. It can consist of your first and last name or a nickname. Type the display name and click **Next**.

3. The next screen asks for your e-mail address. This is a very important step. Carefully enter your e-mail address (it will be something like *username@serviceprovider.com*). Then click **Next**.

4. The next screen asks for the addresses of your Service Provider's mail servers. A box is provider for the Incoming Mail Server (POP) and the Outgoing Mail Server (SMTP) In most cases these will be the same server (see Figure 3.2). Type the appropriate information in each box and click **Next**.

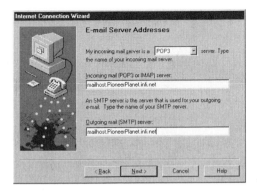

Figure 3.2   You must provide the name of your Service Provider's Incoming and Outgoing mail servers; in most cases they will be the same.

5. The next screen asks you to enter your e-mail account name and your password. Your account name will be the first part of your e-mail address. For instance the *joe* in *joe@domain.com* would be your account name. Your password is the password assigned to you by your Internet Service Provider. After entering this information, click **Next**.

6. The next screen asks you for the type of connection you use to connect to the Internet: modem or a local area network. If you connect using an Internet Service Provider and a modem click **Connect using my phone line**, then click **Next**.

7. The next screen asks you to choose the modem that you will use to connect with. In most cases your PC will only have one modem and the name of that modem will appear in the modem box. Use the drop-down box to select the appropriate modem and then click **Next**.

8. The next step will allow you to configure a dial-up connection to your Internet Service Provider if you have not set one up (see Lesson 5 in this part for help configuring the dial-up feature). Once you complete the dial-up configuration click **Next**. If you have already set up a connection select its name and click **Next**.

9. The next screen verifies that you have completed the configuration process for Outlook e-mail. Click **Finish** to compete the task.

Once you've completed the steps in the Wizard you will be able to send and receive mail using Outlook. However, there are other configuration items that you may wish to set.

Changing Account Information

Outlook makes it easy to edit the account information that was collected by the ICW when you first configured the e-mail client. This is very useful if your e-mail address ever changes or if you need to change your password.

1. Click the **Tools** menu, then click **Accounts**. The Internet Accounts box will appear.

2. Select the account you wish to edit and then click **Properties**. The Mail Account Properties box for the account will appear.

3. The Properties box has five tabs: General, Servers, Connection, Security and Advanced. You can ignore the Advanced tab. To change information regarding your e-mail account, click **General**.

4. The **General** tab includes text boxes for the account name, your name (which will appear in the From box on new e-mail), and your e-mail address. Click in any of the boxes to edit the information (see Figure 3.3).

5. The **Servers** tab is where you supply the name of the incoming and outgoing mail servers and your login information. Click the appropriate box to edit the information.

6. The **Connection** tab allows you to designate which dial-up connection you will use to connect to your Internet Service Provider. Click the **Connection drop-down box** to select the dial-up connection.

7. The Security tab allows you to send a digital ID with your messages, assuring the recipient that the message is from you.

8. When you have completed editing the information in the Mail Account Properties dialog box, click **OK**. You will be returned to the Internet Accounts box. Click **Close** to return to the main Outlook window.

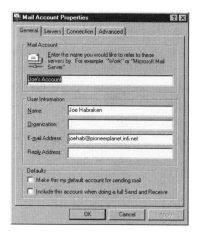

Figure 3.3 The Mail Account Properties dialog box gives you access to all the mail parameters that you set using the ICW.

Completing Outlook's Configuration

Outlook also allows you to set mail parameters involving the how your messages are sent and received. These preferences are set via Mail Options.

1. Click the **Tools** menu, then click **Options**. The Mail Options dialog box will appear. This box has seven tabs: **Send, Read, Spelling, Signature**, and **Security**. Click the appropriate tab to set the features (see Figure 3.4).

2. The General tab allows you to set options such as how often outlook should check for new e-mail and if a sound should be played when a new message arrives. Click the appropriate boxes to make your selections.

3. The **Send** tab allows you to set mail sending options such as the format of your sent messages. You can send messages in HTML or text format. You also have the option of having sent messages routes to a Sent Folder and the text of a received message included in your e-mail reply. To select the various features in the Send box click the appropriate check box.

4. The **Read** tab allows you to set parameters involving new and deleted messages. You can select to have a sound played when new messages arrive or choose to have the Deleted items folder emptied when you exit Outlook. Click the appropriate check box to select a particular feature.

5. The **Spelling** tab lets you set the parameters for Outlook's spelling feature. You can have the spelling checker always suggest spellings for flagged words and have all messages spell checked just before sending. The spelling options can be selected by clicking the appropriate check box.

6. The **Signature** tab allows you to create a text file that will serve as your signature. Many people use the signature file to include their name and phone number or even a personal slogan on all e-mail messages. You can create your signature file in the Signature window or create your signature file using any text editor and then designate the appropriate file in the Signature window.

7. The **Security** tab allows you to set security options for your e-mail. You can choose to add a digital signature to all outgoing e-mail or you can choose to use encryption to protect the e-mail that you send. Click the appropriate check box to make your selections.

8. The Advanced tab alows you to set options that will delete read messages and compact files currently in your outlook folders. Click the boxes to make your selections.

Digital Signature A digital signature stamps all the e-mail that you send with a certificate that confirms that you are the originator of the e-mail message. This is only necessary if you think that someone has been sending e-mail attributed to you.

9. When you have completed your Mail Options changes, click **OK**. The Mail Options box will close and you will be returned to the Outlook window.

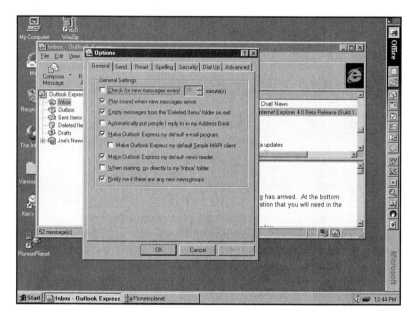

Figure 3.4 The Mail Options dialog box gives you access to mail preferences involving how your messages are sent, the Outlook spelling checker, and e-mail security issues.

Configuring Outlook Express for use is fairly intuitive. If you need additional information on a particular feature use Outlook's help system.

In this lesson, you learned how to configure Outlook Express, the Internet Explorer e-mail client. In the next lesson, you'll learn how to compose and send e-mail using Netscape Messenger.

Composing and Sending E-Mail with Netscape Messenger

In this lesson, you learn how to compose and send e-mail using Netscape Messenger.

Composing E-Mail in Netscape Messenger

You can compose your e-mail in Netscape Messenger either offline or online. The only differences between these two approaches for creating new e-mail in Messenger have to do with how the messages are sent on to your Service Provider's mail server at the end of the process. These minor differences will be discussed later in this lesson.

> **TIP**   **Connect Time**   Composing your e-mail offline can save you money if your payment to your Internet Service Provider is based on your connect time. If you pay a flat fee for unlimited time, however, this isn't an issue, but it is good Internet etiquette to not tie up Service Provider modem lines when you're not sending or receiving messages.

Opening Netscape Messenger

To start the e-mail creation process, you have to start Netscape Messenger. There are a couple of routes to getting the Messenger Window open on your desktop.

1. To Start Netscape Messenger, click the **Start** button, Point at **Programs**, then point at **Netscape Communicator**. The Netscape Communicator group will open.

2. Click **Netscape Messenger**. The Messenger window will open (see Figure 4.1)

TIP **Netscape Communicator**   You can also start Netscape Communicator via the Communicator icon on your desktop. Once Communicator is open, you can start Messenger by clicking the mailbox icon on the toolbar in the lower right of the Communicator Window.

New Message button ———

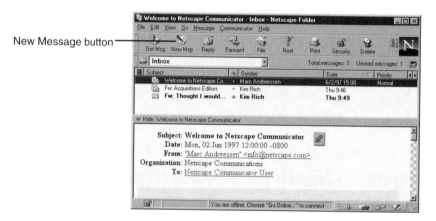

Figure 4.1   The Netscape Messenger Window provides you with all the tools for sending and receiving e-mail messages.

Addressing New E-Mail in Messenger

Once you have the Messenger Window open, you're ready to compose a new e-mail message.

1. Click the **New Message** button. The Composition Window will open (see Figure 4.2). The Composition Window consists of two parts—the Addressing area and the Message area.

2. The Addressing area is where you designate the e-mail address of the person you want to send the message to. Make sure the Insertion point is blinking to the right of **To:**, then type their e-mail address.

TIP **Address Book**   You can also insert e-mail addresses into the To:, CC:, and BCC: boxes using the Messenger Address Book. The Address Book can be set up to hold all your important e-mail addresses. (To insert an address from the Address Book, click the **Address** button on the Composition toolbar.)

Message Sending
Options button

Address message button

Attach Files and
Documents button

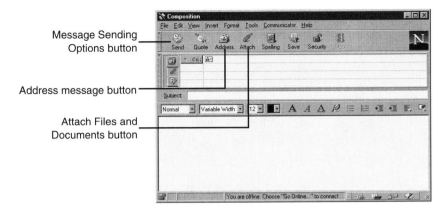

Figure 4.2 The Composition window is where you address and compose your new e-mail message.

TIP **TO:** You can send the e-mail message to as many primary recipients (TO:) as you want. You can either include all the addresses on one line separated by a space or you can use multiple TO: designations in the Address boxes.

You probably noticed that The Addressing area has three buttons in the upper left corner: the Address Message button, the Attach Files and Documents button, and the Message Sending Options button.

- **Address Message** This button allows you to designate whom you are sending your message to (which you just did).
- **Attach Files and Documents** This button allows you to attach files to the e-mail message. You will learn more about sending files with e-mail messages in Part 3, Lesson 13.
- **Message Sending Options** This button allows you to designate the coding method that will be used for items that you attach to your e-mail messages or whether or not you send your e-mail messages encrypted (a way to protect e-mail from being intercepted by nasty hackers on the Net).

TERM **CC** This stands for carbon copy and allows you to copy a message to another e-mail address.

BCC   It stands for blind carbon copy and allows you to copy a message to another e-mail address without the primary recipient of the message knowing it.

After you've designated the person who will receive the e-mail message (designated by their e-mail address) you can also choose to copy the message to another e-mail address. You can copy the message in two different ways—CC: or BCC:. CC stands for carbon copy and the primary recipient of the message will know that you copied the message to another person.

BCC stands for blind carbon copy. This means the message will be copied to another e-mail address, but the primary recipient will not see on their copy of the e-mail message that another person was copied.

To carbon copy your e-mail message to another e-mail address:

1. Click in the box below the TO: e-mail address that you designated. The TO: designator appears in the second box. Click **TO:**, a drop-down menu appears that gives you access to CC and BCC. Click **CC** (see Figure 4.3).

2. Type in the name of the e-mail address that you want to copy the message to (or select an e-mail address from your Address Book by clicking the Address button).

Completing the Message

Once you've designated whom you want to send the e-mail to, you're ready to designate the subject of the message and compose the actual message.

1. Click in the **Subject** text box. Type the subject of your e-mail message. Press the **Tab** key or click in the message area.

2. Type your message in the message area. The formatting toolbar above the message area allows you to select the font or special character attributes that you use in the message. You can also add special formatting to the text like a bulleted list.

Messages in HTML Format   The fonts and other character attributes (such as bold and italic) that can be selected using the formatting toolbar that Messenger provides will only appear in messages that you send in HTML (Hypertext Markup Language) format. And beware that even messages sent in HTML format will not appear with the special font attributes in the e-mail client of the recipient if that e-mail software does not support the HTML format. For more information on configuring Messenger, see Lesson 2 of Part 3.

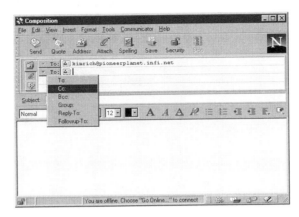

Figure 4.3 The Address message button lets you select the kind and number of recipients you want for your e-mail message.

Sending the Message

Once you've addressed and composed your e-mail message, you are ready to send it. The steps that it takes to get your e-mail to your Service Provider's e-mail server will vary slightly depending on whether you are working offline or online in Messenger.

If you are working offline:

1. Click the **Send** button on the Messenger toolbar (it will say *Send Later* when you place the mouse on it).

2. A dialog box regarding the format of the message will appear if you are sending the message to addresses that are not in your Address Book and designated as being able to receive messages in HTML format. Select the format for the message—**Plain Text and HTML**, **Plain Text Only**, or **HTML Only**—then click **Send** (see Figure 4.4).

3. Your e-mail message will be placed in your Outbox and held until you go online. You will be returned to the Messenger window.

4. To go online and send the message and other messages in your Outbox, click the **Messenger File** menu and select **Go Online**.

Send button ———

Figure 4.4   The HTML Mail Question box asks you to designate a format for your e-mail message.

5. The Download box will appear that lets you choose whether or not new e-mail should be sent, selected newsgroups should be downloaded, or new e-mail for you should be downloaded. Select your choices and then click Go Online.

6. A Connect To box will appear that will dial in to your Internet Service Provider. Type in your password if necessary and then click Connect.

7. A Password Entry Dialog will appear. Type in your e-mail password and the click OK. The e-mail messages in your Outbox will be sent and any e-mail message new for you will be placed in your Inbox.

8. Once you've completed sending your e-mail messages, you can click the Messenger File menu and click Go Offline to close the connection with your Internet Service Provider.

If you are working online:

1. Click the **Send** button on the Composition box toolbar. Your message will be delivered to your Service Provider's mail server and on to the person to whom you addressed the message.

2. To check your sent messages, click the **Inbox** drop-down menu in the Messenger window and select **Sent**. All your sent messages will be listed (this step also applies to working offline).

Whether you work online or offline by default depends on how you set up your preferences for Netscape Communicator.

In this lesson, you learned how to compose and send e-mail messages using Netscape Messenger. In the next lesson, you will learn how to compose and send e-mail messages with Microsoft Internet Explorer.

Composing and Sending E-Mail with Outlook Express

In this lesson, you learn how to compose and send e-mail using Outlook Express.

Composing E-Mail in Outlook Express

You can create your new e-mail in Outlook Express either offline or online. Sending the e-mail will be done using the same procedure, the only difference being when Outlook actually connects to your Internet service provider via your Windows dialup. These minor differences will be discussed later in the lesson.

TIP **Compose Your E-Mail Offline** It will save you connect time and won't tie up modem lines with your service provider.

Opening Outlook Express

To compose new e-mail, you have to start Outlook Express. How the Outlook window looks will depend on how you've configured Outlook Express. You can setup Outlook to either open to the main Outlook Express screen or directly to your Inbox (for more about setting Outlook preferences see Part 3, Lesson 5).

1. To Start Outlook Express click the **Start** button, Point at **Programs**, then click **Microsoft Outlook**. The Outlook Express Window will open.

TIP **Internet Explorer** If you already have Internet Explorer running on the desktop, click the **Mail** toolbar button or the **Go** menu, then click **Mail** to start Outlook.

2. You can configure Outlook to automatically dial a connection, stay offline, or ask you if you wish to dial a connection. If the dial connection box appears select your connection and click **OK**. To remain offline click **Cancel**. You don't have to be online to compose a new message.

3. To open a new message window:

If you are at the Main Outlook screen, click the Compose a Message icon or click the Compose Message button on the Outlook toolbar (see Figure 5.1).

If you are in your Inbox, click the New Message button. A new message window will open.

Compose Message button—

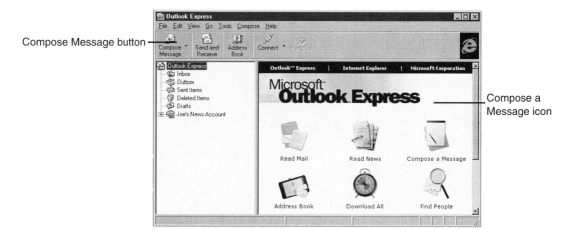

Compose a Message icon

Figure 5.1 The Outlook main screen provides you with two avenues for composing new messages.

Addressing New E-Mail in Outlook

Once you have the new message window open, you're ready to address the e-mail, give it a subject, and actually compose the message itself. The new message window is divided into two distinct panes: the Address pane and the Message pane (see Figure 5.2).

The Address pane is where you designate the e-mail address (or addresses) that you want to send the message to. There are actually three ways that you can include an e-mail address as a destination for the message.

- **To:** This is where you place the e-mail address of the primary recipient of the message. You can include more than one address by separating them with a space.

- **CC:** This allows you to copy (CC stands for carbon copy) the message to another e-mail address. The CC e-mail address will appear on the message that is received by the primary recipient or others that you copy the message to.

- **BCC:** This allows you to blind copy the message to another e-mail address. The Bcc e-mail address will not appear on the message that is received by the primary recipient or others that you copy the message to.

An e-mail message only needs a To: address to send it. To address your new message:

1. Place the insertion point to the right of the address book icon in the **TO:** box, then type the main recipient's e-mail address (see Figure 5.2). You can also select the address from your address book; click the **Address Book icon**. Double-click the address you wish to select in the Address Book and then click **OK**.

2. Place e-mail addresses or address book entries in the CC: and BCC: boxes if appropriate. You can move to these addressing boxes by clicking in the appropriate box or pressing **Tab**.

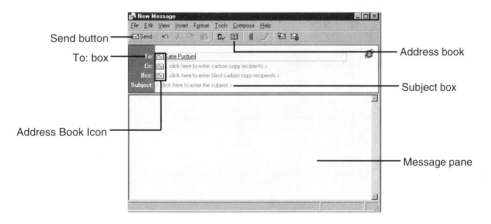

Figure 5.2 The message window is where you address and compose your new e-mail message.

TIP **Address Book** You can also insert an e-mail address into the CC: and BCC boxes using the Address book. To insert the address click the **Address Book** icon in the appropriate address box and then select an e-mail address from the list.

Completing the Message

Once you've designated who you wish to send the e-mail to, you're ready to designated the subject of the message and compose the actual message.

1. Click in the **Subject** text box. Type the subject of your e-mail message. Press the **Tab** key or click in the message area.

2. Type your message in the message area. Remember, e-mail messages are like memos; they are meant to be short and concise (see Lesson 12, Part 1 for more advice on the rules of etiquette regarding e-mail and other e-mail tips).

Sending the Message

Once you've addressed and composed your e-mail message you are ready to send it. The steps that it takes to get your e-mail to your service provider's e-mail server will vary slightly depending on whether you are working offline or online in Outlook Express.

1. Click the **Send** button on the Message window toolbar. If you've configured Outlook to spell check your messages before they are sent, the Spelling box will appear. Spell check your document; upon completion the new message will be placed in the Outlook Outbox. You will be returned to the main Outlook screen or your Inbox.

2. Once the e-mail message is in your Outbox you are ready to send the message to your service provider's e-mail server. Click the **Send and Receive** button on the toolbar.

3. If you are offline, a Dialup window will appear. Connect to your service provider with the appropriate password and click **OK**.

4. Once you are online or if you were already online a status box will appear, showing you the progress of the sending of your e-mail (see Figure 5.3). Once the e-mail is sent to your provider's e-mail server (and onto the Internet), Outlook will check for any new e-mail for you and then close the status box.

Figure 5.3   The Send and Receive status box keeps you apprised of your e-mail transfer.

After you send the e-mail to your Internet mail server, you can compose more new messages, read your new messages, or exit Outlook Express. The great thing about using e-mail software that is integrated with a Web browser like Internet Explorer is that you can browse the Web and then quickly connect to your e-mail account without starting a completely different e-mail client package.

In this lesson, you learned how to compose and send e-mail messages using Outlook Express. In the next lesson, you will learn how to compose and send e-mail messages with America Online.

Composing and Sending E-Mail with AOL

6

In this lesson, you learn how to create an e-mail message.
You'll learn how to edit and apply different styles to the text,
and how to send it.

Create a New E-Mail Message with AOL

You can compose e-mail whether you're connected to AOL (online) or not (offline). The composition process is the same in either case. The only difference is how you send your message, and that's explained later in this lesson.

 TIP   **Save Money!**   Composing your e-mail offline will save you money. Since you aren't connected to AOL, there are no online charges, and you aren't using any of your free hours for the month.

To begin the e-mail process, select **Compose Mail** from the **Mail** menu, or click the **Compose Mail** (pencil and paper) icon on the toolbar. Doing so opens a blank mail form (see Figure 6.1).

 TIP   **Shortcut**   Use the keyboard shortcut **Ctrl+M** to compose mail.

 TIP   **Mac Shortcut**   Mac users can compose mail by using the ⌘+**M** keyboard shortcut.

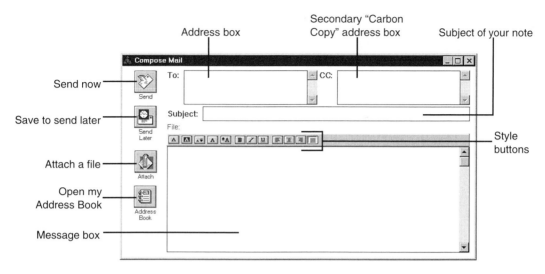

Address box

Secondary "Carbon Copy" address box

Subject of your note

Send now

Save to send later

Attach a file

Open my Address Book

Message box

Style buttons

Figure 6.1   A blank e-mail form.

Filling In the E-Mail Form

Once the blank form is open on your screen, compose your message by following these steps:

1. Click the **To** box and type the screen name(s) of the person(s) to whom you're sending the message. If you're entering more than one name, separate the names with commas: Name, Another name, Yet another name (you'll learn more about screen names later in this lesson).

2. (Optional) Click in the **CC** box and type the screen name(s) of anyone you want to receive a *copy* of the message. Again, if you're entering more than one name, separate the names with commas.

3. Click in the **Subject** box and type a brief description of the message's subject. You only have the amount of space shown in Figure 6.1, so be as brief as possible.

4. Click in the **Message** box and type your message. You have as much or as little space as you need to write your message.

TERM

CC   Short for Carbon Copy, from the days when you had to use carbon paper to make multiple copies of a business letter.

Sending CC copies (step 2) is optional; however, you always need to have the To, Subject, and Message boxes filled before AOL will even *try* to send your message.

Edit and Apply Styles to Your E-Mail

AOL's e-mail editor has many features of a basic word processing program:

- Double-click a word to select that word.
- Drag over two or more words to select longer passages.
- Use your arrow and delete keys to selectively delete characters, spaces, and more.

Also, like a word processor, you can add special formatting to your e-mail messages by using the style buttons found just above the message box.

To choose a style, read the next two steps:

- Select the text you want to format.
- Then click the appropriate style button(s). In order of appearance, the style buttons are:

Text Color	Colors the selected text.
Background Color	Applies a color behind text.
Reduce Font Size	Shrinks the selected text.
Reset Font Size	Makes text your preferred size (see Lesson 3).
Enlarge Font	Makes text bigger.
Bold	Turns text bold.
Italic	Italicizes the selected text.
Underline	Underlines the selected text.
Align Left	Gives text a smooth left edge.
Center	Centers text in your message.
Align Right	Gives text a smooth right edge.
Justify	Gives text smooth left and right edges.

TIP **Color Quick Tip** When you select either of the color options, you'll be asked to select a color from the color palette (see Figure 6.2). Just click the color you want to use, then click OK. To select a custom color, click Define Custom Colors and you can choose from a wheel of all available colors.

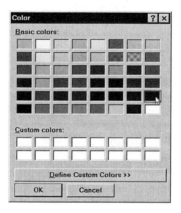

Figure 6.2 Your basic color choices.

You can see an example of all these formats in use in Figure 6.3.

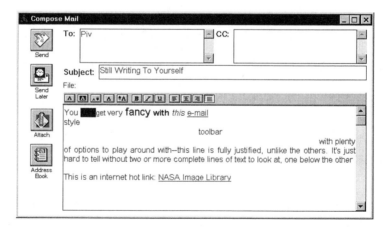

Figure 6.3 Your styling options at work.

That's e-mail composition in a nutshell. You can, however, get even fancier. For example, if you've used your computer to create a beautiful picture, or write a great story, you can attach the file to e-mail and share it with your online friends.

Attaching a File to E-Mail

The process is simple. First, compose and address your mail as described
previously, then:

1. Click the **Attach** button at the left side of the mail form. That gives you the
Attach File dialog box shown in Figure 6.4.

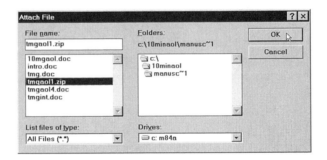

Figure 6.4   The Attach File dialog box.

2. The Attach File dialog box works the same as an Open File dialog box.
Navigate to the file you want to send. Click the file's name, to select it, then
click **OK**.

3. The dialog box will go away, and you'll return to the e-mail form. You'll
see the path statement to the file you selected displayed where it says **File**
on the form, just below the subject box. The file is now attached to your
message.

Path Statement   The map that tells AOL where your file is stored is called
a path statement.

You'll also notice that the Attach button has become a Detach button. If you
change your mind about sending the file, click **Detach** and the file will be
removed from your mail (the actual file is *not* affected, so don't worry).

Send Your Mail

As I mentioned earlier, you can compose mail whether you are currently
connected to AOL or not. However, to send your mail, you must be connected.

While Online

If you choose to compose mail while connected to AOL, sending it off is a simple affair. When you're done composing your letter, simply click **Send**. America Online will think about it for a moment, then it will whisk your letter off for delivery. When you have a file attached to a piece of e-mail, a status box appears, showing you the status of the *upload*.

 Upload The technical term for the process of sending a file from your computer to America Online, or any remote computer.

When the file has been sent, the status box will go away, and the e-mail window will close. A message box appears stating that the file transfer is complete. Click **OK**. At this point, your mail is off and running.

While Offline

You have two options for sending the mail you compose offline: remembering to send it yourself, manually; or by using a FlashSession. Both begin with a single click. When you've finished composing your e-mail, click **Send Later**. You'll get a message that says: **Your mail has been saved for later delivery...** plus some stuff about scheduling a **FlashSession**. For now, just click **OK**.

 FlashSession This is an automated way to send and receive e-mail, files attached to e-mail, and also files from file libraries. FlashSessions are covered in detail in Lesson 7.

 FlashMail This is a term for e-mail messages sent or received via a FlashSession.

The next time you're connected to AOL, select **Read Outgoing FlashMail** from the **Mail** menu. That will open the Outgoing FlashMail dialog box, shown in Figure 6.5.

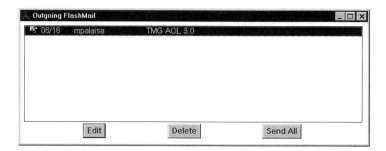

Figure 6.5 One lonely piece of mail, ready for delivery.

To deliver your saved mail, click **Send All**, and all the messages listed are sent at once. Before you send it off, though, you can do some other things with your saved mail:

- You can read and edit your saved mail before sending by double-clicking the piece of mail you want to edit. Make any changes you care to make, then click **Save Changes** or **Send** on the mail form.
- If you've changed your mind about sending a piece of saved mail, you can click the piece of mail you want to eliminate, and then click **Delete**. That mail will be permanently removed from your system—so make sure you mean it before you click **Delete**.

Understanding E-Mail Addresses

Your America Online screen name is your e-mail address. The same is true for anyone else you may meet on AOL. You can also send mail to people on other online services (CompuServe, for example, or the Microsoft Network), or with Internet accounts. The mail just takes a little more addressing. So, if my screen name is *joeguy*, you know my e-mail address (it's joeguy).

If you wanted to send me e-mail, and I had another service, such as the Microsoft Network, you'd address it like this:

> **joeperson@msn.com**

Here's what it means: **joeperson** is my account name on the Microsoft Network. The "**at**" symbol (@) tells AOL that the mail is going to be leaving their system. The "**msn.com**" tells AOL where the mail is going—**MSN** stands for Microsoft Network, and "**.com**" means a **COM**mercial service.

To send e-mail to a friend on CompuServe, you'd address it: *user*@**compuserve.com** where "user" is your friend's member ID number. Prodigy addresses will be *user*@**prodigy.com**. Internet addresses will look like user@*service*.**com**.

Internet addresses have more variation. The "service" portion is the name of the Internet access provider—and there are a lot of providers out there. Some Internet addresses will end with **.com**, others will end with **.edu** (for Education), **.gov** (for Government), and there are still even more variations.

The easiest way to cope with all of these address variations is to be lazy. Just ask your friends to send you e-mail, then you can easily add their addresses to your Address Book, and you'll never have to type one out manually. Lesson 7 explains how to use the Address Book.

Mail sent to *you* from another service should be addressed to *screenname*@**aol.com**, where "screenname" is *your* screen name. Mail sent to me should be addressed to **joeguy@aol.com**, for example.

In this lesson, you learned how to compose and address an e-mail message from scratch. You also learned how to apply styles to your message, how to attach files, and how to send your mail. In the next lesson, you'll learn how to read and respond to mail Using Netscape Messenger, the e-mail component of Netscape Communicator.

Receiving and Replying to E-Mail with Netscape Messenger

In this lesson, you learn how to retrieve your new e-mail messages using Netscape Messenger. You will also learn how easy it is to respond to the messages that you receive.

Receiving New E-Mail

Receiving new e-mail is just a matter of going online with Netscape Messenger and retrieving any messages that are waiting for you on your Internet Service Provider's e-mail server. How you begin this retrieval process will depend on whether or not you are working with Netscape Messenger online or offline.

Retrieving Mail When You're Offline

1. Make sure that you have Messenger open. If you are Offline, click the **File** Menu and then click **Go Online**. The Download box to go online will appear (see Figure 7.1).

2. Click the check box for **Download Mail** then click **Go Online** (see Figure 7.2).

Figure 7.1   Click the Messenger File Menu to Go Online.

Figure 7.2   The Download box is where you select Download Mail.

3. The Password Entry dialog box will appear. Enter your e-mail password in the box and then click **OK**.

 TIP   **Emptying Your Outbox**   If you have mail in your Outbox that you need to send you also can check the box for Send Messages; this will empty your Outbox.

4. Your Connect To box for your service provider will appear. Type in the appropriate password and click **Connect**. As soon as you are connected to the Internet, a status box will appear letting you know that new e-mail is being downloaded to your computer.

5. New e-mail messages will appear in the Messenger Inbox. You can tell the difference between read and new messages because the new message subjects will be in bold. To read a new e-mail message click its **Subject**.

The text for the message will appear in the lower half of the Messenger window.

6. If you want to open a separate window to read the new e-mail message, double-click its **Subject**. A new window opens for the message text (see Figure 7.3).

Figure 7.3 Double-click an e-mail subject to open a window for the message.

Retrieving Mail Online

When you're online retrieving your mail is very easy. In fact, you are only one click away from receiving your new mail.

1. In the Messenger window click the **Get Msg** button. A status box will appear and new e-mail will be downloaded to your Inbox.

2. To read your new messages click the **Subject**, and the text will appear in the Messenger window, or double-click the **Subject** to open a new window for the message.

Replying to an E-Mail Message

After you've received your new e-mail, you can reply to the messages via the Messenger window or a window that you've opened for a particular message. The sequence of steps to create the response is exactly the same.

1. To reply to a message in the Messenger window (or a message window) click the message **Subject**. Then click the **Reply** button on the Messenger.

Select either **Reply to Sender** or **Reply to Sender and All Recipients** as shown in Figure 7.4. A new window will open for your e-mail reply.

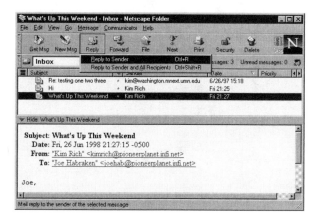

Figure 7.4   Click Reply to send a response to an e-mail message.

2. The e-mail address or addresses for the reply already appear in the appropriate boxes. The subject (with re: added to show it's a reply) and the text from the original message also will appear in the reply window. Add your response by typing it below the original e-mail in the message area.

3. If you want to spell check your reply, click the **Spelling** button. The Spelling box will open and walk you through the process of checking your reply for spelling errors. When the spell check is completed click **Done**.

4. When you have completed your reply, click the **Send** button on the toolbar, as shown in Figure 7.5. If you are online, your message will be sent immediately. If you are offline, the message will be placed in your Outbox until you go online.

Send button—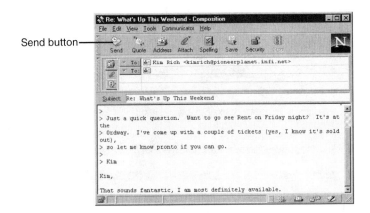

Figure 7.5 After you've completed your reply, click Send to send the e-mail message.

In this lesson, you learned how to receive your new e-mail messages using Netscape Messenger and then reply to them. In the next lesson, you will learn how to receive and reply to new e-mail messages using Microsoft Internet Explorer.

Receiving and Replying to E-Mail with Outlook Express

8

In this lesson, you learn how to retrieve your new e-mail messages using Outlook Express. You will also learn how easy it is to respond to the messages that you receive.

Receiving New E-Mail

To receive your new messages with Outlook Express, you must go online with your Internet Service Provider and download your e-mail from the e-mail server. You can work with Outlook Express offline or online. In either case, connecting to your provider and receiving your new e-mail is very straightforward.

Going Online and Retrieving Messages

1. Start Outlook Express via the **Start** menu or an icon on your desktop. When the Outlook window appears, an Outlook Express startup dialog box will also appear. This box allows you to immediately connect to your service provider and retrieve new mail.

2. To connect to your service provider, click the drop-down arrow in the Outlook Express startup box and select the Dialup Connection to your provider. Then click **OK**. A dialup box will appear, provide any necessary passwords, and then click **Connect**. After you connect to your service provider, you check for your new e-mail in the Outlook window.

TIP **Automatic Connection** You can also configure Outlook so that it automatically connects to your service provider without asking you during startup.
This option can be set in the Dialup tab of the Options dialog box.

3. To open your Inbox at the main Outlook screen, click the **Read Mail** icon.
This will take you to your Inbox. Click **Send and Receive** on the Outlook
toolbar to check for new mail (see Figure 8.1). A status box will open and
new mail will be received by Outlook.

Send and Receive button

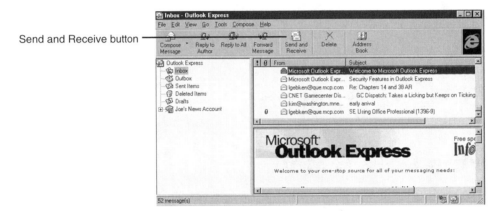

Figure 8.1 Click the Send and Receive button on the Outlook toolbar to receive new
mail.

TIP **Inbox Icon** You can also get to your Inbox by clicking the Inbox button in
the Outlook bar.

4. New messages will appear in your Inbox in bold. To view a new message
click the subject listing for the e-mail and the message will appear in the
Preview pane at the bottom of the Outlook window. If you want to open a
separate window to view the message, double-click the subject in the Inbox
(see Figure 8.2).

If you are already in Outlook Express and want to check for new messages, you
use the same button—Send and Receive. When you do this, you will be connected to your service provider via a dialup box and new messages will be
downloaded.

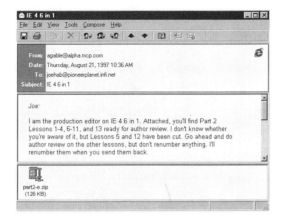

Figure 8.2 Double-click a message subject in the Inbox to open a separate Message window.

TIP **Sending E-Mail from the Outbox** If you have mail in your Outbox that you need to send, clicking **Send and Receive** will also empty your Outbox.

Replying to an E-Mail Message

Once you've received your new e-mail, you can reply to the messages. You can reply to messages in your Inbox window or a window that you've opened by double-clicking a particular message. Whether you reply to a message listed in the Inbox or to a message that you've opened, you will basically follow the same steps to create your reply.

1. To reply to a message in the Inbox, click the message **Subject**. Then click the **Reply to Author** button on the Outlook toolbar. If your message is open in its own window, click the **Reply to Author** button on the toolbar. Both these actions will open up a Reply window (see Figure 8.3).

2. The e-mail address or addresses for the reply already appear in the appropriate boxes. The subject (with re: added to show it's a reply) and the text from the original message will also appear in the reply window. Add your response by typing it above the original e-mail in the message area.

3. You can spell check your reply; click the **Tools** menu, then click **Spelling**. When the spelling check is complete, you are returned to the Reply Window.

333

Send button ───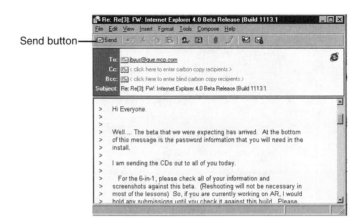

Figure 8.3 Click Reply to Author in the Inbox or in a Message window to open up a Reply window.

TIP **Configuring Outlook** You can configure Outlook so that it automatically spell checks your messages before you send them (including replies). You can set this option in the **Spelling** tab of the **Options** dialog box (see Part 3, Lesson 2 for more about configuring Outlook Express).

4. When you have completed your reply, click the Send button on the toolbar. Your message will be placed in your Outbox. Then all you have to do is click **Send and Receive** to send the e-mail.

Replying to your e-mail messages in a timely manner is good Internet etiquette. You may want to check your e-mail once or twice a day so that you're not inundated with new messages at any one time.

In this lesson, you learned how to receive your new e-mail messages using Outlook Express the Internet Explorer e-mail client and then reply to them. In the next lesson, you will learn how to receive and reply to new e-mail messages using America Online.

Receiving and Replying to E-Mail with AOL

9

In this lesson, you learn how to read and reply to e-mail messages you receive on America Online.

When you send mail, chances are you're going to get some mail back. America Online isn't shy about letting you know when you've received mail. It speaks right up and says, "You've got mail!" All you have to do is read it.

Getting New Mail

You have three options for getting at your new mail. The first is to click the **You Have Mail** button on the AOL Welcome screen (shown in Figure 9.1). Or you can click the mailbox icon on the toolbar, or you can even select **Read New Mail** from the Mail menu.

Figure 9.1 You have mail!

TIP **Ctrl+R** This is the keyboard shortcut for the Read New Mail command.

TIP ⌘**+R** is the Macintosh shortcut for the Read New Mail command.

AOL will think about it for a moment, then present you with your mail.

Reading E-Mail

Whichever way you choose to access it, your list of new mail will appear in a window like the one shown in Figure 9.2.

Figure 9.2 Two new pieces of mail have arrived.

To read an item, click its name in the list box, then click **Read**. You can also double-click an item in the list box to read it. It will open in an e-mail window like the one shown in Figure 9.3.

At the top of the e-mail, you'll find four helpful bits of information. This is called *header* information because it lands at the top (head) of the message. Here is a list of the items in the header of a message.

- **Subject**: What the letter is about. In Figure 9.3, it's "work work work!!"
- **Date**: When the letter was sent (date and time). In the figure, the letter was sent 96-06-20 (or 6/20/96, if you prefer), at 01:31:57 EDT.
- **From**: The screen name of the person who sent it. "Razler" in the figure.
- **To**: The recipient(s), which is "Piv" in Figure 9.3.

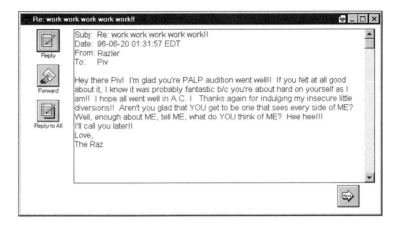

Figure 9.3 Reading your mail.

Of course, if the letter was only sent to you, you probably know who you are. The **To** information is more useful when a letter has gone to more than one person. There's one piece of information missing. Since this note was only addressed to me, there's no **CC** listing. If a Carbon Copy of this note had been sent to anyone else, the recipient's screen name would appear just below the **To** line.

When you're done reading the message, click **Next** (in the lower right corner of the mail form) and AOL will open the next message in your received mail list.

Once you move to the second (or any later) message in the list, you'll also have a Previous button. That button will take you back to the previous message. When you reach the last message in your list, the Next button will disappear (because there's no next message).

Replying to E-Mail

Chances are, you're going to want to reply to some of the mail you get. To answer your mail, open the letter to which you want to respond. Next, click one of the reply buttons on the left of the mail form. You have three options:

Reply	Sends an answer to the author of the original message.
Forward	Sends a copy of this message to someone else.
Reply to All	Sends your response to all the addressees of the original message.

337

When you click **Reply**, you get a standard e-mail form with the **To** and **Subject** boxes already filled in for you. The To box contains the screen name of the original author. The Subject box contains the original subject, with the abbreviation **RE** added to the beginning.

Even though all of this information is filled in for you, you can add or change any of the message contents. None of the text is set in stone. For example, you might want to send a Carbon Copy of your response to someone who did not receive the original mailing.

RE   These letters are the abbreviated form of "regarding," borrowed from business letters and memos.

Just type your message and send it by your favorite method (as explained in Lesson 4). When you click **Forward**, you also get a standard e-mail form. When forwarding a message, the To box is left blank. Type in the screen name of the person to whom you're forwarding the letter. In the message box, type a little introduction to the forwarded message (you know, "thought this might interest you" or words to that effect). Then send it by your favorite method.

If you choose **Reply to All**, it's the same as clicking the Reply button, except all of the original addressees (from both the To and CC addresses) will receive your reply.

Downloading Files Attached to E-Mail

From time to time, friends will send you interesting files attached to their e-mail. When they do, the mail window changes to accommodate the attachment. It will look something like the one shown in Figure 9.4.

Virus Protection   Even though it seems safe to download files from your friends, relatives, and so on, you should still watch for viruses. There are several virus protection programs available on the Net. You are best advised to run downloads through one of these utilities just to be safe.

Mail with an attachment has additional header information, just below the To or CC entries. First, it tells you information about the file, in particular the file name and size. In Figure 9.4, the File information reads: **PAUL.TXT (1968 bytes)**. That tells you that it's a small text file.

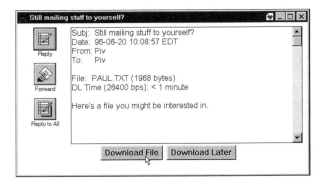

Figure 9.4   Mail with a file attached.

Below that, in the figure, the DL Time information looks like this: **(26400 bps) < 1 minute**. That means that you're connected to America Online at 26,400 bits per second (which is pretty fast) and that it will take less than a minute to send the file to your computer.

 <   This is the mathematical symbol for "less than." The symbol for "greater than" is **>**.

These two tidbits of information will help you decide if you want to download the attachment now, later, or at all. To start the download immediately, click **Download File**. The Save dialog box appears. Choose the directory in which you want the file stored on your computer, then click OK. You'll get a **File Transfer Status** display showing you how the download is proceeding.

When the file has been transferred, you'll get a **Your file has been transferred** message. Click **OK** and then you can continue dealing with your mail, or whatever else you care to do online. If you'd rather wait until you're finished online, click **Download Later**. That will add the attached file to your Download Manager. If you don't want to do anything with the file at all, don't do anything.

In this lesson, you learned how to read and reply to your incoming e-mail using America Online. You also learned how to download files attached to that mail. In the next lesson, you'll learn how to manage all the e-mail files that you send and receive.

Managing E-Mail

In this lesson, you learn how to keep your e-mail in good working order, as well as how to manage the e-mail messages you send and receive.

Getting the Most Out of E-Mail

E-mail is an incredible communication tool that allows you to send messages around the world. However, if you don't manage your messages, both messages sent and received, you won't get the full potential out of this fantastic resource.

Strategies for managing your e-mail can include simple things, such as always including a subject in every message. That way you and those who receive your messages will always know what a particular message is about before they even open it.

Other tactics for getting the most out of your e-mail have to do with how you manage the messages in your Inbox and other mail folders. If you follow a few general rules, you can cut down on possible e-mail clutter.

- Read messages as soon as you receive them. New messages will appear in most e-mail clients in bold. Select the message to read it.
- Reply to messages immediately. If a new message that you read requires a reply, it is e-mail etiquette to do so in a timely fashion. Then you can either delete the original message, or file it elsewhere.
- Delete messages you no longer need. You don't need to keep all of the messages you receive. Keep, or file, the ones that are really important, and delete the rest (see *Deleting Messages* in this lesson).

- File messages you want to hold on to in a special folder. You can create additional folders in which to file your e-mail messages (see *Creating New Mail Folders* in this lesson for more information).

Obviously, some of the strategies for managing your e-mail will be no different than managing a pile of papers on your desk. Some items can be thrown out, and others need to be filed.

E-Mail Software Solutions for Managing Messages

The fact that your e-mail client will have special features for managing your e-mail opens up additional possibilities for maintaining order when chaos is inevitable. Features like sorting, deleting, moving, and creating new folders can make your management tasks much easier.

Sorting Messages in Your Inbox

Every e-mail client will have an Inbox. This is the place where new messages that you receive are stored. One way to keep order in your Inbox is to sort your messages. E-mail clients differ on their abilities to sort your e-mail, however, Microsoft's Outlook Express and Netscape Messenger make this task fairly simple (and use close to the same strategy). In these two mail clients (and many others), you can sort your mail by Sender, Subject, and Date Received. Being able to sort your mail may help you in deciding which e-mail to delete and which e-mail you need to quickly reply to.

To sort your e-mail in Express:

1. Click the appropriate heading box—to sort by sender click **From** (in Messenger click **Sender**). Your e-mail will be sorted in ascending order by the name of the sender.

2. To switch the order of the sort from ascending to descending, click the heading again; in this case, click **From.**

3. You can also sort your e-mail via the View menu. Click **View** then click **Sort**. The different parameters (Sender, Date, and Subject) are listed. You can sort them in ascending or descending order (see Figure 10.1)

Figure 10.1   You can sort your e-mail messages by clicking a particular heading such as Sender, or by using the View menu.

 TIP   **Check Your E-Mail Frequently**   Get in the habit of checking your e-mail at least once a day. This will keep a lot of new e-mail messages from building up in the Inbox.

Deleting Messages

Once you've read and replied to a message, you can either delete it or place it in a special folder for later reference. Deleting an item in a mail client is very straightforward.

1. Select the e-mail message in the Message window.

2. Click **Delete** on the toolbar. The e-mail message is removed from the Inbox.

When you delete a message, most e-mail packages (such as Outlook Express and Messenger) place deleted messages in a special folder either called *Deleted Items* or *Trash*. You can configure your e-mail client to automatically empty the Deleted items or Trash folder when you exit the software as shown in Figure 10.2.

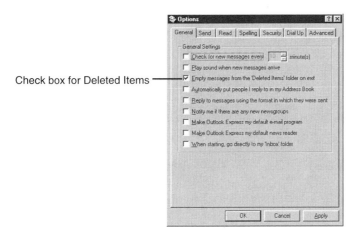

Check box for Deleted Items

Figure 10.2   E-mail clients such as Outlook Express can be configured to automatically empty the Deleted items folder when you exit the software.

Creating Folders

Another way to keep the e-mail clutter under control is to create special folders that hold e-mail messages by subject or send or by some other identifying criteria. Remember, only keep the e-mail that you absolutely must keep. If maintaining only an Inbox works for you, don't create additional folders.

In Outlook Express, it's very easy to create a new folder:

1. Click the **Outlook Express** icon in the Folder pane of the Outlook Window. This will make sure that the folder is created in the main tree of the Outlook folders.

2. Click the **File** menu, then click **New**. A list of possible new items (Message, Folder, Window) will appear; click **Folder**. The new folder will appear in the Folder pane of the Outlook window.

3. Double-click the folder to open it (see Figure 10.3). The folder is empty (you will learn to move messages in the next part of this lesson).

New Folder

Figure 10.3   E-mail clients like Outlook Express provide an easy method for creating new message folders.

343

TIP **Creating Folders** Netscape Messenger allows you to create folders using one of two ways. You can either select the Communicator menu and click **Message Center,** or you can click **File, New Folder** from Messenger's menu bar. Then you will be able to manipulate folders and messages as detailed in this section of the lesson.

Filing Messages in Folders

If you just can't bear to part with certain messages, you can place them in a folder other than your Inbox for safekeeping. Create a new folder in your e-mail client as detailed in the preceding section. Then you just need to copy, or move, the file to the appropriate folder. Outlook Express and Netscape Messenger use very similar menu commands to move and copy files.

1. In your e-mail client's Inbox (in this example, Outlook Express; see Figure 10.4), select a message or messages.

2. Click the **Edit** menu, then click **Move to Folder** (or **Copy to Folder** if you want a copy). The Move box will appear containing all of your folders and their names.

3. Select the appropriate folder and click **OK**. The files will be moved to the folder.

You can select a series of messages by clicking the first one, and then pressing the **Shift** key and clicking the last selection. Multiple messages which are not in a series can be selected by clicking the first message, and holding down the **Control** key while clicking the others.

Figure 10.4 You can easily move e-mail messages to a new folder in an e-mail client like Outlook Express.

TIP **The Inbox Assistant** Microsoft Outlook has an Inbox Assistant that can be used to direct certain types of mail to folders that you've created.

Using some type of strategy for managing your mail will not only make your e-mail experience more pleasant, but it should let you get more out of e-mail as a communication avenue. Well-organized subject folders and a clean inbox can really keep your e-mail client running efficiently.

In this lesson, you learned some of the ways that you can manage your e-mail. In the next lesson, you will learn how to filter the mail that you receive.

Filtering E-Mail

In this lesson, you learn how to filter the e-mail that you receive.

Organizing Your E-Mail Using Filters

You've already learned that keeping your e-mail folders organized will help you to obtain more from your e-mail account. Another way to approach the organization of incoming e-mail messages is through *filtering*. Most e-mail clients allow you to set certain rules that take effect when an incoming message is placed in your Inbox. For instance, if you get a lot of messages from a guy named Joe, you can set up your e-mail software to automatically filter all the messages from Joe into a special folder that could be called *Joe*.

TERM   **Filtering**   A way to set rules so that the e-mail messages you receive are placed in a folder of your choice.

Junk E-Mail and Flames

Another positive aspect of e-mail filtering is that you can deal with junk e-mail without reading it. Sometimes called *Spam*, junk e-mail is unsolicited mail that you get from companies or individuals. Since e-mail is quickly becoming an alternative to regular mail, it's not uncommon for you to end up on someone's mailing list without you knowing it. You can filter these junk messages directly into your Trash or Delete folder.

TERM   **Spam**   This term refers to posting a UseNet message to multiple newsgroups. See Part 4 for tons of information on newsgroups. Spamming is also used to refer to messages that are sent unsolicited to a large group of e-mail addresses. It's the equivalent of the junk mail you receive in your postal mail box.

Another type of annoying e-mail is called the *flame*. A *flame* is an extremely negative e-mail message that is usually in response to a breach of Internet etiquette that you may have unknowingly committed. Flames usually consist of just one message, and sometimes they will give you insight into what you did to deserve such an electronic lecture. However, some "flamers" can be very persistent and will inundate you with mail. You can use e-mail filtering to send these messages right into the Trash bin.

Flame Extremely negative or sarcastic e-mail that you may receive because of your misbehavior as a citizen of the Internet.

Responding to a Flame Sometimes a flame will be nothing more than a nasty message from a nasty person, so you can ignore it. Responding, other than an apology if you were definitely in the wrong, may only make matters worse.

Setting E-Mail Filters

As stated before, most e-mail clients (Outlook Express and Netscape Messenger included) will give you the ability to filter your incoming e-mail messages. You set the rules that the e-mail client uses to actually filter the messages.

The criteria that you set to filter your e-mail messages can be based on information that appears in the following area of the message:

- **TO:** box
- **CC:** box
- **FROM:** box
- **SUBJECT:** box

Filtering criteria in the TO:, CC:, and FROM: box will consist of e-mail addresses. Because it is unlikely that you will want to filter out all messages that are sent to you, you will probably not set rules for the TO: box.

You may want to filter out messages that are sent to you that have been copied to a particular e-mail address. You can set the e-mail address as one of the filter criteria when it appears in the CC: box.

Occasions may exist when you want e-mail from a particular address to go to a special folder or directly to your Delete folder. You can designate e-mail addresses that appear in the FROM: box for this purpose.

You may also want to send e-mail containing certain key words in the SUBJECT: box to be sent directly to a specific folder. The key words themselves would be the rule criteria for this type of filtering.

Filtering E-Mail in Outlook Express

Outlook Express supplies an Inbox Assistant that can be used to set rules for e-mail filtering. The Inbox Assistant can be launched from the main Outlook client window:

1. In the Messenger window, click the **Tools** menu, then click **Inbox Assistant**. The Inbox Assistant box will appear; it displays all the rules that you have set to filter your e-mail.

2. To add new rules click the **Add** button. The Filter Properties box will appear. Type your filter criteria into the appropriate box in the **Filter Properties** box.

3. The Filter Properties box also allows you to designate which folder this rule will filter e-mail into. You can Move mail, Copy mail, Forward mail, even Delete mail without reading. Select the appropriate action by clicking the **check box**. To select the appropriate folder for the rule click **Folder**. A Folder box will appear.

4. Click the appropriate folder in the Folder window and then click **OK**. The Folder box will close and return you to the Properties box (see Figure 11.1).

5. When you've set the criteria for your new rule, click **OK**. The Properties box will close and your new rule will appear in the Inbox Assistant window. To close the Inbox Assistant, click **OK**.

Figure 11.1 In Outlook Express, the Inbox Assistant provides the tools for filtering your incoming messages.

TIP **The Address Book** You can insert e-mail addresses in the CC: or FROM: boxes in the Filter Properties box in Outlook directly from your Windows Address Book.

Filtering E-Mail in Netscape Messenger

Netscape Messenger also provides a very robust mail filtering feature. It allows you to create conditional statements using parameters such as *contains, doesn't contain, is, isn't, begins with,* and *ends with.* For instance, you could create a rule that filters all senders with an e-mail address that begin with *joe* to a particular folder. Or you could filter all e-mail coming from senders in the same domain (such as *aol.com*) into a specific folder using *ends with.*

Messenger allows you to filter mail by sender, subject, body, even the date of the message. To set up filter rules in Messenger, you access the Mail Filters dialog box.

1. In the Messenger window, click the **Edit** menu, then click **Mail Filters**. The Mail Filter dialog box will appear listing all your current filtering rules.

2. To create a new filtering rule, click **New**. The Filter Rules dialog box will appear.

349

3. To create a new rule, name the filter and then use the drop-down boxes to set the criteria for the rule. For instance, you could select **Sender** in the If the box and then **Contains** in the condition box. Typing in a selection criteria in the text box would complete the rule (see Figure 11.2).

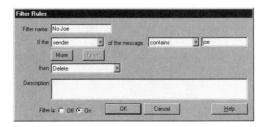

Figure 11.2   In Netscape Messenger, the Filter Rules dialog box is where you set the criteria for filtering your incoming messages.

4. Once you set the criteria for the rule, select the outcome of a match in the Then drop-down box. You can move the message to a particular folder or choose to delete the message. Once you've completed the various criteria for the new rule, click **OK**. You will be returned to the Mail Filter dialog box where your new rule will appear.

5. To close the Mail Filter dialog box, click **OK** and you will be returned to the Messenger window.

Filtering incoming e-mail messages can help you effectively manage the e-mail that you receive. It can also help you immediately deal with potentially offensive e-mail or junk mail.

In this lesson, you learned the basics of filtering the e-mail messages that you receive. In the next lesson, you will learn how to attach a file to an e-mail message.

Finding E-Mail Addresses

In this lesson, you learn how to use World Wide Web resources to find e-mail addresses.

Using the World Wide Web to Find E-Mail Addresses

Sending e-mail using the various e-mail client packages that we've discussed in this book is really straightforward and quite easy. However, if you don't have the e-mail address for a person you want to send a message to, you aren't going to be able to send the e-mail no matter what client software you use.

The World Wide Web provides several e-mail white pages that you can use as resources for finding a person's e-mail address. Examples are Four11, Bigfoot, and Yahoo! People Search. And each of these e-mail white pages has a search feature that you use to locate a person's e-mail address. A list of Web e-mail directories and their Web address is provided as follows.

E-Mail Directory	Web Page Address
Four11	http://www.four11.com
Bigfoot	http://www.bigfoot.com
Internet Address Finder	http://www.iaf.net
Yahoo! People Search	http://www.yahoo/people/search
WhoWhere?	http://www.whowhere.com

You can also do a search on the Web using WebCrawler or any of the other Web search engines available to find additional e-mail directories. Just search for *Email Directories*.

Connecting to an E-Mail Online Directory

Since most of the e-mail directories are reached via the World Wide Web, you will need to start your Web browser to begin your e-mail address search.

1. Connect to your service provider and then start your Web browser (in this case, Netscape Navigator).

2. Type the address of one of the e-mail directories into your browser's Go To or Location box and then press **Enter**. For instance, if you wanted to search the Bigfoot directory, you would type in **http://www.bigfoot.com** and then press **Enter**.

3. Your Web browser will take you to the Bigfoot Web Page (see Figure 12.1). To search for an e-mail address, type the person's name in the Search Name box, then click **Search Bigfoot**.

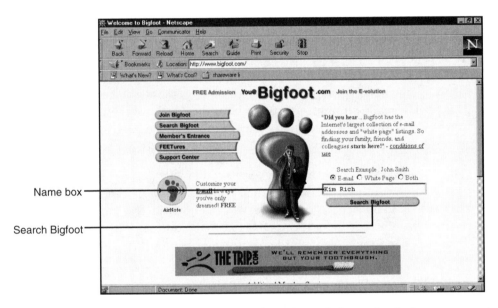

Figure 12.1 Bigfoot is one of a number of e-mail directories that you can use to find e-mail addresses.

4. A results page will be returned showing the e-mail address or addresses associated with the name that you typed in (see Figure 12.2).

5. To send e-mail directly to one of the search matches listed, click the e-mail **address**. Your browser's associated e-mail client will open with the address placed in the TO: box.

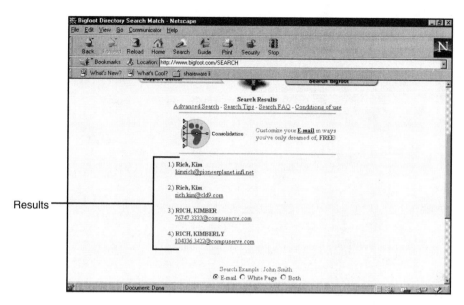

Results ————

Figure 12.2 Since Bigfoot searches by first and last name only, your search may provide more matches than you may really need.

The number of matches you get to your search will depend on how common the name is that you search for. John Smith will probably have a lot more matches than Clarence Magillacutty. If one search engine doesn't give you narrow enough results, you may want to try one of the other e-mail directories.

Another very large database of e-mail addresses is Four11. This e-mail directory also provides for more search parameters, such as name and location, allowing you to narrow the possible matches.

1. Type **http://www.four11.com** in the Go To box of your Web browser and then press **Enter**. You will be taken to the Four11 Web site.
2. Click the **Four11.com Internet White Pages link**. You'll be taken to the Four11 search page.
3. Type the first and last name of the individual. You can also type their city, state, or even the domain that their e-mail address is in if you know it (see Figure 12.3). Once you've typed in the search parameters that you know, click **Search**.

Domain The Domain is the name that is used by the company or organization that maintains a particular Internet Server. For instance Microsoft's domain name is Microsoft.com. Knowing the Domain name portion of a person's e-mail address makes it easier for you to find them.

353

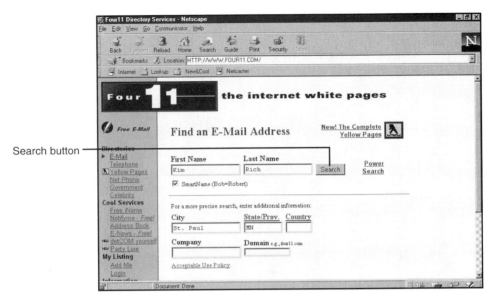

Search button —

Figure 12.3 The Four11 e-mail directory allows you to search by name, city, and state, and the domain name used by the person you are looking for.

> **TIP** When you go to one of the e-mail directory sites on the Web, make sure that you create a bookmark for the site using your Web browser; that way, it will be much easier for you to return to the directory.

Accessing E-Mail Directories Through Your E-Mail Client

Netscape Messenger, the e-mail client in Netscape Communicator, and Outlook Express, the e-mail client in Microsoft Explorer 4.0, both offer you direct connections to some of the global e-mail directories such as Bigfoot and Four11. These directories can be accessed in both of these e-mail packages in very similar ways. It's just a matter of using the command that opens the Address Book for the e-mail client.

For instance, to access e-mail directories in Netscape Messenger, make sure you are connected to your Internet Service Provider and have Netscape Communicator running.

1. With the Communicator Window open, click the **Communicator** menu, then click **Address Book**. The Address Book will open.

2. In the Address Book window, click the **Directory** button on the toolbar (see Figure 12.4).

Directory Button ———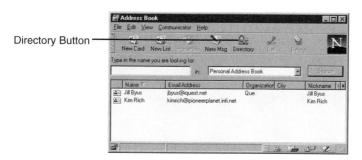

Figure 12.4 You can access several of the global e-mail directories via the Netscape Address Book.

3. A search box will open. A drop-down box gives you access to several e-mail directories. Click the drop-down box and click **Bigfoot Directory**.

4. Additional drop-down boxes let you select your search criteria based on the person's name, e-mail address, and organization. To search by a person's name, click **Name** and **Contains** in the first two boxes and then type in the name in the last text box.

5. You can add additional criteria boxes; click the **more** button. Once you've set all your search criteria, click **Search** (see Figure 12.5).

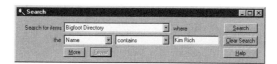

Figure 12.5 Select your search criteria and then type in the item that you want to match such as a name. Your search results will be displayed in the Search Window.

6. The results of your search will be displayed in the Search Window. Select the appropriate result of the search and click **Add to Address Book** to add the address to your e-mail address book. To send e-mail to the address, click **Compose Message**.

7. Once you've completed your e-mail directory searches, you can close the Search box.

355

Internet Explorer's e-mail client, Outlook Express, also allows you to do searches through its address book. Searching while in the e-mail client saves you the trouble of having to start your Web browser and go to a particular site.

In this lesson, you learned how to use the Web and your e-mail clients to access e-mail directories such as Bigfoot and Four11. In the next lesson, you will learn how to attach and send files with your e-mail messages.

Sending Files with E-Mail Messages

In this lesson, you learn how to attach a file to an e-mail message.

E-Mail Attachments

You can send files over the Internet attached to e-mail messages. This allows you to exchange graphics, sounds, even files created in various application packages like Microsoft Word and Excel via your e-mail account.

An attached file can contain just about anything. For example, you might send someone a spreadsheet file, a graphic (like your photo), or even a report in a word processing file. Your recipient will need some way of reading the contents of the file. For example, if you send a Word document attached to an e-mail message, the recipient must have a copy of Word to actually open the file.

Attachment Coding Systems

Since e-mail is normally just a text file, some type of system or process must exist so that your e-mail package sets up the attached file in a way that the person receiving the message can detach it and open it up in the program that you created it with. These processes are referred to as coding, meaning the attachment is coded so that your e-mail client can distinguish it from the text in the e-mail message.

Coding   It puts an attached file in a format that can be recognized by your e-mail client, distinguishing the attachment from the actual e-mail message.

One process that's included in most e-mail programs is called MIME (Multipurpose Internet Mail Extension). The problem with MIME is that it doesn't seem to work very well for people using online services such as CompuServe or AOL.

The most dependable process for sending files over the Internet is called uuencoding. Most e-mail programs (including Outlook Express and Netscape Messenger) automatically uuencode a file when you attach it to an Internet message.

There are some e-mail clients, however, that don't code the attachment for you. This type of e-mail program requires that you code the file before you attach it to the e-mail.

A very good uuencoder is WinCode. It can be downloaded from the Stroud's Consummate Winsock Web site at **http://www.stroud.com** (for more information on downloading files from the Web, see Part 2, Lesson 21).

Zipping Attachment Files

Before you even consider attaching files (especially large graphics or files of even moderate size), you should consider compressing the size of an attached file. An e-mail message with a huge file attached can take forever to send, eating up valuable connect time. Also some e-mail clients will have trouble downloading a message with an enormous attachment.

Shrinking the size of a file before attaching it to an e-mail message is very simple. And one of the best software packages to accomplish this task with is WinZip. WinZip compresses or "zips" a file or files. The result of this compression, a zip file, can then be attached to your e-mail message.

WinZip is shareware and can be downloaded from the WinZip Web site at **http://www.winzip.com/**. The fact that you can zip a number of files together into a "zip archive" and then attach the archive to an e-mail message, makes WinZip a must-have software tool.

Attaching Files to E-Mail Messages

The procedure for attaching files to your e-mail messages is very straightforward. This process is also fairly consistent among the widely used e-mail clients.

1. Create your e-mail message in your e-mail client. Make sure to include a subject heading and to address the message.

2. On the client toolbar will be an attach or insert file button. Click this button. A dialog box will appear that allows you to browse your hard drive and select the file you want to attach to the message.

3. Select the file to be attached and click **OK**. The file will be attached to the e-mail message.

TIP **Attaching E-Mail Messages** For information on attaching e-mail messages to the AOL mail client, see Part 3, Lesson 6, "Composing and Sending E-Mail with AOL."

The way the attachment appears in the e-mail message will depend on the e-mail client that you use. Outlook Express and Netscape Messenger both automatically uuencode the attachment; however, the attachment is represented differently in the message window.

Attachments in Outlook Express

In Outlook Express, files are attached via the **Insert File** button. Attachments appear as an icon in a special pane at the bottom of the e-mail message (see Figure 13.1).

You can check the contents of an attached file in Outlook Express by double-clicking the attachment icon. The file will open in the software that you created the item in. Zip Archives will open WinZip.

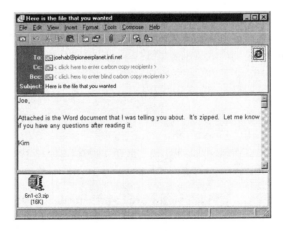

Figure 13.1 Outlook Express represents attached files as an icon in the message window.

359

Attachments in Netscape Messenger

In Netscape Messenger, the Attach button on the toolbar opens the file box where you browse for the file you want to attach to your message.

To view the attachment file name, you must click the Attachment icon below the TO: box in the message window (see Figure 13.2). The file name will appear. Unfortunately, you can't open the file itself from inside the message window.

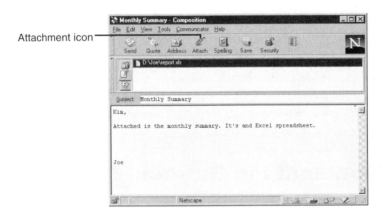

Figure 13.2 Netscape Messenger displays the file name of the attached file when you click the Attachment icon.

Sending the Message and Attached File

Sending your message with the attached file follows the same process for sending any e-mail message. Select Send in your e-mail client and the message and attached file will be on their way. If your e-mail client has a status box for the sending of messages, you will notice that an e-mail message with an attachment will take longer to send.

Attaching files to e-mail messages is a great way to send files quickly and economically. Documents such as your résumé can reach a prospective employer in minutes. And those manuscript pages that you just had to have in on time can be sent at the last possible moment.

In this lesson, you learned how to attach files to your e-mail messages. In the next lesson, you will learn how to retrieve and work with files that are attached to your incoming e-mail messages.

Receiving Files Attached to E-Mail

In this lesson, you learn how to retrieve, open, and save files attached to e-mail messages.

Working with Files Attached to E-Mail Messages

E-mail message attachments are a great way to send and receive files over the Internet. When you receive a message with an attached file, you will need to be able to retrieve and then open the file. Depending on the e-mail client that you are using, the procedure will vary. Some e-mail clients, such as Outlook Express and Netscape Messenger, give you access to the attachment via an icon or a link in the e-mail message. Other mail clients automatically separate the attachment from the message and save it to a predetermined directory on your hard drive (Eudora Light is an example of this type of e-mail client).

 TIP **E-Mail Attachments** If your e-mail client saves the attachment directly to the hard drive, you may have to use WinCode to decode the file and put it in a format that you can work with. Uucoded files will have the extension .uue (for more about WinCode, see Part 3, Lesson 13).

How Attached Files Look

Most e-mail packages will display the file attachment as an icon in the body of the e-mail message. This gives you easy access to the file itself.

More than one icon may appear in a message because you can attach multiple files to one e-mail message; however, the more attachments you have, the longer it will take to send and receive the message.

If you receive a message in Outlook Express that has an attachment, a paper clip icon will appear to the left of the message's subject line in the Outlook window. To view the attachments as icons, double-click the subject of the message to open a Message window. The attached files will appear as icons in a separate pane at the bottom of the Message window (see Figure 14.1).

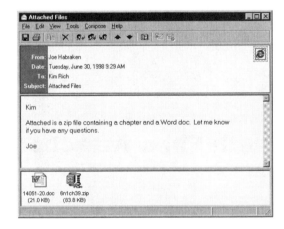

Figure 14.1   In Outlook Express, attached files are represented by icons.

In most cases, the icons will tip you off to what type of attached file you're dealing with. For instance, a Word document would be represented by a typical Word icon. Zipped files (files compressed using WinZip) will appear as a Zip icon.

 TIP   WinZip   Make sure that you have WinZip installed on your PC. It's a valuable tool for zipping and unzipping file archives. You can use it for more than just zipping e-mail attachments. It's a great tool for archiving files that you want to save using a minimum amount of hard drive space.

In Netscape Messenger, attached files are represented by an attachment box in the e-mail message. This box gives the name of the file, the type of file, and the encoding method used. A link is provided to the left of the file that allows you to save the file to your hard drive (see Figure 14.2).

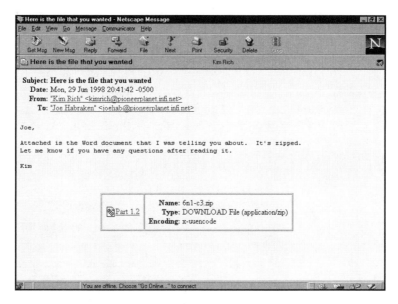

Figure 14.2 In Netscape Messenger, attached file information appears in a box in the e-mail message.

Opening and Saving Attached Files

How you open and save file attachments will vary depending on your e-mail client. Some e-mail software will let you open the attachment before saving the file. Others require that the file be saved and then opened.

One thing that you must keep in mind is that you won't be able to open attached files if you don't have the application in which the file was created installed on your computer. If you receive an Excel spreadsheet as an attachment, you will need Excel to open the file. If you receive a zipped archive, you will need WinZip to open the archive (and then you will need the appropriate application to open the unzipped file).

Opening and Saving Attachments in Outlook Express

Outlook Express provides a very straightforward method of dealing with attached files. You can open and save the file in the Outlook Message window.

To open a file:

1. Double-click the E-Mail Subject to open a Message window. The message and the attachment icons will appear in the new window.

2. To open a particular icon, double-click it. The appropriate application will start and the file will be loaded into the application. In the case of zipped files, WinZip will open and display the files in the archive (see Figure 14.3).

Unzipped files will be loaded into their parent application. This allows you to view the file, modify it, and then save the changes under a different file name.

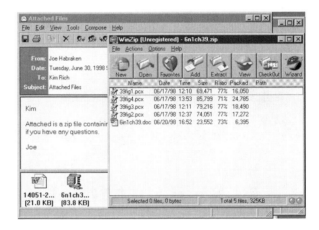

Figure 14.3 WinZip allows you to view and open the files contained in zipped archives.

To save a file:

1. Click the **File** menu, then click **Save Attachments**. The name of the attached file or files will appear. Select the file you want to save. A Save Attachment As dialog box will appear. This allows you to select the folder in which you want to save the file. You can also choose to save the file under a new name.

2. When you have selected the location to which you want to save the file, click **Save**. The file will be saved to your hard drive.

 TIP **Outlook Express** Since Outlook Express allows you to double-click attached file icons and open them in their parent application, you can save the file immediately after opening it. Use the application's **File** menu and the **Save As** command.

Opening and Saving Attachments in Netscape Messenger

Netscape Messenger also automatically decodes attached messages. You can open or save an attached message when you are in the Message window. The set of steps to open or save are identical except for one step when you determine whether you want to save the file to your hard drive or open the file in its parent application (a Word attachment in Word).

Saving or opening the attached file in Messenger:

1. Open the message with the attached file. The attached file information will appear in a box at the end of the message. A link for opening or saving the attached file will appear to the left (highlighted in blue) of the file information.

2. Click the attached file's link. A dialog box will appear asking you whether you wish to open or save the file (see Figure 14.4).

   Open it This will open the file in its parent application.

   Save it to disk The attachment will be saved as a file on your hard drive. A dialog box will appear giving you the option of changing the file name choosing the location to save the file.

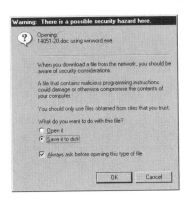

Figure 14.4 In Netscape Messenger, you can open or save an attached file by clicking the attachment link.

Managing Attachments

When you receive attachments, you should treat them like e-mail messages; meaning process them immediately. You should save attached files to folders that allow you to find the files later. If you need to rename an attachment so that it is easier to find later, do so.

E-mail messages with file attachments can take up a lot of disk space. Make sure that you delete the messages and the attachment once you've read the message and saved or opened the attachment. Using some of the e-mail management techniques that you picked up in Lesson 10 will also help you manage your file attachments.

In this lesson, you learned how to open and save files attached to e-mail messages. In the next lesson, you will learn about UseNet discussion groups.

Newsgroups

Understanding
Newsgroups

In this lesson, you learn the basics of using newsgroups to read and post messages on the Internet.

What Are Newsgroups?

Newsgroups are discussion groups where people can share knowledge, insights, and concerns. Users can find help; ask and answer questions; and even post graphics and other file types. There are over 20,000 Internet newsgroups covering such topics as politics, current events, software, automobiles, pets, tattoos, movies, supermodels, and romance.

To access a newsgroup, you need to use a special program called a newsreader. You use the newsreader to connect to an Internet news server, subscribe to your favorite newsgroups, and read messages posted by others. You can then reply to someone's posting or start a discussion by posting your own question or message. Figure 1.1 shows a list of messages posted in a typical newsgroup.

Internet Explorer, Netscape Communicator, and America Online all come with their own newsreaders, which are covered in the lessons in this Part.

Newsgroups, Newsreaders, and News Servers   A *newsgroup* is an online bulletin board, where people can read posted messages and post replies or start discussions. A *newsreader* is a program that allows a person to visit a newsgroup and read and post messages. The *news server* is a feature of the Internet, which makes newsgroups accessible.

List of posted
messages

Content of the
currently selected
message

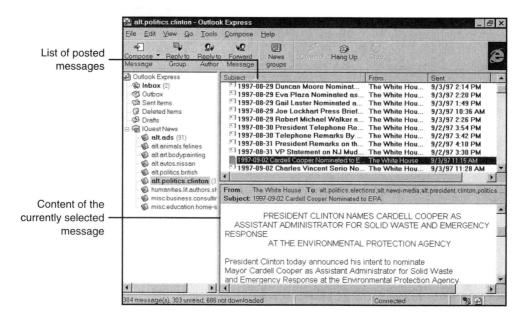

Figure 1.1   You can read and post messages in over 2,000 newsgroups.

Connecting to a News Server

Before you can read and post messages in newsgroups, you must first connect to a news server. Your Internet Service Provider should have given you the address of its news server. The address typically looks something like **news. internet.com**. You must then enter this address in your newsreader, so it can connect to the news server. Figure 1.2 shows a news server address entered in Outlook Express.

For detailed instructions on how to set up and configure your newsreader for your news server, see Part 4, Lesson 2, "Setting Up a News Server in Outlook Express," or Part 4, Lesson 3, "Setting Up a News Server in Netscape Collabra." If you are using America Online's Internet access, see Part 4, Lesson 4, "Accessing Newsgroups from AOL."

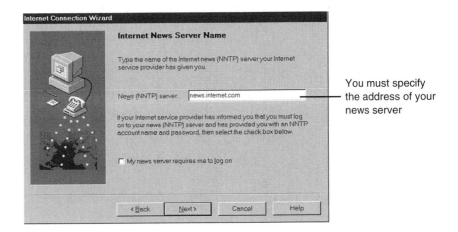

You must specify the address of your news server

Figure 1.2 Before you can access newsgroups, you must give your newsreader the server's address.

Subscribing to Newsgroups

Once you have supplied the news server's address, you can download a list of available newsgroups from the server. Most newsreaders have a Get Newsgroups command or a similar command. Downloading a list of newsgroups can take several minutes, but when the operation is complete, the newsreader displays a list of newsgroups you can access, as shown in Figure 1.3. As you can see, the newsreader displays the number of messages in the newsgroup, so you can determine how active the newsgroup is.

Most newsreaders provide tools for finding and subscribing to newsgroups that interest you. You can search the long list of newsgroups by entering search terms, such as pets, cars, or politics, to narrow the list. When you find a newsgroup that catches your eye, you can subscribe to it. This places the newsgroup on a shorter list of subscribed newsgroups, so you can access it more quickly later. See Part 4, Lesson 5, "Subscribing to Newsgroups," for details.

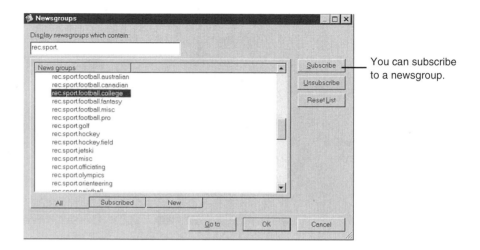

Figure 1.3 Your newsreader downloads a list of all available newsgroups.

Subscribe To mark a newsgroup, so you can select it from a short list of newsgroups that interest you.

Reading Messages

When you click the name of a subscribed newsgroup, the newsreader displays a list of *headers*, descriptions of the posted messages. Most newsreaders display a two-paned window, showing the header list in one pane, and the contents of the selected message in the other pane. To read a message, click its header. Or, you can double-click the header to view the message in its own window, as shown in Figure 1.4. For detailed instructions on how to read newsgroup messages, see Part 4, Lesson 6, "Reading Newsgroup Messages."

Posting Replies and New Messages

Posting a reply or starting a discussion is as easy as sending an e-mail message. You click a button to post your reply or message, enter a description of the message, type the message itself, and click the **Post** or **Send** button. However, you do have a few choices on how to post your reply or message:

- Post your reply or message publicly to have it appear in the list of messages, so all visitors of the newsgroup can read it.

- Post your reply privately, by sending an e-mail message to the person who posted the original message. This ensures that the person will receive your reply. Sometimes, a person specifically requests that you reply via e-mail.

- Post your reply publicly and privately via e-mail. This places your message in the newsgroup, so all visitors can read it, and sends a copy via e-mail to the person who posted the original message.

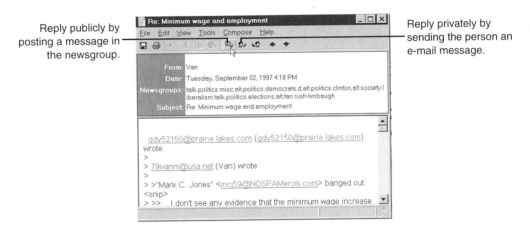

Reply publicly by posting a message in the newsgroup.

Reply privately by sending the person an e-mail message.

Figure 1.4   You can display a message in its own window.

Working with Attached Files

For the most part, newsgroup postings are simple text messages. However, you might encounter newsgroups where people commonly exchange files. For instance, in an application newsgroup, you may find program files that include patches or macros designed for that application. You might also find newsgroups where people post graphic files (pictures of their cats, sample photographs, and so on).

Most newsreaders display a link or icon that you can click to download or view the attached file. Simply click the icon or link. If you have a player for the selected file, the player will run and start playing the file. If no player is assigned to that file type, a dialog box appears, prompting you to save the file to disk.

TIP **HTML Postings** The newest breed of newsreaders supports HTML, the coding system used to format Web pages. With an HTML-friendly newsreader, you can add fancy formatting to your messages and insert links and graphics. This gives your message the look and feel of a Web page. You can also use your HTML newsreader to view HTML-coded postings. Both Netscape Collabra and Outlook Express News support HTML.

 Patch A fix for an application. Programmers commonly develop a patch to repair a bug in an application or add a new feature. Some software companies prefer to call them "service paks."

In this lesson, you learned newsgroup basics. In the next three lessons, you will learn how to access newsgroups using Microsoft's Outlook Express, Netscape's Collabra, and America Online.

Setting Up a News Server in Outlook Express

In this lesson, you learn how to run Outlook Express News and configure it to access a news server.

Setting Up Your News Server Connection

Internet Explorer 4 comes with an e-mail program and a newsreader called Outlook Express. You use the same interface to send and receive both e-mail and newsgroup messages. However, before you can use the newsreader features in Outlook Express, you must enter settings to specify which news server it should use and how to connect to it.

Your Internet service provider should give you access to its news server and provide you with the server's address. The news server is like a newspaper delivery person, bringing newsgroup messages to your computer. In order to read and post messages in newsgroups, you first have to connect to your news server. (You might also need a username and password to log in to the server.)

 TIP **Common News Server Addresses** If your service provider did not specify a news server, and you can't find out the news server's address, guess. You can usually just add "news." to the beginning of your service provider's domain name entry. For example, if the general domain name is internet.com, the news server address should be news.internet.com.

The first time you run Outlook Express News, it runs the Internet Connection Wizard, which leads you through the process of setting up your news server.

Take the following steps to run Outlook Express News for the first time and set up your news server connection:

1. Perform one of the following steps to run Outlook Express News for the first time and start the Internet Connection Wizard:

In Internet Explorer, open the **Go** menu and select **News**.

Click the **Launch Mail** icon in the Windows 95 taskbar, or select **Start**, **Programs**, **Internet Explorer**, **Outlook Express**. Then, open the **Go** menu and select **News**.

2. The first Internet Connection Wizard dialog box appears. Type your name as you want it to appear when you post messages to a newsgroup. (This can be your real name, or if you prefer to remain anonymous, you can type a nickname.) Click **Next**.

3. Type your e-mail address, so people can reply to the messages you post by sending you an e-mail message. Click **Next**. You are now prompted to type the address of your news server.

4. In the **News (NNTP) Server** text box, type your news server's address (for instance, news.internet.com). If your news server requires you to log on using your username and password, select **My news server requires me to log on**. Click **Next**. See Figure 2.1.

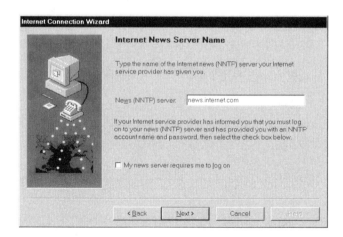

Figure 2.1 You must provide your news server's address.

5. If the server requires you to log on, select one of the following logon settings, and click **Next**:

 Log On Using if your news server requires you to enter a name and password to connect. Enter the required name and password in the appropriate text boxes.

 Logon Using Secure Password Authentication (SPA) if your news server requires you to connect using a digital certification.

6. Type a descriptive name for your news server (for example, Internet News) and click **Next**.

7. Click **Connect Using My Phone Line** or **Connect Using My Local Area Network** to specify how you connect to the Internet. Click **Next.**

8. Click **Use an Existing Dial-Up Connection**, and click the Dial-Up Networking connection you use to connect to the Internet. Click **Next**.

9. Click the **Finish** button. The Outlook Express dialog box appears, asking if you want to download a list of newsgroups from the server.

10. Click **Yes**.

Most news servers offer access to thousands of newsgroups, so it may take several minutes for Outlook Express to download the list of newsgroups. See Lesson 5, "Subscribing to Newsgroups," for details on downloading a list of newsgroups.

When Outlook Express is finished, it displays a dialog box listing available newsgroups. Click **OK** to close the dialog box, or skip to Lesson 5 to learn how to subscribe to newsgroups in the list.

Adding and Changing News Servers

If you have access to other news servers, or if you pick a new Internet Service Provider, you may need to add, delete, or change the settings of a news server. To add a server, take the following steps:

1. Open the **Tools** menu and select **Accounts**. The Internet Accounts dialog box appears, as shown in Figure 2.2.

2. Click the **News** tab. This tab lists any installed news servers.

3. Click the **Add** button, and select **News**. This starts the Internet Connection Wizard.

4. Take the steps in the previous section to use the Internet Connection Wizard to enter settings for the news server.

The Internet Accounts dialog box also provides buttons for removing servers you no longer use, changing a server's properties (such as its domain name or logon information), and marking a news server as the default server.

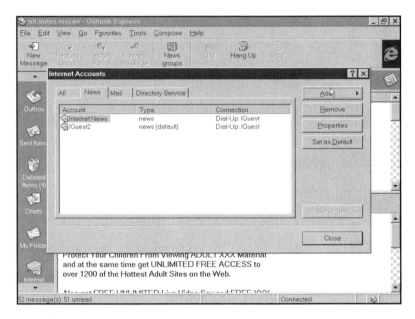

Figure 2.2 The Internet Accounts dialog box provides tools for managing one or more news servers.

The Default Server Outlook Express News allows you to set up more than one news server. However, only one server acts as the default server. If you've set up more than one server, you must mark it as the default server before using it to open newsgroups. Select the server, and click the **Set As Default** button.

CAUTION

Viewing Newsgroups from Outlook Express

Before you can view messages posted in newsgroups, you must subscribe to some newsgroups, as explained in Lesson 5. However, before we cover that topic, you should be aware of the various ways to run Outlook Express, and how to access the newsgroups folder. You can run Outlook Express by performing any of the following steps:

- In Internet Explorer, open the **Go** menu and select **News**.
- If you installed Internet Explorer 4 and your taskbar has an icon named **Launch Mail**, click the icon.
- Change to the Internet Explorer Suite program group, and double-click **Outlook Express**. (In Windows 95, open the **Start** menu, point to **Programs**, **Internet Explorer**, and click **Outlook Express**.)

The Outlook Express window appears, as shown in Figure 2.3. As you can see, you use the same Outlook Express window to view e-mail and newsgroups. When you set up your news server connection, Outlook Express displays a new folder for the server in the bottom of the left pane.

Click the icon for the news server. Because you have not yet subscribed to newsgroups, nothing happens. However, after you subscribe to newsgroups, the names of the subscribed newsgroups will appear in the upper-right pane.

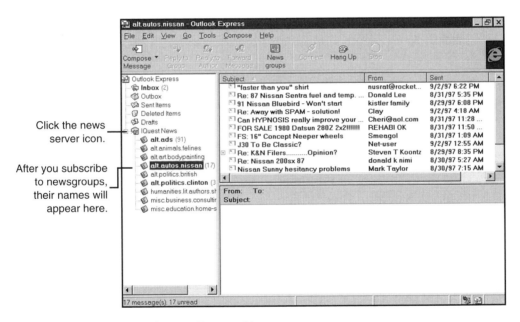

Click the news server icon.

After you subscribe to newsgroups, their names will appear here.

Figure 2.3 Outlook Express News.

Running Outlook Express News from Internet Explorer

Once you've installed Outlook Express News, you should set it up as your default newsreader. That way, whenever you choose to read a newsgroup from another application, Windows will automatically run Outlook Express News. To set up Outlook Express News as your default newsreader, take the following steps:

1. Open the **Tools** menu, and select **Options**. The Options dialog box appears.
2. Click the **General** tab.
3. Make sure there is a check in the box next to **Make Outlook Express My Default News Reader**.
4. Click **OK**.

To access newsgroups from Internet Explorer using Outlook Express News, you must set up Outlook Express News as your preferred newsreader in Internet Explorer. Take the following steps:

1. Run Internet Explorer.
2. Open the **View** menu, and select **Internet Options**. The Options dialog box appears.
3. Click the **Programs** tab, as shown in Figure 2.4.
4. Under messaging, open the **News** drop-down list, and select **Outlook Express News**. This tells Internet Explorer that whenever you click a link for a newsgroup, Internet Explorer should run Outlook Express News.
5. Click **OK**.

Now that Internet Explorer is set up to use Outlook Express News, you can open newsgroups from Internet Explorer by clicking a link for the newsgroup or by entering a newsgroup URL in the Address text box. Newsgroup addresses start with news: but do not include forward slashes. For example, type **news:alt.comedy.british** in the Address text box, and press **Enter**. Internet Explorer runs Outlook Express News, connects to the newsgroup, and displays a list of messages posted to the newsgroup.

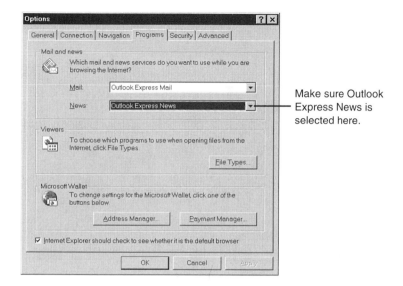

Make sure Outlook Express News is selected here.

Figure 2.4 You can set up Outlook Express News to run automatically from Internet Explorer.

 TIP **Go News!** You can quickly switch from Internet Explorer to Outlook Express News by opening Internet Explorer's **Go** menu and selecting **News**. If you are in Outlook Express Mail, simply click your news server in the folder list on the left.

In this lesson, you learned how to run Outlook Express News and set it up to access your news server. Skip to Lesson 5, "Subscribing to Newsgroups," to learn how to download a list of newsgroups and pick the newsgroups that interest you.

Setting Up a News Server in Netscape Collabra

In this lesson, you learn how to run Netscape Collabra and configure it to access a news server.

Starting Netscape Collabra

Because Netscape Collabra is a component of Netscape Communicator, there are all sorts of ways to run Collabra. To run Collabra by itself in Windows 95, open the **Start** menu, point to **Programs**, point to **Netscape Communicator**, and click **Netscape Collabra**. Netscape Collabra appears, as shown in Figure 3.1.

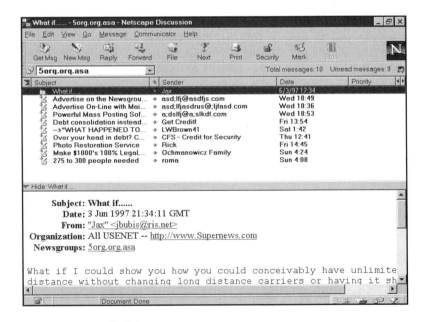

Figure 3.1 Netscape Collabra.

You can also run Collabra from the other Communicator components:

- In Navigator, Messenger, or Composer, open the **Communicator** menu and click **Collabra Discussion Groups**.
- In the Component bar, click the **Discussion Groups** button.
- To display a window for creating a message to post, open the **File** menu (in any of the Netscape Communicator components), point to **New**, and click **Message**.
- To have Messenger start automatically when you double-click the Netscape Communicator icon, open the **Edit** menu, and select **Preferences**. Click **Appearance**, and then, under **On startup, launch**, click **Collabra Discussions**.

Adding and Connecting to a News Server

To read messages posted in a newsgroup, you have to tell Collabra which news server you want to use. Hopefully, your service provider already supplied you with the domain name (address) of its news server. If you don't have this information, get on the phone to your service provider and find out. For a temporary solution, try **secnews.netscape.com**, which allows public access.

 TIP **News Server Domain Name** If your service provider did not specify a news server, you can usually just add "news." to the beginning of your service provider's domain name entry. For example, if the general domain name is internet.com, the news server address should be news.internet.com.

Once you have the information you need, take the following steps to set up Collabra to use the news server:

1. Open the **Edit** menu, and select **Preferences**. The Preferences dialog box appears.
2. Click the plus sign next to **Mail & Groups**, to expand the list of options.
3. Click **Groups Server**. This displays options for setting up and configuring the news server, as shown in Figure 3.2.
4. Click inside the **Discussion groups (news) server** text box, and type the domain name of your service provider's news server.
5. Don't change the entry in the Discussion group (news) folder text box, unless you have some good reason for changing it. This entry tells Collabra where to store information about the newsgroups you decide to read.

383

6. Make sure **Ask me before downloading more than 500 messages** has a check mark next to it. This prevents Collabra from downloading more message descriptions than you have time to wait for.

7. Click **OK** to save your changes.

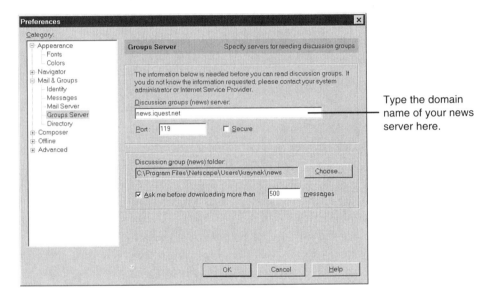

Figure 3.2 You must specify the domain name of your news server.

Accessing Newsgroups from Navigator

Communicator offers a couple of ways to open a newsgroup and read its postings. If you're in Navigator and you pull up a page that has a link for a newsgroup, simply click the link. Navigator automatically runs Collabra, which then connects to the newsgroup and displays a list of messages in that group. Double-click the message description to display the contents of the message.

Another way to connect to a newsgroup from Navigator is to enter the URL of a newsgroup in the Location text box, as shown in Figure 3.3. Of course, you have to know a newsgroup's URL before you can enter it. The URL for a newsgroup must start with **news:** (no forward slashes). Here are some URLs to try (although your news server may not provide access to all of them):

news:alt.comedy.british

news:humanities.lit.authors.shakespeare

> news:hawaii.sports
>
> news:alt.startrek.borg
>
> news:sci.anthropology

When you type the URL and press Enter, Navigator automatically starts Collabra, connects to the newsgroup, and displays a list of recently posted messages. You can then select a message to display its contents.

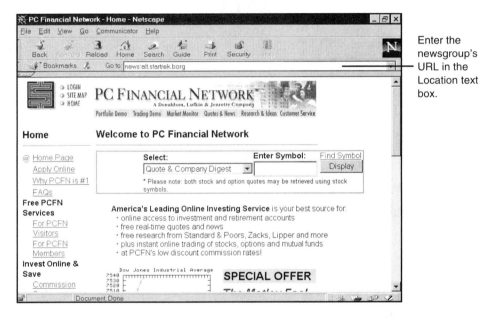

Enter the newsgroup's URL in the Location text box.

Figure 3.3   You can access newsgroups from Navigator.

The more standard way of connecting to newsgroups is to have Collabra download a list of available newsgroups from your news server. You can then select a newsgroup from the list.

In this lesson, you learned how to run Netscape Collabra and set it up to access your news server. Skip to Lesson 5, "Subscribing to Newsgroups," to learn how to download a list of newsgroups and pick newsgroups that interest you.

Accessing Newsgroups from AOL

In this lesson, you learn how to read and post messages in Internet newsgroups through your AOL account.

Connecting to Internet Newsgroups via AOL

Newsgroups are very similar to AOL's message boards, except on a worldwide scale. In newsgroups, you can read messages posted by millions of people all over the globe, and post your own replies and messages, as explained in Lesson 1, "Understanding Newsgroups." To access newsgroups through AOL, you use AOL's Internet Connection, as instructed in the following steps:

1. Run America Online.
2. Click **Internet Connection** on the Channels display.
3. When the Internet Connection window opens, click the **Newsgroups** button. The Usenet Newsgroups window appears, as shown in Figure 4.1.

 Usenet   Short for User's Network, the name of a major collection of newsgroups on the Internet.

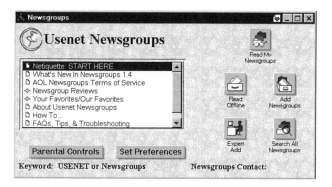

Figure 4.1 AOL's Usenet Newsgroups window.

Reading Newsgroup Messages

To read the newsgroups, click **Read My Newsgroups**. This opens the window shown in Figure 4.2. Since there are so many newsgroups out there, AOL starts you out with a list of about a dozen. These are mostly related to using the newsgroups, computer topics, and a few general interest subjects, such as pets and travel. Practice with these to start.

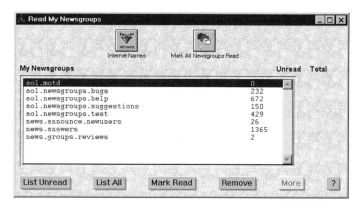

Figure 4.2 Your list of Newsgroups.

To open a newsgroup, follow these steps:

1. Double-click the name of the newsgroup in the My Newsgroups list. AOL displays a list of the messages posted to the selected newsgroup.

2. Scan the list to find a topic of interest.

3. When you find one, double-click its name. The message will open in a window like the one shown in Figure 4.3.

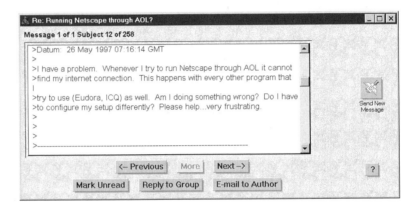

Figure 4.3 A newsgroup message.

When you look at the message display, you'll see the similarities between the newsgroups and AOL's message boards. They work very much the same. When you've read through the message, the buttons at the bottom of the window give you a number of options:

- **Previous** takes you to the message before the current one.
- **More** displays the rest of the current message (if it's very long).
- **Next** takes you to the message after the current one.
- **Mark Unread** flags a message you have already read as unread, making it easier to find the message again later. (When you've read a message, AOL marks it as read and won't display it again in order to cut down on newsgroup clutter.)
- **Reply to Group** lets you post a reply to the message. Your reply appears in the newsgroup, where anyone who visits the newsgroup can read it.
- **E-mail to Author** sends an e-mail reply to the author only, not the newsgroup.

Replying to a Newsgroup Message

A newsgroup posting may inspire you to post a reply to the message. Take one of the following steps to post your reply or send a private response via e-mail:

- Select **Reply to Group** to post a message to the newsgroup. You'll get a reply form like the one shown in Figure 4.4. The form will already be addressed to the appropriate newsgroup, and the subject will already be filled in for you. Simply type your response in the text box at the bottom, then click **Send**. If you care to, you can send an e-mail copy of your reply to the author. Click the check box labeled **Copy author of original message via e-mail** before clicking the Send button.

- Click **E-mail to Author** to send a message to the author only. You'll get a standard e-mail form, pre-addressed to the author of the message. See Part 3, Lesson 6, "Composing and Sending E-Mail with AOL," for details on sending e-mail messages.

Click the Send button.

Type your reply in the message area.

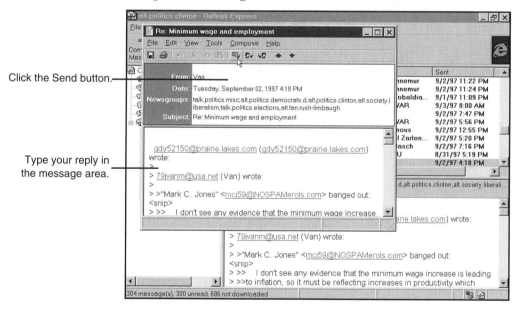

Figure 4.4   The newsgroup response form.

Starting a New Discussion

Newsgroups can ramble all over the place. If you can't find information you're looking for, or otherwise want to start a new discussion in the newsgroup, take the following steps to post your message:

1. On any message window, click **Send New Message**. You'll get a pre-addressed form like the one shown in Figure 4.4, but the Subject box will be blank.
2. Click in the **Subject** text box.
3. Type a brief description of your message.
4. Hit the **Tab** key. The insertion point moves to the message area.
5. Type the body of your message.
6. Click **Send**.

Adding and Deleting Newsgroups

Once you've explored the newsgroups that are already in your list (back in Figure 4.2), you'll probably want to add other newsgroups, and maybe delete some of the ones that are already there. The following sections provide detailed instructions on how to add and delete newsgroups.

Adding a Newsgroup

As you learned in Lesson 1, the Internet offers over 20,000 newsgroups. To add one of these newsgroups to your list, take the following steps:

1. In the Usenet Newsgroups window (refer to Figure 4.1), click **Add Newsgroups**.
2. Scroll through the list of available groups until you find one that you feel is interesting.
3. Double-click the newsgroup name. That opens a list of the newsgroup topics.
4. Click the topic that interests you. You can browse some of the messages by double-clicking the name to see if you really want to add it to your list.
5. Select **Add**. The selected newsgroup will be listed the next time you open Read My Newsgroups.

Deleting a Newsgroup

Although the Internet offers many newsgroups, some are not very active, and others are not quite what you expected. To reduce the clutter on your newsgroups list, you should delete the newsgroups you no longer access. Take the following steps to remove a newsgroup:

1. In the Usenet Newsgroups window (refer to Figure 4.1), click **Read My Newsgroups**.

2. Click the name of the newsgroup you want to delete.

3. Click **Remove**.

Managing Your Newsgroups

People post thousands upon thousands of messages to newsgroups every day. A lot of them will be of no interest to you. To hack through the underbrush of unwanted messages, you have two options:

- If the current crop of messages in a single newsgroup isn't of interest to you, click the newsgroup name in the My Newsgroups list (refer to Figure 4.2). Then click **Mark Read**. That marks all the messages in that group as having been read, and you won't see them again unless you click **List All**.

- If all of your newsgroups are yielding little interest to you, you can mark every message in all of your newsgroups as read, hiding them all. Click **Mark All Newsgroups Read** above the My Newsgroups list (refer to Figure 4.2).

Reading Newsgroup Postings Offline

If you spend a lot of time reading newsgroups online, and thus running up your AOL bill, you may want to consider reading your groups offline. To read messages offline, you must first set up AOL's Flash Sessions feature. You can then mark the newsgroups whose messages you want to download. When you activate the Flash Session, AOL will download messages from the selected newsgroup, and automatically disconnect.

The following sections explain how to set up AOL Flash Session and use it to download newsgroup messages so you can read them offline.

FlashSession   An AOL feature that lets you sign on, automatically send
and retrieve e-mail messages, download files, send and receive newsgroup
postings, and automatically sign off. This allows you to reduce your connect
time and hourly online charges. Although you can schedule FlashSessions, the
following section, "Setting Up AOL's FlashSession Feature," explains how to
initiate FlashSessions manually.

Automatic AOL   At the time this book was being written, America Online
was busy developing version 4.0, in which it has renamed FlashSession,
"Automatic AOL."

Setting Up AOL's FlashSession Feature

Before you can download and read newsgroup postings offline, you must set up
AOL's Flash Session feature. Take the following steps:

1. Open AOL's **Mail** menu and select **Set Up FlashSession**. The first time
   you select this command, the Welcome to FlashSessions dialog box appears. If you receive the FlashSessions dialog box, instead, click **Walk Me
   Through**.

2. Click the **Continue** button. The FlashSessions Walk-Through dialog box
   appears, asking if you want to download e-mail messages during the
   FlashSession.

3. Click **Yes** to download e-mail messages or **No**, if you do not want to
   download e-mail messsages. Another dialog box appears, asking if you
   want to download any files that may be attached to incoming e-mail
   messages.

4. Click **Yes** or **No**. The next dialog box asks if you want to send e-mail
   messages, which you have composed offline, during the FlashSession.

5. Click **Yes** or **No**. You are now asked if you want to use Download Manager
   to automatically download marked files during the Flash Session.

6. Click **Yes** or **No**. The Download Manager is not covered in this book. The
   next dialog box is the one we are looking for; it asks if you want to download messages from selected newsgroups.

7. Click **Yes**. You are now asked if you want to post newsgroup messages
   and replies, which you have composed offline, during the FlashSession.

8. Click **Yes**. The Screen Names dialog box appears, prompting you to enter
   your screen name and password.

9. Enter the requested information, and click the **Continue** button. The Schedule FlashSessions dialog box appears, asking if you want to schedule an automatic FlashSession.

10. Click **No**. (Automatic FlashSessions are not covered here, but you can go ahead and choose **Yes**, and follow the on-screen instructions, if you wish.) Assuming you clicked **No**, the Congratulations dialog box appears, indicating that you have successfully set up a FlashSession. Click **OK**.

Reading Messages Offline

Now that you have a FlashSession set up, you can mark newsgroups for offline reading. Take the following steps to read messages offline:

1. In the Usenet Newsgroups window, click **Read Offline** (refer to Figure 4.1). A window appears, displaying a list of your newsgroups.

2. Click the name of the newsgroup you want to read offline.

3. Select **Add**.

4. Repeat steps 2 and 3 for each newsgroup you want to read offline, or click **Add All** if you want to read all of your newsgroups offline.

5. Click **OK**.

6. Exit the Newsgroups window and any message boards you are connected to. (If the Newsgroup window is open, AOL cannot retrieve messages.)

7. Open the **Mail** menu and select **Activate FlashSession Now**. The Activate FlashSession Now dialog box appears.

8. To disconnect from AOL when AOL is done downloading the messages, click **Sign Off When Finished**, to place a check in the box.

9. Click **Begin**. AOL downloads the messages, and places them in your Personal Filing Cabinet. If you chose to disconnect when finished, AOL automatically signs you off when it is done.

CAUTION

Too Many Messages By choosing to read messages offline, you can get a lot of newsgroup messages, filling up your hard drive. To stop downloading a particular newsgroup, follow the preceding steps, but click **Remove** in Step 3.

All of the messages posted to the selected newsgroups will be downloaded to your computer and stored in your Personal Filing Cabinet. The Personal Filing Cabinet is an organizational tool to help you keep track of all the information you send and receive from America Online.

To read your messages offline, take the following steps:

1. Sign off from America Online, unless you chose to have FlashSession automatically disconnect you.

2. Click the **Personal Filing Cabinet** icon on the toolbar, or open the **File** menu and select **Personal Filing Cabinet**. AOL opens your Filing Cabinet (see Figure 4.5), which contains folders for Download Manager, Favorite Places, Mail, and Newsgroups.

3. Double-click the Newsgroups folder to view a list of your newsgroups. The folder displays a subfolder for each newsgroup.

4. Double-click the subfolder for the newsgroup whose messages you want to read. A list of message descriptions appears.

5. Double-click a message description to display the contents of the message.

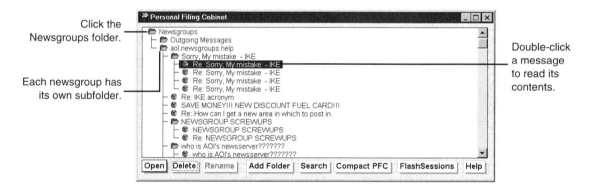

Figure 4.5 The Personal Filing Cabinet.

You can use the buttons across the bottom of the Personal Filing Cabinet window to Open, Delete, or Rename any item in the Filing Cabinet (except folders that AOL needs to operate, such as the Files To Download folder).

In this lesson, you learned how to read and post messages to an Internet newsgroup in America Online. In the next lesson, you will learn how to subscribe to newsgroups using Microsoft's Outlook Express News or Netscape Collabra.

Subscribing to Newsgroups

In this lesson, you learn how to add newsgroups to a list of your favorite newsgroups to make them easily accessible.

Subscribing to a Newsgroup

When you find a newsgroup that interests you, you should *subscribe* to it. When you subscribe to a newsgroup, your newsreader places the newsgroup name on a short list of newsgroups, as shown in Figure 5.1. You can then select the newsgroup to view a list of posted messages. The following sections show you how to subscribe to newsgroups in Outlook Express News and Netscape Collabra.

 Subscribe Subscribing to a newsgroup simply makes it more convenient to access a newsgroup. Subscribing in newsgroups is not like setting up a Web site subscription to have information delivered automatically to you. Nor is it like subscribing to a mailing list to have updated material delivered to you via e-mail.

 Subscribing in AOL To subscribe to newsgroups in America Online, refer to Lesson 4, "Accessing Newsgroups from AOL."

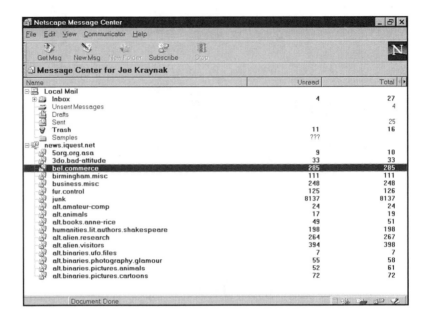

Figure 5.1   Subscribing to newsgroups places the newsgroups on a short list.

Subscribing to Newsgroups in Netscape Collabra

Once you've set up your news server, as explained in Lesson 3, you can use the server to download a complete list of newsgroups. From this list, you can select the newsgroups you want to subscribe to. Take the following steps to subscribe to newsgroups in Netscape Collabra:

1. Establish your Internet connection, and run Netscape Collabra. The Netscape Message Center appears, and highlights your news server.

2. Click the **Subscribe** button in the toolbar. The Subscribe to Discussion Groups dialog box appears, as shown in Figure 5.2. If this is the first time you have chosen to subscribe to discussion groups, Collabra downloads a list of all available groups. This may take several minutes.

3. Scroll down the list, and scan it for groups that might interest you. If you see a plus sign next to a newsgroup name, you can click it to view additional subgroups.

TIP **Search for Newsgroups** The list of available newsgroups may contain thousands of newsgroups. To narrow the list, click the Search for a Group tab, and type a search string (for instance, **dog**, **auto**, or **politic**) to narrow the list. Click **Search Now**.

4. When you find a newsgroup that interests you, click its name, and click the **Subscribe** button. Or click the dot in the Subscribe column next to the desired newsgroup. The dot changes into a check mark, indicating that you have subscribed to the newsgroup.

5. Click the **OK** button to return to the Message Center.

Click a plus sign to see a list of subgroups.

Click the dot next to a newsgroup name to subscribe to it.

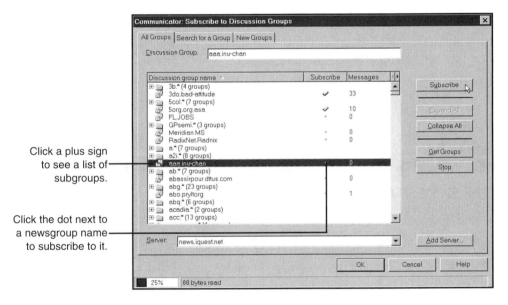

Figure 5.2 You can subscribe to newsgroups by selecting them from a long list of available newsgroups.

Viewing Your Subscribed Newsgroups

When you return to the Message Center, your news server (in the folder list on the left) has a plus sign next to it. Click the **plus sign**. The Message Center displays the names of all the newsgroups you subscribed to (refer back to Figure 5.1). You can double-click a newsgroup's name to display a list of messages posted in that newsgroup.

Removing Newsgroups from Your Subscriptions List

To unsubscribe to a newsgroup, you can delete it from the Message Center. Just click the newsgroup's name, and press the **Delete** key. You can also use the Subscribe to Discussion Groups dialog box by taking the following steps:

1. Run Collabra to display the Message Center window.

2. Click the **Subscribe** button. The list of newsgroups appears.

3. Click the check mark next to the name of the newsgroup you want to unsubscribe from. The check mark turns back into a dot, indicating that the newsgroup is no longer on the list.

TIP   **Right-Click Newsgroup Access**   Right-click a newsgroup name to view a context menu, which allows you to open the newsgroup (discussion group), search its messages, remove the newsgroup (unsubscribe), and perform other actions.

Subscribing to Newsgroups in Outlook Express News

Once you have set up your news server in Outlook Express News, you can download a list of newsgroups and subscribe to the ones that catch your eye.

You can subscribe to newsgroups in the Newsgroups dialog box. Take the following steps:

1. Run Outlook Express, open the **Go** menu, and select **News**.

2. Click the **News groups** button. This displays a list of all available newsgroups, as shown in Figure 5.3. If this is the first time you clicked the News groups button, Outlook Express may take several minutes to download the list of available newsgroups.

TIP   **Search for Newsgroups**   To narrow the list of available newsgroups, click in the Display newsgroups which contain text box, and type a search string (for instance, **dog**, **auto**, or **politic**).

3. In the list of available newsgroups, click the newsgroup to which you want to subscribe.

4. Click the **Subscribe** button. A newspaper icon appears next to the newsgroup's name, and the newsgroup appears on the Subscribed tab.

TIP **Double-Click to Subscribe** In the Newsgroups dialog box, you can quickly subscribe or unsubscribe to a newsgroup by double-clicking its name.

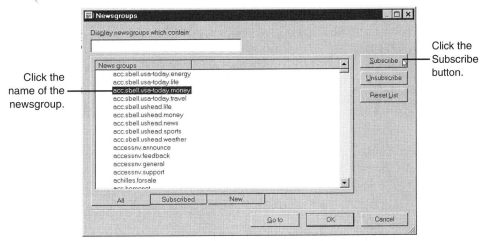

Click the name of the newsgroup.

Click the Subscribe button.

Figure 5.3 You can subscribe to newsgroups in Outlook Express.

Viewing Your List of Subscribed Newsgroups

When you subscribe to a newsgroup, Outlook Express displays the newsgroup's name in the folder list, directly below the folder icon for your news server. If there is a plus sign next to the news server folder, click it to expand the list (see Figure 5.4).

Click a newsgroup's name to view a list of messages posted to that group. In Lesson 6, "Reading Newsgroup Messages," you will learn how to display the contents of the listed messages.

Messages
posted in
currently
selected
newsgroups

News server folder

Click a newsgroup
to display a list of
posted messages

Subscribed
newsgroups

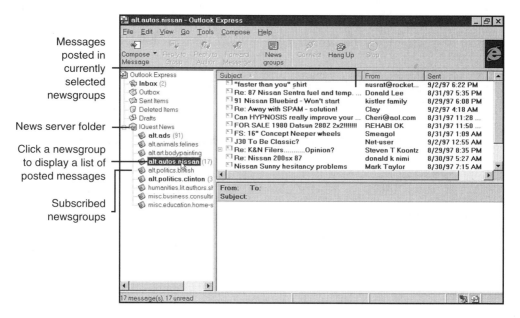

Figure 5.4   Outlook Express displays a list of subscribed newsgroups.

 TIP   **Outlook Bar**   If the folder list is not displayed in the left pane, you can turn it on. Open the **View** menu and select **Layout**. Under Basic, turn off **Outlook Bar** and turn on **Folder List**.

Removing a Newsgroup from the Subscriptions List

If a newsgroup is not very active, or you just lose interest, you should remove the newsgroup from the subscriptions list. You can click the newsgroup name and then press the **Delete** key to remove it from the list. You can also unsubscribe from newsgroups using the Newsgroups dialog box:

1. Click the **News groups** button in the Outlook Express toolbar. The Newsgroups dialog box appears.

2. Click the **Subscribed** tab. A list of only subscribed newsgroups appears.

3. Click the name of the newsgroup you want to remove from the subscriptions list, and click the **Unsubscribe** button.

4. Click **OK**.

In this lesson, you learned how to subscribe to your favorite newsgroups in Outlook Express News and Netscape Collabra. In the next lesson, you will learn how to read messages posted in a newsgroup.

Reading Newsgroup Messages

In this lesson, you learn how to pull up a list of newsgroup messages and read them in Collabra or Outlook Express News.

Reading Newsgroup Messages in Collabra

Now that you know all about connecting to a news server and subscribing to newsgroups, you probably want to read some of the messages you've found. To read messages in Netscape Collabra, take the following steps:

1. Run Collabra, if it's not already running. This displays the Netscape Message Center window.

2. Click the **plus sign** next to your news server's name. A list of subscribed newsgroups appears.

3. Double-click the name of the newsgroup whose postings you want to view. The Netscape Discussion window appears, displaying a list of messages in the selected newsgroup.

4. Double-click a message to display its contents. The message appears in its own Netscape Message window (see Figure 6.1).

5. Click the **Next** button to read the next unread message. (You can select options from the **Go** menu to read the next or previous message.)

Click Next to display
the next message.

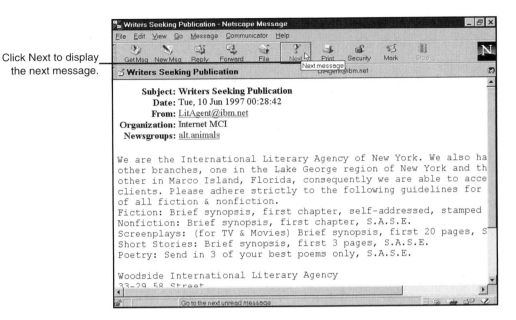

Figure 6.1 You can display a message in its own window.

Another way to read messages is to divide the Netscape Discussion window into two panes (it may already be divided into two panes). If the window displays a single pane, click the **blue triangle** in the lower-left corner of the window to display the message contents pane, as shown in Figure 6.2. Whenever you click a message description in the upper pane, the contents of the message appear in the lower pane. You can use the drop-down list just above the message list to select a different subscribed newsgroup or to change to your Inbox folder or another folder.

TIP **Article, Newsgroup, Message Center** When you double-click a newsgroup in the Message Center, the Discussion window appears, showing a list of messages in the selected newsgroup. If you then double-click a message, the Message window appears. Below the Netscape N logo in the Message and Discussion window is a button you can click to quickly switch to the previous window. In the Message window, click the button to go back to the Discussion window. In the Discussion window, click the button to return to the Message Center.

403

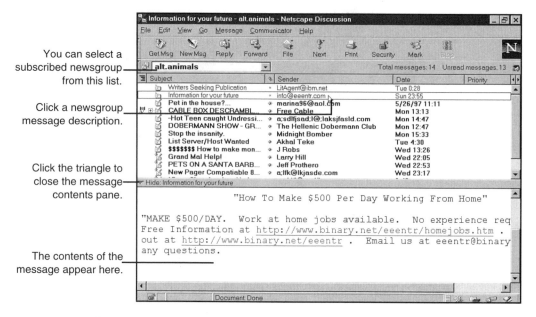

You can select a
subscribed newsgroup
from this list.

Click a newsgroup
message description.

Click the triangle to
close the message
contents pane.

The contents of the
message appear here.

Figure 6.2 You can display a list of messages and the contents of the selected message in a single window.

Viewing Replies to Posted Messages

As you are reading messages, you might notice that some message descriptions have a plus sign next to them. This indicates that someone else has posted a reply to the original message. Click the **plus sign** to view the reply(ies). You can then click the description of the reply to view its contents. To collapse the list of replies, click the **minus sign** to the left of the original message. See Figure 6.3.

A message and its replies are called a *thread*. To skip from one thread to another, open the **Go** menu and select **Next Unread Thread** (or press the **T** key). This allows you to proceed through the list of unread messages without having to view each message.

Thread A collection of messages and replies. By grouping messages and their replies together, Collabra makes it easy to follow an ongoing discussion.

Click the plus sign to view a list of replies.

Click the minus sign to hide replies.

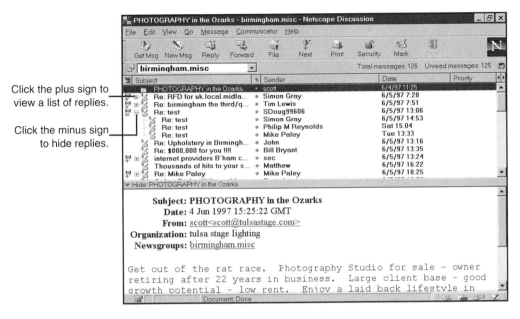

Figure 6.3 Collabra groups messages with their replies.

Sorting and Searching for Messages

If you connect to a newsgroup that contains hundreds of messages, sifting through the list may be time-consuming. To help, you can sort the messages. Simply click the heading above the column whose entries you want to sort. For example, to sort by name, click the **Sender** column heading. To sort by message description, click the **Subject** heading. You can change the sort order (for instance, from A-Z to Z-A) by clicking again on the column heading.

If you know of a specific subject or sender that you want to search for in the message list, you can use Collabra's search tool to hunt down messages. Take the following steps:

1. Open the **Edit** menu and select **Search Messages**. This displays the Search Messages dialog box, as shown in Figure 6.4.

2. Open the **Search for items in** drop-down list, and select the specific newsgroup you want to search.

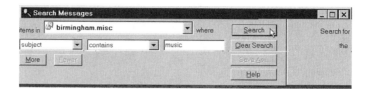

Figure 6.4 Collabra lets you search for messages by sender or subject.

3. Use the next three controls to specify what you want to search for. In the example, shown below, we are about to search the body of messages that contain "stan laurel." (Some servers allow searches on a limited number of fields; for example, you may be able to search only the Subject field, not the Body.)

4. You can click the **More** button and enter additional search instructions to narrow the search.

5. Click the **Search** button. Collabra performs the specified search, and displays a list of newsgroup messages that it found. Double-click a message description to read the message.

> **Other Newsgroup Management Options** The Netscape Message window offers many options for sorting and displaying messages. Refer to Part 4, Lesson 10, "Managing Newsgroups and Messages," for details.

Reading Newsgroup Messages in Outlook Express

Once you have subscribed to some newsgroups in Outlook Express, you can start reading messages in those newsgroups. Take the following steps:

1. Run Outlook Express News or Mail. The Outlook Express window appears.

2. In the folder list (on the left), click the button for your news server. This displays a list of subscribed newsgroups.

3. Click the name of the newsgroup where the messages you want to read are located. The upper-right pane displays descriptions of messages posted to the selected newsgroup, as shown in Figure 6.5.

4. To view a message, click its description. The contents of the message are displayed in the lower pane.

5. You can double-click a message description to view the contents in a separate window.

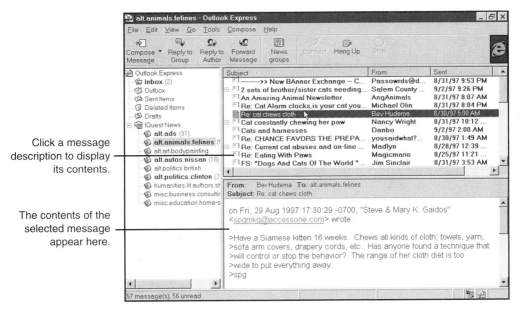

Click a message description to display its contents.

The contents of the selected message appear here.

Figure 6.5   Outlook Express displays a three-paned window, showing a list of messages and the contents of the selected message.

Following a Discussion

Occasionally, someone will post a message that inspires a long discussion or at least a couple of replies. When this happens, Outlook Express News tries to keep the related messages together so you can follow the discussion. To the left of the original message, you'll see a plus sign (+). Click the **plus sign** to display the related messages. You can then read these messages by clicking them.

When you click the plus sign, it turns into a minus sign. You can click the **minus sign** to collapse the list of replies, so only the original message appears in the list of messages.

TIP **More Than 300 Postings?!** Outlook Express is set up to download up to 300 headers (message descriptions) in each newsgroup. If there are more than 300 postings, you can view additional headers by selecting **Tools**, **Get Next 300 Headers**. To have Outlook Explorer initially download a different number of headers, open the **Tools** menu, select **Options**, click the **Read** tab, and enter the desired number in the **Download ___ Headers at a Time** text box.

Finding and Sorting Newsgroup Messages

If you connect to a newsgroup that contains hundreds of messages, you may have trouble sifting through the list to find messages on specific topics. To help, you can use the Find tool. Take the following steps:

1. Open the **Edit** menu and select **Find Message**. This displays the Find Message dialog box, as shown in Figure 6.6.

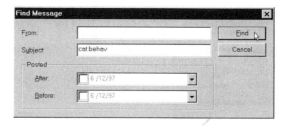

Figure 6.6 Outlook Express lets you search for messages by sender or topic.

2. Take one of the following steps:

To search for messages posted by a specific person, enter the person's username in the **From** text box.

To search for messages on a particular topic, click in the **Subject** text box, and type one or two unique terms to indicate what you are searching for.

3. (Optional) Use the **Posted After** and **Before** options to search for messages posted only between specified dates.

4. Click the **Find** button. Outlook Express performs the specified search, and highlights the description of the first message it finds that matches your search instructions.

5. To find another message that matches your search instructions, open the **Edit** menu and select **Find Next**, or press **F3**.

Outlook Express sorts messages according to the times they were sent, displaying the most recent messages last in the list. However, there may be times when you want to sort messages by sender or by description or reverse the sort order. Although the View/Sort By submenu contains sorting options, there's an easier way to sort messages. Take the following steps:

1. Right-click the heading for the column you want to sort (for example, right-click **From**). This displays a pop-up menu that allows you to sort in **Ascending** (A to Z, 1 to 10) or **Descending** (Z to A, 10 to 1) order.

2. Select the desired sort order. Outlook Express rearranges the message descriptions to conform to the specified sort order.

You can also add or remove columns from the list. Take the following steps to add or remove columns:

1. Open the **View** menu, and select **Columns**. This displays the Columns dialog box, which has two lists: Available Columns and Displayed Columns.

2. To add a column, click its name in the **Available Columns** list, and click the **Add** button.

3. To remove a column, click its name in the **Displayed Columns** list, and click the **Remove** button.

4. Click **OK**.

 TIP **Moving Columns** You can rearrange the columns in the Columns dialog box by clicking on a column name in the **Displayed Columns** list and using the **Move Up or Move Down** button. An easier way to move a column is to drag the column heading to the left or right in the Outlook Express window.

In this lesson, you learned how to read posted newsgroup messages. In the next lesson, you will learn how to post replies to messages you have read and start your own discussions.

Posting a Message or Reply

In this lesson, you learn how to post a reply to a message you have read, and how to start your own discussion.

Replying to Newsgroup Messages

Before you post messages to a newsgroup, familiarize yourself with the newsgroup. Hang out, and read existing messages to obtain a clear idea of the focus and tone of the newsgroup. Reading messages without posting your own messages is known as *lurking*. Newsgroups encourage lurking, because it provides you with the knowledge you need to respond intelligently and to avoid repeating what has already been said.

You can reply to a message by posting your reply in the newsgroup, by sending a private reply via e-mail, or by posting and sending an e-mail reply. (Check the original message to determine if the sender requested a reply method.) The following sections explain how to reply publicly or privately to posted messages.

Posting a Public Reply

When you post a reply to a newsgroup, your message appears in the newsgroup, where anyone can read it. The person to whom you are replying will have to check the newsgroup to read your reply. To post a reply publicly, take the following steps:

1. Select the message to which you want to respond.

2. Click the **Reply** button (in Collabra), and select **Reply to Group**, or click the **Reply to Group** button in Outlook Express. A new message window appears, with the newsgroup's address and the subject description filled in for you, as shown in Figure 7.1.

3. Type your message in the message area at the bottom of the window.

4. Click the **Send** or **Post** button. Your newsreader sends your reply as instructed.

Click the Post Button.

Type your message here.

This message will be posted to a newsgroup.

The description of the message to which you are responding appears here.

Figure 7.1 You can post your reply publicly in the same newsgroup.

 TIP **Newsgroup Etiquette** To avoid getting verbally battered in a newsgroup, follow a few simple rules. Don't insult any person or attack any topic of conversation. Post messages that pertain to the newsgroup and topic of conversation (read the entire conversation before adding your own two cents). Don't advertise in a newsgroup unless the newsgroup is especially designed for advertising. If there's a FAQ (frequently asked questions list), read it. And, don't shout by using all capital letters in your message.

Replying Privately via E-Mail

Many users specifically request that you reply to their messages via e-mail. This saves them the trouble of having to sift through a long list of messages to find your reply, and it keeps your reply confidential. If you reply via e-mail, your reply goes only to the person who posted the original message. To reply privately via e-mail, take the following steps:

411

1. Select the message to which you want to respond.

2. Click the **Reply** button (in Collabra), and select **Reply to Sender**, or click the **Reply to Author** button in Outlook Express. Your newsreader automatically starts the e-mail program and displays a new message window, with the person's e-mail address and the subject description filled in for you, as shown in Figure 7.2.

3. Type your message in the message area at the bottom of the window.

4. Click the **Send** button. Your e-mail program sends your reply to the specified e-mail address.

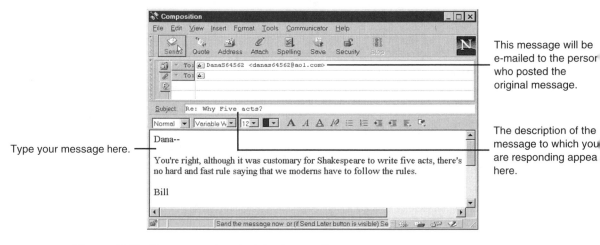

Type your message here.

This message will be e-mailed to the person who posted the original message.

The description of the message to which you are responding appears here.

Figure 7.2   You can reply privately via e-mail.

Starting Your Own Newsgroup Discussion

As you gain experience in a particular newsgroup, you might decide to venture out and start your own conversation. To start a discussion, take the following steps:

1. Select the newsgroup in which you want to post your message. A list of posted messages appears.

2. Click the **New Msg** or **Compose Message** button. The window that appears is very similar to the window you use to reply to messages, except in this dialog box, the Subject text box is blank.

3. Click in the **Subject** text box, and type a description for your message.

4. Click in the big text box at the bottom of the window, and type your message.

5. Click the **Send** or **Post** button. Your message is posted in the active newsgroup. You can now check the newsgroup on a regular basis, to see if anyone has replied to your message. And don't be surprised if you receive replies via e-mail!

TIP   **Check Your Spelling**   Most newsreaders now come with a spelling checker. Before sending your message, use the spelling checker to check your message for typos and misspelled words. In most cases, you can click the Spelling button in the newsreader's toolbar or select the spelling checker from one of the menus.

Formatting Your Messages with HTML

Ninety percent of the newsgroup messages you encounter are simple text messages. However, like most features of the Internet, newsgroups are becoming more Web-like, allowing users to post messages containing fancy text, links, embedded graphics, and other objects. If you have a relatively new newsreader, it probably supports HTML, allowing you to jazz up your messages.

Make Your Messages Universally Accessible   Be careful when posting HTML-coded messages. Although your newsreader may support HTML, many people who access the newsgroup may be using a less capable **CAUTION**   newsreader.

Both Netscape Collabra and Outlook Express News support HTML codes. When you create a new message using either of these newsreaders, you will see a formatting toolbar just above the message area, as shown in Figure 7.3. You can click its buttons and use its drop-down lists to format text, add links, and insert graphics, just as if you were using a full-featured word processor. You will also see a Format menu that offers additional formatting options.

Format menu

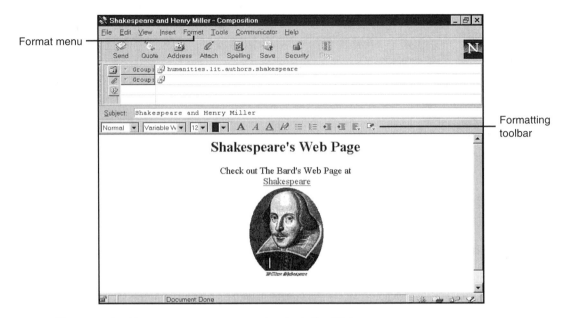

Formatting toolbar

Figure 7.3 You can post messages that look like Web pages.

Although these advanced formatting tools give your newsgroup postings an enhanced look, they may pose problems for people using other newsreaders. To make your messages accessible to all, you can disable HTML formatting. Take one of the following steps:

- In Outlook Express, you can disable HTML coding for individual messages. In the new message window, open the **Format** menu and select **Plain Text**. A dialog box appears, asking you to confirm. Click **Yes**.

- In Outlook Express, set **HTML** coding or **Plain Text** as the default for new messages. In the Outlook Express News window, open the **Tools** menu, and select **Options**. Click the **Send** tab, and select **HTML** or **Plain Text**.

- In Netscape Collabra, you can disable HTML coding for new messages. Open the **Edit** menu and select **Preferences**. Under Mail & Groups, click **Messages**. Click **By Default, Send HTML Messages**, to remove the check from the box.

In this lesson, you learned how to post a reply to a newsgroup message you've read and how to start your own discussion. In the next lesson, you will learn how to download and send files as attachments.

Working with Attached Files

In this lesson, you learn how to save and play files attached to newsgroup messages, and how to attach files to messages you post.

Receiving and Sending Files in Newsgroups

In some newsgroups, people like to trade files instead of simple text messages. In gaming newsgroups, for instance, gamers may post shareware versions of their favorite games or add-ons that make the game more challenging and fun. In a photography newsgroup, you might find digitized landscape photos or portraits.

In the past, swapping files in newsgroups was difficult. You usually had to download several parts of a coded message, assemble the parts to create one file, and then decode the file you just created. With the latest newsreaders, however, the process has become as easy as transferring files on the Web. The following sections show you how to send and receive attached files in Collabra, Outlook Express, and America Online.

Downloading File Attachments in Collabra

Collabra is capable of displaying inline images, such as GIFs and JPEGs (graphics), text files, and HTML-coded documents (Web pages). If a message contains an embedded graphic, Collabra displays the graphic right in the message viewing area (see Figure 8.1).

If Collabra cannot display an attached file, it displays a link for the file, just as you might see on a Web page. You can then click the link to display the Save As dialog box and save the file to your hard drive.

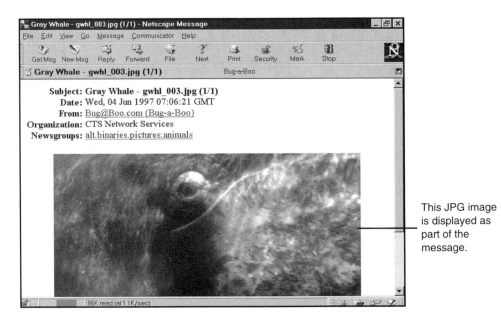

This JPG image is displayed as part of the message.

Figure 8.1 In Collabra, newsgroup messages can look a lot like Web pages.

You can change the way Collabra displays attachments. Open the **View** menu, point to **Attachments**, and click **Inline** to display attachments as part of the newsgroup message, or **As Links** to display them as highlighted text you can click. If you choose to have attachments displayed as links, you can access the file by performing one of the following steps:

- Click the link as you would in Navigator. Collabra opens the program associated with the file type, and displays the file in that program. If no file association has been set up for the selected file type, Collabra prompts you to save the file.
- Right-click the link, and choose the Save command to save the file to your hard drive. You can then open or run the file later.

Downloading File Attachments in Outlook Express

If you click a message title, in Outlook Express, you see a paper clip icon just above the message area, as shown in Figure 8.2. Click the paper clip, and then click the file's name to open it. Assuming that this file type is associated with an application, Outlook Express News runs the application and opens the file. (Because Internet Explorer can play most media file types, such as JPG and GIF files, Outlook Express News will use Internet Explorer or one of its add-ons to play most file types.)

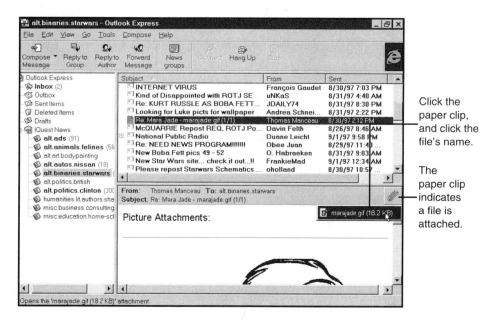

Click the paper clip, and click the file's name.

The paper clip indicates a file is attached.

Figure 8.2 You can open attached files in Outlook Express News.

You can associate file types with applications installed on your system, but you can't do it from Outlook Express News; you have to create file associations in My Computer or Windows Explorer. To set file associations in Internet Explorer, refer to Part 2, Lesson 17, "Installing and Using Helper Applications."

TIP   **Decoding Messages**   Some users post files that consist of several parts. Next to each message, you might see something like 0/3, 1/3, 2/3, 3/3, indicating the various parts. To view a file such as this, you must decode it. Select all the parts of the message by Ctrl-clicking them. Then, open the **Tools** menu, and select **Combine & Decode**. Drag the parts of the messages so they are in the correct order (from 0 to 3, for instance), and click **OK**.

Downloading Attached Files in America Online

America Online comes with the equivalent of a secret decoder ring, which can decode most of the file attachments you'll find in newsgroups. To download and decode an attached file, take the following steps:

1. From the list of newsgroup messages, double-click the message that has the attached file. (The message description typically indicates if a file is attached.) America Online displays the dialog box shown in Figure 8.3.

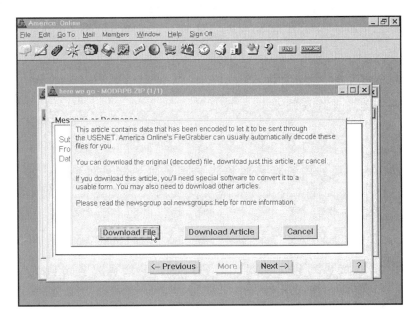

Figure 8.3   When you choose to read a message that has a file attachment, AOL prompts you to save the file.

2. Click the **Download File** button. The Download Manager dialog box appears.

3. Use the Download Manager to pick the drive and directory in which you want the file saved, and click the **Save** button.

If you click the Download File button and get a message indicating that Parental Controls have restricted your ability to download binary files, you can turn off the control from the main account name. Take the following steps:

1. Open the **Members** menu, and select **Parental Control**.

2. Click the **Custom Controls** button.

3. Click **Newsgroups**, and click the **Newsgroup Controls** button.

4. Select your screen name, click **Edit**.

5. Click **Block binary downloads**, to remove the check from its box.

6. Click the **Save** button. Click the Close (X) button to back out of the Parental Control dialog boxes and return to newsgroups.

Attaching Files to Your Newsgroup Postings

Although most newsgroup messages contain simple text, you can attach files to the messages you post. Perhaps you'd like to share a digitized photo or sound recording with the group, or you have a file that contains information, which the group might find helpful. Whatever the case, you can post the file along with your message.

Drag-and-Drop Attachments

The easiest way to attach a file to your message in Outlook Express is to create the message and then drag the file's icon into the message area of the new message window. You can drag the file My Computer, Windows Explorer, or File Manager. This places an icon for the file at the bottom of the window.

Netscape Collabra also supports drag-and-drop attachments, but you can't just drag the icon into the message area. Instead, click the Attach Files & Documents tab, as shown in Figure 8.4. Then, drag the file's icon into the blank area to the right of the tab.

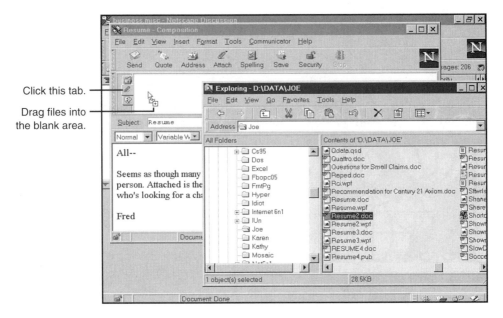

Click this tab.

Drag files into the blank area.

Figure 8.4   You can drag the files you want to attach to the Attach Files & Documents area in Collabra.

Using the Button Bar or Menu Commands

Most newsreaders also allow you to attach files to your messages by using a command on the button bar or menu bar. Take the following steps to use this technique to attach files in Outlook Express or Netscape Collabra:

- In Outlook Express, click the **Insert File** button (the button with the paper clip on it) in the New Message toolbar. Use the Insert Attachment dialog box, to select the file from your hard drive, and click **Attach**.

- In Netscape Collabra, click the **Attach** button and click **File**. Use the Enter File to Attach dialog box to select the file from your hard drive, and click **Open**.

Attaching Files in America Online

Although America Online is on the cutting edge of most Internet technologies, it lags when it comes to attaching files to newsgroup messages. In America Online, you have to attach files the old-fashioned way, by encoding the files with a special UUencode program.

First, obtain the UUencoder. One of the best encoders for Windows is WinCode, which you can obtain at **http://www.members.global2000.net/snappy/ wincode.html.** If you can't find WinCode, or you use a different operating system, search for a UUencoder at any of the following Web sites:

www.stroud.com

www.tucows.com

www.shareware.com

www.windows95.com

TIP **QuickFind** You can search for a UUencoder in America Online. Enter the keyword **Quickfind**, and use the QuickFinder to search for UUencode.

Once you have the UUencoder, install it, and use it to encode the file you want to send. The following steps lead you through the process with WinCode, but the steps will differ slightly if you use another encoder:

1. Run WinCode. (You can double-click its icon or select it from the Windows 95 Start, Programs, Wincode menu.)

2. Click the **Encode a Data File** button on the left end of the toolbar. The File to Encode (UUE) dialog box appears, prompting you to select the file you want to encode.

3. Select the drive, folder, and file name of the file you want to encode, and click the **Clipboard** button, as shown in Figure 8.5. This places the encoded version of the file (the coding consists of numbers, letters, and symbols) on the Windows Clipboard, to save you the steps of having to copy the text from a separate file.

Encoding the file creates a text file that a UUdecoder can translate. Once the file is encoded, you can paste it into your outgoing message. Create the message, as explained in Part 4, Lesson 4, "Accessing Newsgroups from AOL." Then, right-click at the bottom of the message area, and select the **Paste** command. You can then send the message as you normally do.

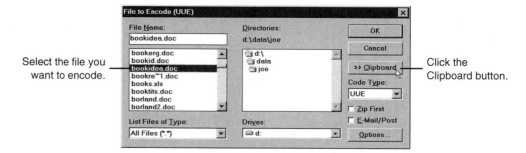

Select the file you
want to encode.

Click the
Clipboard button.

Figure 8.5   You can send the UUencode results to the Clipboard and then paste it into your message.

In this lesson, you learned how to download files attached to newsgroup messages and send file attachments. In the next lesson, you will learn how to read newsgroup messages offline.

Reading Newsgroup Messages Offline

In this lesson, you learn how to download newsgroup messages and read them offline, to reduce online connect time and charges.

Reading Messages Offline

If your Internet service provider charges you by the hour, lurking around in newsgroups can become an expensive habit. To save yourself some connect time, you can download newsgroup messages and read them later. The sections in this lesson show you how to work offline with Outlook Express and Netscape Collabra. If you are accessing newsgroups through America Online, see Part 4, Lesson 4, "Accessing Newsgroups from AOL," for details on working offline with the FlashSessions feature.

Reading Messages Offline in Outlook Express

By default, Outlook Express News downloads only the message headers (the title of each message). It does not download the message contents until you click the header. To have Outlook Express News download all messages in a newsgroup, take the following steps:

1. Select the newsgroup that contains the messages you want to read offline.

2. Open the **Tools** menu, point to **Mark for Retrieval**, and select **Mark All Messages** (to download all the messages in the newsgroup). See Figure 9.1. Outlook Express displays icons next to the messages, indicated that they have been marked for downloading.

3. Open the **Tools** menu, and select one of the following options:

   Download this Account downloads all messages in all newsgroups marked for retrieval. If you set up more than one account (more than one news server), Outlook Express downloads messages in newsgroups only for the selected account.

   Download this Newsgroup downloads all messages only in the selected newsgroup.

   Download All downloads all messages in all newsgroups marked for retrieval. If you set up two or more news servers, Outlook Express retrieves messages from all the servers.

 TIP   **Download Account**   If you subscribe to just a few newsgroups, you may want to download all the messages in all your subscribed newsgroups for the selected news server. To do so, open the **Tools** menu and select **Download Account**. If you have several news servers set up, you can download all of the messages for all of your subscribed newsgroups by selecting **Download All**.

4. The Download Newsgroup dialog box appears. Make sure **Get marked messages** is checked and click **OK**.

5. Wait until all the messages have been downloaded and then click the **Hang Up** button in the toolbar to disconnect from the Internet. You can now read the messages offline. The following sections explain some of the more advanced offline reading features that Outlook Express offers.

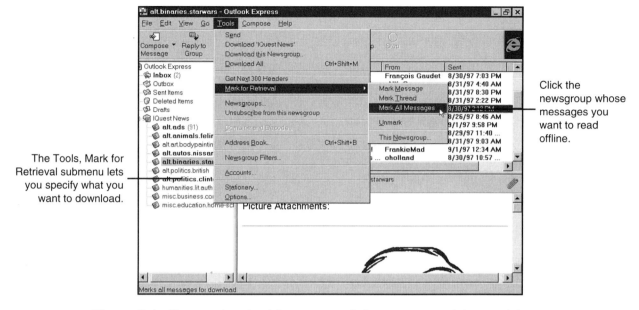

The Tools, Mark for Retrieval submenu lets you specify what you want to download.

Click the newsgroup whose messages you want to read offline.

Figure 9.1   You can download the contents of all messages, and then read them offline.

Downloading Selected Messages

You can often tell whether or not you want to read the contents of a message by looking at its description (header). And it doesn't make much sense to download the contents of a message which you have no intention of reading. Outlook Express lets you download only those messages you intend to read. To mark and download the contents of selected messages, take the following steps:

1. Click the name of a newsgroup. Outlook Express displays a list of message headers in that newsgroup.

2. Click the **Hang Up** button in the toolbar. This disconnects you from your news server and from the Internet.

3. Click the header for a message you want to read, and **Ctrl+click** additional headers.

425

4. Open the **Tools** menu, point to **Mark for Retrieval**, and click **Mark Message**. An arrow icon appears to the left of each selected message. (If you are connected to the Internet, Outlook Express immediately retrieves the contents of the marked messages.)

5. Open the **Tools** menu, and select **Download this Newsgroup**. The Download Newsgroup dialog box appears, prompting you to specify the items you want to download.

6. Select **Get Marked Messages**, and click **OK**. Outlook Express connects to the Internet and to your news server, and retrieves the contents of the marked messages.

7. You can now disconnect from the Internet and read the messages offline. Click the **Hang Up** button.

Additional Offline Reading Options

Earlier in this section, you learned how to download all the messages in a selected newsgroup and only selected messages. But what if you want to download a single thread (a message and all its replies) or just the new messages? Outlook Express provides several options that allow you to perform these specialized offline reading tasks:

- You can mark all messages for retrieval. Select the newsgroup, and then open the **Tools** menu, point to **Mark for Retrieval**, and select **Mark All Messages**.

- To unmark a message, click its header, and **Ctrl+click** any additional headers you want to unmark. Open the **Tools** menu, point to **Mark for Retrieval**, and click **Unmark**.

- To retrieve the contents of all related messages in a discussion, click the original message. Open the **Tools** menu, point to **Mark for Retrieval**, and click **Mark Thread**, as shown in Figure 9.2.

Keep in mind that you can mark messages and threads for retrieval while offline. To retrieve the messages, open the **Tools** menu, and select **Download this Account**, **Download this Newsgroup**, or **Download All**.

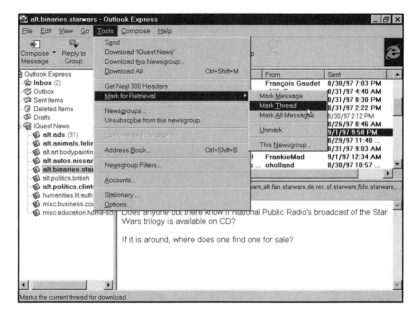

Figure 9.2   The Tools, Mark for Retrieval menu offers several options for retrieving and reading messages offline.

Going Offline with Netscape Collabra

Like Outlook Express, Collabra allows you to download messages from selected newsgroups and then read those messages offline. Here's what you do:

1. In the Message Center, open the **File** menu and select **Go Offline**. The Download dialog box appears.

2. Click the **Select Items for Download** button. A list of subscribed newsgroups appear, as shown in Figure 9.3.

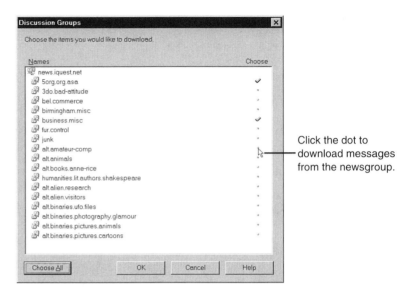

Click the dot to download messages from the newsgroup.

Figure 9.3   You must tell Collabra what to download before going offline.

3. Under Choose, click the dot next to each newsgroup you want to read offline. The dot changes into a check mark. Click **OK**.

4. Make sure **Download Discussion Groups** is selected. You can also choose to download mail and send mail messages before going offline.

5. Click the **Go Offline** button. The Downloading Articles dialog box appears, displaying the downloading progress.

6. When downloading is complete, you can disconnect from the Internet and read your messages offline. To go back online, open the **File** menu and select **Go Online**.

In this lesson, you learned how to download and read newsgroup postings offline. In the next lesson, you will learn how to organize newsgroups and messages.

Managing Newsgroups and Messages

In this lesson, you learn how to organize newsgroup messages, remove newsgroups, and clear old messages from your system.

Organizing Your Newsgroup Window

E-mail and newsgroups expedite your communications with the rest of the digitized world. But these programs also pack your disk with hundreds of messages. In this lesson, you will learn how to use the tools in your newsreader (Outlook Express or Netscape Collabra) to clear messages off your hard drive, reorganize your folders, and remove some of the newsgroups you don't use.

Removing Subscribed Newsgroups

The first step in organizing your newsgroups is to delete any newsgroups you no longer access from the subscriptions list. In Outlook Express, you can remove newsgroups by taking any of the following steps:

- Click the folder for the news server in the folder list. Right-click the name of the newsgroup in the folders list, and select **Unsubscribe from this newsgroup**.
- Click the **News groups** button in the toolbar, and click the **Subscribed** tab, as shown in Figure 10.1. Click the newsgroup you want to remove, and click the **Unsubscribe** button. Click **OK**.

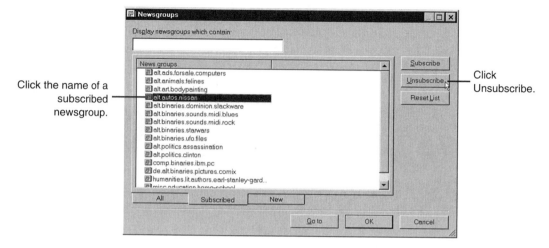

Click the name of a subscribed newsgroup.

Click Unsubscribe.

Figure 10.1 Use the same dialog box you used to subscribe to newsgroups for removing them.

In Netscape Collabra, you can remove groups from the subscriptions list by performing the following steps:

1. Go to the Message Center. (From any Communicator component, you can go to the Message Center by opening the **Communicator** menu and selecting **Message Center**.)

2. Click the **plus sign** next to your news server to display a list of subscribed newsgroups.

3. Click the name of the newsgroup you want to remove. You can **Ctrl+click** additional newsgroup names to select them.

4. Open the **Edit** menu and choose **Delete Selection**. Collabra displays a dialog box asking for your confirmation.

5. Click **OK** to remove the newsgroup. Repeat this step if you selected more than one newsgroup in Step 3.

TIP **Right-Click Removal** To quickly remove a newsgroup in Collabra, right-click its name, and select **Remove Discussion Group**. Click **OK** to confirm.

Organizing Your Messages in Outlook Express

Outlook Express uses a few folders to group related messages. All the e-mail messages you receive are placed in the Inbox folder. Messages you send are placed in the Outbox, until you click the **Send and Receive** button. And Outlook Express creates a separate folder for messages in each newsgroup you subscribe to.

As you send and receive messages, you will eventually need to clean up these folders—delete and sort messages, move messages to other folders, and perhaps even create your own folders. The following sections explain how to perform these message management tasks.

To manage folders and messages, you should turn on the folder list. Select **View**, **Layout**, make sure **Folder List** is checked, and click **OK**.

Making New Folders

Outlook Express lets you create your own folder for grouping messages. To create a folder, take the following steps:

1. Right-click the icon for the folder below which you want the new folder placed, and select **New Folder**. The Create Folder dialog box appears, as shown in Figure 10.2.

Type a name for your folder. ——
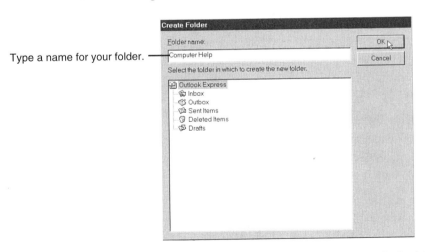

Figure 10.2 You can create your own message folders in Outlook Express.

2. In the **Folder Name** text box, type a name for the folder. At this point, you can also choose to place the new folder below a different folder.

3. Click the **OK** button. You now have a new folder in which you can move messages you want to save.

Folder in a Folder If you create a subfolder (for instance a folder under the Inbox folder), Outlook Express may not display it immediately. Click the plus sign next to the main folder to display a list of its subfolders.

CAUTION

Deleting and Moving Folders and Their Contents

If you no longer use a folder you created, delete it. It's pretty easy, so be careful. Check to make sure you don't need any messages in the folder. Click the folder, and then click the **Delete** button or press the **Delete** key. Click the **Yes** button to confirm the deletion.

You cannot delete or move any of the original folders: Inbox, Outbox, Sent Items, Draft, or Deleted Items. However, you can move a folder you created. Simply click and hold the folder icon and drag it over the desired folder (or over Outlook Explorer at the top of the list).

TIP **Renaming Folders** You can change a folder's name. Click the folder's name, and then click it again. The name appears highlighted. Type the new name. You cannot rename the Inbox, Outbox, Sent, Items, or Deleted Items folder

Selecting, Moving, Copying, and Deleting Messages

Before you can move, copy, or delete messages, you must select them. If you know how to select files in My Computer, Windows Explorer, or File Manager, the following list is review material for you:

- To select a single message, click it.
- To select additional messages, **Ctrl+click** them.
- To select a group of neighboring messages, click the first message in the group, and hold down the **Shift** key while clicking on the last message.
- To select all the messages, open the **Edit** menu and click **Select All**, or press **Ctrl+A**.

Once you've selected the messages, you can copy, move, or delete them by performing any of the following steps:

- To delete messages, click the **Delete** button in the toolbar. This doesn't actually delete the message—it simply moves the message to the Deleted Items folder. You can undelete the message at any time by dragging it from the Deleted Items folder to the Inbox or another folder. To delete messages permanently, delete them from the Deleted Items folder.

- To copy messages, open the **Edit** menu and select **Copy to Folder**. A dialog box appears, showing the names of all the folders, as shown in Figure 10.3. Click the name of the folder to which you want to copy the messages, and click **OK**.

- To move messages, open the **Edit** menu and select **Move to Folder**. A dialog box appears, showing the names of all the folders. Click the name of the folder to which you want to move the messages, and click **OK**.

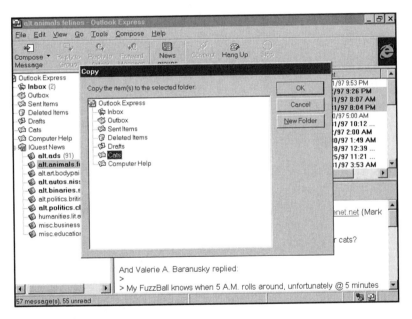

Figure 10.3 Select the folder to which you want to copy selected messages.

TIP **Disabling the Deleted Items Folder** You can tell Outlook Express to automatically remove items from the Deleted Items folder whenever you exit. Open the **Tools** menu, select **Options**, and click the **General** tab. Click **Empty Messages from the 'Deleted Items' Folder on Exit** to place a check in its box. Click **OK**.

433

Compacting Folders to Save Disk Space

As you delete messages from folders, Outlook Express removes the message but leaves a gap where the message used to be. This gap consumes disk space. To remove these gaps, you should *compress* your folders whenever you do any major clean up. To compress a folder, take the following steps:

1. Click the folder that you want to compress (usually the Inbox, Sent Items, or Deleted Items folder).

2. Open the **File** menu, point to **Folder**, and click **Compact**. The Compacting dialog box appears, showing the progress of the operation. When the dialog box retreats from the screen, the folder is compacted.

3. Repeat the operation to compress other folders.

 TIP **Automated Compression** Whenever you start Outlook Express, it automatically checks your folders to determine if they should be compressed. If you have a lot of wasted space, Outlook prompts you to compress.

Cleaning Out Newsgroup Messages

If you've downloaded a bunch of newsgroup messages to read offline, they're probably still on your hard drive. You can delete them as explained earlier, but if you have some heavy-duty cleaning to do, there's a better way to clear them from your system. Take the following steps:

1. In Outlook Express, click the name of any of your news servers. (Most people have only one news server.)

2. Open the **File** menu, and select **Clean Up Files**. The Local File Cleanup dialog box appears.

3. Open the **Local file(s) for** drop-down list, and select the news server whose files you want to clean up, or select **All Servers (All Files)**.

4. Click one of the following buttons:

> **Compact** removes wasted space, but leaves the message descriptions (headers) and content intact.

Remove Messages deletes the message contents, leaving only the message descriptions intact. You can then retrieve a message by connecting to your news server and clicking the description.

Delete removes the message contents and descriptions, cleaning up the entire mess.

5. A dialog box appears, showing the progress of the clean up, and then you are returned to the Local Cleanup dialog box. Click the **Close** button.

Organizing Messages in Netscape Collabra

To organize your newsgroups, you need two Collabra windows: the Discussions window (for working with individual messages) and the Message Center (for working with newsgroups). The Message Center provides better tools for creating and managing the various folders in which Messenger stores messages: the Inbox, Outbox, Drafts, Sent, Trash, and newsgroup folders. The following sections show how to use the tools available in each of these windows to manage your newsgroups and messages.

You can go to the Message Center by clicking on the Message Center button, just above and to the right of the viewing area in the Discussions window, or by selecting **Communicator, Message Center** from any of the other Communicator programs (or press **Ctrl+Shift+1**). To display the Discussions window, double-click a newsgroup in the Message Center.

Organizing Messages with Folders

The first step in reorganizing your messages is to create a folder. Each newsgroup already has a separate folder, but you may wish to create a folder for important messages you want to save. To create a folder, take the following steps:

1. Go to the Message Center.
2. Click the folder below which you want the new folder to be created. To place the folder on the same level as the Inbox folder, click **Local Mail** at the top of the folder list.

3. Open the **File** menu and select **New Folder**. The New Folder dialog box appears, prompting you to type a name for the folder.

4. Type a name for the folder, and click **OK**. The new folder appears. You can now copy and move messages to this new folder, as explained in the next section.

Selecting Messages

Before you can delete, copy, or move messages, you must select them. You can select a single message by clicking on its name in the Discussions window. To select additional messages, hold down the **Ctrl** key while clicking on their names. You can select a range of neighboring messages by clicking on the top message in the range, and then holding down the **Shift** key while clicking on the bottom message in the range. The **Edit**, **Select Message** menu offers the following commands for selecting messages:

Thread   Selects all messages that have the same title.

Flagged   Selects all messages that you've flagged. To flag a message (mark it as important or as a message you want to respond to later), select the message, open the **Message** menu, and click **Flag**.

All Messages   Selects all messages in the currently open folder.

Moving Messages

After selecting the messages, you can quickly move them to a different folder. Take the following steps:

1. Right-click any one of the selected messages to display a context menu.

2. Point to **File Message**, and click the folder in which you want the selected messages moved. Collabra immediately moves the messages to the selected folder.

Another way to move messages is to click the **File** button in the toolbar, and then select the folder from the file list, as shown in Figure 10.4.

You can click the File button and select the destination folder.

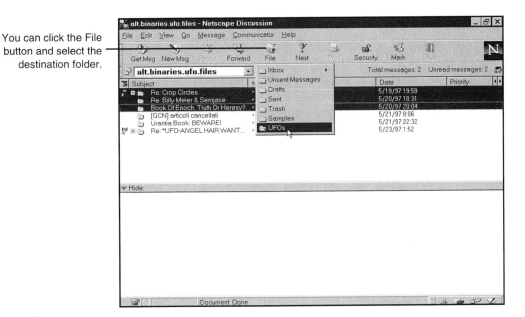

Figure 10.4 You can easily move selected messages to another folder.

Deleting Messages

To delete messages, first select them, and then click the **Delete** button in the toolbar, or press the **Del** key. The deleted messages are sent to the Trash folder. If you delete a message by mistake, you can move it from the Trash folder to one of your other folders, as explained in the previous section. To permanently delete messages, delete them from the Trash folder.

TIP **Taking Out the Trash** You can quickly delete all the messages in the Trash folder. Open the **File** menu and select **Empty Trash Folder**.

As you delete messages from folders, Messenger removes the message but leaves a gap where the message used to be. This gap consumes disk space. To remove these gaps, you should *compress* your folders whenever you do any major clean-up. To compress your folders, open the **File** menu and select **Compress Folders**.

In this lesson, you learned how to organize newsgroups and messages. In Part 5, you return to the Web, where you will learn how to publish your own creations.

Creating Web Pages

Overview
of HTML

In this lesson, you learn what you can and cannot do with HTML.

What Is HTML?

HTML (HyperText Markup Language) is the language of the World Wide Web. Every time you access a Web document, you're accessing a document someone wrote in HTML. All the document formatting you see in Web documents is done with HTML, and the hyperlinks you follow so easily by clicking with your mouse are set up using HTML, too. Those colorful images you see on the Web, those flashy forms you've filled in, and those scrolling banners are also products of the HTML language you'll learn about in this part. HTML is easy to learn, and by the time you've finished the lessons in this part, you'll be creating professional-quality HTML documents.

Figure 1.1 shows the HTML coding behind a typical Web page. As you can see, an HTML-coded document isn't much to look at. It consists of the text you see on the Web page, along with many bracketed codes that tell the Web browser how to display the text, where to insert graphics, how to display links, and more. Figure 1.2 shows the same page displayed in Internet Explorer.

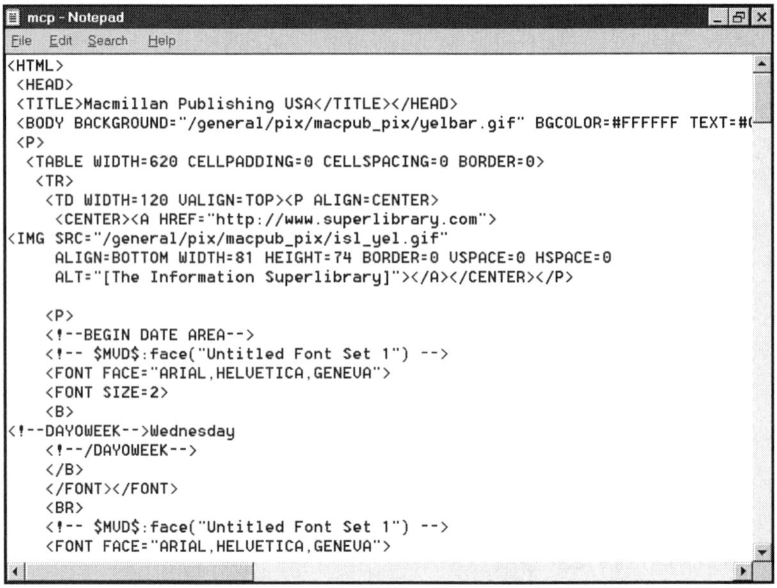

Figure 1.1   The HTML codes behind a typical Web page.

Figure 1.2   The same page as it's displayed in Internet Explorer.

Here's a short list of the major features of HTML:

- *Document formatting* uses various typeface styles, a range of headlines, and a new feature called *frames*.
- The capability to include *hyperlinks* that point to other Web documents, multimedia files, or services on computer systems all over the Internet.
- A wide range of *list layout* capabilities.
- The capability to create *tables* and *preformatted text*.
- The capability to *embed graphical images* right in an HTML document, which can be hyperlinks to other documents.
- *Clickable image maps* with hot spots to take you various places depending on where in the image you've clicked.
- Inclusion of *interactive features* such as fill-in forms and programs that involve the user.

You've probably seen all these features and more on the Web. In this part, you'll learn how to create your own HTML documents, which include these same features. Whether you're learning because your company or organization wants to go on the Web or just because you're curious, you will learn the basics of this language.

Limitations of HTML

Before we go into the nuts and bolts of HTML, however, we need to go over some fundamental limitations of the language, not to discourage you from learning and using it, but to give you an overall perspective on what you can expect.

Not a Typesetting Language

Despite recent changes in the HTML language that allow you to control line justification, typeface size, graphical image placement, and the flow of text around images, HTML is still not a full-blown typesetting language. What your HTML documents look like when people view them still isn't subject to your total control, as it would be in printed documents. And you can lead a user to a graphical image, but he won't necessarily look at it; many users who use slow links to the Internet disable image display to speed up downloads.

Physical Differences in Hardware

There's a wide variety of computer systems, with various hardware and capabilities, and each one will affect your HTML document in a different way.

Hardware differences are the most important limitation affecting HTML. Your PC may have a nice, color monitor with a 15-inch screen, but the engineers in your company probably have higher resolution, 20-inch screens on high-end workstations for their CAD design, your graphic designers may have high-end Macintoshes, and the folks in the back office use PCs with monochrome screens, or even dumb terminals, to do word processing or data entry. Every one of these pieces of hardware has different capabilities, yet each one is potentially capable of accessing the World Wide Web and looking at your documents written in HTML.

Dumb Terminals Minimal-capability computer terminal screens with keyboards. They don't display color, or any kind of graphics—just letters and other characters.

You don't expect monochrome displays to deal with color, you can't expect low-resolution displays to render graphical images well, and those dumb terminals can't do anything but display plain text in just one boring fixed font. Color and type fonts differ as well. These physical differences mean that your HTML documents will get rendered differently from PC to workstation to terminal. For example, if your corporate public relations policy dictates the company logo be a precise shade of red and of certain aesthetically pleasing proportions, expect your graphical image of it to get rendered in different shades of red, orange, and pink, as well as in black-and-white, and in different proportions on different machines; on a dumb terminal, it won't be displayed at all.

Choosing Personal Preferences

If you've played on the Web very much, you've probably noticed your Web browser has some *user-settable features*. You can, for instance, select from a range of font styles and sizes available on your system, based purely on your personal preferences. Also, you can set your browser to delay the loading and display of images in an HTML document. If you do, the HTML author's images are replaced by generic placeholders that you must click to reveal the original image. (This feature is designed to minimize the time it takes to load and render a document and is of most benefit to users whose network connections are over slow, dial-up links; see Lesson 5, "Using Anchors and Links," for more on this problem.) Finally, you can resize your Web browser display, and the documents you view will take the new size of the display, resulting in reformatting the document's text to fit the new size.

Viewing HTML Documents in Different Browsers

Viewing your HTML documents in different Web browsers can give you a better feel for the differences. Figures 1.3 and 1.4 show how the same HTML document can be rendered differently, even on the same hardware, using different browsers. Figure 1.3 shows the page displayed earlier, in Figure 1.2, as it is rendered in NCSA Mosaic. Figure 1.4 shows the page displayed in a nongraphical Web browser.

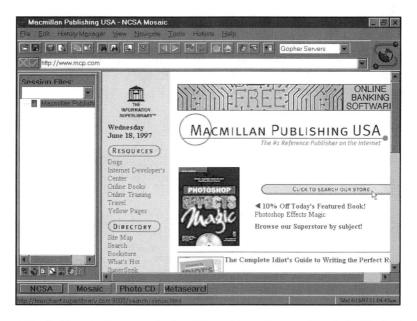

Figure 1.3 In Mosaic, the page looks different from the way it looks in Navigator.

New changes in the HTML language and the way browsers interpret it have removed many early limitations, but, as you can see, some remain. Do these limitations mean you shouldn't bother learning some of the more advanced HTML codes?

Before you answer that question, remember all the Web surfing you've done and how impressed you've been with what you've seen. The HTML language, despite its remaining limitations, is highly capable, and hopefully, you'll agree its capabilities outweigh its limitations. The lessons in this part show you how to get the most out of HTML. One way of working with these limitations is to think of your documents not in terms of physical things, like where the lines break or specific font styles, but rather in a larger, more general sense.

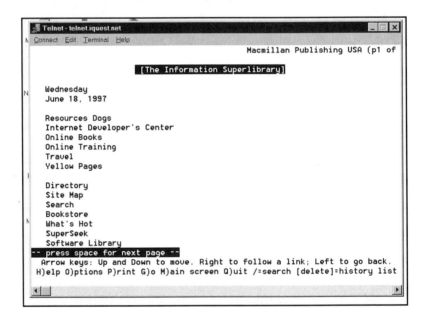

Figure 1.4 The same page displayed in a non-graphical browser called Lynx.

This lesson introduced you to HTML. Even with the limitations we've mentioned, you can achieve quite impressive things with HTML. In the next lesson, you'll learn how to make a simple HTML Web page by typing some basic codes.

Creating a Simple HTML Document

In this lesson, you create your first HTML document, and learn about the tools you can use that are already on your computer system.

Tools for Creating and Editing HTML Documents

What tools do you need? HTML documents are *plain text (ASCII)* files with special markup codes embedded right in the text. This means HTML files contain nothing but letters, numbers, punctuation marks, and other printable characters—plus HTML markup codes.

Although some specialized tools for creating and editing HTML documents are available (we'll look at them in Lesson 11, "Helper Applications and Plug-Ins for Multimedia"), you can begin creating HTML immediately with tools you already have on hand. These include:

- Your computer's built-in text editors, such as the Microsoft Windows Notepad, DOS edit, Windows Write, Macintosh TeachText/SimpleText, UNIX vi or emacs, or VAX/VMS edt.
- Your favorite word processor, such as Microsoft Word, WordPerfect, or any other program you use, used in plain text or ASCII mode. (If you have the latest version of Word or WordPerfect, you have a high-powered HTML editor on your system.)

In fact, you can use whatever tool you're comfortable with for creating documents, making the HTML learning process much less of a chore. You can focus on learning and creating HTML, without having to learn a special tool at the same time.

Select whatever editor you're going to use to create your HTML document. The examples in this book show the Windows Notepad editor, but you can use any editor that can create and edit plain ASCII text files. If you're using a regular word processor, such as Microsoft Word, WordPerfect, or Write, be sure to remember to use the **Save As** feature to save the documents in plain ASCII text. Or, if you have a version that is HTML-ready, you can use its advanced features to convert your documents into HTML and even publish them on the Web.

TIP   **Use the Extension**   It's a good idea to use the ".html" (or ".htm" on PCs) file name extension when saving HTML documents. Later, you'll be able to tell what kind of documents they are. More importantly, visiting Web browsers will be able to tell what kind of documents they are and open them as Web pages instead of as text files.

You may want to bring up an empty document in your chosen editor and follow along with this lesson.

What Does HTML Look Like?

What distinguishes an HTML file from any other plain-text file is the presence of simple *markup codes* called HTML tags. These codes are typed right into a document; they control the formatting and layout of your finished document, specify hyperlinks to other documents, and other things we'll cover.

HTML markup codes are surrounded by special markers to set them off from the substantive text of the document. You just type them in, using HTML's two key symbols to signal markup instructions. These symbols are the *angle brackets*, < and >. You type these characters on most computer keyboards using **Shift-,** (comma) and **Shift-.** (period).

An important thing to note about HTML markup codes is they are not case-sensitive, <body> is the same as <bODy> or <boDy> or <BodY>. Most HTML authors use uppercase consistently for HTML markup codes because it makes the markup stand out visually from the actual text of the HTML document, easing the chore of proofreading.

Codes and Tags   HTML codes are commonly referred to as *tags*. Same thing, different name.

What HTML Tags Are Required in Documents?

Before we start, let's note some basic HTML tags that must appear in all HTML documents. These include a declaration of the fact that your document is an HTML document, a title, and some tags that divide your document into logical parts.

 Logical Parts? Different Web browsers render your HTML documents in different ways—color, type fonts, size, and so on—requiring you to think of your documents as logical entities, not physical ones, recognizing that the physical look varies from one viewer to another and from one computer to another. The basic HTML markup tags you'll learn in this lesson divide individual documents into logical parts, or sections.

The <HTML> Tag

Every HTML document must begin and end with the <HTML> tag, declaring the document an HTML document. No matter what else your HTML document contains, it must contain these tags. The HTML markup tag pair looks like this:

```
<HTML>
My First HTML Document
</HTML>
```

Always wrap your HTML documents with the beginning and ending **<HTML>** tags (*container tags*). If you omit the end or closing code, the starting code will affect all text from that point forward in the document.

 TIP **Forward Slash** Remember the closing tag requires the forward slash to mark it as a closing tag.

The <HEAD> and <BODY> Tags

All HTML documents are divided into two logical parts—the *head* and *body*. Web browsers need to distinguish between them to interpret your documents properly. Generally speaking, the head part of an HTML document includes *general information about the document*, while the body is its actual content. So, we'll extend the preceding example to include the **<HEAD>** start and stop tags.

449

```
<HTML><HEAD>
```

...the matter making up the head section

```
</HEAD>
My First HTML Document</HTML>
```

As you can see from the addition of the pair of **<HEAD>** tags here, HTML tags can appear on the same line with other tags.

Let's add the **<BODY>** tags to complete the logical division of your HTML document, since all HTML documents must have both a **<HEAD>** and a **<BODY>** section:

```
<HTML><HEAD>
```

...the matter making up the head section

```
</HEAD><BODY>
My First HTML Document
</BODY></HTML>
```

Your document is wrapped with the **<HTML>** start and stop tags, then divided into two pieces, marked off with the **<HEAD>** and **<BODY>** start and end tags, nested inside the overall pair of **<HTML>** tags. Each of these tags must appear in pairs: **<HTML>** and **</HTML>**; **<HEAD>** and **</HEAD>**; and **<BODY>** and **</BODY>**. (There are very few unpaired HTML tags.)

The <TITLE> Tag

There is one last required HTML tag, the **<TITLE>** tag. As you've noticed while using the Web, your Web browser's title bar always displays a title for each document it encounters. The title displayed is taken from the content of the **<TITLE>** tag in the original HTML document. If you do not include a title, nothing catastrophic will happen, but the title bar will display the page's URL instead of a title.

Always appearing *within the **<HEAD>** section* of your HTML document, the **<TITLE>** tags also come in pairs, surrounding the text you've entered as the title of your document. Let's make one last change to our example document to add these tags:

```
<HTML><HEAD><TITLE>The Title of the Document</TITLE>
</HEAD><BODY>
```

```
My First HTML Document
</BODY></HTML>
```

Our little HTML document is now complete, containing all the tags an HTML document must have. In fact, the document is a legal HTML document, and you can actually display it in your Web browser.

Pretty basic document, isn't it? Well, yes, it is, but you've just completed your first HTML document.

If you've been working along in your own editor, now is the time to save your document, just as you'd save any other document. The required HTML markup tags make your document an HTML document. If you're using a regular word processor, don't forget to save it in plain text. For a file name, use something like "**first.html**" (or "**first.htm**" if you're on a PC). We can now take a look at the document, using a Web browser.

CAUTION

Web Page Titles In Lesson 16, "Testing and Publishing Your Web Page," you will learn how to place your page on the Web. If you know which service you will use as a home for your page, ask to determine if you must use a special file name for your Web page. In many cases, the service will require you to name the document index.html, default.html, or home.html. These are the default names used on most Web servers; when a user accesses the directory in which the page is stored, it automatically looks for a file using one of these names.

Displaying and Previewing Your HTML Document

You know you can use your Web browser to view documents from World Wide Web servers across the Internet, but you may not realize you can use the same browser to view documents on your own computer system. This is a critical part of your work in creating HTML documents, because it enables you to preview, and *debug*, your documents before letting anyone else see them.

To view a local HTML document with your Web browser:

1. Pull down the **File** menu and select **Open Page** or **Open** (Open Local in some browsers). A dialog box appears, prompting you for a file name. Figure 5.1 shows the dialog box used by Netscape Navigator.

451

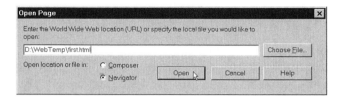

Figure 2.1 You can use the File, Open command to open a Web page on your hard drive.

2. Type in the name of the HTML document you saved, or use the familiar browse feature to locate and select the document.

3. Click the **Open** or **OK** button. Your Web browser brings up your HTML document.

If you've typed in the HTML document we've been working on in this lesson, the display in your Web browser should be much like Figure 2.2. Of course, there's not much to this document. You see the title of the document displayed in the browser's Title bar, and the one line of text we've entered.

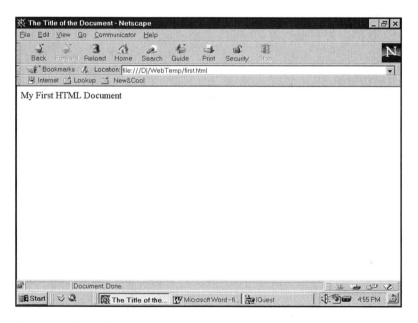

Figure 2.2 Your first HTML document.

In this lesson, you learned how to use some basic, paired HTML tags required in all HTML documents. In the next lesson, you will learn how to add headings and paragraphs.

Inserting and Formatting Headings and Running Text

In this lesson, you learn to create headings, use type styles, and insert paragraph tags in your HTML documents, as well as how to use text colors.

Creating Headings

You can create headings of various sizes in your HTML documents using heading tags. The setup of HTML supports six levels of headings, using the tags **<H1>** through **<H6>**. An HTML heading is very simple:

```
<H1>This is a Level-One Heading</H1>
```

Surround the heading text with start and stop heading tags.

For smaller heading type sizes, use a larger number (for example, **<H2>** or **<H5>**). Headings create an automatic line break in your documents (see the following for more on line breaks), and wrap over multiple lines. You should note the smaller heading sizes—generally **<H3>** and above—are rendered on most Web browsers in a type size that's actually smaller than regular text. See Figure 3.1 for a sample of **<H1>** through **<H6>** headings.

Recent changes in HTML standards have added the capability of centering your headings, using an additional HTML tag called an attribute (you'll use HTML attributes again in later lessons). To center a heading, use this markup:

```
<H1 ALIGN="CENTER">This is a Level-One Heading</H1>
```

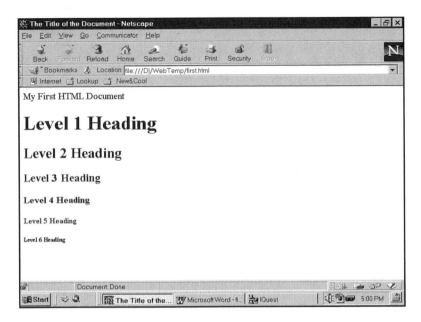

Figure 3.1   HTML headings.

 TIP   **Netscape's <CENTER> Tag**   Netscape has its own method of centering text, including headings, in HTML. To center a heading for the Navigator browser, use this construction:

<CENTER><H1>This is a Level-One Heading</H1></CENTER>

The <CENTER> tag works for both Internet Explorer and Netscape Navigator.

Controlling Type Styles and Character Formatting

You have a great deal of control over type styles/character formatting matters, like boldfacing and emphasized text and, in Navigator, some control over font sizes. Later in this lesson, you'll also learn about controlling text colors. It's useful to think of *logical* and *physical* typeface formatting.

 TERM   **Physical or Logical?**   When you use a word processor, it's set up to use the capabilities of your specific printer, and your documents access the physical capabilities of the printer, such as printing in, say, italics. Because you

454

can't know the capabilities of the Web browser used by every single reader of your HTML documents, the HTML language allows for logical control of typeface/character formatting. Logical typeface tags in HTML are read by a Web browser and interpreted according to the browser's capabilities.

Table 3.1 shows some HTML logical and physical typeface/character formatting tags. Use the logical tag in virtually all cases. As usual, all tags require closing tags at the end of the affected text (<STRONG> requires </STRONG>, and so on).

Table 3.1 Logical and Physical Character Formatting Tags

Meaning	*Logical Tag*	*Physical Tag*
Bold/Emphasis	**<STRONG>**	**<B>**
Italic	**<EM>**	**<I>**
Fixed Type	**<CODE>**	**<TT>**

Both Netscape Navigator and Internet Explorer use an HTML extension for changing the font size of part of an HTML document. Judicious use of font changes can enhance your HTML documents. The following HTML markup generates Figure 3.2.

```
See how <font size=2>fonts <font size=3>can <font size=4>change in
<font size=5>Netscape Navigator.
```

Formatting Paragraphs

Paragraphing in HTML takes some getting used to. As we've said, the different Web browsers, running on different computers with different graphical capabilities render documents differently. For one thing, they pretty much decide for themselves how to wrap lines of text in a displayed HTML document, and the end-of-line characters you may have put into an HTML document (by pressing the Enter key) will likely be ignored. Similarly, while you may include blank lines in your HTML source document, intending them to mark paragraph endings, the user's browser ignores them. You must explicitly mark a paragraph.

The paragraph tag in HTML is **<P>**, and it goes at the beginning of a new paragraph, except where there is some other line break. (Multiple <P> tags are ignored, so you can't use them to add extra blank lines.) Here is an HTML fragment showing use of the paragraph tag:

```
<HTML><HEAD><TITLE>Paragraphing</TITLE></HEAD>
<BODY>Here is some text.
<P>Here is a new paragraph</P></BODY></HTML>
```

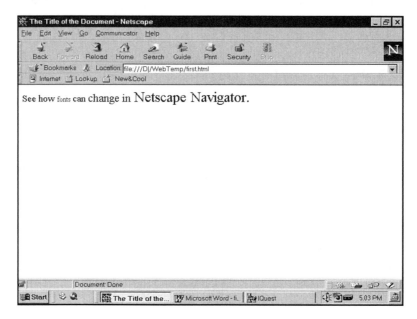

Figure 3.2   Netscape font size changes.

 TIP   **Closing tag—</P>**   The end-of-paragraph tag </P> is optional, since a beginning-of-paragraph tag is always a logical end-of-paragraph tag. This is one of the few tags that does not need to be used in pairs.

Any HTML tag that creates a line break, such as a heading, results in the text immediately following the line break becoming a new paragraph, so the **<P>** tag isn't needed in these cases.

Listing Other Line Breaks

Because the paragraph tag causes a blank line to be displayed in a Web browser's rendering of your document, you also need a way to cause a line break to occur without an attending blank line. The **
 (line break)** tag does this for you. Here's an HTML fragment showing its use, as well as clarifying the difference between it and the **<P>** tag:

```
For more information, contact:

<P>John Doe<BR>

123 Main Street<BR>

Htmltown, USA 55555

<P>Resumption of document text...
```

When rendered, this is displayed with a blank line before "John Doe," but with line breaks (no blank line) between the lines of the address, and a new paragraph (with blank line) after the ZIP code line. See Figure 3.3. You can use multiple <BR> tags to force multiple blank lines in your document.

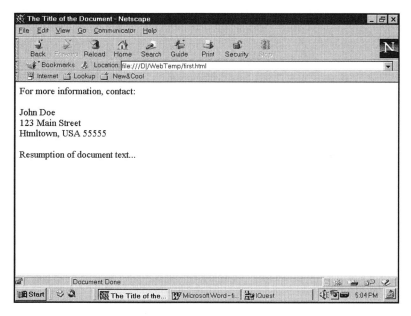

Figure 3.3   Paragraphs and line breaks.

Be aware that several other HTML tags, by definition, always create line breaks. As noted previously, headings always break the text and start a new line. Paragraph tags always, of course, create a line break. Similarly, lists (see Lesson 6, "Inserting Lists"), preformatted text (see Lesson 7, "Inserting Tables"), and some of the logical formatting tags create line breaks. In these cases, you don't need to include line-break (or paragraph) tags. However, preformatted text does not recognize the Enter keystroke as an end of paragraph.

> **TIP**   **<NOBR> tag**   Netscape also supports a <NOBR> tag to suppress any line break Navigator might otherwise include in displaying an HTML document, while the <WBR> Netscape extension provides a "suggested" line break that only gets used if necessary. <NOBR> is useful if breaking the line will cause confusion, such as in a program listing.

Text Colors

You can specify the color of text in your HTML documents. This mechanism is based on the notation of colors by using the RGB (red, green, blue) colors found in all color video monitors. Individual colors are specified by using three separate numbers (one each for red, green, and blue), each in the range of 0 through 255. For example, pure black (that is, the lack of any red, green, or blue) is expressed as three zeros, or "0 0 0," while white is expressed as "255 255 255," because white is created by full saturation of all three primary colors. In between, colors are created based on setting each of the three primary colors to a value between 0 and 255. Royal blue, for instance, is expressed as "65 105 225."

To set text colors in HTML, grab your scientific calculator (or pop up your Windows calculator in scientific mode) and convert your three decimal color numbers into hexadecimal. You can also use the Windows 95 Paint program to select colors and display their hex equivalents. Here is a short HTML fragment that sets the text color to royal blue, illustrating the number conversion of the 65, 105, 225 triplet:

<BODY TEXT="4169E1">

As you can see, this HTML tag is inside the <BODY> section of your HTML documents. As such, it controls the text color for all the text on the page. To change the color of a range of text, use the <FONT COLOR=></FONT COLOR> tags. The example uses the hexadecimal equivalents of the three numbers 65 (41), 105 (69), and 225 (E1) to express the color royal blue.

With the same mechanism, you can specify different colors for your basic document text and the text of your hyperlinks (see Lesson 5, "Using Anchors and Links") in your HTML documents.

CAUTION

Colors, Colors, and More Colors   Simple arithmetic indicates there's a vast range of possible combinations of these color designations. It's a lot easier to choose your colors if you can see them. There are a couple of Web sites where you can do just that. First, check out **http://www.onr.com/user/lights/colclick.html**. Next, try **http://www.reednews.co.uk/colours.html** or **http://alberti.crs4.it/colori/f108.html**. Also, UNIX systems generally have a list of colors and their decimal number equivalents in the file /usr/lib/X11/rgb.txt (/usr/openwin/lib/rgb.txt on Sun systems). This is a plain-text file you can read.

This lesson covered fundamental typeface/character formatting issues, and showed you how to create headings and paragraphs. In the next lesson, you'll learn about Uniform Resource Locators, which help you to specify locations on the World Wide Web.

Creating Documents with URLs

4

In this lesson, you learn about Uniform Resource Locators, or URLs, the pointers in HTML documents that lead to various services on the World Wide Web.

What Is a Uniform Resource Locator?

The *Uniform Resource Locator*, or URL, is the key to locating and interpreting information on the Internet. URLs are a standard way of describing both the location of a Web resource and its content. URLs in HTML documents help you locate Web resources, regardless of whether it's another document on your local computer or on another computer halfway around the world. To create HTML documents with hyperlinks in them, you need to understand the basics of URLs.

Hyperlinks   The colored words and phrases you've seen in Web documents. Clicking hyperlinks lets you jump to the location pointed to by the link. Some hyperlinks do not appear as colored text. They may appear as underlined text, or the Web page author may have chosen to use a graphic to act as the hyperlink.

The HTML language uses a standard syntax for expressing an URL. It looks like this:

> **protocol://domainname:portnumber/path**

As you can see, there are three parts to this syntax:

- **protocol** is followed by a colon and two forward slashes (there are a couple of exceptions to the requirement for the slashes, as you will see later).

- **domainname** is where the service is located and the optional **portnumber**, followed by a single forward slash.
- **path** is normally a document or file on the computer, but it may also be other kinds of resources, as you will see.

Here's an example URL, showing the required parts:

http://www.yourcompany.com/home.html

 Connections   Internet services use imaginary wires to connect services between imaginary plugs (ports) on two computers. These virtual connections are managed by the network software using an abstraction called *port numbers*. Except where you need to include one in an URL, you really don't need to know anything more than how to recognize the URL.

Creating an URL

To create an URL, you type its various component parts as if you were typing a sentence without spaces. The following steps lead you through the process:

1. Identify the service name you will include in your URL. The most commonly used one is the http service.

 HyperText Transfer Protocol (http)   The way Web servers and clients communicate over the network.

2. Identify the **Internet location** of the resource. This is an Internet hostname, such as **www.yourcompany.com**.

3. Identify the name of the resource, such as a document name, file name, or other resource. An example might be **home.html**.

Using the examples in the preceding listing, we can construct an URL that might represent your company's home page:

http://www.yourcompany.com/index.html

Examples of Different Service URLs

This section provides example URLs covering some of the major URL types.
Each example is an actual World Wide Web resource that you can access using
your Web browser. This is not a complete list of URL types.

The http URL

The **http** URL represents a document available from a World Wide Web server.
Here is an example of Netscape's download page:

http://www.netscape.com/download/index.html

What Is That Forward Slash?   All URLs use the **forward slash (/)** to
specify documents. Even if you're setting up your Web server on a PC, use the
forward slash in your URLs, *not* the *backslash* (\), to specify the path to a file or
document.

Figure 4.1 shows the result of using the preceding http URL example. Notice the
URL in the Location box near the top of the screenshot.

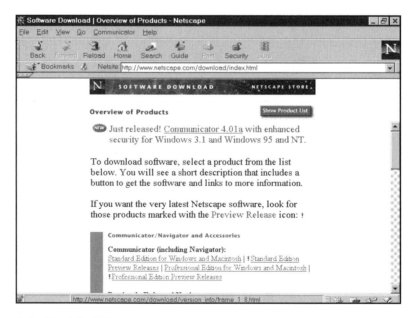

Figure 4.1   The http URL.

The ftp URL

ftp represents the Internet file transfer protocol service. Here is an example:

ftp://gatekeeper.dec.com/pub/

Note here that we have specified not a file name, but rather, a directory name (pub/). ftp URLs can also specify file names. This URL is an archive of no-cost software maintained by the Digital Equipment Corporation for customers and others; it's freely accessible.

The telnet URL

Telnet allows you to remotely log in to a computer system and use your local screen and keyboard as a terminal. Here is an example:

telnet://madlab.sprl.umich.edu:3000

The telnet URL is an exception to the three-part rule; it has only the service name and the hostname.

This URL has an extra twist—specification of an Internet "port number," in this case ":3000" (note the colon). For normal telnet services, you don't need to specify a port number (nor do you need a port number in most other URLs). This is a service known as the "Weather Underground."

The news Address

This represents the UseNet news service. UseNet is a vastly distributed bulletin board service (BBS) organized into literally thousands of special interest subject areas. Following is an example of a news address :

news:comp.infosystems.www.authoring.html

Figure 4.2 shows a sample listing. This example is a newsgroup dedicated to the discussion of HTML authoring. As you'll note, each article shows up as a hyperlink, which you can select and view. While this screenshot shows Netscape Collabra, other newsreaders present UseNet news in different ways.

CAUTION

Where Are the Forward Slashes? The news address is an exception to the rule requiring the two forward slashes in the first of the three parts of the address; only the colon and the newsgroup name are required. News is not a bona fide protocol, such as ftp or http.

463

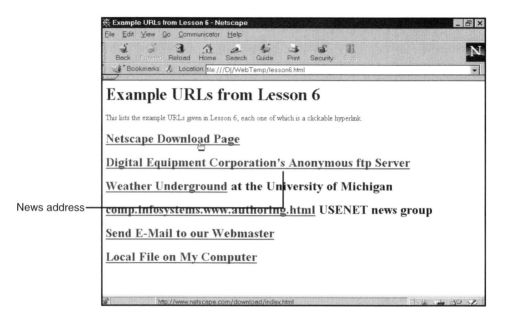

Figure 4.2 The news address.

The mailto Address

This represents the Internet electronic mail (e-mail) service. The mailto address is supported by most Web browsers. Use a mailto address in your HTML documents so readers can send you e-mail simply by clicking the hyperlink. Here is an example:

mailto:webmaster@www.yourcompany.com

The file URL

This represents a file located on your own computer. Here is an example:

file://winword6/html/myfile.htm

Where's the Last "l" in that URL? DOS allows only three characters in a file name extension, whereas other systems, such as UNIX systems, allow more. This URL refers to a file on a PC. If you have Windows 95, MacOS, or Windows NT, you can use the entire .html extension when naming your documents.

CAUTION

Other URL Types

There are several other, less commonly used, URL types. These include the **WAIS** (Wide Area Indexing Servers) **URL**, for doing keyword searches in WAIS databases; **gopher**, a text-based, menu-oriented predecessor to the World Wide Web; and others. WAIS keyword support has been, for the most part, supplanted by other Web services called Search Engines, while gopher services are becoming more and more rare.

This lesson has covered Uniform Resource Locators: what they look like and their syntax. We've seen the various kinds of URLs and the Internet services they represent. In the next lesson, you learn how to use URLs to insert hyperlinks in your HTML documents.

Using Anchors and Links

In this lesson, you learn to use tags and URLs to create hyperlinks to local and remote documents and services on the Web.

What Is a Hyperlink?

You've no doubt used hyperlinks as you've tooled around the World Wide Web in Part 2, "The World Wide Web." Your knowledge of HTML tags and URLs, along with the new anchor tag to be introduced in this lesson, will enable you to add highlighted hyperlinks to your HTML documents.

 Click and Go *Hyperlinks* are the colored/highlighted/underlined words and phrases you see in Web documents. When you click them, you jump to other documents on the local Web server or documents, or to services somewhere out on the Internet, across town, or halfway around the world.

The Anchor HTML Tag

Hyperlinks are based on the *anchor* HTML tag. Like all HTML tags, the anchor tag must open with the < symbol and close with the > symbol. Here is the general syntax:

```
<A ATTRIBUTE="target">Highlighted Text</A>
```

Let's take this apart and look at it, piece by piece. First, the matter inside the opening set of angle brackets, **<A ATTRIBUTE= "target">**.

- There are two parts, separated by the = sign. The part on the right side is shown inside double quotation marks (this isn't a strict requirement in all situations, but it's a good rule to follow).

- On the left side, substitute either **HREF** or **NAME** for ATTRIBUTE. HREF signifies a hyperlink, whereas NAME signifies a marked place in the document (we'll focus on HREF here, then cover NAME a little later).

- The HREF command inside an anchor tag announces that the text on the right side of the = sign is the **target** of a hyperlink. Generally, your anchor tag will look like this:

  ```
  <A HREF="target">Highlighted Text</A>
  ```

Let's now turn to the part of the anchor we've labeled "Highlighted Text</A>" in our example:

- Before you can select a hyperlink in a Web document, you must be able to see some *highlighted text* that is somehow connected to the hyperlink. It's this part of the anchor tag that specifies the word or phrase to appear as highlighted in the HTML document. Add this as shown here:

  ```
  <A HREF="target">Highlighted Text to Appear</A>
  ```

- Note the closing **</A>** in the example; this is the end of your anchor tag. When the HTML document is displayed, the material represented by "Highlighted Text to Appear" in the preceding example appears highlighted, and will be an active hyperlink.

 TIP **Assemble the Link** Putting the anchor link together, including the material on both sides of the "=" sign, is what produces your highlighted hyperlink.

Linking to Local Documents

The simplest hyperlink is one that points to another document on the same computer. Let's say you have two HTML documents in the same directory, named doc1.htm and doc2.htm. To enable the user to jump from the first to the second document, you'd add an anchor tag in doc1.htm like this:

```
<A HREF="doc2.htm">Highlighted Text to Appear</A>
```

Below is a very simple, complete HTML document that illustrates a simple anchor tag pointing to a local document (that is, a file on your own computer).

467

This link will also work if you place both documents in the same directory on your Web server.

```
<HTML><HEAD>

<TITLE>Simple HTML Doc with Local Link</TITLE>

</HEAD><BODY>

<H1>HTML Document with a Hyperlink to a Local File</H1>

Welcome to my HTML document.

<P>You can try out <A HREF="doc2.htm">my hyperlink</A> by clicking
here.

</BODY></HTML>
```

Where's the Link?   If you've typed this example document and tried it out, you probably got an error message. This is because the target document, named *doc2.htm* in this example, hasn't been created yet.

Figure 5.1 shows what this document looks like in your Web browser. Clicking the hyperlink (the phrase "my hyperlink") opens the new document (assuming the document exists and is in the same directory as the page that contains the link).

What If the Target Document Is in a Different Directory?   The example assumes both documents are in the same directory. If you need to reference a document in a different directory, simply change the target part of the anchor tag to include the directory path. For example, if doc2.htm is in the subdirectory subdir1, your anchor would read:

<A HREF="subdir1/doc2.htm">

Note the use of the forward slash, not the backslash. You can, of course, use either a full directory path, such as **http://www.mcp.com/myfiles/subdir1/ doc2.htm** or relative path, such as **./subdir1/doc2.htm**, depending on how you've organized your directories and subdirectories.

Linking to Specific Places in a Document

Now that you know how to link to another document, you may want your hyperlink to point to a specific spot in the target document, instead of just to the document itself. Fortunately, this is easy in HTML. As noted previously, there are two commands that may be part of an anchor link. For this purpose, you'll use the NAME command. Syntax is simple:

```
<A NAME="spot">
```

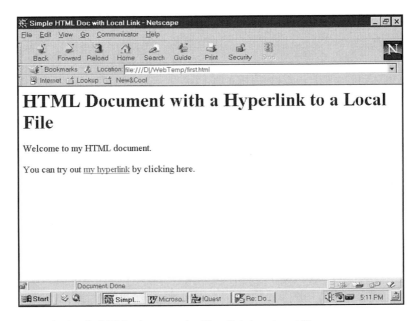

Figure 5.1 A simple HTML document with a link to a local file.

This anchor represents a marker in your target document to the spot where you want the hyperlink in the first document to point. For example, here's an HTML fragment from a target document with a marked spot:

```
<A NAME="xmarks">X Marks the Spot</A>
```

Moving back to your first document, you can use an anchor to create a hyperlink to this spot in your target document:

```
Additional <A HREF="doc2.htm#xmarks">information</A> on creating link
to specific areas of a Web page.
```

As you can see, this is a normal hyperlink to a local document, but with one difference: the addition of "#xmarks" to reference the spot you've marked in the target document. Clicking the hyperlink in your first document jumps you not only to the target document, but also right to the marked spot in it. You can fine-tune your HTML documents by enabling users to jump to a precise spot.

469

Incidentally, you can also use the jump-to-a-spot feature of HTML within a single document. Just enter the spot marker (**<A NAME="spot">**), then create your hyperlink in the same document, like this:

<A HREF="#spot">

Here's an HTML fragment, showing this feature within the same document.

```
This page provides access to an assortment of tools and information
for

WebMasters (people who run WWW servers or who create hypertext

markup lanaguage (HTML) documents for WWW servers).

<P>From this page, you can

[ Some text deleted ]

<LI>Learn about the <A HREF="#htmlrefs">Hyper Text Markup
Language</A></LI>

[ Some text deleted ]

<A NAME="htmlrefs"><H2>Hyper Text Markup Language (HTML)
</H2></A>
```

Figure 5.2 shows the page from which this HTML fragment is taken. As you can see, there's a list of hyperlinks; our fragment is the fifth item on that list.

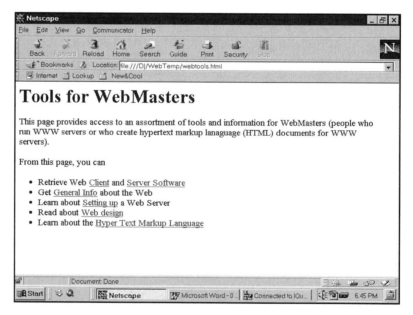

Figure 5.2 HTML document with jump-to-spot links.

As you can see, this is a full hyperlink, with "#htmlrefs" as the target of the link. The last line of the HTML source fragment is the target of this hyperlink. You'll note the use of the "<A NAME="htmlrefs">." Selecting the hyperlink jumps you to the destination, within the same document, as shown in Figure 5.3. Note the appearance of the "#htmlrefs" in Netscape's URL box.

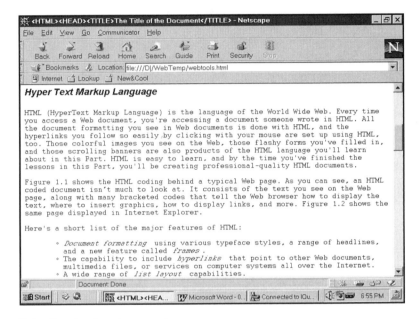

Figure 5.3 Destination document.

Linking URLs

We can now turn to links that point to documents or other resources on remote systems. To do this, we'll use the *Uniform Resource Locator* representing the remote document. Let's look back at the first URL example we discussed in Lesson 4:

http://www.netscape.com/download/index.html

Creating a hyperlink containing this URL is pretty straightforward, using what we've learned about anchors:

```
<A HREF="http://www.netscape.com/download/index.html">Netscape
Download Page</A>
```

As you can see, we've simply dropped the complete URL into the target slot (to the right side of the = sign) in our hyperlink anchor tag.

The phrase "Netscape Download Page" is highlighted, and you can jump all the way to Netscape's download page with just a click of your mouse.

Other URLs work exactly the same way. Here's the second example, the DEC anonymous ftp server:

<A HREF="ftp://gatekeeper.dec.com/pub/">Digital Equipment Corp's ftp Server</A>

The following is an excerpt from an HTML document containing links to all the URL examples covered in Lesson 4. A Netscape rendering of that HTML document is shown in Figure 5.4.

```
<HTML><HEAD><TITLE>Example URLs from Lesson 6</TITLE></
HEAD><BODY><H1>Example URLs from Lesson 6</H1>

This lists the example URLs given in Lesson 6, each one of which is a
clickable hyperlink.

<H2><A HREF="http://www.netscape.com/download/index.html">Netscape
Download Page</A></H2>

<H2><A HREF="ftp://gatekeeper.dec.com/pub">Digital Equipment
Corporation's Anonymous FTP Server</A></H2>

<H2><A HREF="telnet://wudlab.sprl.umich.edu:3000">Weather
Underground</A> at the University of Michigan</H2>

<H2><AHREF="news:comp.infosystems.www.authoring.html">comp.
infosystems.www.authoring.html</A> USENET news group</H2>

<H2><A HREF="mailto:webmaster@www.youcompany.com">Send
E-Mail to our Webmaster</A></H2>

<H2><A HREF="file://winword6/html/myfile.htm">Local File on My
Computer</A></H2>

</BODY></HTML>
```

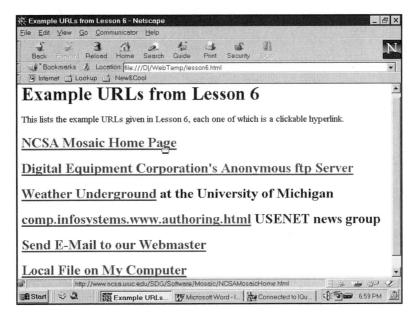

Figure 5.4 Hyperlinks to Lesson 4 example URLs.

Absolute and Relative URLs By now, you've figured out that hyperlinks to local documents are actually little URLs, but without the normally required service name and Internet host name. When referring to documents that use the same service name and host name as the parent document, you can use *relative* URLs. Using relative URLs allows you to move whole HTML document trees from one place to another, even to another computer, without having to go back through all the documents and changing the absolute URLs.

In this lesson, you've combined what you learned in Lesson 4, "Creating Documents with URLs," to create hyperlinks in your HTML documents by using Uniform Resource Locators. We'll return to HTML formatting and layout in the next lesson, as we turn to adding lists to your HTML documents.

Inserting Lists

6

In this lesson, you learn how to insert bulleted, numbered, and definition lists in your Web page.

Kinds of Lists

It's useful to have your HTML documents contain formatted lists of items, in addition to ordinary paragraphs. HTML supports several different list formats, each with enough variations to give you a wide range of capabilities. These include:

- Bulleted lists, called *unordered lists* in HTML
- Sequentially numbered lists, called *ordered lists*
- Glossary lists, sometimes called *definition lists*

HTML has markup tags for each of these kinds of lists.

Formatting Bullets (Unordered Lists)

Bulleted lists highlight each item on a list by adding a typographical bullet or other distinctive marker. In HTML, you create bullets using the unordered list markup tag, together with the generic **<LI>** tag (the latter tag, as you'll see, is used in all types of HTML lists). Here is an HTML fragment containing an unordered list:

```
<UL><LI>First Bulleted Item</LI>
<LI>Second Bulleted Item</LI>
<LI>Last Bulleted Item</LI></UL>
```

By now, you're familiar enough with HTML markup syntax to recognize the start and stop **</UL>** markers for the overall list, as well as the markers for the individual items **<LI>**.

Although the list-close marker **</UL>** is always required, the existing HTML standard doesn't require the closing **</LI>**, and most current Web browsers just ignore them. Nonetheless, rather than learning exceptions to general HTML rules, it's a good idea to just go ahead and use the list item close marker. Future changes in the HTML standard may require it.

Figure 6.1 shows an unordered list, as well as an ordered list (see next section). As you can see, list items need not be confined to a single line of text. You can use several lines of text, creating hanging indents. Also, you can use paragraph markers **<P>** and **</P>** to create multi-paragraph, bulleted lists.

Mixing Tags   Be careful when mixing other HTML tags within your lists. In particular, note that line-breaking HTML tags, such as the <BR> tag or a headline tag, may have undesirable effects on your lists.

Hanging Indents   Bulleted lists produce hanging indents. In other words, the paragraph begins with a bullet, and each line of the paragraph is indented from the left margin, rather than returning to the margin. The whole paragraph "hangs" directly below the bullet.

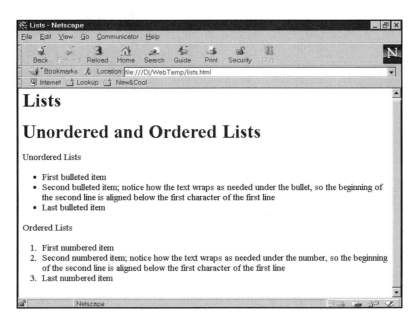

Figure 6.1   Unordered and ordered lists.

If you're not happy with the default bullets you get with an unordered list, you have two other choices. Using an HTML unordered list *attribute*, you can select one of two other bullet types, the *square* and *hollow circle* types. Here's an HTML fragment showing use of the square bullet type.

```
<UL TYPE=SQUARE>
<LI>First Item</LI>
...
</UL>
```

As you can see, the attribute "TYPE=SQUARE" appears immediately after the open-list tag, within the angle brackets. To use the hollow circle bullet type, use "TYPE=CIRCLE." The default bullet type for unordered lists is "TYPE=DISC" and is not required.

 Attributes HTML attributes specify characteristics that apply to HTML tags. Thus, the TYPE attribute for unordered lists defines the type of bullet to be used within the list. You'll see more HTML attributes as we go along.

Formatting Numbered (Ordered) Lists

Instead of bullets, you may want to have your lists *numbered*. HTML's ordered list tag **<OL>** enables you to do just that—and automatically numbers your items for you. Here's an example HTML fragment:

```
<OL><LI>First Numbered Item</LI>
<LI>Second Numbered Item</LI>
<LI>Third Numbered Item</LI></OL>
```

Note the use of the standard <LI> and </LI> tags for the individual, list items. Also, your ordered list is automatically numbered when it's interpreted and displayed by your user's Web browser, so you don't need to type any numbers in your HTML document; it will be automatically renumbered if you change it later, or add or delete items. Figure 6.1 shows both an ordered and unordered list as interpreted and displayed.

The latest HTML standards have added a couple of useful attributes for ordered lists. First, as you might guess, there is a TYPE attribute that enables you to select the kind of numbering to use. You can choose from ordinary Arabic numbers, Roman Numerals (in large or small letters), and alphabetical letters, in upper- or lowercase. Use the TYPE attribute, as shown in Table 6.1.

Table 6.1 Numbered List Attributes

Code	Attribute
<OL TYPE=1>	Arabic Numbers (the default; not required)
<OL TYPE=a>	Lowercase Letters
<OL TYPE=A>	Uppercase Letters
<OL TYPE=i>	Small Roman Numerals
<OL TYPE=I>	Large Roman Numerals

CAUTION

Just in Case Throughout this book, use of all uppercase characters has been recommended for your HTML markup. Although this remains a good idea, you can see the ordered list numbering types are case-sensitive.

There may be instances when you'd like to control the starting number used in an ordered list. The new **START** attribute does this for you. Here's an example HTML fragment, calling for an ordered list to use large Roman Numerals and to begin numbering with the VII, illustrating use of multiple attributes at once.

```
<OL TYPE="I" START="7">
...
</OL>
```

CAUTION

All Gaul Is Divided into Three Parts You must use an Arabic number (that is, 1, 2, 3, and so on) to define an alternative starting number in a list, even though you may have specified a Roman Numeral or Letter numbering type.

Creating Glossary Lists

A glossary listing allows you to include a description of each item listed. The HTML tag **<DL>** denotes such a list, but uses a couple of other tags to format the glossary listing. The others are **<DT>**, *definition term*, and **<DD>**, *definition data*. Here's a sample HTML fragment:

477

```
<H1>HTML List Elements</H1>

<DL><DT>The UL Tag</DT>

<DD>Creates an unordered, or bulleted, list</DD>

<DT>The OL Tag</DT>

<DD>Creates an ordered, or numbered list</DD>

<DT>The LI Tag</DT>

<DD>Used in both unordered and ordered lists to denote list items.
</DD>

<DT>The DL Tag</DT>

<DD>Create a glossary or dictionary list</DD>

<DT>The DT Tag</DT>

<DD>Delineates a term on a definition list</DD>

<DT>The DD Tag</DT>

<DD>A definition on a dictionary or glossary list</DD></DL>
```

Figure 6.2 shows the rendering of this example, and a quick summary of the HTML list tags.

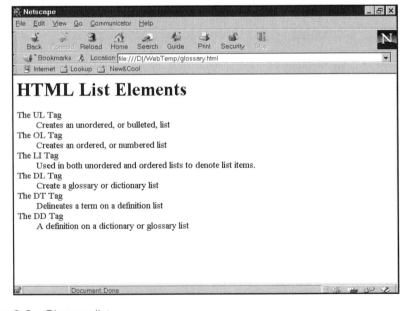

Figure 6.2 Glossary list.

New List Features in HTML

A couple of overall list features have been added in the latest HTML standard. These are general features, and they apply to all types of lists.

- The **<LH>** tag provides an automatic List Header by printing a title for your list.
- The **COMPACT** attribute causes your list to be rendered in a smaller font.

Here's a small HTML fragment that illustrates both these new features.

```
<UL COMPACT>
<LH>New HTML Tags</LH>
<LI>List Header</LI>
<LI>Compact Spacing</LI></UL>
```

Nesting Lists

You can also nest lists, even different kinds of listings. (A nested list is a list within a list.) For example, the following HTML fragment shows a two-level unordered list:

```
<UL><LI>List Item Number 1</LI>
<LI>List Item Number 2</LI>
<UL><LI>Item 2 sub-item A</LI>
<LI>Item 2 sub-item B</LI></UL>
<LI>List Item Number 3</LI></UL>
```

Some Web browsers, as shown in Figure 6.3, will render nested lists using different types of bullets; others just use more bullets. This figure also shows a nested list, using both ordered and unordered list tags; the HTML fragment follows.

```
<OL><LI>Apples</LI>
<UL><LI>Granny</LI>
<LI>Golden Delicious</LI></UL>
<LI>Oranges</LI>
<UL><LI>Navel</LI>
<LI>Juice</LI></UL></OL>
```

479

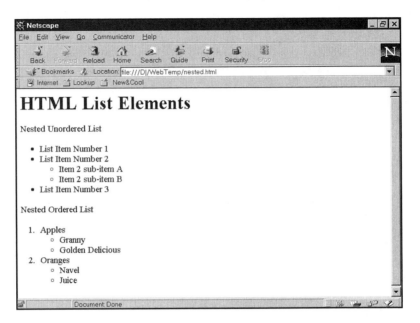

Figure 6.3   Nested lists.

Count Your Tags   Be sure to count your HTML tags when you're nesting them. If your list doesn't display the way you expect it to, you've probably miscounted your pairs of stop and start tags.

CAUTION

Also, when nesting lists (or nesting other HTML tags, for that matter), make sure the logical operations of one tag don't cancel out those of another. For example, you wouldn't succeed trying to nest an *unordered* list in the middle of a *directory* list, since the former would break up the across-the-screen formatting of the latter. When in doubt, use your Web browser to preview your HTML document before putting it on the Web.

This lesson covered the various kinds of lists you can put into your HTML documents. In addition, you've learned that lists can be nested to create useful effects. In the next lesson, you will learn how to arrange text in columns, using tables.

Inserting Tables

In this lesson, you learn how to use HTML tags to create on-screen tables. Tables are used not only for tabular data, like columns of numbers, but also to control image placement and text alignment.

Why Use Tables

Although headings, paragraphs, and lists can handle most text, occasionally, you need a little more control over text and graphic layout. Tables give you this control. They allow you to place text and numbers in rows and columns, and allow you to position a graphic precisely on a page. In addition, tables force Web browsers to display text in your intended layout, taking some of the guesswork out of positioning text and graphics.

Table Talk An HTML table, like any other printed table, consists of columns and rows of information.

Table Basics

It's best to think of HTML tables as *text spreadsheets*, like Lotus 1-2-3 or Excel. Spreadsheets consist of horizontal *rows* and vertical *columns* of information, which can be formatted according to your needs. The intersection of a row and a column is called a cell. An HTML table won't do math like Lotus 1-2-3, but if you're familiar with the basics of spreadsheets, you should be on familiar ground here. HTML table markup can be used for what most people think of as tabular information, such as columns of numbers. While we'll start out our tables discussion with just such data, because it's the best way to introduce tables, we'll move into sophisticated use of table markup for images and other data shortly.

Using Heading, Row, and Data Tags

HTML uses the **<TABLE>** markup tag to signify a table. An HTML table has three main markup tags: **<TH>** for table heading; **<TR>** for end of a table row; and **<TD>** for table *data* (that is, the information in a cell), as well as several kinds of cell-alignment attributes. Here's an HTML fragment with a very simple table:

```
<TABLE>
<TR><TD>Row 1, Column 1</TD>
<TD>Row 1, Column 2</TD></TR>
<TR><TD>Row 2, Column 1</TD>
<TD>Row 2, Column 2</TD></TR></TABLE>
```

This prints a simple two-row, two-column table.

Vertical and Horizontal Headings   Table heading is a bit of a misnomer; it applies both to vertical column headings and horizontal row labels.

Let's modify our previous example fragment to add some real information:

```
<H1>Consolidated HTML Consultants, Inc.</H1>
<H2>1994 Profit and Loss (Actual and Forecast)</H2>
<TABLE><TR><TH>First Quarter</TH>
<TH>Second Quarter</TH><TH>Third Quarter</TH>
<TH>Fourth Quarter</TH></TR>
<TR><TD>12% Profit (Actual)</TD>
<TD>2% Loss (Actual)</TD>
<TD>5% Loss (Actual)</TD>
<TD>8% Profit (Actual)</TD></TR>
<TR><TD>11% profit (Forecast)</TD>
<TD>2% profit(Forecast)</TD>
<TD>3% loss (Forecast)</TD>
<TD>5% profit (Forecast)</TD></TR></TABLE>
```

Here, we added four *headings* for our quarterly report of profit and loss, and added two rows of actual *data*, along with a couple of descriptive headlines. Figure 7.1 shows our table.

Table headings ———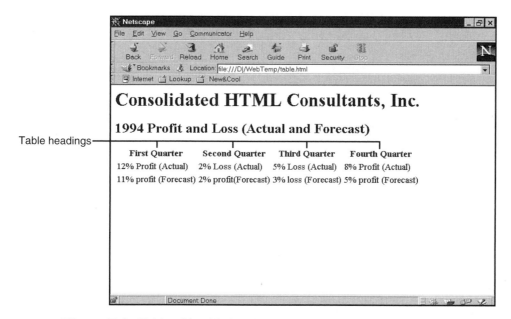

Figure 7.1   Table with table headings added.

Adding Alignment

One of the first things you'll notice about the table (besides the slightly different, bolded typeface automatically added for the table headings—a nice touch) is the formatting of the cells. The contents of each table heading and table data cell are centered, which is the default alignment for table headings. The **<TH>** and **<TD>** tags each support the **ALIGN** attribute, which gives you control over the justification of the contents. Simply insert the attribute into the markup tag. For example, to use left alignment, use **<TH ALIGN="LEFT">**; for right justification, use **<TD ALIGN="RIGHT">**. As with other HTML attributes, you should surround table attributes with double quotes.

Controlling Columns and Rows

There are a couple of additional attributes supported by both the **<TH>** and **<TD>** markup tags. You can control the width and height of columns and rows using the *COLSPAN* and *ROWSPAN* attributes. For example, **<TH ROWSPAN**

=3> creates a table heading that is three rows high, while **<TD COLSPAN=2>** creates a cell that's two columns wide. Imaginative use of the COLSPAN and ROWSPAN attributes allows you to create quite complex tables.

Creating a Complex Boxed Table

Figure 7.2 shows a complex table, using both the COLSPAN and ROWSPAN attributes. You'll notice this table is neatly boxed. It's very simple to box your tables with the *BORDER* attribute of the <TABLE> markup tag. To box your table, start out with **<TABLE BORDER>. <CAPTION>** is an HTML tag, which you can use to add a title to your tables. Like, **<TD>**, and **<TR>**, **<CAPTION>** is valid only within a **<TABLE>** tag and can specify your table title like this:

```
<CAPTION>Title of the Table</CAPTION>
```

Figure 7.3 shows the HTML markup, which creates the table in Figure 7.2. The table in Figure 7.2 is only an example. The **<TABLE>**, **<TR>**, **<TH>**, and **<TD>** tags have many more attributes than those listed in the figure.

Border Width   You can control the border width (that is, the on-screen thickness of the border itself) for Netscape Navigator or Internet Explorer with the *WIDTH* attribute. For example, to make your border 3 screen pixels wide (the default is 1 pixel), use **<TABLE BORDER WIDTH=3>**.

CAUTION

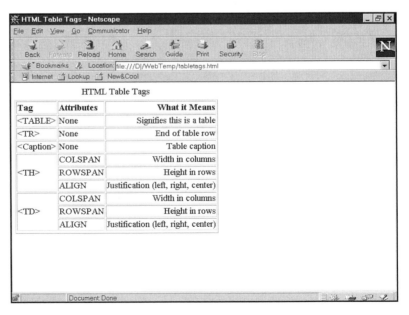

Tag	Attributes	What it Means
<TABLE>	None	Signifies this is a table
<TR>	None	End of table row
<Caption>	None	Table caption
<TH>	COLSPAN	Width in columns
	ROWSPAN	Height in rows
	ALIGN	Justification (left, right, center)
<TD>	COLSPAN	Width in columns
	ROWSPAN	Height in rows
	ALIGN	Justification (left, right, center)

Figure 7.2   Complex, boxed table.

Figure 7.3 HTML markup for a complex, boxed table.

Table Width and Alignment

Current HTML standards give you a good deal of control over the width and alignment of tables, though there are some slight variations between the standards and how Netscape Navigator implements them.

Table Width

The *WIDTH* attribute, together with the optional *UNITS* attribute, control table width. By default, table width is expressed in printer's *en* units, with each unit being equal to half the point size of the current type. You can express table width in more commonly understood terms by using the UNITS attribute with either *PIXEL* (screen pixels) or *RELATIVE* (a percentage of the page width). To create a table that occupies half the width of the page, use HTML markup like this:

```
<TABLE WIDTH="50%" UNITS="RELATIVE">
```

Earlier, you learned about the COLSPAN and ROWSPAN attributes, which allow you to set the size of cells in your tables. You can also use the new *WIDTH* attribute within individual table cells to control cell width. Here's an example:

```
<TD WIDTH="50%">Cell Entry</TD>
```

485

In this example, the cell will span 50 percent of the table width. If the user resizes the browser window, the cell width changes according to the width of the table.

Table Alignment

Table alignment is one of the new features of the HTML 3.2 standard, and some of its specifications aren't yet implemented in all Web browsers. You'll need to experiment with these and see how different browsers deal with them.

Basic table alignment is controlled using the ALIGN attribute. For example, to center a table on your viewer's page, begin your table markup like this:

```
<TABLE ALIGN="CENTER">
```

Other values for table alignment include *LEFT, RIGHT, JUSTIFY* (fit the width of the page), and *BLEEDLEFT* and *BLEEDRIGHT*. The latter pair are used when other, non-table text flows around your table. (You'll learn about text flow in Lesson 9, "Adding Images to Your Documents.")

CAUTION

Web Browser Support   Not all browsers support all HTML 3.2 table-alignment attributes. You'll need to experiment with a couple of Web browsers to see where they stand in this area. Do note, however, Netscape's general <CENTER> tag can be used to center any text, including tables.

Advanced, Creative Use of HTML Tables

Use of HTML table markup to create simple rows and columns of numbers might seem fairly limited. After all, you don't need a table of data in every HTML document. In fact, many sophisticated HTML authors use table markup to overcome HTML's other limitations in document layout. The key point to remember is that table cells can contain almost anything, including images, hyperlinks, and most other HTML markup.

In fact, use of HTML table markup creates many of the striking Web pages you've probably seen. Figure 7.4 shows the Microsoft Internet Explorer (IE) home page (**http://www.microsoft.com/ie/**). If you take a look at the HTML source for this page, you'll see it consists entirely of tables, some of which are nested inside other tables. While you'll want to use your Web browser's View Source capability to study this code, let's look at a couple of pieces of it to get an idea of what they've done here.

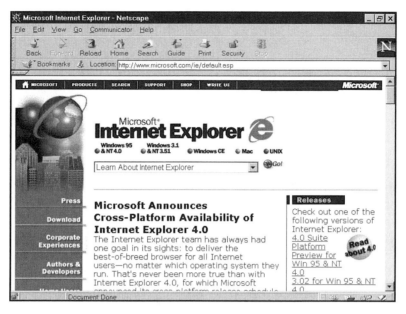

Figure 7.4   Internet Explorer Home Page, Featuring Table Markup.

The first thing you notice about the IE home page is the black navigational bar across the top, which Microsoft's HTML authors have created as an HTML table. The table has two **<TD>** tags, one each for the left and right sides of the button bar, and is placed against a black background (you'll learn about background colors in the next lesson). The left **<TD>** tag, for example, contains the six clickable buttons labeled "Microsoft," "Products," "Search," "Support," "Shop," and "Write Us," as well as two other transparent GIF image files.

Take a detailed look at the HTML source for this table. You'll see several important capabilities:

- Inclusion of the images shows images can be placed inside table cells, with full control of height, width, and alignment, using **<IMG>** attributes.

- Images and other data inside of a table cell can also be clickable hyperlinks, using the HTML anchor tag.

- Alignment of the table is fine-tuned by using a new **<TABLE>** attribute, *CELLPADDING*.

Just below the black navigation bar on the IE home page, you'll see that the rest of the page is little more than a large, three-column table. As you can see, the table allows graphics and text to live side-by-side. Here's the HTML markup for this last table:

```
<TABLE CELLPADDING="0" CELLSPACING="0" BORDER="0" WIDTH="152"
BGCOLOR="#336699">
<TR><TD ALIGN=LEFT WIDTH="152" BGCOLOR="white">
<IMG WIDTH="151" HEIGHT="221" SRC="/ie/images/ULG_iehome.jpg"
ALT="Internet Explorer" BORDER=0><BR>
<A HREF="/ie/press/"><IMG BORDER=0 WIDTH=152 HEIGHT=16 SRC="/ie/mac/
images/press.gif" ALT="Press"></A><BR>
<IMG WIDTH=152 HEIGHT=23 SRC="/ie/mac/images/redln.gif"
ALT="line"><BR>
<A HREF="/ie/download/"><IMG BORDER=0 WIDTH=152 HEIGHT=15 SRC="/ie/
mac/images/downld.gif" ALT="Download Internet Explorer"></A><BR>
<IMG WIDTH=152 HEIGHT=23 SRC="/ie/mac/images/greenln.gif"
ALT="line"><BR>
<A HREF="/ie/corp/"><IMG BORDER=0 WIDTH=152 HEIGHT=32 SRC="/ie/mac/
images/corpexp.gif" ALT="Corporate Experiences">
</A><BR>
<IMG WIDTH=152 HEIGHT=23 SRC="/ie/mac/images/blueln.gif"
ALT="line"><BR>
<A HREF="/ie/authors/"><IMG BORDER=0 WIDTH=152 HEIGHT=33 SRC="/ie/
mac/images/a&d.gif" ALT="Authors and Developers">
</A><BR>
<IMG WIDTH=152 HEIGHT=23 SRC="/ie/mac/images/yellowln.gif"
ALT="line"><BR>
<A HREF="/ie/homeuser/"><IMG BORDER=0 WIDTH=152 HEIGHT=16 SRC="/ie/
mac/images/homeusers.gif" ALT="Home
Users"></A><BR>
<IMG WIDTH=152 HEIGHT=23 SRC="/ie/mac/images/redln.gif"
ALT="line"><BR>
<A HREF="/ie/logo/"><IMG BORDER=0 WIDTH=152 HEIGHT=17 SRC="/ie/mac/
images/getlogo.gif" ALT="Get The Internet Explorer Logo"></A><BR>
<IMG WIDTH=152 HEIGHT=23 SRC="/ie/mac/images/greenln.gif"
ALT="line"><BR>
</TD></TR>
<TR><TD ALIGN=LEFT WIDTH="152" BGCOLOR="white"><IMG WIDTH=140
HEIGHT=3200 SRC="/ie/images/bluehome.gif" ALT=""><IMG WIDTH=12
HEIGHT=3200 SRC="/ie/images/wht.gif" ALT=""></TD></TR>
</TABLE>
```

As you can see, most of the table attributes you've learned are used, along with a couple of new ones. Compare this markup to what you see in Figure 7.4.

In this lesson, you focused on HTML tables, with basic table setup information, as well as examples of sophisticated table markup, by using images and other HTML capabilities within tables to create striking effects. In the next lesson, you will learn how to use preformatted text.

Preformatted Text

*In this lesson, you learn how to use HTML markup to format
tabular material without using HTML table markup.*

Why Use Preformatted Text?

You learned in the last lesson how to use HTML table markup to create tabular
material and to fine-tune the layout of your Web pages using table markup.
Some older Web browsers, however, don't support tables, or they do so only
partially, or display them slightly differently. Still others (NCSA X Mosaic for
UNIX) allow users to turn table support on and off, while another (NCSA
WinMosaic) allows users to set table display preferences that may cause your
tables to be displayed differently than you intended. If users who will be
viewing your Web pages use older Web browsers, you'll need to consider
another way of preserving essential layout, such as tables in your HTML
documents. The following section explains an alternative to using tables.

Controlling Table Layout with the
<PRE> Tag

Before the development of HTML table standards, the sure way to retain the
formatting of your tables was to use *preformatted text*. If viewers of your HTML
documents don't have table-capable browsers, such as the Lynx nongraphical
browser, or browsers with limited/configurable table support, such as NCSA
Mosaic, you'll want to know how to set up preformatted text.

Generally speaking, HTML ignores the extra white space you'd normally use in a table to create rows and columns; the **<PRE>** HTML tag *preserves* it. This is where tabular material comes in, since tables have specific spacing/whitespace needs in order to create and line up the rows and columns. Here's a simple fragment of HTML using the <PRE> tag to create a small table, much like the one you created in the last lesson.

```
<PRE>Row 1     Column 1     Column 2     Row 2     Column 1     Col-
umn 2</PRE>
```

As you can see, this is a simple two-row, two-column listing. Without the preformatting tags, this text would run together on a single line, with no extra white space, like this:

```
Row 1 Column 1 Column 2 Row 2 Column 1 Column 2
```

The <PRE> tag causes this text to be rendered in the tabular format you want.

CAUTION

My Columns Don't Line Up   When working with preformatted text, it's not a good idea to use tabs to create white space. Web browsers differ in the way they interpret the Tab character, so you should use multiple spaces to make sure columns of material line up. In the example above, we used exactly five spaces between the columns. Unfortunately, this can get tedious.

Let's re-create the Consolidated HTML Consultants table from the last lesson using preformatted text.

```
<HTML><HEAD><TITLE>Consolidated HTML
Consultants</TITLE></HEAD><BODY>

<H1>Consolidated HTML Consultants, Inc.</H1>

<H2>1994 Profit and Loss (Actual and Forecast)</H2>

<PRE>

First Quarter         Second Quarter      Third Quarter
Fourth Quarter

_ _ _ _ _ _ _ _ _ _ _ _ _ _ _ _ _ _ _ _ _ _ _ _ _ _ _ _ _ _ _

12% Profit (Actual)    2% Loss (Actual)    5% Loss (Actual)
8% Profit (Actual)

11% profit (Forecast)  2% profit(Forecast) 3% loss (Forecast)
 5% profit (Forecast)</PRE><BODY></HTML>
```

490

Here, we used standard HTML headline markup to add *headings* for our quarterly report of profit and loss, and used preformatted text to add column headings, a horizontal ruler, and two rows of actual *data*. Figure 8.1 shows our table. As you can see, you can come pretty close to the table formatting you learned in the last lesson with some imaginative use of HTML. However, tables created using preformatted text cannot have borders.

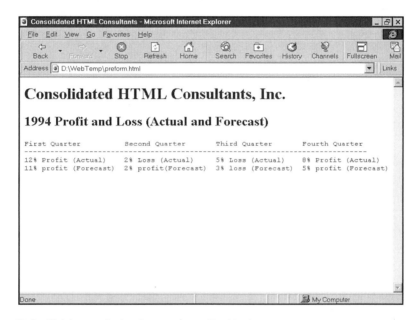

Figure 8.1 Table created using preformatted text.

 TIP **Converting Existing Documents with Tables** In Lesson 15, "Simplify Your Life with HTML Editors," you'll learn about a package called rtftohtml, which allows you to convert existing documents that have been saved in the Microsoft Rich Text Format into HTML. Where such documents have tabular material in them, it'll be converted to preformatted text to preserve the spacing.

In this lesson, you learned how to create tables for Web browsers that do not support the HTML tables feature. In the next lesson, we'll turn to the inclusion of colorful images in your HTML documents.

Adding Images to Your Documents

9

In this lesson, you learn to include colorful images, such as your company logo, in your HTML documents, and to make them hyperlinks.

Adding an Inline Image

There are two sorts of images used in HTML documents. Those that appear directly in your document are called *inline images*. Other images, called *external images*, are discussed below.

Most Web browsers can handle just a few kinds of inline images:

- **Graphic Interchange Format (GIF)** images.
- **X Window** images (normally found on UNIX systems), called **X-Bitmap (XBM) images**, a black-and-white image type.
- Color **X-Pixelmap (XPM)** images, another X Window image type.
- **Joint Photographic Experts Group (JPEG)** image type.

Other image types not directly supported by a browser are treated as external images, viewable with a *Helper application* or *plug-in*, add-on software covered in Part 2, Lessons 15 to 17.

As with other HTML markup, you include an inline image using markup tags. The minimal image inclusion tag is this:

```
<IMG SRC="filename">
```

As you can see, image inclusion requires the attribute SRC, since it specifies your image. Also, to the right of the equal sign, is the file name of the image.

If you are pointing to an image stored on a remote server, include the domain name of the server and the path to the graphic file (for instance, **http:// www.mcp.com/public/graphics/picture.gif**).

The **<IMG>** tag has several other optional attributes. Here's a brief listing of the major ones:

- **ALT** specifies alternative text when the image is in the process of loading, when it only partially loads, or when the image can't be viewed.
- **ALIGN** specifies the physical alignment of the image on the page.
- **HEIGHT** and **WIDTH** specifies the size of the image.
- **ISMAP** specifies the image is a clickable image map.

Microsoft Internet Explorer Internet Explorer has added the **DYNSRC** attribute to the **<IMG>** tag. This adds real-time video to a Web page.

CAUTION

Providing ALT Text

Users with slower connections to the Internet, such as dial-up modem connections, often turn off auto-loading of images. Others use *text-only* Web browsers, such as *Lynx*, which have no graphical capabilities. The *ALT* attribute allows you to specify a text string to appear in place of the image for these users, in order to make your pages usable in these circumstances. For example, if you've included your company's logo, provide alternative text for users with nongraphical browsers like this:

```
<IMG ALT="[Company Logo]" SRC="mycompany.gif">
```

Web pages consisting of nothing but a clickable image map are completely useless to a nongraphical browser, so it's a good idea to include the ALT attribute in all **<IMG>** tags.

Using Align

Although you've learned you have limited control over the rendering of documents in HTML, you can control the alignment of your inline images with the *ALIGN* attribute, which can have one of five values. Here's an example:

```
<IMG ALT="[Logo]" ALIGN="middle" SRC="company.gif">
```

493

Other ALIGN values are top, bottom, left, and right; you can include both vertical and left/right alignment with a second ALIGN attribute. Top, middle, and bottom are relatively subtle differences, since the alignment reference point is the single line of text on which the **<IMG>** tag is placed. Using ALIGN="middle" means the *middle of the image* will line up with the *middle of the line of text*.

Left and right alignment are more dramatic controls, and they allow for the text on your HTML pages to flow around inline images.

Figure 9.1 shows an image aligned with each of the ALIGN attributes.

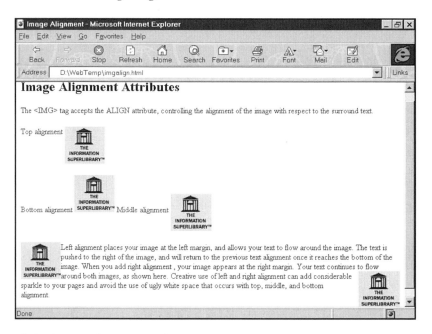

Figure 9.1   Image alignment attributes.

Using HEIGHT and WIDTH

Ordinarily, Web browsers have to download images before they can identify their on-screen size. This results in delays in the display of your HTML documents, as the user's browser waits to learn the size of images before displaying the text of the document. You can reserve space for your inline images using the HEIGHT and WIDTH attributes, causing your HTML documents to load faster, as Web browsers leave enough space for the images, and go ahead with the text while the images are downloading.

CAUTION

No Height or Width Don't try to use HEIGHT and WIDTH as a means of resizing your images on-the-fly. These attributes merely let a browser reserve on-screen real estate for your image. Specifying a height and width that is more than 30 percent smaller or larger than the actual image may result in it being distorted. If you need to change the size of your images by more than 30 percent, use a graphics package.

Both HEIGHT and WIDTH are specified using screen pixels, and should be the same size as the actual image. For example, the clock images in Figure 9.1 are 64-by-64 pixels. Here's an HTML fragment using HEIGHT and WIDTH:

```
<IMG ALIGN="LEFT" HEIGHT="64" WIDTH="64" SRC="mcp.gif">
```

ISMAP

The final **<IMG>** tag attribute is *ISMAP*. We'll cover this exciting feature in the next lesson; for now, just note that it allows you to include *image maps*, inline images that have areas designated as hyperlinks, so that clicking different parts of the image causes different links to be accessed.

Making an Inline Image a Hyperlink

In Lesson 5, "Using Anchors and Links," you learned how to use the HTML anchor **<A>** tag to create highlighted hyperlinks leading to other documents or to URLs representing services elsewhere on the Internet. Sophisticated HTML authors frequently use inline images themselves as hyperlinks by inserting the <IMG> tag within the anchor. Here is an example:

```
<A HREF="http://sales.mycompany.com/"><IMG ALT="[Sales
Department Logo]" ALIGN="LEFT" HEIGHT="32" WIDTH="32"
SRC="sales.gif">Sales Department</A>
```

In this example, we've included a hyperlink to an URL pointing to Sales' Web server. The text "Sales Department" is the hyperlink. Note, however, that we have inserted the complete **<IMG>** tag, with several attributes, *between* the URL and the highlighted text. When you view this in a browser, you'll see not only the normal clickable text highlight, but also the image itself is highlighted. This means you can click directly on the image to access the hyperlink.

Thumbnail Images Link to External Images

Besides the obvious uses of images as hyperlinks, you can also link a small inline image, sometimes called a *thumbnail image*, with a larger, *external* version of the same image. This saves on the network bandwidth required to load the HTML document. If the reader wants to, he or she can click the hyperlinked thumbnail to see the larger image. Here is an example anchor:

```
<A HREF="bigimage.gif"><IMG ALT="[Logo]"SRC="thumbnail.gif">View
Large Image (150kb)</A>
```

As you can see, we've linked directly to another image, along with adding a reference to the image size to tip off the user to the fact that clicking the thumbnail will download a large file.

Image Backgrounds

Many Web authors create pages with image backgrounds. This is easy to do, and can spice up your HTML document without using up bandwidth. To add a background image, use the *BACKGROUND* attribute, like this:

```
<BODY BACKGROUND="mybg.jpeg">
```

As you can see, BACKGROUND is an attribute of the overall HTML **<BODY>** tag. The trick to image backgrounds is the tiling (repeated display) of one small image to create the overall background.

What Happens When a User Can't View Images?

We've already covered use of ALT for including text to display in place of inline images for nongraphical Web browsers. Not only is it always a good idea to include the ALT attribute, you should always include text hyperlinks as alternatives to image links for the same reasons. Presenting a Web page with nothing but a lot of [IMAGE] links is most unfriendly to those with plain-text browsers. And, as we'll see in the next section, there are other reasons for providing text-based alternatives to images, even to users with graphical browsers.

Other Image-Related Considerations

Many people who access the World Wide Web do so over high-speed network links, but many others use dial-up modems and telephone lines. Even with the incredible advances in modem technology over the past few years, today's fastest modems are still very slow compared with local area networks (LANs) and leased digital lines. Images can be very large. They take time to transfer over the link between the user and the server where they reside. It will take longer to retrieve and render your document if it contains many large images. This may only be a few seconds on your LAN, but may be much longer over a modem link. Experts disagree on the appropriate image size, or the overall size of a page with multiple images. Nevertheless, you need to recognize that slow-loading Web pages often result in impatient users going elsewhere.

The capability for Web browsers to begin displaying the text of HTML documents while the images are still being downloaded was a great step forward, especially for users with slow links like modem connections. Nonetheless, as an HTML author, you need to be aware of the trade-offs involved in adding images to your HTML documents.

Always provide text-only alternatives to your images (or use the ALT attribute). For image maps, always use a text-only alternative, and provide them near the top of the page for easy access. Make sure your HTML documents are fully functional in a text-only environment, so when your images aren't available, all your hyperlinks still work. The hyperlink to the company sales department in the previous paragraph is a good example: It contains *both an image and high-lighted text*, either of which can be selected to follow the hyperlink. Whether it's viewed with a graphical or nongraphical browser, the hyperlink works and all necessary explanatory text is shown. Similarly, image maps need to be accompanied by text-based alternatives.

There's another important consideration in adding images to your HTML documents. Even if all your customers have high-speed network links, there are issues of quality involved, too. Inclusion of a large number of images can create an overall look that may not be appealing to visitors. Imagine the worst commercial strip in your town or city, with signs scattered helter-skelter, car dealerships, and fast-food restaurants, and make sure your Web pages don't look like it.

Obtaining Graphics to Use in Your Pages

At this point, you may be wondering where you can get some images to place on your Web pages. You can pick up images from the Web itself by using your Web browser's Save Image As or Save Picture As command. In most cases, you right-click the image you want, and then click the Save command. However, if the image is original art, you must first obtain permission to use the image on your page.

You can also create original images using 3-D, paint, and image manipulation software, such as Paint Shop Pro, ImageMagick, Photoshop, and others. You can also use a scanner and scanner software or take images from clip-art collections. Remember, your images must be in one of the standard formats in order for them to be usable as inline images.

CAUTION

Remember the Copyright   If you take images from a clip-art collection or collection on the Web or use a scanner, be sure to observe any copyright requirements.

In this lesson, you learned the basics of images in HTML. You learned how to add and align inline images; how to include alternative text for users without Web browsers or those with low-bandwidth links; and how to hyperlink inline images to other documents or external images. In the next lesson, you'll learn how to use graphics as image maps.

Creating
Clickable
Image Maps

In this lesson, you learn how to use one of the most exciting features of HTML: clickable image maps.

Understanding Image Maps

You've undoubtedly seen *clickable*, or *hot* images on the Web. These are images with hyperlinks built right into them, so that when you click the image, you jump to another HTML document. Even more exciting, depending on where in the image you click, you go to a different URL. An example might be a floorplan of an office building, in which clicking a suite in the map might generate a detailed floorplan of that suite.

There are two ways of using image maps, one of which is new to the HTML 3.2 standard. First, traditional *server-side* image maps are controlled by the Web server from which they come. Second, *client-side* image maps are activated by your own Web browser based on HTML markup in the document containing the map. Client-side image maps offer substantial advantages, but are only supported in the latest releases of Netscape and Explorer. As a result, you'll want to be familiar with each.

Layout of Image Maps

Both methods are based on the same preliminary measurement and layout of your image hot spots. Image map hot spots are laid out using screen pixel coordinates on a horizontal-vertical axis. That is, if there is a rectangular area in the image you want to be a clickable area, you'll need to get the coordinates of two corners of the rectangle and record them. Although this is a potentially tedious process, there are a couple of shareware programs available that make it easy—*Mapedit* (for PCs and UNIX systems, available at **http://www.boutell.com/mapedit/**), *LiveImage* (available at **http://www.mediatec.com/**), and *Map THIS!* (**http://galadriel.ecaetc.ohio-state.edu/tc/mt/**). These packages use graphical interfaces in which you use your mouse to outline the hot spots right on your image, capturing the coordinates. They automate much of the process of setting up image maps. Figure 10.1 shows a *Mapedit* session; note the toolbar at the top of the image, with buttons for drawing rectangles, polygons, and circles.

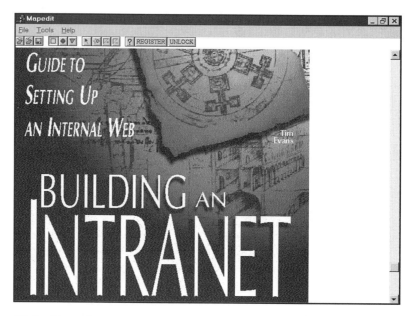

Figure 10.1 Mapedit.

 TIP **Keep It Small** As with other images in your Web pages, keep your image maps small, so people won't lose patience with lengthy downloads. You'll also want to provide a plain-text alternative to your image maps to ensure everyone can use them.

Once you have your coordinates, create an image map file containing them and URLs to correspond to them. Here's an example:

```
rect http://www.company.com/bk1.html 150,337 177,346rect
http://www.company.com/bk2.html     184,286 220,314rect
```

```
http://www.company.com/bk3.html    330,102 350,150default
http://www.company.com/bookhelp.html
```

As you can see, each entry contains a keyword for the shape of the hot spot (in this example, *rect*). Next, you see familiar URLs. Finally, the file contains the coordinates of your hot spots, with x-y coordinates for the upper-left and lower-right of the rectangles. (Polygons require four or more coordinates, while circles require just a center coordinate and a radius.) You'll want to add a *default* URL, as shown, to be accessed when the user clicks outside of your hot spot(s).

TIP **On Automatic** Mapedit, Map This!, and LiveImage create the image map file for you based on your selected hot spots.

Setting Up Server-Side Image Maps on Your Web Server

If you're using server-side image maps, now's the time to get your local Webmaster involved. Each clickable image map available on your Web server needs to be registered with the server before it will be active. To do this on NCSA, Apache, and other NCSA-based servers, add it to a file called **imagemap. conf**, stored in the **conf** subdirectory. (Check your server documentation for details, or for instructions for setting up image maps on other Web server software.) Here's a sample entry:

bookshelf : /web-docs/bookshelf.map

This file is very simple. On the left of the colon is a *nickname* by which you want the map known to the server; you use the nickname in your HTML markup. On the right is the directory path on your server to the map file you created earlier by hand or with Mapedit or WebMap.

HTML Markup for Image Maps

The simplest step in setting up your image maps is your HTML document markup. Markup for server-side and client-side image maps differs, although you can use both. The following sections cover both methods.

HTML Markup for Server-Side Image Maps

Let's look at HTML containing markup for a server-side image map first, then build our way to client-side markup. The following HTML fragment sets up an image map we've nicknamed bookshelf.

```
<A HREF="http://www.yourcompany.com/cgi-bin/imagemap/bookshelf"><IMG
ALT="[Bookshelf Image]"SRC="bookshelf.
gif" ISMAP></A>
```

CAUTION

Single Anchor   It's very important that you note this HTML fragment is a single anchor (hyperlink), beginning with **<A>** and ending with **</A>**. The image reference, and all the other markup, are *within* the anchor.

The URL in this fragment is a little strange. In addition to the familiar URL service name, we've tacked on **cgi-bin/imagemap/bookshelf**. The cgi-bin directory on your Web server contains a program called *imagemap*. (You'll learn more about the cgi-bin and what it contains in Lesson 12, "Fill In Forms and CGI Scripts.") Here, we've called the image map program with our *bookshelf* nickname.

Second, we've added the *ISMAP* attribute to show the image is a clickable image map. Web browsers recognize the ISMAP attribute. When users click an image map, the coordinates of the click location are sent to the Web server and the image map program runs, sending back the URL associated with the hot spot.

HTML Markup for Client-Side Image Maps

While server-side image maps work with your image hot spot coordinates stored on the Web server, client-side maps include them right in the HTML document. Let's look at an example, then take it apart.

```
<MAP NAME="bookshelf"><AREA SHAPE="RECT" COORDS="150,337,177,346"
HREF="http://www.yourcompany.com/bk1.html">
<AREA SHAPE="RECT" COORDS="184,286,220,314"
HREF="http://www.company.com/bk2.html"></MAP>
```

This is quite an HTML mouthful, so let's dissect it. First, note the new HTML tag **<MAP>** and its attribute *NAME*, where we've used the now-familiar *bookshelf* nickname. The **<AREA>** tag (two of them are shown) is also a new one, as are its two attributes, *SHAPE* and *COORDS*. AREA signifies an image map hot spot, while SHAPE and COORDS define it.

Slight Difference   Note the syntax of the numerical coordinates is slightly different from that of the image map file shown previously, with commas, rather than spaces, separating the pairs of coordinates.

CAUTION

You need one more bit of HTML magic to associate your marked-off image map with the image itself.

```
<IMG ALT=[Bookshelf Image] SRC="bookshelf.gif" USEMAP=#bookshelf>
```

Most of this is familiar to you, as it signifies an inline image. What's new is the *USEMAP* attribute, new in HTML 3.2. Much like ISMAP, which you used earlier in your server-side image map markup, USEMAP tells your Web browser a client-side image map nicknamed *bookshelf* is to be used. The browser will locate your <MAP> markup and the *bookshelf* nickname. When the user clicks an image hot spot, the browser retrieves the URL associated with the hot spot coordinates.

Using Both Server- and Client-Side Image Maps

If part of your Web server's clientele is using Web browsers that don't support client-side image maps, you may want to use both methods so everyone can take advantage of your image maps, regardless of their Web browser. Here's an example:

```
<A HREF="http://www.yourcompany.com/cgi-bin/imagemap/bookshelf"><IMG
ALT="[Bookshelf Image]" SRC="bookshelf.
gif" ISMAP USEMAP="#bookshelf"></A>
```

Here, both kinds of image map markup are included. Older Web browsers, which don't understand client-side image maps, will just ignore the unknown markup (including the **<MAP>** tag) and zero in on what they know about,

<ISMAP> and the server-side imagemap markup. Newer browsers are smart enough to choose the client-side method when both are presented.

CAUTION

Keep In Sync   You'll need to make sure your Webmaster keeps the server-side image map files on the Web server in sync with the client-side image map markup in your HTML code. If your coordinates or images change, for example, the changes need to be reflected in both locations.

Which to Use, Server- or Client-Side Image Maps?

As you might have guessed from the foregoing section, the Web browser being used by your Web server's clientele may dictate the need for you to have both server- and client-side image maps (or only server-side maps).

Client-side image maps have substantial advantages, and you should use them to the extent you can. The reason is the Web browser doesn't send the coordinates of the mouse click off to the Web server for interpretation by the image map cgi-bin program. Rather, since the URLs associated with the hot spot coordinates are right in the HTML markup, all the coordinate processing is done by the browser, which directly retrieves the URL. In server-side image maps, the browser sends the coordinates to the server, which looks them up in the server image map file, then sends back the URL associated with them. A busy or remote server, or a busy network, can delay response with server-side image maps.

In this lesson, you learned how to spruce up your Web pages with clickable image maps. The next lesson covers Web browser Helper applications and plug-ins for the inclusion of multimedia—video and sound—in your HTML documents.

Helper Applications and Plug-Ins for Multimedia

In this lesson, you learn how helper applications and plug-ins allow you to incorporate multimedia (audio and video) into your HTML documents.

Helper Applications and Plug-Ins

You learned how to use helper applications and plug-ins with your Web browser in Part 2, "The World Wide Web. These are separate programs Web browsers use to deal with data they retrieve from a Web server that isn't directly supported. Most Web browsers support HTML documents, plain text, and inline images, but they require other programs for multimedia, like sound, video, and other kinds of data.

 Helper Applications These take the data Web browsers can't interpret and deal with it, displaying unsupported images or playing sound or video files, calling up a new window to display the data.

 Plug-Ins Plug-ins perform much the same role as helper applications, but are more tightly integrated into newer Web browsers (Netscape and Explorer). Rather than popping up a new window for the multimedia data, it's displayed right in the browser window.

HTML Markup for Multimedia

You already know most of what you need to include multimedia in your HTML. You know how to use hyperlinks in your documents, pointing to other documents or to Internet services. Creating a hyperlink to an audio, video, or other multimedia file works exactly the same way. Here's an example that includes both:

```
<HTML><HEAD><TITLE>Audio and Video</TITLE></HEAD>

<BODY><H1>Audio and Video</H1>

You can view a movie clip of <A HREF="http://www.hawaii-
50.com/hawaii.mpg">

beautiful Hawaii</A> or <A HREF="http://www.hawaii-
50.com/ocean.au">listen to the roar of the surf</A>.
```

As you can see, this example uses hyperlinks to point to these multimedia files; these links are the same as any other hyperlink. There are no special HTML markup tags or other HTML-specific requirements to link in these or any other kind of multimedia files. You just create the links and you're done. Users with suitably equipped computers (you need a sound card and speakers to listen to audio clips) will be able to view and hear your multimedia links, via either a helper application or a plug-in.

Size Concerns   Even very short audio and video clips can be extremely large, in the range of megabytes (millions of bytes) in length. This is much larger than most of the images you will be adding to your HTML documents. Technology is working toward making even these large files easy to download over slow network links.

Browsers, Helpers, Plug-Ins, and MIME

Web servers are set up to know about a list of common *file types*, including most widely used types of multimedia files, using a mechanism called *MIME*, or *Multipurpose Internet Mail Extensions*. When a Web server sends data to a browser, it first consults its list of MIME file types, then tells the requesting client what type of data is coming.

MIME   You may have run across MIME in the context of e-mail, where it's used to allow attachment of nontext files to e-mail messages for transmission over the Internet, which normally requires all e-mail to be in plain text. Eudora is one MIME-compliant, e-mail package.

The Web browser reads the incoming file type information and tries to process it. If the data type isn't directly supported by the browser, the browser consults its list of helper applications/plug-ins to see if any support the incoming data type. In other words, if a Macintosh Web browser is configured to use a QuickTime video viewer to render incoming QuickTime video, the browser recognizes the incoming data as a QuickTime movie and calls up the QuickTime viewer to play it.

CAUTION

Download Disappointment   You might click a multimedia link and wait for several minutes while a video or audio file downloads, only to be greeted by an error message. This is usually an indication that the multimedia format isn't supported on your computer, the Web browser wasn't set up to use the correct helper application/plug-in, or that the helper application/plug-in was not installed. Some recent browsers will ask you what to do with the data, while in some cases, you'll be prompted to download the plug-in on the spot.

Fortunately, most Web browsers come with a pre-set list of MIME file types and the file types are associated with the correct helper applications/plug-ins. Users can always add to this list, but the critical step is getting and installing the necessary helper applications and plug-ins.

Which Is Best—Helper Applications or Plug-Ins?

You might be wondering right now why you need to know about both helper applications and plug-ins, and whether you can't just go with the latest rage, plug-ins. For multimedia purposes, plug-ins do offer the best mechanism, but only if everyone accessing your HTML documents is using a Web browser that supports plug-ins. Users with older browsers still need to use the traditional helper application mechanism to view multimedia.

Helper applications have a strong advantage over plug-ins in a different area, however. The helper application is typically much more flexible and adaptable to a wide variety of computer software applications. Virtually any software package can be set up quite easily as a Web browser helper application. Building a plug-in is a heavy-duty programming job, while setting up, say, WordPerfect as a helper application, is a simple point-and-click process. Helper applications can be especially valuable on a corporate intranet, because you can create shareable document libraries, a spreadsheet gallery, or other organizational resources. For more information about helper applications and intranets, see

Building an Intranet (ISBN 1-57521-071-1), by Tim Evans, published by Que's sister imprint, Sams.net.

"Intranet" Is Not a Typo The term *intranet* is used to refer to the use of World Wide Web and related networking technologies inside a company to create internal corporate Webs for the purpose of the corporation's own work. You need not be connected to the Internet to have an intranet, though you may do both.

New Multimedia Features in Internet Explorer

Although Internet Explorer supports both helper applications and plug-ins, it also supports another means of viewing multimedia. New HTML markup tags, supported by Explorer alone, allow you to add *soundtracks* and *inline movies* to a Web page. Using the **<BGSOUND>** tag, you can add an audio file that's played whenever the HTML document containing it is accessed. The new *DYNSRC* attribute to the old standby <IMG> tag refers to an inline movie. Neither <BGSOUND> nor DYNSRC require a helper application or plug-in; Explorer itself renders the soundtrack or inline movie in the main Explorer window.

Your HTML markup for soundtracks and inline movies is just what you'd expect when using these new tags. Here's a fragment from Blue Hawaii, modified to include both:

```
<BGSOUND="http://www.bluehawaii.com/ocean.wav">

<IMG DYNSRC="http://www/bluehawaii.com/hawaii.avi">
```

Explorer will display the video inline, as well as play the audio soundtrack.

The Work Continues <BGSOUND> and DYNSRC are formalized in the HTML 3.2 standard, but Microsoft continues to work on new multimedia features in Internet Explorer. Your copy of Explorer may support new capabilities by the time you read this.

In this lesson, you learned how to use some basic HTML tags to insert links for playing multimedia files. In the next lesson, you will learn how to create HTML fill-in-the-blank forms for gathering user input and the scripts they call up to process the user's input.

Fill In Forms and CGI Scripts

In this lesson, you learn how to create forms to gather user input and use CGI scripts to process the user input.

Getting User Input with Forms

In addition to including hyperlinks and images in your HTML documents, collecting user input with forms is probably the most important feature of HTML. You can get input from users and feed it to computer programs for almost any purpose, such as taking orders or updating a database.

Simple Forms Created Automatically

Although there are HTML tags for creating forms, the simplest form gets created automatically by a Web browser when it encounters a single markup tag, **<ISINDEX>**. It collects user input for a program that processes it. Here's a complete HTML document that illustrates use of **<ISINDEX>**:

```
<HTML><HEAD><TITLE>Address Book</TITLE><ISINDEX>
</HEAD><BODY>

<H1>Address Book</H1>

Type a name or partial name in the box above to search the address
book database. Just press return when you've entered the name to
start the search.

</BODY></HTML>
```

Figure 12.1 shows the document in a browser. As you can see, the form itself and the text beginning with "This is a searchable index." is not in our HTML document. Instead, it's automatically inserted by your Web browser when it encounters **<ISINDEX>**. We've not included any reference pointing to a program to search the address book database. You'll learn how to do this later in this lesson.

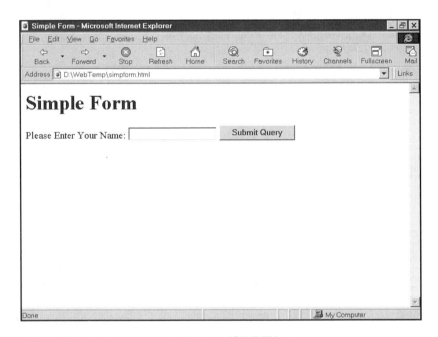

Figure 12.1   Simple form created with the **<ISINDEX>** tag.

Creating Advanced HTML Forms

More advanced HTML forms must be declared with the **<FORM>** markup tag.

I Declare   You'll recall from Part 4, Lesson 8, "Working with Attached Files," the use of the <HTML> tag as a declaration of the document's HTML content; here we use <FORM> to announce that the HTML document is also a form.

```
<FORM ACTION="URL">Contents of Form</FORM>
```

We've shown the **<FORM>** tag with its *mandatory attribute*, ACTION. We'll discuss the ACTION attribute later, but bear in mind that an HTML form collects information from the user. The ACTION attribute specifies what to do with the information.

Within an HTML form, you include markup tags to create the form that will collect user input. This is done with a new HTML tag and two new attributes:

- **<INPUT> tag**. Collects and saves the data for the user so it can be passed off later.
- **NAME attribute**. Attaches an identifying label to the information, to be used by the CGI mechanism.
- **TYPE attribute**. Signifies the type of action to be taken with the data.

In addition, since you're going to pass the collected information to another computer program, you must have a way the user can indicate completion of the form. Here is a simple <INPUT> markup, added to the previous <FORM> fragment to add these features:

```
<FORM ACTION="URL"><INPUT NAME="datalabel1">Rest of Form<INPUT
TYPE="submit"></FORM>
```

In this fragment, we've added NAME and TYPE attributes to the two <INPUT> tags.

There are several ways to collect information from a user. These include simple *fill-in-the-blanks*, *checkboxes*, *radio buttons*, and *pull-down* or *scrollable menus*. We'll look at each in turn.

Radio Buttons The push buttons on most car radios can be set to select different stations. Pressing one of them not only selects the station you want, but deselects all others. Radio buttons (often referred to as *option buttons*) in HTML forms work the same way.

Applying Fill-In-the-Blank

Having a user fill in a blank is the simplest way to get information. The *TEXT* attribute accomplishes this:

```
<FORM ACTION="URL">
Please Enter Your Name:
<INPUT TYPE="text" SIZE=20 NAME="yourname">
<INPUT TYPE="submit"></FORM>
```

Here, we've created a simple one-line box, 20 characters wide, and asked the user to type into it. In addition, we've provided a simple button for the user to click to submit the information. Let's take a look at this basic form in Figure 12.2.

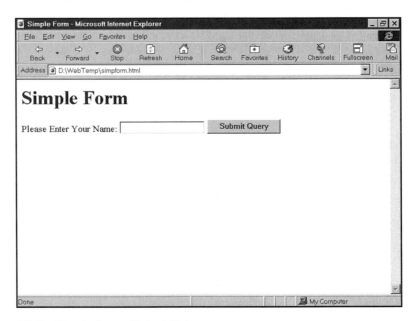

Figure 12.2   Simple form with text fill-in.

Using Check Boxes and Radio Buttons

In addition to a simple text box, it's useful to present the user with a set of *predefined choices*. HTML forms provide a couple of ways to do this. The *CHECKBOX* attribute allows the user to select one or more of several choices, while the *RADIO* attribute allows the choice of just one of several. Like the *TEXT* attribute, both of these require the additional attribute *NAME*, and both allow you to preselect default selections for the user. Here's a piece of HTML containing both:

```
<H1>Build-it-Yourself Sundae</H1>
<FORM ACTION="URL">
<P>Choose Your Favorite Ice Cream Flavor(s):
<INPUT TYPE="CHECKBOX" NAME="choices"
VALUE="chocolate" CHECKED>Chocolate
<INPUT TYPE="CHECKBOX" NAME="choices"
VALUE="vanilla">Vanilla
<INPUT TYPE="CHECKBOX" NAME="choices"
```

```
VALUE="strawberry">Strawberry</P>
<P>Choose a topping (only one, please):</P>
<P><INPUT TYPE="RADIO" NAME="topping"
VALUE="hotfudge">Hot Fudge<BR>
<INPUT TYPE="RADIO" NAME="topping"
VALUE="marshmallow"
CHECKED>Marshmallow<BR>
<INPUT TYPE="RADIO" NAME="topping"
VALUE="butterscotch">Butterscotch<BR>
<INPUT TYPE="RADIO" NAME="topping"
VALUE="pineapple">Pineapple</P>
<P><INPUT TYPE="submit" VALUE="Order Sundae">
<INPUT TYPE="reset"></P></FORM>
```

This is a fairly long listing, with several new items in it, so let's take a look at Figure 12.3, which is a snapshot of the resulting form. As you can see, there are two main selection areas, each one presenting several choices. In the first, the user can choose one, two, or all three choices; Chocolate, however, is the default choice, signified by the use of the *CHECKED* attribute. You'll notice in Figure 12.3 that the "chocolate" button is already selected (it displays in a different color). In the second selection, using *RADIO* buttons, the user is allowed only one choice; selecting any one turns off any other. There's a default selection here as well.

We've added a new clickable box to the bottom of this form, next to the Order Sundae button, labeled Reset. *Reset* returns the form to its default selections, just in case you can't decide and want to start over. In addition, we've replaced the generic "submit query" text with our custom "Order Sundae" string, using a *VALUE* attribute. You'll also note we've laid out the choices in two different ways, one horizontal and the other vertical, using the **<P>** (paragraph) and **
** (line break) tags.

Let's touch for a moment on the other VALUE attributes in the previous form. When the user has completed and submitted the form, these values get passed to the CGI program for which the form is the front end.

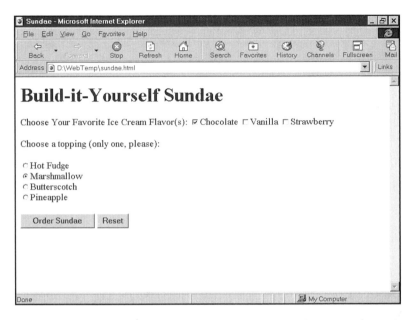

Figure 12.3 The user can choose as many check boxes as he wants, but only one radio button.

Providing Pull-Down Menus and Scrollboxes

If check boxes or radio buttons aren't satisfactory, there are other ways to lay out choices, using the **<SELECT>** tag and its companion **<OPTION>**. You can provide users with pull-down menus and scrollboxes with multiple choices. Let's rework our Build-it-Yourself Sundae form using these tags, so you can see the difference.

```
<H1>Build-it-Yourself Sundae</H1>

<FORM ACTION="URL">

Choose Your Favorite Ice Cream Flavor(s).

Press CTRL-Click for multiple flavors:<BR>

<SELECT NAME="choices" MULTIPLE>

<OPTION SELECTED>Chocolate

<OPTION>Vanilla

<OPTION>Strawberry
```

```
<OPTION>Cookies 'n Cream</SELECT>
<P>Choose a Topping (Only One, Please)
<SELECT NAME="topping">
<OPTION SELECTED>Marshmallow
<OPTION>Hot Fudge
<OPTION>Marshmallow
<OPTION>Butterscotch
<OPTION>Pineapple</SELECT><P>
<INPUT TYPE="submit" VALUE="Order Sundae">
<INPUT TYPE="reset">
```

Figure 12.4 shows the revised form. You'll note the first selection shows the four choices in a box, from which the user can select one or more items. (Had there been more choices than four, we could have used a scrolling box.) In the second selection, the button labeled "Marshmallow" covers a menu; clicking it raises a menu of the four choices. As before, defaults are already set.

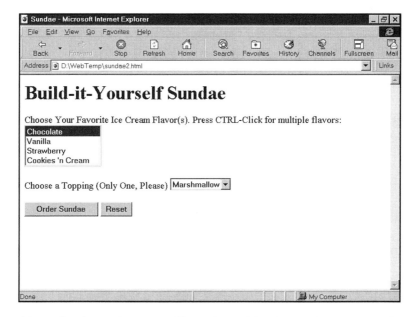

Figure 12.4 Our form takes on a different look with selection boxes and pull-down menus.

Collecting Extended User Input

There's one final—and very useful—HTML element for collecting user input. We've already seen the *TEXT* attribute, which provides a single-line text box. Suppose, however, you want more than just a single line, and you can't predict just how much information the user might enter. *TEXTAREA* allows you to provide a free-form, multi-line text box in which users can type to their hearts' content.

TEXTAREA requires a *NAME* attribute, and allows for sizing, both in width (**COLS**) and height (**ROWS**). Here's an HTML fragment illustrating this:

```
<H1>Suggestion Box</H1>

<P>Please type your comments into the box below, pressing RETURN at
the end of each line. When you are finished, press <EM>Submit Sugges-
tion</EM>. Press <EM>Reset</EM> to clear the form and start over.</P>

<TEXTAREA NAME="comments" COLS=40 ROWS=8></TEXTAREA>

<P><INPUT TYPE="submit" VALUE="Submit Suggestion">

<INPUT TYPE="reset"></P>
```

The *TEXTAREA* element is shown in Figure 12.5. Here, we've provided an 8-line, 40-row box for comments.

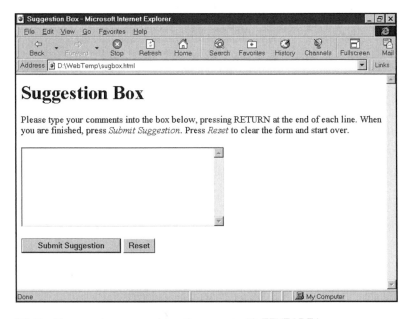

Figure 12.5 Users enter as much as they want with TEXTAREA.

Other Forms Stuff

There are several other things you can do with HTML forms, including:

- Prompt the user for a user name and password, before permitting the form data to be submitted.
- Include some hidden information (neither entered nor seen by the user) for session tracking.
- Include clickable images inside the form.
- Use paragraph and other HTML formatting, such as lists, to lay out forms.

Using Common Gateway Interface (CGI)

Now that you know how to collect information with HTML forms, we can spend a bit of time learning about processing it. As we mentioned previously, the basic concept is taking the information entered on the form and passing it to the Web server. The *Common Gateway Interface (CGI)* is the standard way of doing so. Our form examples have contained a so-far unexplained ACTION= "URL" attribute. For CGI-based forms, the URL is always the name of a CGI program on the Web server, usually located in the cgi-bin directory. (You'll recall that we mentioned the cgi-bin directory in Lesson 6, "Inserting Lists"when discussing the image map program.) An example ACTION attribute might be:

```
ACTION="http://www.yourcompany.com/cgi-bin/get_sundae.exe"
```

 cgi-what? cgi-bin (cee-gee-eye-bin) is short for Common Gateway Interface binary program—that is, a computer program.

You can write CGI programs in almost any programming language, including UNIX shell scripts, DOS batch files, Visual BASIC, AppleScript, the C language, or others. Whatever language you use, a CGI script must accept as input the information the user has entered into your form, then process it in some way. The program may send the information in an e-mail message, for instance, to enter the data into a database, or to generate an order. Here's a simple UNIX shell script (included with the NCSA httpd server software) that prompts the user with a form for a month and year. The script displays a calendar for the selected month and year in the user's Web browser window.

```
#!/bin/sh
CAL=/bin/cal
echo Content-type: text/html
echo
if [ -x $CAL ]; then
if [ $# = 0 ]; then
cat << EOM
<HTML><HEAD><TITLE>Calendar</TITLE>
</HEAD><BODY>
<H1>Calendar</H1>
<ISINDEX>
To look up a calendar month, type the month followed by a space then
the year. Example: <code>3 1993</code> would give the calendar for
March 1993.
EOM
else echo \<PRE\>
$CAL $*
echo \</PRE\>
fi
else echo Cannot find cal on this system.
fi
cat << EOM
</BODY></HTML>
EOM
```

UNIX shell programming is beyond the scope of this book. The most interesting thing about this program is that it *creates HTML code on-the-fly*. Notice the use of the UNIX cat command to output the HTML code contained in the script. Most cgi-bin scripts, regardless of the programming language they're written in, do this sort of dynamic HTML code generation when they run.

Perl   Short for Larry Wall's *Practical Extraction and Report Language*, Perl is the most widely used language. It's freely available for most systems on which Web servers run, including PCs and Macs.

A special, and widely used, kind of CGI processing involves processing the information, then returning the results in the form of HTML so the user can see it. (Usually, this repeats the information the user has entered for verification, before actually sending it off.) To do this, your CGI script must not only pass off the user information for processing but format its output in HTML—including all necessary markup tags, as the previous calendar script shows. The user's Web browser receives the HTML-formatted information and dynamically renders it for viewing. You can examine the cgi-bin subdirectory on your Web server for examples of CGI scripts and programs.

Security Risk   CGI scripts represent a potential security risk. You should consider using the *password TYPE* attribute on your forms to ensure that only authorized users can enter information. Your Webmaster should also make sure the CGI scripts themselves aren't subject to abuse by unscrupulous people who might try to damage or otherwise compromise your Web server. Be sure to read the CGI documentation online at NCSA, **http://hoohoo.ncsa.uiuc.edu/ cgi/overview.html**.

We've covered quite a bit of complex information in this lesson about HTML forms for gathering information from users. Also, we touched on the Common Gateway Interface for writing programs that take the information entered into forms and process it. In the next lesson, you will learn how to control the Web browser window with *frames*.

Creating Frames

In this lesson, you learn how to use frames to divide the Web browser window into sections.

Frames

When Netscape Communications released version 2 of Navigator in early 1996, the Web browser bar had clearly been raised. Netscape frames was a new feature that attracted immediate attention, and Web pages using it popped up all over the Internet. Microsoft jumped on the bandwagon and added frames support to Internet Explorer, though it made changes in its implementation, making it partially inconsistent with Netscape's version.

What Are Frames?

Netscape frames (support for which is also in Netscape versions 3 and 4) are much like the split-screen video tricks used by television networks to retain viewers between shows. You've seen these, where part of the TV screen shows the ending show's credits, while the other part shows a teaser for the next show. Unlike the TV version, though, Netscape's frames allow each portion of the window to be independent of the others, and of course, Netscape frames are interactive.

Frames can contain ordinary HTML markup, can be scrollable, and can even hold clickable images or image maps. While you interact with one frame, the content of the other frames remains on-screen. Figure 13.1 shows a typical page with frames.

Basic Frames Used to Create HTML Markup

As you've probably guessed, HTML markup to create frames uses a new tag, namely **<FRAMESET>**. Use the **<FRAMESET>** tag within an ordinary HTML document to define a frame to be called by that document. Let's look at the steps for creating an HTML document with frames.

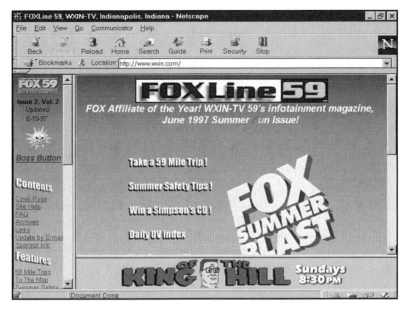

Figure 13.1 Frames divide the browser window into sections.

First, you need to define the number, orientation, and size of each frame to be created. Do this with one of two **<FRAMESET>** attributes, *COLS* (for vertical frame dividers) and *ROWS* (for horizontal dividers). Here's an example fragment that creates two frames, oriented vertically, each using half the browser window.

```
<FRAMESET COLS="50/,50/">
```

You can also specify absolute values in pixels for *COLS* and *ROWS*, rather than percentages of the window as we've done here. To do so, leave off the trailing slashes shown for each value. The number of values you enter here defines the number of frame divisions.

Next, you need to specify URLs for the documents that are to be displayed in each of your frames. Let's add two URLs to the fragment above, and also wrap basic HTML housekeeping markup around it to complete the document:

```
<HTML><HEAD><TITLE>First Frame Document</TITLE></HEAD>
<FRAMESET COLS="50/,50/">
<FRAME SRC="frame1.htm">
<FRAME SRC="frame2.htm">
</FRAMESET></HTML>
```

521

Here, we've specified a couple of local documents, *frame1.htm* and *frame2.htm*, as the source for what's to appear in our frames. You can also use a full URL here, if your document resides elsewhere. Note also the closing **</FRAMESET>** tag.

Before your frames document is ready to be viewed, you need to create the two other HTML documents to be called by it. Here's *frame1.htm*:

```
<HTML><HEAD><TITLE>Left Frame</TITLE>
</HEAD><BODY><H1>This is the Left Frame</H1>
Click within this frame to make it active.
</BODY></HTML>
```

As you can see, this is simple HTML. Here's *frame2.htm*, which is slightly more complex, but still nothing you haven't already seen:

```
<HTML><HEAD><TITLE>Right Frame</TITLE>
</HEAD><BODY><H1>This is the Right Frame</H1>
<IMG ALIGN="LEFT" SRC="test.gif">Frame documents are ordinary HTML
documents, and they can contain anything an HTML document can,
including inline images and regular text.
<A HREF="foo.htm">hyperlinks</A>.</BODY></HTML>
```

Figure 13.2 shows our first frames document. Notice the two files called by it are displayed in separate panes, or frames, of the Navigator window.

CAUTION

Corpus Delecti?   Notice there's no **<BODY>** tag in the example HTML document. This is OK, as the **<FRAMESET>** tag substitutes for **<BODY>**.

Advanced Frames HTML Markup

As you can see from Figure 13.1, you can divide your window into more than two frames. You can create multiple frames by nesting one set of **<FRAMESET>** tags inside another. Here's a short example that introduces you to the things you can do with nested **<FRAMESET>** tags.

```
<HTML><HEAD><TITLE>Home</TITLE></HEAD>
<FRAMESET COLS="30/,70/">
<FRAMESET ROWS="80/,20/">
<FRAME SRC="framelinks.html">
<FRAME SRC="framenav.html">
```

```
</FRAMESET>

<FRAME SRC="http://home.netscape.com" NAME="main">

</FRAMESET></HTML>
```

It's easier for you to interpret this if you look at Figure 13.3. You'll first notice one large frame on the right, and two smaller ones on the left, divided horizontally with the ROWS attribute.

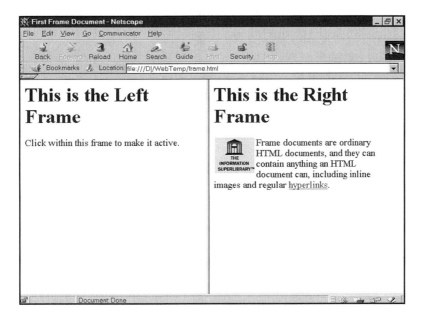

Figure 13.2 Basic Frames document.

The second **<FRAMESET>** tag (third line of the HTML code example) divides the left frame in two, splitting the frame 80/20. Each **<FRAME>** tag has an HTML document as its source. The example, loading two local files and one URL (the Netscape Home Page), shows how you can create custom Web pages with frames that incorporate remote sites. Note the Location box at the top of the screenshot, showing the loaded document is our local file, named *homeframe.html*, not the Netscape Home Page we've loaded in the right frame.

The frames feature has a nifty capability of letting hyperlinks in one frame load documents in a different frame. You may have noticed the 'NAME="main"' markup in the next-to-the-last line of our example. We're going to use that now. Here are just a couple of lines from the HTML document that creates the upper-left frame, framelinks.html:

```
<H1>Quick Links</H1>
<UL>
<LI><A HREF="http://home.netscape.com/home/whats-new.html"
TARGET="main">What's New</A></LI>
</UL>
```

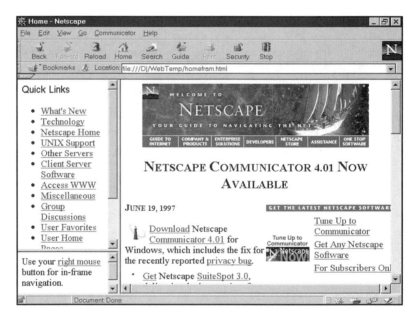

Figure 13.3 Nested Frames.

As you can see, this line also contains the "main" label. (This works a lot like the jump-to-spot feature about which you learned in Part 5, Lesson 5, "Using Anchors and Links.") The relationship between this label in the two HTML documents allows a link clicked in the upper-left window to be loaded into the other window, as shown in Figure 13.4. The two left frames have stayed in place, while the new document, Netscape's What's New page, was loaded in the right-hand window.

Over the Bounding Main Use of the word "main" in the example shouldn't imply there is a concept of a "main" frame. All frames are created equal, even if they have different sizes. We could just as easily have used "right" or "zipfiz" as **CAUTION** the label. It's just a means of labeling frames so the HTML documents can link one frame to another when loading documents.

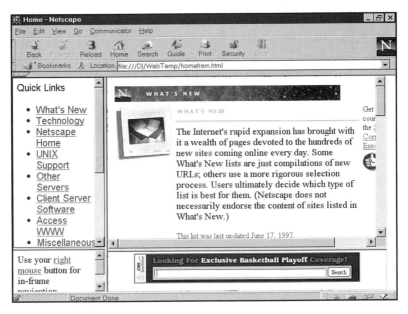

Figure 13.4 Display of selected hyperlink directed to another window.

Wither (*sic*) Frames?

While the right mouse button is a perfectly good way of getting around in frames, users find this disconcerting at best. Netscape's been unable to get the word out about this, probably because it's not quite as intuitive as the Back button. As a result, users are having a good deal of trouble navigating frames, and many Webmasters are abandoning this once-promising feature. As if that weren't enough, Microsoft introduced incompatibilities when it implemented frames for Internet Explorer. The final death knell for frames may have been sounded when Netscape itself removed frames markup from its own Home Page.

Status of Frames in the HTML 3.2 Standard

The frames-related HTML tags are not included in the HTML 3.2 standard. Since the World Wide Web Consortium is funded by major companies, including both Microsoft and Netscape, the standards committee was unable to resolve differences between the two companies over frames. As other lessons in this part show, this is not an isolated phenomenon.

In this lesson, you've learned how to add snappy-looking frames to your Web pages. The capabilities of frames seem quite attractive, but users have found problems navigating them. In the next lesson, we'll turn to cutting-edge (possibly bleeding-edge) HTML features for adding banners, marquees, and color to your Web pages.

Using Banners, Marquees, and Color in Your HTML Documents

In this lesson, you learn about exciting new HTML features that will liven up your documents, including marquees and the use of color for backgrounds and text.

Introduction

Recent activity in the HTML standards process, along with the cut-throat competition of Netscape and Microsoft, have resulted in a near-bewildering array of snappy new HTML features. Let's try to make sense of a couple of these, even though HTML continues to develop at a breakneck pace, and these features may change, merge, or even disappear by the time you read this. Worse, these features are a potential minefield in the war between Microsoft and Netscape, and you'll need to pick and choose among the features carefully, based on the audience of your HTML documents and their browsers.

Marquees

A Microsoft innovation, marquees allow you to place scrolling text on a Web page. When the user opens your page, the text starts to scroll from left to right or right to left across the screen, like the famous Times Square news-headline ticker.

HTML Markup for Marquees

The <MARQUEE> tag is used for marquees, along with several attributes, the most important of which are:

- **ALIGN**, controlling the placement of the marquee on-screen.
- **BEHAVIOR**, controlling the type of marquee display.
- **DIRECTION**, controlling the direction of a scrolling marquee.

Other Marquee attributes include those relating to color, height and width, the number of times the marquee text repeats, and others. For a detailed listing, see Microsoft's HTML workshop at **http://www.microsoft.com/workshop/author/ newhtml/**.

Let's look at a sample piece of HTML markup containing a marquee:

```
<MARQUEE ALIGN="TOP" BEHAVIOR="SLIDE" DIRECTION="RIGHT">We, the
people of the United States.</MARQUEE>
```

Here, the marquee appears at the top of the Explorer window, with the text sliding from right to left. Since Marquees generate moving text within the Explorer window, it's not possible to show one in a screenshot.

CAUTION

Too Much of a Good Thing Internet Explorer marquees can, like the Netscape **<BLINK>** feature and the new animated images supported in both Netscape and Explorer, turn people off of your Web pages. Continuously blinking or scrolling text and animated images get users' attention perhaps too well, as the changing parts of the page tend to draw the viewer's eyes toward them, distracting from the rest of the page. Be sure to keep this in mind as you view pages with marquees.

Marquees in the HTML 3.2 Standard

As with frames, the HTML 3.2 standard does not mention marquees, no doubt for the same reasons.

It's always a good idea to check out the state of the HTML standards process. The best place to look for information about the current standards is on the World Wide Web Consortium's Web site, **http://www.w3.org/**. You'll also want to visit the Microsoft HTML workshop site mentioned previously, as well as Netscape's site at **http://developer.netscape.com/library/documentation/ htmlguid/index.htm**.

You'll also find a quite valuable HTML standards resource maintained by Sean Bolt at **http://www.etsimo.uniovi.es/html_3.2/** . Not only will you find a complete listing of the HTML 3.2 standards, but you'll also find a searchable database of HTML elements and attributes. You can do searches on any combination of current and past standards, including the Netscape- and Explorer-specific additions. This is a great place to find out how browser support for new HTML elements compares.

At the time this book was being written, the author, Sean Bolt, was going through a transitional period (he was finding a new home for his page). To find out the latest address of the page, go to **http://webpages.marshall.edu/~rogers8/new.html**.

Color on Your Web Pages

Originated by Netscape, colors (both text and background) are now part of the HTML 3.2 standard. As with text colors, background colors are specified with an attribute to the <BODY> tag, namely **BGCOLOR**. The HTML 3.2 standard calls for use of three hexadecimal numbers to express color selections, the same as you saw in Lesson 3. Creating an HTML document with a pure white background looks like this:

```
<BODY BGCOLOR="FFFFFF">
```

If you want something more soothing, try this cool green background:

```
<BODY BGCOLOR="EEFFFA">
```

CAUTION

Colors Out of Whack?   You'll recall our discussion of how different computer hardware affects the rendering of your Web pages. Color is especially sensitive to users' video cards and monitors. Low-end, low-resolution cards or monitors won't give true color in all cases and, of course, monochrome monitors don't give any colors at all. Be sure to test-view your HTML documents that use color on as many different systems as you can, to get an idea of how your color selections actually get displayed. You may have to stick with less-subtle colors.

Text Colors Redux

Along with background colors and the basic text colors, you can also selectively and separately control some parts of the text in your documents in other ways. For instance, you can use text colors to *vary the look of the hyperlinks* in your Web pages.

As you know from using a Web browser, the hyperlinks in Web pages appear in a different color than the rest of the text, and they usually change to a different color after you've visited them. The HTML 3.2 standard allows you to control each of these colors. You can define the color of text representing ordinary hyperlinks, the color of visited hyperlinks, and the color the text changes to when the user clicks it for the first time. As with your text and background color selections, all three of these are controlled by new attributes of the general HTML <BODY> tag. Here's a list:

- **LINK**, referring to an unvisited hyperlink.
- **VLINK**, referring to a visited hyperlink.
- **ALINK**, referring to an activated hyperlink.

Quick Change   The last, ALINK, is a bit tricky to understand. What it does is change the color of text representing a hyperlink as the user clicks it. Depending on how quickly the link loads, however, the user may not see this
CAUTION   color change but for a split second.

Here's an example that uses all three, as well as background and ordinary text color specifications:

> <BODY BGCOLOR="EEFFFA" LINK="CC0000" VLINK="000055"
> ALINK="FF3300" TEXT="000000">

Here, the ALINK and VLINK attributes are set to pale red and dark blue, respectively. Ordinarily, unvisited links are set to be bright red. In addition, the page has plain black text on a cool green background.

Tan (Shoes) and Pink (Shoelaces)?   Watch the combinations of your text and background colors. A potential problem, besides garish color contrasts, is a combination in which your text disappears into the background color
CAUTION   because there's not enough contrast between the two colors.

Finding Colors

Earlier you learned how to use your calculator or the Windows 95 Paint program to convert colors into the hexadecimal numbers used here. You can find a nifty, clickable color palette (shown in Figure 14.1) on the Web at **http:// www.hidaho.com/colorcenter/cc.html**. Clicking a color shows its hexadecimal equivalents. In addition, you'll actually see the on-screen background and text change as you test colors.

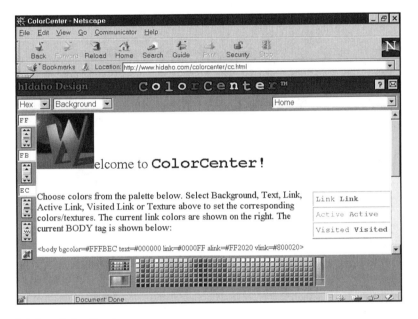

Figure 14.1 Color Center.

TIP **For UNIX Users Only** UNIX users can use the command-line bc utility to do quick decimal-to-hex conversions. Here's an example, shown with the standard dollar sign UNIX shell prompt:

```
$ bc
ibase=10
obase=16
158 * 1
```

continues

continued

9E

...

<CTRL-D>

$

As you can see, the ibase and obase commands within bc set the input and output base (decimal and hexadecimal, respectively, in the example). You then simply multiply any decimal number by 1 to get its hex equivalent. Continue doing such multiplications until you have all your hex numbers. As with most UNIX utilities, pressing **Control+D** exits bc.

In this lesson, you learned about cutting-edge HTML features for adding marquees to your Web pages and for giving your page more color. In the next lesson, you'll learn how to specialize HTML editors to simplify the job of creating and editing Web pages.

Simplify Your Life with HTML Editors

In this lesson, you learn about several HTML editors and other tools for creating HTML documents.

Creating Web Pages the Easy Way

In the previous lessons, you learned how to create Web pages the old fashioned way—by typing the HTML codes in a standard text editor. It's important to learn the codes. If you open a page and find that it has funky line breaks, missing links, and graphics that have gone AWOL, you need to know how to go behind the scenes with HTML markup and fix the problem.

However, there are many tools available to help you code your documents. The current breed of word processors, including Microsoft Word, have tools that allow you to convert existing Word documents into HTML Web pages, insert graphics and links, add background colors, and add other objects unique to the Web. In addition, Internet Explorer 4 and Netscape Communicator 4 each come with advanced tools for creating, editing, and publishing your pages.

With these tools, instead of typing HTML codes, you simply type text and insert graphics as you would in any word processor or desktop publishing application. These *Webtop publishing* applications include commands for inserting graphics, links, anchors, headings, and other objects. They also allow you to quickly format text by selecting a formatting option from a toolbar or menu. You insert objects and format the text, and the application automatically inserts the codes for you. Most HTML editors also support *WYSIWYG editing*, so you can view the appearance of the page as you create it.

WYSIWYG   Pronounced "wizzy-wig," WYSIWYG is short for What You See Is What You Get. With WYSIWYG, your page appears on-screen as it will appear in print or as displayed in a Web browser. WYSIWYG editors have the advantage of allowing you to drag graphics and text on-screen and to move them around on a page.

There are three basic kinds of HTML editors/editing tools:

- *Tricks* and *add-ons* for your own word processor for editing HTML.
- Tools to *convert* existing documents to HTML.
- Full-blown, *WYSIWYG HTML editors*.

Tricks, Add-Ons, and Converters

You can use your word processor to create HTML, and get a leg up on the task with one or more of the following tricks, add-ons, and converters.

Word Processor Tricks and Add-Ons

If you've been using your word processor to create HTML documents, you already have the ability to create some tools to make HTML editing easier. You've probably already thought of them, but let's mention them anyway. All modern word processors have features for creating and reusing commonly used procedures. These are usually called *macros*. It's a very simple matter to create macros for each of the major HTML markup tags, then save them for later. Each time you need to add an HTML markup code to your document, you can just grab your pull-down macro menu, or hit whatever function key your word processor uses, and zap in the required tag.

If you have Word, you can also store HTML codes as AutoText entries. AutoText allows you to create your own typing shorthand. For example, you can create an AutoText entry for a code sequence, such as the following, to create a bulleted list:

```
<UL>
<LI></LI>
<LI></LI>
<LI></LI>
<LI></LI>
```

```
<LI></LI>
</UL>
```

You could then assign the AutoText entry to the keystroke **ul**. To insert this series of codes, you simply type **ul** and press the **F3** key. All you have to do to complete the list is type your list entries between each pair of **<LI></LI>** codes, and delete the pairs you don't use.

Macros   Word processors allow you to record and save these as a series of keystrokes, then play them back to automate repetitive tasks.

You can also create (or obtain on the Internet) document *templates/stylesheets* for HTML markup. Even simple word processor *global search-and-replace* features can help speed up creation of HTML documents.

Microsoft Internet Assistants

Microsoft has a no-cost *Internet Assistant (IA)* add-on for its Word 6.0 package for Windows PCs and Macintoshes (Word 7.0 for Windows 95 has IA built in). IA allows WYSIWYG creation and viewing of HTML documents, as well as support for graphics and hyperlinks pointing to other Web services, and conversion of standard Word documents to HTML. An HTML editor that looks and acts like Word, IA also includes a built-in Web browser (Internet Explorer, of course).

Microsoft has added features to Internet Explorer to support special Word formatting (such as text flowing around graphics) that isn't supported in other Web browsers. They've also made available, at no cost, a *stand-alone viewer* for Word documents. *Word Viewer* can be used as a Helper application with other browsers like Mosaic or Netscape Navigator. You can retrieve IA and Word Viewer on the Web at **http://www.microsoft.com/msword/internet/ia**.

TIP   **Also Offered**   Microsoft also has Internet Assistant add-ons and read-only viewers for PowerPoint, Excel, and Access. They're available at the Microsoft Web site. The latest versions of these products, included in Microsoft Office 97, have built-in support for Web page creation, editing, and publishing.

Document Converters

You no doubt already have documents you'd like to have available on your Web server. Converting common word processor documents to HTML is a simple, two-step process.

First, most word processors have a *Save As* feature that saves documents in alternative formats. One such common format is called the *Rich Text Format*, or *RTF*. RTF makes documents portable, while preserving document formatting.

Although RTF was developed by Microsoft, it's widely supported and converting from RTF to most any other format is fairly simple. You may have used it to convert from one word processor format to another, such as from Word to WordPerfect. A shareware software package called *RTFTOHTML* (for UNIX systems, PCs, and Macintoshes) is available to, as the name suggests, convert RTF documents to HTML. You'll find the conversion less than perfect, especially if you have complex tabular material or graphics in the original documents. Nevertheless, the main job of converting the documents to HTML is done well. You'll find these packages on the Web at **http://www.sunpack.com/RTF/latest/**.

The main advantage of the two-stage RTF conversion process is that you can convert your existing documents to HTML quickly and easily. The disadvantage, as with word processor macros, is you're still not working in a WYSIWYG environment. In addition, you should expect to have to do some cleanup editing of the resulting HTML documents.

Besides this two-step *RTFTOHTML conversion method*, there are several other document converters. Of particular interest are those that convert from FrameMaker, a widely used desktop publishing package, to HTML. These include a commercial package called *WebWorks Publisher* from Quadralay and several freeware packages, *Frame2htmL* and *WEBMAKER*. Release 5 of FrameMaker has built-in HTML support, and includes a copy of *WebWorks Publisher* Lite, a limited-function version of the Quadralay product, for converting older Frame documents. Also, Interleaf, Inc.'s *Cyberleaf* converts not only among different word processor formats, but also from any of them to HTML. If you need to convert from PageMaker, try the Netscape plug-in converter from Adobe for the PageMaker desktop publishing package (**http://www.adobe.com/ prodindex/pagemaker/details.html**).

Finally, there are a wide variety of other programs that convert from one text format or another to HTML, including those that convert from the TeX and

LaTeX formatting languages widely used by scientists and mathematicians, from UNIX *nroff/troff* and *man* pages, and from other lesser-known formats.

Full-Blown HTML Editors

If you're ready to move on from your text editor or word processor, you may want to look at one of several full-blown HTML editors. These operate in a more or less WYSIWYG environment, rendering your document formatting pretty much as it will look in a Web browser. This is a crowded market, so let's take a quick look at just a few of the major editors.

Netscape Composer

Netscape Composer is Netscape Communicator's HTML editor. Formerly available only in Netscape Gold, Composer takes a central role in the Communicator package, allowing you to not only open and edit pages on the Web, but also publish your pages and add HTML tags to e-mail and newsgroup messages. Composer also allows you to quickly create Web pages by starting with an existing template or using its online Web Page Wizard.

To start Composer, take any of the following steps:

- Select **Netscape Composer** from the Windows 95 **Start**, **Programs**, **Netscape Communicator** menu, or from a program group.
- Open the **Communicator** menu in any of the other Communicator components (Messenger or Collabra, for instance) and select the **Page Composer** option.
- To edit an existing page, you can open it directly in Composer. In Navigator, select **File**, **Open Page**. Type the URL of the page you want to open, and make sure **Composer** is selected. Click the **Open** button.

Figure 15.1 shows Composer in action. As you can see, Composer allows you to preview the page as you create it. Composer offers a feature-packed toolbar, which provides quick formatting options, and buttons for inserting links, graphics, and tables. It even offers a button for publishing your page on the Web.

Buttons for inserting graphics, links, tables, and more

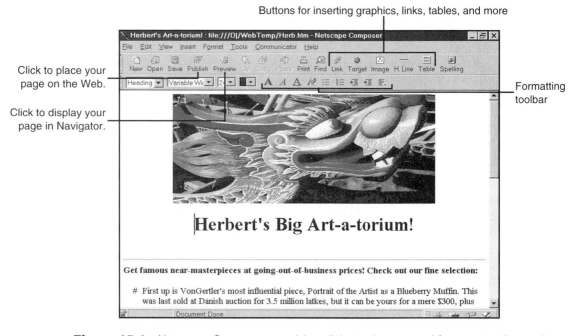

Click to place your
page on the Web.

Click to display your
page in Navigator.

Formatting
toolbar

Figure 15.1   Netscape Composer provides all the tools you need for constructing and publishing Web pages.

TIP   **Drag-and-Drop Editing**   One of the best features of Composer is that it supports drag-and-drop editing. You can drag files from your file manager window into the Composer window to insert files. You can also drag text, graphics, and links from existing Web pages (displayed in Navigator) onto your Web page (displayed in Composer).

Microsoft FrontPage Express and FrontPage

Not to be outdone, Microsoft has included its own Web page creation tool, called FrontPage Express, in its new Internet Explorer 4.0 Suite. FrontPage Express is a less robust version of Microsoft's FrontPage, an application that provides more advanced tools for setting up and managing Web sites.

Like Composer, FrontPage Express supports toolbars and pull-down menus for common HTML-editing tasks (see Figure 15.2). And, of course, FrontPage Express supports all the Internet Explorer HTML extensions. To run FrontPage Express, select **FrontPage Express** from the Windows 95 **Start**, **Programs**, **Internet Explorer** menu, or from a program group.

As you can see in Figure 15.2, FrontPage Express offers a Formatting toolbar, containing controls that allow you to quickly apply formatting to text, and a Standard toolbar, which contains buttons for inserting links and graphics. In addition, FrontPage Express' menu bar contains an Insert menu for inserting links, graphics, marquees, video clips, and other objects, and a Format menu which provides additional options for formatting text and links.

Figure 15.2   Microsoft FrontPage Express is like a desktop publishing application for the Web.

TIP   **Move Up to FrontPage**   If your Web page needs are modest, FrontPage Express should suffice. However, if you're chosen to be the Webmaster at your company, you should move up to Microsoft FrontPage. If you are accustomed to FrontPage Express, the move to FrontPage will be relatively easy. FrontPage offers all the tools available in FrontPage Express, but includes additional tools for creating and managing a *web*, a collection of interconnected Web documents.

SoftQuad HoTMetaL

SoftQuad *HoTMetaL* is available in both a no-cost version (**http://www.sq.com/**) and a commercial version, the latter of which is called *HoTMetaL PRO*. HoTMetaL PRO Version 4 is available for Windows 95 and Windows 3.1 PCs and should be available for the Macintosh by the time you read this; the freeware version is available for these platforms, as well as some UNIX systems, while version 3 of the PRO package is available for Windows, Macintosh, and some UNIX systems. HoTMetaL has the familiar Windows look, with pull-down menus, an extensive toolbar, and a scrolling text area. In addition, HTML markup codes are highly visible and hyperlinks are plainly marked. The PRO version has a Netscape Frames editing feature, as well as the capability to import common word processing formats.

Sausage Software's HotDog

One of the most popular commercial HTML editors for Windows PCs is called *HotDog*, from the Australian firm Sausage Software. Like HoTMetaL, HotDog uses pull-down menus and an extensive toolbar to make creation of HTML documents easier. Of particular note, HotDog offers the following:

- A drag-and-drop *File Manager* for inserting links, graphics, and other documents.
- A *text color picker*, which allows you to preview your text and background colors.
- The capability to group multiple HTML documents into a *Project*, allowing group manipulation of all the files included.

Calling itself the "Switzerland of the Web," Sausage Software has taken a position of neutrality in the HTML standards wars. All features of the HTML 3.2 standard are supported, along with all of the Netscape and Microsoft extensions. To help you negotiate the several standards, HotDog displays nonstandard HTML markup in different colors, with separate colors for Netscape Navigator- and Internet Explorer-only tags. Figure 15.3 shows HotDog. HotDog also includes an interactive image map package, called *MapTHIS!*. You can download trial versions of HotDog at **http://www.sausage.com/**.

Adobe PageMill for Macintosh and Windows 95

PageMill is far and away the favorite Macintosh HTML editor. The latest release of PageMill (Version 2.0) has support for many of the latest HTML enhancements, including frames, tables, and animated images. As an added bonus, PageMill comes with a collection of clip art, sounds, page templates, and animations to help you quickly create a professional-looking Web page.

The package also supports WYSIWYG editing, including internal support for Netscape-style plug-ins, allowing dynamic viewing (what you hear is what you get?) of multimedia files right in the editor. With Macintosh-style drag-and-drop support, PageMill features a built-in spelling checker and integrated image support, and built-in support for Java and corporate database connectivity. Client-side image maps are supported, as is a new feature called *PlaceHolders*. This feature allows drag and drop of dynamic Web elements, such as CGI scripts, right into open HTML documents.

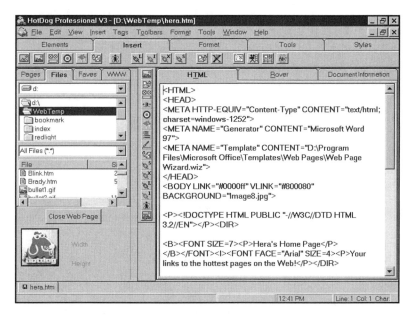

Figure 15.3   HotDog with Drag-and-Drop File Manager.

On the minus side, PageMill doesn't have all the integrated "Web publishing" features other HTML editors, including Netscape Composer and Microsoft FrontPad, and others have. These other packages allow the direct upload of documents to Web servers right out of the HTML editor via pull-down menus. With PageMill, you'll still have to move your finished files over to your Web server manually. For more information about PageMill, see Adobe's Web site, **http://www.adobe.com/**.

This lesson has covered quite a lot of ground concerning HTML editors. We've discussed the pros and cons of using plain-text editors, word-processor tricks and add-ons, document converters, and full-blown WYSIWYG HTML editors. In the next lesson, you learn how to test and publish your page on the Web.

541

Testing and Publishing Your Web Page

In this lesson, you learn how to check your Web page for misspellings, typos, and code errors, and how to place your page on the Web.

Checking and Testing Your Web Page

Before you place your page on the Web, where millions of people can check it out, you should check it, as you would check any document you intend to make public. First, check the page in your word processor or HTML editor for spelling errors or typos. Most of the newer HTML editors have their own spelling checkers. In FrontPad or Netscape Composer, you can start the spelling checker simply by clicking the **Spelling** button in the toolbar. Use the resulting dialog box to correct any misspellings or typos.

You should also open your page in your Web browser, and check to make sure it looks right. Check the position and appearance of graphics, make sure your text contrasts with any background colors you have used, and, most importantly, click every link to make sure it pulls up the correct linked page (see Figure 16.1). Because most HTML codes come in pairs, one of the most common mistakes is to omit the closing code in a pair. If you run into problems, check your paired codes.

If you are using an HTML editor, such as FrontPad or Netscape Composer, click the **Preview** button to view the page in your browser. Be sure to save the page one last time before opening it.

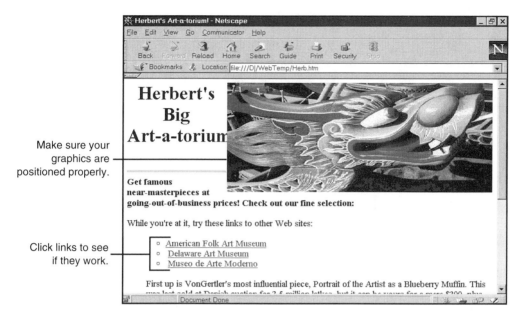

Make sure your graphics are positioned properly.

Click links to see if they work.

Figure 16.1 You should check your page before placing it on the Web.

CAUTION

Check After Publishing You should check your page before placing it on the Web, and after you place it on any associated files on the Web. If you have links or codes that point to local files, those files may be misplaced when you upload your page and other files to the Web. By checking the page when it is on the Web, you ensure that it will work for visitors.

Finding a Home for Your Page

Before you can publish your page, you need to make sure you have somewhere to place your Web page. The best place to start is to call your Internet service provider. Most providers make some space available on their Web servers for subscribers to store personal Web pages. Call your service provider, and find out the following information:

- Does your service provider make Web space available to subscribers? If not, maybe you should change providers.

- How much disk space do you get, and how much does it cost, if anything? Some providers give you a limited amount of disk space, which is usually plenty for one or two Web pages.

- What is the URL of the server you must connect to in order to upload your files? Write it down.

- What username and password do you need to enter to gain access to the server? (This is usually the same name and password you use to establish your Internet connection.)

- In which directory must you place your files? Write it down.

- What name must you give your Web page. In many cases, the service requires you to name your home page **index.html**, **default.html**, **home.html**, or something similar. This tells the Web browser that when it accesses your directory on the server, it should open this page by default.

- Are there any other specific instructions you must follow to post your Web page?

- After posting your page, what will its address (URL) be? You'll want to open it in your Web browser as soon as you post it.

Now, if your service provider does not offer Web page service, run your Web browser, connect to your favorite search page, and search for places that allow you to post your Web page for free. These services vary greatly. Some services require you to fill out a form, and then the service creates a generic Web page for you (you can't use the page you created in Composer). At others, you can copy the HTML-coded document (in Notepad or WordPad) and paste it in a text box at the site. A couple other places will let you send them your HTML file and associated files. Find out what's involved. Figure 16.2 shows a typical form you might fill out to place your page on the Web.

 TIP **Publishing at GeoCities** GeoCities (at **http://www.geocities.com/**) is a popular place to publish Web pages. At GeoCities, you join a community (or neighborhood) where you more or less fit in. You can then upload your Web page and files to the GeoCities site using FTP. Uploading with FTP is described later in this lesson.

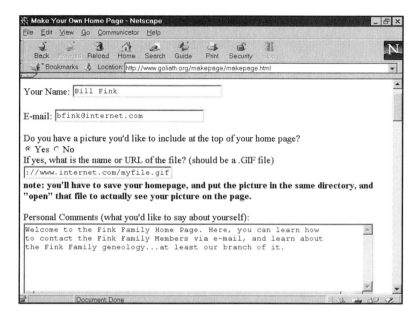

Figure 16.2 Some sites allow you to place a simple page on the Web by filling out a form.

Publishing Your Page with Netscape Composer

In order to publish your page, Composer needs to know your username, your password, and your Web site address. When you have that information, follow these steps to configure the publisher:

1. Open Composer's **Edit** menu and select **Preferences**. The Preferences dialog box appears.

2. Click the + in the box next to Composer to expand the item, and then click the **Publishing** item. The form displayed in Figure 16.3 appears.

3. The Maintain Links option and the Keep Images with Page option are both turned on by default. Leave them on to ensure that your page's links will work and that any associated graphic files will be shipped along with your page.

4. In the **Enter a FTP or HTTP Site Address to Publish To** text box, type the address of the FTP or HTTP (Web) site to which you want to upload your

file(s). This address consists of the URL of the server plus the path to the directory. Here's an example:

ftp://ftp.internet.com/pub/users/webpages/

5. If you are uploading your page to an FTP server, click in the second text box under Default Publishing Location, and then type the URL you must use to open the page in a Web browser.

6. Click **OK** to save your settings.

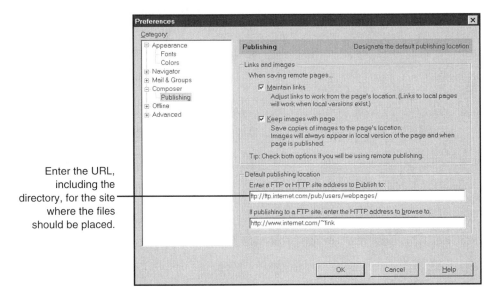

Enter the URL, including the directory, for the site where the files should be placed.

Figure 16.3 Tell the publisher where you want the page sent.

You can use Composer to publish any pages you have, whether they were created with the Web page editor or with any other tool. You can even mix pages from different sources. Just make sure that all of the pages you want to publish are in the same directory on your hard drive before you begin. To publish your pages, follow these steps:

1. Establish your Internet connection, run Composer, and open the page you want to place on the Web.

2. Click the **Publish** button, and the Publish dialog box appears (see Figure 16.4).

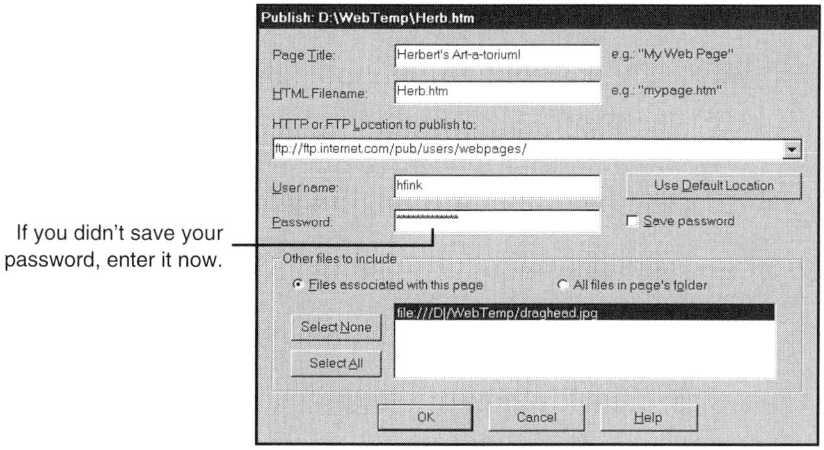

If you didn't save your
password, enter it now.

Figure 16.4 The Publish Files dialog box.

3. If the **HTTP or FTP Location to Publish to** is blank, open the drop-down list, and select the desired location, or click the **Use Default** button to insert the address you entered under Preferences.

4. If this is the first time you are publishing a page, enter your username and password in the appropriate text boxes. To have Composer save this information (for the next time you publish a page), click **Save Password**.

5. To publish just this one page, click the **Files Associated with This Page** option button, which uploads the HTML file for this page, along with all of the files for graphics on the page. To publish all the pages in the current directory, click the **All Files in Page's Folder** option button.

6. Click **OK** to start the publishing process. Composer connects to the Internet (if you are not already connected). The Publishing Page dialog box appears, listing the name of each file as it is uploaded and showing the number of files that have been uploaded in relation to the total number to be uploaded. When all the files have been uploaded, this box disappears. Congratulations! Your material is now out on the Web!

Using Microsoft's Web Page Publishing Wizard

If you've created your Web page using FrontPad or any of the applications in the Microsoft Office 97 suite, you can use Microsoft's Web Publishing Wizard to place your page on the Web. Web Publishing Wizard is included on the

547

Microsoft Office 97 CD, or you can pick up the latest version on the Web at the following address:

http://www.microsoft.com/windows/software/webpost/

After downloading the file, you can click it to run the installation program. You can then run the Wizard and use it to publish your page on the Web. Take the following steps:

1. Run the Web Publishing Wizard. In Windows 95, click **Start**, **Programs**, **Microsoft Web Publishing**, **Web Publishing Wizard**. You are prompted to select the folder in which your Web files are stored.

Place All Files in One Folder The Web Publishing Wizard will place your Web page and all related files (including graphics) on the Web. Make sure your Web page and related graphics are all in the same folder, and are separate **CAUTION** from other files.

2. Take one of the following steps:

Click **Browse Folders** if your service provider allows you to place an entire folder on its Web server. (Some service providers allow you to place only a single page on the server.) Use the resulting dialog box to select the folder in which your files are stored.

Click **Browse Files** if your service provider allows you to place only a single file on the Web server. Use the resulting dialog box to select your Web page file.

3. Click **Next**. The Wizard asks you to type a name for the Web server.

4. Type a name to describe the server, and click **Next**. The next dialog box asks you to specify the URL and directory in which you want to place your page. (You should have obtained this information from your service provider.)

5. Enter the URL of the FTP or HTTP server you want to publish to. This includes a path to the directory in which the files will be placed (see Figure 16.5). Click **Next**. The Enter Network Password dialog box appears.

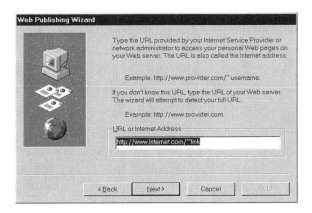

Figure 16.5 The Wizard needs to know where to place the file(s).

6. Type your username, and then tab to the **Password** text box, and type your password. Click **OK**. The Wizard starts to transfer your file(s), and displays a dialog box to indicate when the process has been completed.

TIP **Select File(s) First** There's another way to start the Wizard in Windows 95. Run My Computer or Windows Explorer, and select the file(s) you want to place on the server. Right-click one of the selected files, point to **Send To**, and click **Web Publishing Wizard**.

Uploading Files with FTP

If your service provider indicates that you must upload your Web page and associated files to an FTP server, you can use an FTP program to perform the transfer. The following steps show you how to use WS_FTP to upload files (you can get a copy of WS_FTP at **http://www.ipswitch.com/Products/WS_FTP/index.html**). Once you have installed the program, take the following steps:

1. Connect to the Internet, and double-click the WS_FTP icon to run the program.

2. The Session Properties dialog box shown in Figure 16.6 appears. If this dialog box does not appear, click the **Connect** button.

3. Click **New**.

4. In the **Profile Name** text box, type a description of the FTP server (you can type anything here).

549

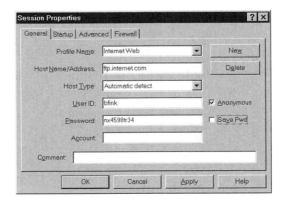

Figure 16.6 Set up a connection to the FTP site.

5. In the **Host Name** text box, type the address of the FTP server (for example, **ftp.internet.com**).

6. Remove the check mark from the **Anonymous Login** check box, type your username in the User ID text box, and type your password in the **Password** box.

7. Click **Save** and click **OK**. WS_FTP connects you to the FTP server and places you in the default directory.

8. After you connect to the FTP site, change to the directory your service provider told you to use for your Web page file(s). (Just double-click a directory name to change to it; the directories on the FTP site should be shown on the right side of the WS_FTP window.)

9. On your Local System (shown on the left side of the WS_FTP window), change to the directory that contains your Web page and any associated files, as shown in Figure 16.7.

10. In your list of Web page files, click the file you want to upload. **Ctrl**+click any additional files. Click the right arrow button to start uploading the selected file(s).

11. After the file(s) is completely uploaded (it may take a long time depending on the speed of your modem or network connection and the amount of traffic at the FTP site), click **Cancel** to cancel the connection. Then click **Exit** to exit WS_FTP. Finally, disconnect from the Internet.

Change to
the required
directory on
the FTP
server.

Select the
file(s) you
want to
upload.

Click the right
arrow to start
uploading.

Change to
the directory
on your drive
that contains
your Web
file(s).

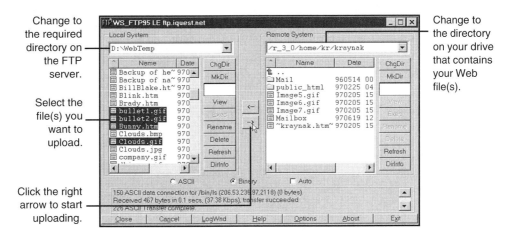

Figure 16.7 Set up your directories for the upload.

Placing Your Page on America Online

America Online has its own Web page editor that you can use to create and publish your page on the Web. You simply run Personal Publisher, and then use it to select a template and fill out a form. Take the following steps to create and publish a page using Personal Publisher:

1. Press **Ctrl+K**, and enter the keyword **Personal Publisher**. The Personal Publisher window appears.

2. Click the **Create a Page** icon. The Templates window prompts you to select a template.

3. Click the icon for the desired template. Personal Publisher displays a form, asking you to enter a title and headline, as shown in Figure 16.8.

4. Enter the requested information, and click **Next**.

5. Continue entering information and clicking the **Next** button until you have completed your page. When the page is complete, you will see a View button at the bottom of the window.

6. Click **View** to preview your page. You can then click **Edit Page** to add or delete from your page. Or, click **Publish** to place your page on the Web.

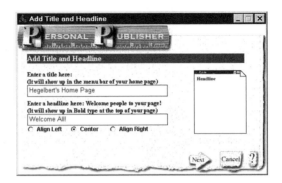

Figure 16.8 With Personal Publisher, you can create a simple page by filling out forms.

In this lesson, you learned what to check for before placing your page on the Web, and you learned various ways to upload your page to a Web server. In the next lesson, you will learn how to spread the word about your Web page so others will visit.

Announcing Your Web Pages to the World

In this lesson, you learn how to make your Web pages known to the outside world.

Going Public with Your Page

Once your HTML documents are up and running on a Web server, you'll want the world to know about them. Fortunately, there are a large number of forums for this kind of announcement. Most of them are Web *Search Engines*, searchable indices of Web resources. Let's look at Search Engines, then at other means of announcing your Web pages.

Search Engines and Your Web Pages

A large number of searchable indices have grown up on the Web. While each is different, and get their information from a different mix of sources, Search Engines have much in common. Generally, you have the ability to type in one or more search strings (in some cases, you can enter natural language concepts) and have the Search Engine look for your specifications in its database. Netscape users know about the Net Search button, usually displayed near the top of the standard Netscape browser window, which accesses a whole page of Search Engines. Figure 17.1 shows part of the results for a search on the word "cigars" in *Excite* (**http://www.excite.com/**).

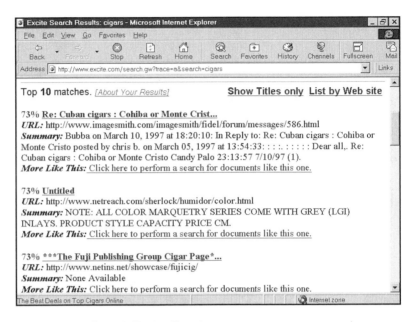

Figure 17.1   eXcite Search Engine Results.

Adding Your Web Pages to Search Engines

While each Search Engine seeks to be unique in some way, all allow users to add URLs to them, usually through a fill-in form. Most don't charge for such listings, though there are some which do. Either is a grand way of publicizing your own Web pages.

In Search Of   Of course, you can use the Search Engines themselves to look for announcement services; see, for example, **http://www.yahoo.com/ Computers_and_Internet/World_Wide_Web/Announcement_Services/**.

The Yahoo! Search Engine's add-an-URL form asks you to categorize your Web page, and also requests comments. What you enter helps build up Yahoo!'s keyword database, so be sure to use good descriptions of your pages. Other services don't require you to enter this information. Instead, they send out a *spider* (sometimes called a *robot*) to access and search the URL you've entered for keywords to add to their database. Spiders typically will follow all links in the URL you've specified, so all your Web pages will get indexed as well.

Before we move on, you need to know a few more things about Yahoo!. First, if you use the service, you'll see it's indexed down to what seems infinite detail. The Web is populated by a vocal minority of people who actually like this sort of endless indexing, so you may want to wander around in Yahoo! until you find just the right place for your service. Every Yahoo! page has the Add hyperlink on it, and when you click it from a place in the index hierarchy, the category on the fill-in form will be filled in for you.

TIP **Leveraging-Submit-It** This is a good example of a no-charge service through which you can add your Web page URLs to multiple Search Engines at the same time; see **http://www.submit-it.com/**. *AAA Internet Promotions* is a commercial service that will add your URL to many Search Engines' databases. You can visit AAA Internet Promotions at **http://www.websitepromote.com/**. Some of these allow literally anything to be posted, from business listings to adult entertainment to radical politics. As a result, you may find yourself with some pretty strange bedfellows if you put information about your Web resources on some of these.

What's New Pages

What's New pages are a Web tradition. Many Web sites use them for announcements of new pages and services; you'll probably want to set one up for your own Web site. The great ancestor of all What's New pages (NCSA What's New) is no longer available, though you can look through its archives at **http://www.ncsa.uiuc.edu/SDG/Software/Mosaic/Docs/whats-new.html**. You've probably also noticed the What's New navigational button in Netscape. Unfortunately, where Netscape used to allow submissions to its What's New page, this no longer seems to be the case. It would appear the explosive growth in the Web has overwhelmed both organizations' What's New process and new submissions aren't being accepted. What gets chosen for the page, like who gets into *Planet Hollywood*, is anybody's guess: The page's maintainers know what they want, and recognize it when they see it.

Yahoo!, the Search Engine described earlier in this lesson, has a What's New page at **http://www.yahoo.com/new/**. Clicking the Add URL button on this page takes you to Yahoo!'s standard fill-in form. Near the bottom of the Yahoo! What's

New page, you'll find a week's worth of daily listings of new pages; each daily entry lists as many as 2,000 new listings, so it would appear anything new that's added shows up here.

Similarly, the *WebCrawler* Search Engine has a What's New page at **http://webcrawler.com/select/nunu.new.html**. You can use WebCrawler's overall URL submission form to add your Web site to the database, but there's no guarantee it'll get added to the What's New page. Figure 17.2 shows the WebCrawler What's New page; note the New Sites This Week clickable image near the top of the page.

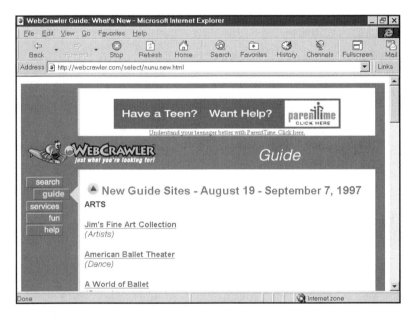

Figure 17.2 WebCrawler What's New Page.

UseNet Newsgroups

You'll want to announce your HTML resources on the mother of all computer bulletin boards, UseNet (also called NetNews). If you have access to NetNews, post a message about your resource to the newsgroup **comp.infosystems.www.announce**. This newsgroup is *moderated*, which means your announcement won't go out onto UseNet right away. Instead it'll be e-mailed to the newsgroup moderator, who will review it to make sure it conforms with the newsgroup's charter, and then post it. The newsgroup's charter, describing its purpose and the procedures for posting to it, is posted to the group periodically. Also, look for the FAQs (Frequently Asked Questions) that are posted on a regular basis; one important such posting is titled "FAQ: How to Announce Your New Web Site."

You can also post an announcement of your Web resource to the newsgroup **comp.internet.net-happenings**, which is an unmoderated newsgroup. Whatever you post there appears without any review or editing.

Other Means of Announcing Your Web Resources

If you're planning on doing business on the World Wide Web, don't overlook your normal advertising channels. If, for example, you advertise your services in computer-related publications, be sure to include the URL for your company's home page in your advertisements. Pick up any computer publication and you'll see ads with URLs in them. You may even want to include your URL in mainstream advertisements, regardless of media. The 1996 Summer Olympics, for example, featured its Web site heavily in its (and its commercial sponsors') on-air promotions. A significant—and growing—portion of television commercials and print media advertisement seem to include URLs, and, more and more, you're hearing radio commercials intoning URLs.

If you're a regular Internet E-Mail or NetNews user, you already know people frequently include *signature tags* on their E-Mail messages and NetNews postings. Consider adding the URL to your Web server in your own signature tag. Some Web Search Engines scan every UseNet posting, looking for URLs, which then get added to the searchable databases; just by having your URL in your signature file, yours gets added every time you post. This is much like an online business card; every time you send e-mail or post netnews, you'll be promoting your Web resources. Speaking of business cards, don't forget your printed one.

Sign It! It's common for Internet users to attach a small signature to all their e-mail messages and NetNews postings. This may give their postal address, phone number, or other similar information. In addition, many people use it for personal expression, including a favorite quotation, piece of song lyric, or other material they believe to be cute, funny, or otherwise significant. Many of these are tedious, juvenile, and significant only to the poster, so be sure to keep yours relevant—and short!

In this lesson, you learned how to publicize your page on the Web.

Readers interested in extending their Web sites into corporate intranets may want to check out Tim Evans' best-selling book *Building an Intranet*, also published by Macmillan Computer Publishing, ISBN 1-57521-071-1. You can preview *Building an Intranet,* and other Macmillan books, at the Macmillan Information SuperLibrary on the Web at **http://www.mcp.com/**. Also, you can find more information about Tim Evans, and his other Web-related books, at **http://www.tkevans.com/tkevans.html**.

WWW
Directory

WWW Directory

Internet Yellow Pages

The World Wide Web is chock full of interesting places to visit. There are Web sites covering everything from UFOs to Personal Finance. The following directory is designed to provide you with a guide to some of the most exciting and informative Web pages. To find several Web sites that cover a particular topic, use the alphabetized categories provided in the Web directory. For instance, if you're interested in information about the weather, check out the sites listed in the Weather category under W.

You will find that the Web can be interesting, informative, and a great deal of fun. And when you're transported to a Web page that's really your cup of tea, remember to add it to your favorites list on your Web browser.

Alternative Medicine

Ask Dr. Weil
www.drweil.com

You've seen this guy's face all over *Time* and *Life* magazines and now he's taken the Web by storm with his Ask Dr. Weil site. Each day Dr. Weil posts a new alternative medicine topic dealing with everything from AIDS, cancer, and arthritis to the common cold, dry skin, and headaches. All of this information is generated through questions sent into the site from curious readers.

In addition to Dr. Weil's daily topic, viewers can browse the site for FAQs, previous topic discussions, optimum health recipes, a searchable database of diseases, treatments and remedies, and a referral page with links to professional organizations.

New Age

www.newage.com

A companion to the popular health magazine, New Age features a Holistic Health Forum where readers can search for topics, books, clinics, and schools online. The Holistic Health Directory can also help you find a practitioner in your state who specializes in any one of over 100 areas of alternative medicine. These range from acupressure to yoga therapy.

Mother Nature's General Store

www.mothernature.com

If you're looking for alternative medicinal products, Mother Nature's General Store stocks it all including: aromatherapy, hair and skin care, vitamin regimens, homeopathy, and herbal products. In addition to being a great source for actual alternative medicine products, this site also provides resourceful forums and a comprehensive online research library.

Health Trek

www.healthtrek.com

Visit the Health Trek Shopping Mall for the best health products and foods. Search for books on dozens of health topics, or drop in and read the monthly newsletter. Whether you are exploring the Botanical Reference, visiting the online Doctor's Office, browsing the Treatment Library, or stopping by the Learning Center, Health Trek is the definitive online resource for "exploring the alternatives."

Alternative Medicine Digest

www.alternativemedicine.com

This site provides one-stop shopping for information on alternative medicines and cures. The Digest tracks the latest and greatest in medical research of an alternative bent and then summarizes the information in an online journal. This site also provides links to alternative medicine books, alternative medicine radio programs, and an online chat area.

HealthWorld Online

www.healthy.net

Offering a map of "HealthWorld Village" as a navigational tool, this site has information on nutrition, fitness, and other wellness issues. You can click the "Nutrition Center" map icon and peruse a variety of topics including the use of herbs in the kitchen and vegetarian cooking. A bookstore offers the online purchase of alternative medicine books and a health food store gives you access to various food products. The site is dedicated to "self-managed care," and offers resources so everyone can participate in the maintenance of their own wellness.

Acupuncture

www.acupuncture.com

This site is by far the most informative and diverse site in terms of alternative therapies and medicines. Focusing on traditional Chinese therapies, including acupuncture, herbology, Qi Gong, Chinese nutrition, Tui Na, and Chinese massage, this site offers valuable information and treatment for three focused audiences, which include consumer, student, and practitioner.

Animals

ASPCA

www.aspca.org

Animals are often one of the most overlooked facets of American life. Whether you are discussing your family pet, or the beautiful American bald eagle, the American Society for the Prevention of Cruelty to Animals is the animal world's biggest friend. On this Web site, you'll find everything from pet care tips, to animal services, to newsletters devoted to the animal lover. This is a complete animal lover's site with information on overpopulation and a calendar of events geared toward pet lovers and people who study animals. You also can join the ASPCA and find e-mail links to other animal organizations.

PETA

www.envirolink.org/arrs/peta

This page offers a list of tips to help you take care of your pet. It provides a guide to proper treatment of different injuries and diseases for all animals. It's a must-see for anyone who owns, or cares for, animals.

Holistic Health

www.cyberark.com/animal/

This is a great page to learn about products and services that help you take care of animals. It's one of the most complete sites on the Web dedicated to home care of animals.

Animals, Animals

www.pacificablue.com/animals/

If your interests lie in learning about animals from all over the world, then this site is the place to visit. It also includes sound bites and videoclips of various animals.

Animal Species

www.fws.gov/%7Er9endspp/mammals1.html

This site offers a complete listing of all endangered wildlife and fish residing in the United States. Each description also provides links for more information.

Auto Racing

RaceZine

www.primenet.com/~bobwest

If you're looking for the fastest auto racing news around, then RaceZine is the answer. This site features news on all the major racing organizations, plus sound bites and archived pictures of some of the top teams in the world. This site isn't a rehash of wire service stories, but offers an in-depth look at various teams in NASCAR, CART, and the NHRA. It also offers trivia contests and links to some of the other top racing sites on the Web. However, don't come here looking for the latest race results. This site is more focused on features and the history of auto racing. There are, however, plenty of links to sites that offer up-to-the-minute race results.

SpeedNet

www.starnews.com/speednet/

From the auto racing capital of the world comes the most informative racing-related page on the Net. The *Indianapolis Star*'s SpeedNet page features complete results and news of all the major racing organizations in the world.

NASCAR

www.nascar.com

If NASCAR is your thing, then the NASCAR home page is a dream come true. This page offers up-to-date results, a history of the sport, and it features stories about top drivers.

CART

www.cart.com

Championship Auto Racing is one of the fastest forms of racing in the world, and this page gives current results on all races. It also includes features on all CART drivers.

IRL

www.indyracingleague.com

A league fighting for survival has one of the top pages on the Net. It features news from the Indianapolis Motor Speedway and links for both IRL and NASCAR events.

Baseball

Major League Baseball @Bat

www.majorleaguebaseball.com

This is the official home of the Boys of Summer on the Web. From here, you can link to all of the Major League teams as well as their minor league affiliates. At the right time of year, you can participate in voting for the All-Star Game. There's a Virtual Ballpark tour that takes you to the park. There are special sections and events for young fans, and everyone will enjoy special treats like the tribute to Jackie Robinson in the 1997 season. Look for trivia contests and giveaways all over the site, including the This Week In Baseball (TWIB) area. And if you are in a shopping mood, browse the Clubhouse Shop for apparel from all of your favorite teams.

Classic videoclips from baseball history and current highlights await at the video section of @Bat. You'll have to install some extra software to see these. They are free and instructions are included. Once you can view these highlights, you'll have your pick of great plays like "The Catch" and different newsclips from every week of the current season.

Fastball
www.fastball.com

This site features incredibly detailed coverage of the Major Leagues as well the minors. You won't miss a single story with baseball news that is provided directly from the AP wire. There are chats with players and other personalities from the game, and you can join the action with interactive fun and games.

Instant Sports
www.instantsports.com

Don't tell my boss, but this site is one of my favorite ways to waste time on a summer day at the office. With Instant Ballpark at Instant Sports, you can see an animated version of every game. Every 30–90 seconds, the animation is updated and shows the progress of the game.

Baseball Statsweb
www.baseballstats.com

This site is the ultimate source for settling any bet on baseball stats. Every stat for every pitcher, batter, and team in the modern era is here. Ty Cobb's lifetime batting average is .366. There are a million more stats where that came from.

Major League Rotisserie Baseball
www.fantasysports.org

Hundreds of Web sites offer fantasy baseball leagues, so it's hard to pick just one that will appeal to everyone. But I'll recommend Major League Rotisserie Baseball. Use any of the Web search engines to find your favorite fantasy league.

Basketball

NBA.com
www.nba.com

The NBA season and playoffs may only run eight months a year, but the NBA.com Web site is available to you 24 hours a day, 365 days a year. It provides you with your pro hoops fix. In season, you find highlights, scores, game summaries, previews, interviews, and more basketball news than you could ever possibly read. In the off-season, be sure to check here for draft news, player trades and signings, as well as news from the training camps. If you want to join the action, you'll find a variety of interactive forums, including chats with other fans (even players and coaches stop in sometimes).

On Hoops
www.onhoops.com

This site is a self-proclaimed alternative NBA site. The proprietors are hard-core fans and want to provide a Web site with a different view of the NBA. Take a look and see what you find. Then you can be the judge of which site is better.

College Hoops Insider
www.collegehoopsinsider.com

For my money, the best basketball isn't played by guys with multimillion dollar contracts, but on the floors of college halls around the country. If you want the most complete scores, stats, and news on every Division 1 A basketball program, this is the best site.

National Wheelchair Basketball Association
www.nwba.org

Basketball is a game that almost anyone can play, especially with some determination. If you are looking for a local wheelchair league, or just more information about wheelchair basketball in general, the NWBA is the premier organization. They have leagues for men, women, and children at all levels of play.

WNBA.com

www.wnba.com

You've seen the commercials, and you know they've "got next." Women's professional basketball is one of the fastest growing pro sports. With the backing of the NBA, it looks like a sure hit. This site looks very similar to the NBA site, and you'll find a lot of similar features here.

Beauty

Redbook Beauty and Style

homearts.com/rb/toc/00rbbec1.htm

Redbook has taken the information and advice from the magazine world and upgraded it to a virtual beauty community. The Redbook Beauty and Style site provides visitors with tips, advice, forums, and bulletin boards to help every woman become more aware of beauty products and secrets. This site is not just a takeoff of its magazine or a high-tech advertising teaser: It is a full information center. It provides tips for women of all ages. Redbook knows that not everyone has time to spend hours in the beauty salon, so they update the site with new articles on how to save time and still look great. Redbook also covers other topics, such as how to look your best though the upcoming weather, finding the perfect scent for your personality, how to care for your clothes, and how to rescue your hair from a bad hair day.

@Hairnet

www.hairnet.com/html/home.html

Get the latest news on the hair and salon industry at Hairnet.com. This site reviews the latest hair styles, the best hair care products, and it connects you to the best salons in your area. This is a must–see before you visit your salon.

Beauty Spot

www.beautyspot.com

Beauty Spot is a great online beauty store, which will help you pick and order the best products. Then they arrive at your door, and you never have to leave your computer! Beauty Spot serves both women and men with great advice and products.

Paula Begoun—The Cosmetics Cop

www.cosmeticscop.com

Before you buy any more cosmetics, make sure you visit Paula Begoun's site. Begoun is known as the "Cosmetics Cop" because she exposes the cosmetics industry's secrets to help beauty consumers make the wisest buying decisions. She posts many reviews of new beauty products, as well as large excerpts from her books, such as *Don't Go to the Cosmetics Counter Without Me.*

Cover Girl

www.covergirl.com

Cover Girl's beautifully designed site helps its visitors become customers by providing them with the latest news, tips, and makeup advice. You can fill in a questionnaire, and the "beauty advisor" will tell you which Cover Girl colors and products will work best for you and your lifestyle.

Beer

All About Beer Online

www.allaboutbeer.com

All About Beer Magazine sponsors this Web site which contains a wealth of information about the beer industry. It offers a generous sampling of feature articles from the printed magazine. There are large sections of beer-tasting notes, advice on the art of home-brewing, what food to eat with which beers, and how to cook food with the ingredients you normally find in beer. One of the best columns is "Jackson's Journal," in which famed beer expert Michael Jackson (not the pop musician) details his trips throughout the world looking for the perfect beer. All About Beer Online also contains international news about the beer industry, information on beer-related stocks, and keen insights into beer advertising campaigns.

The Beer Info Source

www.beerinfo.com

The Beer Info Source has a rich collection of links to Web sites that deal with all aspects of the beer industry, such as beer-tasting clubs, home-brew organizations, magazines, books, and retailers. You can also search their virtual library for listings of brew pubs and beer festivals around the world.

Brew Your Own

www.byo.com

This Web site contains select articles from current and back issues of *Brew Your Own* magazine if you're looking for beer recipes, articles on the beer industry, or answers to tough questions like, "What's the difference between Laaglander and Klages dry malt?".

BrewCrafters

www.brewcrafters.com

BrewCrafters has everything you need to make your own home-brew—brewpots and cookers, yeast and hops, bottles, caps, and rubber stoppers. You can order everything online via e-mail or call their toll free number.

BreWorld

www.breworld.com

BreWorld is the largest European Internet site devoted to beer. It contains information on international beer festivals, meetings, and breweries. You can also find tips and recipes for brewing other alcoholic beverages, like hard cider and perry.

Books

BookWire

www.bookwire.com

"The man who does not read good books has no advantage over the man who can't read them." —Mark Twain.

This incredible site offers everything a book lover could possibly want, whether your taste is for mysteries, nonfiction, fine literature, poetry, or even computer books. BookWire is a rich and well organized resource where you can consult hundreds of book reviews, read complete books they have online, and check to see if your favorite author will be appearing in a bookstore near you. BookWire also has a lot of publishing news, including a link to *Publishers Weekly* magazine (referred to by those in the know as "PW"), and a comprehensive list of awards and critics' choices.

New York Times Book Review
www.nytimes.com/books/home

The New York Times book review has ruined more aspiring writers then a mean-spirited high school writing teacher. It's also made many writers. The Web site contains over 50,000 book reviews from the past 17 years. You'll have to subscribe to the Web version of the *The Times* before you can use it, but subscriptions are free.

The Literary Web
avery.med.virginia.edu/~jbh/litweb.html#rev

The Literary Web contains hundreds of links to Web sites that deal with literary fiction and poetry. It is well organized and covers a lot of ground, from online books to book clubs, journals, and writers' resources.

Publishers Weekly Interactive
www.bookwire.com/pw/pw.html

This site is sponsored by the leading magazine for the publishing industry, *Publishers Weekly*. The magazine and the Web site specialize in publishing industry news, early reviews of upcoming books, the *PW* bestsellers' list, and classified ads for publishing jobs.

Amazon.com
www.amazon.com

If you want to buy a book online, you can't beat Amazon.com. Search their database of more than 2.5 million titles, read descriptions and reviews, and then order your book at a discount.

Camping

CampNet America
www.campnetamerica.com

As the ultimate camping resource on the Web, CampNet America can tell you the best places to camp, how to get there, what to do once you get there, and much more! With more than 12 areas focusing on all of your camping needs, this site includes a listing of RV parks, a campground locator, a complete listing of national and public parks, camping and outdoor supplies, log cabin rentals, travel clubs and associations, the CampNet Traveler's Journal, and the Campfire Forum. It even includes recipes you can use on your next camping adventure. All of this is located right at your desktop. With cool links to AAA's Map 'N' Go (an online trip router), *USA Today*'s Weather site, and First Aid Online, CampNet America is a one-stop-shop for all your camping needs.

Wrolin Camping 'Round the World
www.wrolin.com/campindx.htm

Should your camping adventures lead out of the country, the Wrolin Camping 'Round the World site can help you find campgrounds in virtually any country in the world. From the rustic outback of Australia to the sunny beaches of the Virgin Islands, you'll find some of the best and most beautiful camping spots the world has to offer.

Coleman
www.coleman-eur.com

Let the oldest and most trusted name in camping gear outfit your next camping trip. Coleman camping supplies brings you a complete catalog of camping and hiking paraphernalia, including tents, lanterns, coolers, sleeping bags, camping stoves, and more.

Harvest Foodworks
www.harvest.on.ca

So roasting weenies and marshmallows over the fire can get a little boring…. Spice up your camping menu with zesty, healthy recipes and products from Harvest Foodworks. You'll find a complete index of recipes for breakfast, snacks, lunch, dinner, and desserts, plus a complete product line of healthy alternative camping meals.

Intercamp: Summer Camp & Resource Directory
www.intercamp.com

Parents, take note, because you can't pass this one up. With a listing of more than 2,000 summer camps searchable by price, location, specialty and Web sites,

Intercamp can help you solve your child's summertime blues. You'll also find convenient chat rooms and a special section on summer camp gear for your kids.

Car Buying

Edmund's
www.edmunds.com

Edmund's knows the automobile industry. They've been publishing automobile buying guides since 1966. So if you're in the market for a new or used car, don't even think about stepping onto a dealer's lot without visiting the Edmund's Web site first. For new cars, they list the base price, prices for all the options, and most importantly, what the dealer really paid for the car. You'll also find exact details on the car's interior and exterior dimensions, safety features, performance data, fuel efficiency, warranties, and how much it costs to insure it. Once you've found the car you want, Edmund's will even help you locate a dealer near you.

AutoVantage
www.cuc.com

AutoVantage is a free service. They work with over 2,300 car dealers to give you a prenegotiated discount on a new car. Simply fill out their form online, and AutoVantage will tell you what dealer to go to for the best price.

Yahoo! Classifieds
classifieds.yahoo.com/auto.html

Search for cars, trucks, and motorcycles that are for sale anywhere in the United States by individual owners and dealers. You can even print out a map that tells you how to get there.

Consumers Car Club
www.carclub.com

Consumers Car Club membership is free when you apply on their Web site. Members get access to special automobile pricing information, financing programs, and insurance discounts.

AutoSeek

www.autoseek.com

If the thought of negotiating with a car dealer makes you break out in hives, then check out AutoSeek. This is a free service that will locate the car you want and negotiate the purchase or lease amount that you want to pay.

Comics

VR-1 Digital Comics

www.vr1.com/comics

As one of the first online comics to hit the Internet, VR-1 Digital Comics has several series to interest the diehard comic junkie. Stories run from serious to silly, and they all take full advantage of what modern Internet technology can offer.

Doonesbury Electronic Town Hall

www.doonesbury.com

If your tastes run a little more mainstream, visit Mike, Zonker, and the rest of the crew from Walden Puddle. Here you'll see flashbacks of comic strips of the past with a short list of what happened in the real world on that day. This dates all the way back to the strip's inception in 1977. After getting hit with a heavy dose of nostalgia from the flashback, you may want to test your knowledge of Doonesbury trivia, or buy your own memories, with a bit of Doonesbury paraphernalia.

The Dilbert Zone

www.unitedmedia.com/comics/dilbert

This is the center of the *Dilbert* universe, where you can get as close to "Nerdvana" as possible, without ever leaving the safety of your cubicle. Here, you'll find sage advice from the Dogbert Oracle, micromanagement tips straight from Dilbert's boss, and many other time wasters. You'll get your daily *Dilbert* comic fix as well.

Calvin and Hobbes

www.uexpress.com/ups/comics/ch/

United Press Syndicate, publishers of Calvin and Hobbes, have devoted an entire section of their Web site to the child in all of us. You'll find information about the strip's creator Bill Waterson, his creations Calvin and Hobbes, letters to Bill, and links to some Web pages created by some of the comic's many fans.

This Modern World

www.well.com/user/tomorrow/

This popular alternative comic strip is often seen in the online literary magazine, *Salon*. At the creator, Tom Tomorrow's site, you'll have access to an archive of interviews and articles giving you information about what goes into the creation of each week's strip, as well as links to a vast library of "This Modern World's" episodes.

Celebrities

People Online

www.people.com

No other celebrity site focuses more on famous people than, you guessed it, *People* Online. The interface design is modeled after the design of the printed magazine, and there are plenty of photos, cool graphics, and intriguing articles with daily updates. You'll find some of your familiar *People* Magazine features, such as "Picks and Pans," and you'll be able to check out back issues without ever having to subscribe or sort through the library. Of course, if you would like to subscribe, you can do that at the site, too. Look through the *People* Online "Peephole" to get a sneak peak at the latest activities of your favorite celebs.

Ask Mr. Showbiz

www.mrshowbiz.com

Need information about the hottest, most notable stars? Ask Mr. Showbiz! Catch daily exclusive stories on your favorite celebrities, Hollywood's top headlines, television, video, movie reviews, and daily updated feature photos. Go to Star

Bios to find biographies, real names, astrological signs, credits, and educational backgrounds. There's even a Star Bios Top Ten list of the week's most accessed celebrities at Mr. Showbiz!

Celebsite

www.celebsite.com

Find your favorite star at Celebsite. You can link to Celebsite from Mr. Showbiz or vice versa. Use a search engine to type in the names of the celebrities you'd like to locate. You can also browse alphabetically or even by category. Get recent news and birthday information on your favorite celebrities, check out your horoscope, send fan mail, or get more scoop on a featured celebrity.

Celebrity Four11

www.four11.com

Go to **www.four11.com** and choose Celebrity to link to e-mail and mailing addresses for your favorite celebrities. If you are looking for a quick, easy way to contact an actor, author, business leader, entertainer, government politician, model, sports star, or other star, this is the quickest way to get in touch with the person of your choice.

Sports Celebrity Network

www.sportspin.com

If you want intense coverage of football, basketball, baseball, hockey, golf, auto racing, field hockey, or tennis, you can't miss the Sports Celebrity Network. This site provides daily updates of athlete and team news, and articles featuring your favorite sports personalities.

Community Service

Peace Corps

www.peacecorps.gov

The Peace Corps site is loaded with information about the achievements of this organization. There is a complete list of the countries that the Corps has helped, and is continuing to help. Many of the countries listed have links detailing the work that is being done there. You can read all about the Peace Corps volunteer programs and how you can become a volunteer. Links describe the various work that volunteers do as well as the areas of expertise that are sought. The complete application process is detailed online.

Habitat for Humanity
www.habitat.org

You don't have to be Bob Vila to help the Habitat for Humanity build homes. At this site, find out how to get involved with the Habitat for Humanity in your area. An online search engine will help you find a local affiliate in any of the 50 states and 53 countries.

United Way of America
www.unitedway.org

At this site, you can find out about the many United Way programs. Locate your local United Way by state and see what new things the organization is doing. Football fans will certainly be interested in the section describing the long-standing efforts the NFL has made for this organization.

Idea List
www.idealist.org

This provides a huge directory of over 10,000 nonprofit groups and their Web sites. They also include a section on tools for nonprofit organizations describing ideas for fundraising, using computers, using the Internet, nonprofit management techniques, and much more.

Rotary International
www.rotary.org

Use this Web site to better understand the mission of the Rotary Club. If you are interested, search for a club that meets in your area. The history of the organization and current news are a few of the many topics you may explore here.

Chat

Talk City

www.talkcity.com

Talk City is a live chat environment with a strong sense of the global community. There's literally something for everyone here, with chat rooms covering topics of all kinds from politics to music.

Talk City stresses the safety of their community, providing "clean, well-lighted places for conversation on the Internet." What that means is that all chat areas are moderated by community standard advisors who maintain a family friendly atmosphere. Finding others who share your interest is easy at Talk City. A click on the Communities button brings up a list of all the communities on Talk City with a description of what they cover.

Yahoo! Chat

chat.yahoo.com

Yahoo! isn't just a search engine. At Yahoo! chat, you can use the iChat plug-in, Java or html, and your Web browser to chat with others on the Internet. There are 10 general subject areas to choose from, with several rooms in each area dealing with specific topics. Users can create their own rooms as well.

State of Insanity

soi.hyperchat.com

The chat at this site is not insane, as the name suggests. This online community has rooms created and moderated by its users. Think of it as a cybercommune that's open to the public. There's plenty to experience here, and some of the conversation is really meant for the ears and eyes of adults.

Chat Central

chat.nstate.net

Chat Central is another online community run by folks who want to keep the site safe for chatting. The sponsor of the site makes it clear that no vulgarity and other inappropriate behavior will be tolerated. The one downfall is that occasionally you might find yourself banned from Chat Central because of the actions of someone else using your ISP.

World League of Air Traffic Controllers

www.geocities.com/CapeCanaveral/1140/

Not all chatting on the Internet is done through communities like Talk City. The World League of Air Traffic Controllers is a group of air traffic contollers that meet monthly to discuss the concerns of their industry at Yahoo! Chat. This site provides a meeting schedule and agendas.

Children's Toys

Dr. Toy's Guide

www.drtoy.com

Dr. Toy's online guide to children's toys is jam-packed with information on the latest toys on the market. This site comes complete with descriptions about the newest toys. It also lists the top toys from previous years. It has a list of summer activities to help keep your kids occupied during the long summer days. This site is a must-see for parents with children ranging in ages from 2 to 14.

Learning

www.difflearn.com

This page specializes in learning materials and educational toys geared toward children with special needs, but any parent will enjoy the material described here.

Legos

www.lego.com

What child doesn't enjoy the creativity of building that comes with playing with Legos? This site has all the new Lego products complete with pictures.

Yo-Yo

www.socool.com/socool/yo-yo.html

No childhood is complete without a yo-yo. This page teaches all those cool yo-yo tricks, and it has a complete listing of yo-yo products.

Games Kids Play

www.corpcomm.net/~gnieboer/gamehome.htm

From Red Rover, Red Rover to flashlight tag, this site offers complete descriptions on all those wonderful childhood games that make you want to stay young forever.

Cigars

Cigar Aficionado

www.cigaraficionado.com

Whether you're a seasoned cigar connoisseur or looking for a good first smoke, your stop should be *Cigar Aficionado* magazine's Web site. Here you'll find a wealth of information that is easy to access. Their database lists over 1,000 cigars with ratings, tasting notes, and prices. You can find restaurants around the world that are cigar-friendly, and tobacco shops complete with addresses and phone numbers. Learn how cigars are made or how to store them so they'll last. But that's just the beginning. *Cigar Aficionado* has links to articles on art, music, fashion, fine jewelry, drinks, and all the other status accessories.

Cigar.com

www.cigar.com

Cigar.com features a wide range of articles about how to select a good cigar, the legendary men who make cigars, and the famous people who enjoy cigars. You'll also find a great collection of links to places where you can smoke cigars and buy cigar accessories.

The [Internet] Smoke Shop

www.thesmokeshop.com

Now that cigars are in vogue again, you may order your favorite smoke and end up on a long backlist. But this won't happen at The [Internet] Smoke Shop. You can see exactly what they have in stock, and then order appropriately. Best of all, freshness is guaranteed.

Smokerings.com

www.smokerings.com

If there was a secret password to get into Smokerings.com, it would probably be "fun." This site is full of great quotes about cigars, jokes, trivia contests, and interesting facts. Don't pass this one by!

ALT.SMOKERS.CIGARS FAQ

www.cigargroup.com/faq/

This site is the best source on the Web for answers to all your technical questions about tobacco, how cigars are made, how to choose a cigar, how to store it, and most importantly, how to enjoy it.

Computers

ZDNet

www.zdnet.com

ZDNet is a great comprehensive computer resource on the Web. It has all the news about the latest hardware and software, product reviews and recommendations, and links to downloading software. Shoppers can find ratings of PC hardware and software vendors for quality, customer satisfaction, service and repair, technical support, and other key measures. If you are thinking about buying a new PC anytime soon, look here to see how fellow consumers rate the products. Check out the Healthy PC area for tips on keeping your PC running in tip-top shape and for troubleshooting advice when something goes wrong.

Que

www.quecorp.com

The Que Web site is where you should always go in order to obtain information about technical references on every computing topic. Many of the books have sample chapters available for online previewing.

clnet
www.cnet.com

This is another complete computer news site from the makers of the clnet TV shows. There are reviews of hundreds of software and hardware products. The "How to" section has a great collection of tips and tricks for getting the most out of your software and making your own hardware upgrades.

Dell
www.dell.com

If you've ever thought about ordering a PC online, Dell's site is a great place to put those thoughts to work. You can completely customize any Dell offering on this site, and get an exact price quote for your new system. Then order it online or call them and talk to a sales representative.

TuneUp
www.tuneup.com

Try this service for 60 days for free. You can find answers to thousands of frequently asked computer questions. The site also features one-on-one answers to your specific questions from trained PC technicians. After the 60-day free trial, the service does cost a few dollars a month.

Conspiracies

60 Greatest Conspiracies of All Time
www.conspire.com

Feeling paranoid? Then hop over to the online version of this popular book (Citadel Press Book, $18.95). You'll find several chapters of the book online for a sneak preview. The site is rich in conspiracies including UFOs, Paranoia, Madness, and Subversion. You'll find sections detailing the most up-to-date "bizarreness" as well as archives. You can also check out the Rant-o-Rama for weird articles from the late David Koresh of Waco fame, to Lyndon LaRouche, the perennial Presidential candidate who always has several conspiracy theories up his sleeve.

The Conspiracy Pages
w3.one.net/~conspira

Voted by *Hotwired* as a "Netizen Fresh Link," this conspiratorial site talks about the genocide of native Americans and the Biblical Rapture Index. This site tends to focus on government covert conspiracies.

Gonzo Links—Your Online Guide to Millennia
www.capcon.net/users/lbenedet/

Gonzo is a powerful site with hundreds of links to in-depth conspiracy. You'll find a section on "current news" conspiracies as well as UFOs. The Spooks section, which details the National Security Agency and the CIA, is rich with critical stories. And for you "the sky is falling" Chicken Littles, there is a Panic Culture site filled with apocalyptic links.

Disinformation
www.disinfo.com/

Do you think the world is ruled by a handful of capitalistic elites? If you answered yes, then cruise over to the Disinformation site. This Web page maintains that your six o'clock news is dictated by powerful corporate interests; to counteract this daily corporate propaganda, the page offers, the "real news" (at least according to the site) about everything from genetic altering to mind control.

Art Bell
www.artbell.com/

Art Bell is the premier talk radio host of UFOs and other extraterrestrial matters. His two radio programs—Dreamland and Coast to Coast AM—have developed almost cult followings. Although you can hear his shows in select cities through the wee hours of the night, you can hear him whenever you want by using Real Audio on his Web site. Tune into his show "Live or Go Back," and listen to the archived shows at your leisure. Bell interviews many of the leading UFOlogy experts, including a crowd favorite Richard C. Hoagland, former NASA scientist, who is a proponent of life on Mars.

Contests, Sweepstakes, and Lotteries

Sweepstakes Online

www.sweepstakesonline.com

Because Web sites and Web pages change every day, the contests that are here today are likely to be gone when you read this. So the best place to start when you are looking for contests and sweepstakes is a site that lists and reviews them all. Sweepstakes online has links to hundreds of contests as well as some special contests of their own. They also have a subscription available for an e-mail newsletter with up-to-the minute news for sweepstakes fans.

Publisher's Clearing House

www.pch.com

Save yourself a stamp and enter the famous Publisher's Clearing House Sweepstakes online. You can enter once a day, and there are additional Internet-only prizes. And yes, you can subscribe to the magazines while you are entering.

Prizes.com

www.prizes.com

Once you register and set up an account here, you can play lots of free "scratch and win" type games. Prizes range from tokens that are exchanged for real prizes or cash. Some games require payment.

PLUS Lotto

www.pluslotto.com

As with most lotteries, this is a contest where you must pay to enter. If you are playing from the U.S., be sure to read the prize amounts in U.S. dollars, not foreign currency. And be sure you are familiar with the rules and are comfortable giving your credit card number in order to enter.

Lottery News Online

www.lotterynews.com

Lottery players don't have to play games on the Internet to get some use out of the Web. With Lottery News Online, you can get results from several state lotteries and PowerBall. It also has a list of links to other sites with other lottery results and "official" lottery pages.

Cooking

Cookbooks On/Line

www.cookbooks.com

If you don't have space for a shelf full of cookbooks, Cookbooks On/Line is the site for you. Over one million recipes await you in an easy-to-use, searchable database. Access to the database is free, but you must register for your user ID and password.

The Food Network's CyberKitchen

www.foodtv.com

The companion Web site to cable's Food TV network offers all the variety of the network's programming. Here you'll find recipes, food news, and, of course, information about your favorite Food TV shows. You can get your cooking questions answered by their Cyberchef, and go to their Cybermarket gift show, if all the browsing has made you hungry.

The Dinner Co-op Home Page

dinnercoop.cs.cmu.edu/dinnercoop/

The Dinner Co-op is about 15 people, all Carnegie-Mellon graduates who love food. The Co-op home page has an extensive collection of recipes, menus, links to stores, farmers' market directories, and their very own downloadable cookbook.

Judy's Flavors of the South

www.ebicom.net/~howle/

If you want a little spice in your cooking, visit Judy's Flavors of the South. The chile pepper is Judy's emphasis: "variety is not the spice of life…the chile is!" There are special recipes here (without chile peppers), and tons of links to other homespun cooking pages.

Foodwine.com

www.foodwine.com

Home to the electronic Gourmet Guide (eGG), foodwine.com has recipes and much more. Interviews with nationally recognized chefs give you help in the kitchen and monthly columns help with meal planning and provide insight into the world of food and wine.

Education—Colleges and Universities

CollegeEdge
www.collegeedge.com

What do you need in order to prepare for your future? Whatever you need, you can find it at the award-winning CollegeEdge Web site. Use the advanced college search feature to explore the most suitable institutions. This is available through AT&Ts WorldNet™ service for only $19.95 per month. With the convenience of the CollegeEdge Web Apps feature, you can apply to colleges and universities electronically! Also, there's no need to worry about life after college since you can also explore employment opportunities and acquire advice on careers, as well as academic majors. Perhaps, the greatest deal of all is the opportunity to add $1,000.00 to your college fund. So hurry to apply for the CollegeEdge scholarship.

Resource Pathways College Information Community
www.collegeguides.com

If you're looking for a great resource suitable for your academic and financial needs, visit Resource Pathways, Inc. Only the best college choices, admissions, and financial aid resources make their recommendations list. This site provides current, comprehensive data. The prices of available resources vary, but are well worth the money.

CollegeNET
www.collegenet.com

Get ready to soar through the skies with CollegeNET, rated one of Lycos' top five college search resources. Whatever your college search needs are, you can rest assured that you'll be fine in flight with CollegeNET. You can directly apply to 34 of 38 universities listed at this site. Check out the 3-D VRML tour while you're visiting.

U.S. News.edu
www.usnews.com/usnews/edu/home.htm

The U.S. News site is great for college-bound students. Acquire detailed information about choosing and applying to colleges, as well as available financial aid. An even greater value is the information on jobs and careers after graduation. The post-graduate student can access information on the GRE, GMAT, and LSAT. Try subscribing to the .edu newsletter.

Purdue University
www.purdue.edu

I couldn't let you slip through this Web directory without showing you an example university site. Purdue, home of the Big Ten Boilermakers, sports a site full of the details you need to check out the various disciplines and application processes. Contact students and faculty, and find out more about the great campus life in West Lafayette, Indiana.

Education—K-12

Discover Learning
www.discoverlearning.com

Here's a site that meets the needs of parents, teachers, and students alike. From the catchy section area names like Student Skull Camp and Parent Brain Dump to the feature articles, this site is interesting to look at and to read. There is a community forum for speaking your mind on educational topics, an area devoted to facilitating the creation of online learning sites, and a large set of links to other interesting educational resources. My favorite part is "Free Speak" where students can answer a creative question like "If you were asked to make a "Top Ten" list of the people you regard as the all-time greatest people, whom would you rank first and why?" Check out this site and see the answers that students have given.

The Jason Project
www.jasonproject.org

The Jason Project Web site allows students and teachers to participate in an annual scientific expedition via the Web. Logs and highlights of past expeditions to sites, including hydrothermal vents in the Mediterranean sea and a lava flow in Hawaii, are also online.

Federal Resource Center for Special Education

www.dssc.org/frc

This Web site has information about conferences and technology for parents and teachers of students who are in Special Education programs. There are links to resources about disabilities defined under the Individuals with Disabilities Education Act as well as links to many other types of special educational needs.

AskEric

ericir.syr.edu

Through AskEric, teachers, administrators and other educators can seek educational information and receive a personalized response researched by a trained individual. Users can also search the Eric databases, which include lesson plans and information guides.

Family Education Network

www.families.com

Parents with Web access have no excuse for not being involved in their child's education. This site has suggestions for parents and how they can get involved at school. It also features home-schooling resources. There are opinion polls, chat areas, and other interactive features on the Web site.

Encyclopedias and Reference

Britannica Online

www.eb.com

If you have school-age children, this site is the replacement for any printed encyclopedia you may have ever considered buying. There's a seven-day free trial period before you have to pay a yearly subscription to use this. But you'll probably find that the subscription price is a small one to pay for the wealth of information here. The site is loaded with high-quality reference material, articles, pictures, and multimedia. And best of all, it's all constantly updated.

Grolier Multimedia Encyclopedia Online
gme.grolier.com

This is the Web home of the popular CD-ROM-based Grolier Multimedia Encyclopedia. All of the pictures, sounds, and other multimedia that you would expect to find are here. As with the Britannica site, there is a subscription fee and a free trial period.

The Electric Library
www.elibrary.com

The Electric Library is a huge collection of searchable current reference materials. They have the complete text of thousands of books, newspapers, magazines and other sources online in a searchable format. This is a great source of the most current and accurate information available on the Web. Try the free trial, and see if this is for you or your family.

The World Factbook
www.odci.gov/cia/publications/nsolo/wfb-all.htm

The CIA publishes this yearly electronic World Factbook containing a huge amount of reference information about other countries. Maps, flags, population, natural resources, government, economy, and much more are detailed for every country.

Knowledge Adventure Encyclopedia
www.adventure.com/encyclopedia

This site isn't intended to compete with the comprehensive commercial Web encyclopedias. It offers a smaller selection of very fun and interesting information on topics of interest to children, including dinosaurs, bugs, and space.

Finding People

1-800-U.S. Search
www.1800ussearch.com

1-800-U.S. Search is a fee-based service, charging from $29.99 to $59.95 to locate someone for you. All you need is the person's name you want to locate, although the more information you have (previous address, telephone number, Social Security number, and so on), the better your chance of locating them. 1-800-U.S. Search uses a wide variety of public records, including Postal Office information, lists of telephone numbers, magazine subscription lists, marketing databases, driver's license records, and voter registration information. If you have a credit card, you can fill out a search form online and submit your query immediately. 1-800-U.S. Search does not use a secure server, however.

Four11
www.four11.com

Four11 can help you contact someone by finding the person's e-mail address for you. This is a free service, although it is not as reliable as 1-800-U.S. Search.

Find-It!
www.iTools.com/find-it

Find-It! can help you locate lots of different things on the Internet, including someone's name, e-mail address, service provider, and video phone listing.

Internet Address Finder
www.iaf.net

This service is similar to Find-It!, except that you can enter a user's e-mail address into the Internet Address Finder in order to get information about the person.

Info Space
www.accumail.com/iui/index.htm

Info Space enables you to search for government resources, businesses, and individuals. It can tell you someone's Web site address, e-mail address, phone number, and street address.

Fishing and Hunting

Fish and Game Finder

www.fishandgame.com

Fish and Game Finder Magazine offers one of the best fishing and hunting sites on the Net. This site offers complete up-to-date news, fishing reports, hunting information, and a marketplace where you can find any fishing or hunting equipment you might need. The site offers information on fishing tournaments throughout the country as well as feature articles from the actual magazine. Whether you are a weekend angler, or a more serious hunter, this site provides everything you need to make the experience more enjoyable.

The Fishing Hole

www.roanoke.infi.net/~dolores/fish.html

If you are looking specifically for fishing information, this page offers state-by-state fishing reports, the latest in fishing news, and all the equipment you'd ever need. A must-see for all fishermen.

Sporting Adventures

www.spav.com

This site is geared toward informing and educating hunters and fishermen about the various conservation groups. It also offers a complete fishing guide.

Tackle Towne

www.saint-james.com/captain.html

Capt'n Mike's Tackle Towne is one of the best sites to visit when you're looking for the latest and greatest fishing and hunting equipment.

Outdoors Online

www.ool.com

This is a great site for the serious outdoorsman. It offers fishing and hunting information as well as legislative news geared toward hunters.

Food

Epicurious

food.epicurious.com

Epicurious is the site "for people who eat." Actually it's more than eating; it's drinking and playing with your food as well. You'll find tips for outdoor grilling, a grill guide, and over 150 recipes. You'll also find directions to dozens of festivals around the country where you can sample your favorite food and drink.

Los Angeles Times Food News

www.latimes.com/HOME/NEWS/FOOD

Los Angelenos have benefited from the *L.A. Times* food section for generations; now the online version shares that information with everyone. Not only will you find detailed reviews of area restaurants (handy for your next trip to L.A.), you'll also find recipies, cooking tips, and helpful articles covering everything from spices to kiwi fruit.

PastaNet

www.pastanet.com

You'll find everything you've ever wanted to know about pasta at PastaNet from its history (yes, it did come from China) to its composition (anything from wheat to seaweed). This entertaining and informative site is certainly one to add to a food lover's bookmark list. You'll even find 10 rules for preparing better pasta. You'll no longer have an excuse for cooking soggy noodles.

Godiva Chocolates

www.godiva.com

This is the chocolate center of the Internet universe. Godiva's Web site is a treasure chest of cocoa. You'll find recipes and descriptions of everything in Godiva's line. If you're daring, you'll want to try the Chocolate Meter to see how much you really love chocolate. And after you're finished cruising around their pages, you can order some chocolate of your own.

Insect Recipes
www.ent.iastate.edu/Misc/InsectsAsFood.html

Insects, as this page cheerfully tells us, can be delicious and nutritious. While eating insects may be unthinkable by many, the folks at Iowa State have come up with dozens of ways to serve our creepy crawly friends as your next meal. In addition to the recipes, you'll find detailed nutritional information about some of the more popular insects, links to insect "treats" at the University of Kentucky, and a link to a place where you can purchase chocolate-covered crickets.

Football

NFL.com
www.nfl.com

Every pro football fan will want to start their exploration on the Web at the National Football League's NFL.com site. This site has complete news from the NFL year-round, statistics for teams and individual players, and chat areas for fans to communicate with one another. In season, you'll find up-to-the minute scores on game day, as well as TV times and schedules for coverage. There are areas of the site devoted to the playoffs and to the big finale—the SuperBowl.

Dick Butkus Football Network
www.dickbutkus.com

One of the NFL all-time greats has taken to the Web at this site. Look for his inside perspective and commentary which gives this site a unique slant.

Collegeball.com
www.collegeball.com

Here's your chance to get involved in one of the longest running college football "office pools" on the Internet. Pick your teams each week and see how you stack up against the competition. Ranking the games by order of your confidence in your picks makes for an additional challenge here.

The College Football Hall of Fame

collegefootball.org/index.html

Check out this site for a virtual tour of the College Football Hall of Fame. You can view information about all of the Hall of Famers, search for them by category or accomplishment, and find out about events scheduled around the Hall of Fame.

Edge NFL Matchup

www.nfledge.com

In season, this site has plenty of game reviews to keep you busy. And don't forget, if you didn't obtain enough football news from this site, check out any of the sports news sites listed in the Sports News section of this book.

Games

The Game Cabinet

www.gamecabinet.com

With all the video and computer games in the market, you might wonder if there's room in this world for an old-fashioned game of chess or checkers. The Game Cabinet, a monthly e-zine, gives you information about all those games that don't require microchips and a television set. The site has regular features covering everything from the latest in gaming news to a "Stump the Net" section. This is where the Cabinet's editors challenge you to identify obscure games or solve scenarios encountered in games such as chess, Okey (a Turkish card game), or Carom (a wooden board game).

Social Recreation Resources

www.pacifier.com/~shaffer/games/games.html

Some games aren't much fun if played alone or with one other person. Occasionally, you need a crowd to get your game going. This site, which started as a BYU class project, deals specifically with "social" or party games. If you want more information on "Duck, Duck Goose" or "Dragon Tail Tag," this is the place to go.

Chess Space

www.chess-space.com

Chess is one of the oldest and more popular strategy games in the world. It is a game that most of us have played at least once in our lives. Chess Space is a site where every chess aficionado should visit. With an easy-to-use search utility, visitors can find tons of information about this popular game, even where to play it on the Internet.

The WWW Backgammon Page

www.statslab.cam.ac.uk/~sret1/backgammon/main.html

The WWW Backgammon Page is the most popular Backgammon site on the Internet, and has mirror sites in the U.S., Greece, Portugal, South Africa, and Russia, in addition to its home site in the UK. Everything from Backgammon rules, book reviews, and a list of Backgammon clubs can be found here.

The Scottish Tiddlywinks Association

www-groups.dcs.st-and.ac.uk:80/~ben/tiddlywinks

The home of the alt.games.tiddlywinks newsgroup FAQ, and promoters of the modern game of Tiddlywinks, The Scottish Tiddlywinks Association's home page is the center of Tiddlywinks information on the Net. Tournament listings and rules of the game are easily obtained.

Gardening

Garden Escape

www.garden.com

With so many stunning photographs, valuable gardening information, and great products, Garden Escape is simply a gardener's online paradise. Sponsored by *Garden Escape* magazine, this site is bound to hold your attention for hours, and it will keep you coming back for all your gardening concerns. Search through hundreds of flowers, vegetables, and herbs available online, or just tiptoe through the tulips at your own speed. Whether you need to buy plants and flowers, start a garden from scratch, tend a dying plant, landscape a yard, keep on top of gardening news, talk to fellow gardeners, check out the gift store, or read the online magazine, Garden Escape is your one-stop-shop for gardening needs.

The Great Exotic Seed Company

www.gen.com/exoticseeds

Move over beets and marigolds, and make room for some of the most exotic seeds available from around the world. Choose from fragrant flowers, nuts and fruits, cacti, rainforest plants, and even natural insect repellent plants, all available for online ordering. And you'll be surprised by the low, low prices!

GardenTown

www.gardentown.com

Whether you want to brag about your six-foot sunflowers, or commiserate about your herb garden that went to the dogs, GardenTown is the place to go for garden chat. Pull up your watering can and choose from several types of chat rooms and forums. And don't forget to visit the Town Library and the GardenTown Gallery.

Plant of the Week

www.lclc.com/plantof.htm

This is a great site to bookmark and visit every once in a while in order to check out the Plant of the Week. Each week, you'll find a new plant, complete with picture, botanical and common name, size, description, uses, and other comments. You can also look up past Plant of the Week features.

Better Homes & Gardens

www.bhglive.com/gardening/index.html

As a long and trusted household name, Better Homes & Gardens offers a wide variety of gardening resources including Garden Features where you can get tips, hints, and suggestions from the Better Homes and Gardens editors. It also includes Garden Talk, where you can join reader discussions; Garden Map, where you check out the most detailed plant hardiness maps; and much more.

Government

Thomas

thomas.loc.gov

If you're a C-Span junkie, a political activist, or just want to be a knowledgeable citizen, then aim your browser at Thomas, the legislative tracking service provided by the Library of Congress. Named after Thomas Jefferson, this service tracks bills before the U.S. House of Representatives and the U.S. Senate. You can search for bills sorted by topic, title, and number and follow the bill of your choice through the various committees that have jurisdiction over it. The Web site also contains historical documents such as the Constitution and Federalist Papers. Thomas supplies Congressional member names complete with phone numbers and office addresses.

United States Government Printing Office

www.access.gpo.gov

On the surface, the Government Printing Office doesn't sound too exciting (you might say that about government in general), but this site is chock full of government documents ranging from the latest Food and Drug Administration regulations to full text of the U.S. government budget. Check out the latter and see where your tax dollars are going.

The White House

www.whitehouse.gov

Well, what's a tour in government without a stop at the White House? Here, you will find not only what Bill and Al are up to, but what the entire executive branch has been doing. All sorts of government information can be accessed at this site, including access to Social Security, student aid, small business assistance, and countless other federal programs. Don't forget to read some of the transcripts of White House press briefings; they can be humorous.

National Air and Space Museum

www.nasm.si.edu

One of the more popular Washington tourist sites is the National Air and Space Museum of the Smithsonian Institution. The same exhibits that you can see live are now at this Web site. Find great color pictures (fast downloading time) of aircraft from the early Wright Brothers years to modern-day space flight.

Guns

The National Rifle Association
www.nra.org

Guns and the National Rifle Association (NRA) are almost synonymous. The word "gun" stirs up many different emotions—both pros and cons. The NRA site is the definitive site to find out the latest news on gun safety, legislation, and national statistics. The site also includes a page covering the laws of every state related to owning and carrying a firearm. The NRA site always contains links to the latest news stories from around the nation and world covering gun ownership and use. The site goes much further than gun ownership and contains information about crime prevention programs in general. The NRA page is a great place to start for anyone who owns a gun or is thinking of purchasing a gun.

Doug's Shooting Sports Interest Page
www.users.fast.net/~jasmine/

This site is an excellent place to find out about all types of shooting sports. It covers Olympic shooting sports, trap and skeet shooting, and many others. If you are interested in any type of shooting sport, this is the Web page for you.

Women's Firearm Network
www.amfire.com/wfn.html

Women are increasingly becoming a gun buyers. The percentage has increased a great deal just in the last year. In fact, gun manufacturers are offering handguns made specifically for women. This page is tailored to the specific issues related to women using firearms. It contains helpful information for women who carry and use firearms.

The Gun Page
www.prairienet.org/guns/

The most important issue with using any type of firearm is SAFETY FIRST! This page contains the universal safety rules all gun owners should observe. This page says it best, "A gun never 'goes off' unless something causes it to do so." This site contains a list of the most important gun safety rules that must become second nature of all gun owners.

National Shooting Sports Foundation
www.nssf.com

If you are interested in shooting sports of any type, the National Shooting Sports Foundation (NSSF) is the organization for you. The NSSF is for the hunter as well as the serious competition target shooter. This organization was formed by business leaders and hunting industries.

Health—Men's

Men's Fitness
www.mensfitness.com

Men's Fitness magazine has one of the most comprehensive sites online dealing with men's health issues. In addition to select feature articles from the magazine, this site also includes information about the best sports equipment on the market, nutritional information, tips on how to improve your health, and an excellent interactive forum. The site also has a tip of the day that focuses on everything from exercise to political information. This is a great site to visit for men interested in improving their health and getting the most out of their bodies.

Health—Men's
www.menshealth.com

Men's Health magazine covers this topic in great detail. This site is more geared toward subscribers but still offers complete coverage of key issues.

Prostate Cancer
www.prostate-online.com

Prostate cancer is one of the most serious health issues for men, and this site covers the topic in great detail. This is a must-visit for men of all ages.

Ask the Dietitian
www.dietitian.com

This site is complete with tips on how to improve your diet as well as and what foods to avoid. It also has a listing of the side effects of alcohol.

Fertility

www.dash.com/netro/nwx/tmr/tmr0595/fertility0595.html

Fertility problems are one of the most worrisome problems facing couples today. This site explores fertility issues from the male perspective.

Health—Women's

Women's Wire

www.women.com/body/

The Women's Wire is one of the top sites dealing with women's health issues. This site contains a top news article each day dealing with anything from skin cancer to profiles on healthy diets. The site also contains tons of information from sex experts to nutrition experts that will help keep any woman in tune with her body. One of the best parts of the site, however, is an interactive page where you can talk directly with doctors in the field.

OBGYN.net

www.obgyn.net

This site is for everyone from medical professionals to women just wanting information on their health. It is provided by physicians, so you definitely receive a professional health perspective at this site.

Women's Health

www.nytimes.com/women/

The New York Times offers a comprehensive page dealing in 29 topics of special concerns to women. The women's health forum on this page is of special interest.

Women's Health Interactive

www.womens-health.com

This site is an interactive learning environment geared toward the exchange of ideas and advice. It also has a great health assessment page.

Healthgirl

www.nethealthgirl.com.au/

This is an extremely fun page on a serious topic. Women of all ages will get a kick out of how the page deals with all types of health and beauty concerns.

Herbs

Algy's Herb Page

www.algy.com/herb/index.html

This is the most comprehensive site available for information on planting herbs, cooking with herbs, healing with herbs, and decorating with herbs. Algy's Herb Page features special sections including herbal products, herbal news, and a complete herbal library. Take a walk through The Garden and discover helpful gardening tips, or visit The Store for herbal oils, art, soaps, plants, seeds, and books. Feeling hungry? Sit a spell in The Kitchen to explore the culinary uses of herbs and exchange recipes online. Not feeling up to par? Visit The Apothecary and find an herbal remedy for whatever ails you. Explore The Potting Shed where you can exchange seeds with other readers, or stop in The Greenhouse to join a live online chat.

The Herb Finder

www.woodny.com/garden/herbfinder.html

This searchable database sponsored by Ithaca Gardens can help you locate the name of virtually any herb in existence. Or if you just want to browse, use the alphabetical listing to find sizes, uses, and pictures of all the herbs in the database.

Herbal Information Center

www.kcweb.com/herb/herbmain.htm

The Herbal Information Center and Vitamin Directory will provide you with a complete listing and detailed summary of the most popular medicinal herbs available including Feverfew, Echinacea, Ginseng, St. John's Wort, and many more. You'll also find a General Store for online ordering and an Herbal Book Shoppe.

Seeds of Change

www.seedsofchange.com

Order the best in organic, traditional, heirloom, and antique flower, herb and vegetable seeds from Seeds of Change's online store. Search the database for hundreds of seed varieties grown by certified organic farmers.

American Botanical Council

www.herbalgram.org

Stay abreast of herbal news by checking out what the American Botanical Council is up to. Read about current education and research projects, subscribe to the HerbalGram (The Journal of the American Botanical Council and Herb Research Foundation) or browse current book reviews.

History

The History Channel

www.historychannel.com

This Web site is sponsored by The History Channel cable television channel. Like the television channel, the Web site brings together images, video, and descriptions of historical events to teach you about the world in a fun and engaging way. The Exhibits section is full of rich, multimedia displays that usually focus on a historical place like Ellis Island and Jerusalem. The Classroom section has free classroom materials, study guides, and videos. The Events Calendar lists historical reenactments, special museum exhibits, conferences, and other events happening in the U.S. and U.K. The TV Listings is a convenient way to check The History Channel's programming schedule so that you don't miss your favorite shows. If you want to read more about the things you've learned here, check out The History Store which sells books, videos, and authentic historical documents.

Exploring Ancient World Cultures

eawc.evansville.edu/index.htm

This site focuses on ancient history from the Uruk culture (3450 BCE) to medieval Europe. Here, you'll find complete ancient texts, a useful chronology, maps, images, and descriptive text. There is also a great collection of links to other ancient history Web sites.

Military History
www.thehistorynet.com/MilitaryHistory/

This Web site is sponsored by *Military History* magazine and focuses on famous wars and battles throughout history. Here, you'll find articles and book reviews from the current magazine and 4 years' worth of back issues.

Art History Resources on the Web
witcombe.bcpw.sbc.edu/ARTHLinks.html

The name of this Web site does not do it justice. It contains an incredible wealth of images, history, and analysis of artwork from prehistoric cave paintings to Greek pottery, medieval manuscripts, Gothic architecture, Baroque paintings, and 20th century pop art.

The History Net
www.thehistorynet.com

The History Net contains a diverse collection of historical information, from the usual types of images and descriptive text, to recorded speeches, eyewitness accounts, and interviews with the people who lived through historical events.

Hobbies

CraftSearch
www.craftsearch.com

CraftSearch is really four sites in one, combining online catalogs of craft, hobby, quilting, and sewing sites. If you want to find a craft or hobby site quickly, this is the site to visit. CraftSearch has a total of 3,200 sites to choose from and they can be searched two ways. First, you can search their pages by ZIP Code. By entering the first three digits of a ZIP Code, CraftSearch will bring up a listing of all the sites that have those three digits in their ZIP Code. This is a great way for finding hobby supplies in your area.

Nerd World-Hobbies
www.nerdworld.com/nw565.html

Don't let the title scare you. This listing of hobby sites covers everything that CraftSearch doesn't. You'll find links to sites that deal with yo-yo tricks, slot car racing, and model railroads, just to name a few topics. Nerd World's hobby page makes a great companion to CraftSearch.

Hobby Craft Network

www.hobby-craft.com

It seems there are cable networks for everything these days. This companion site to the upstart Hobby Craft Network (HCN) has information about their programming and links to other hobby resources. Tune into HCN's Web site and look for it on a cable system near you.

National Model Railroad Association on the Web

www.mcs.net/~weyand/nmra

The home page of the National Model Railroad Association (NMRA) has everything for the novice or veteran model railroader. Here, you'll find tips for creating a new layout, a detailed reference library, and links to magazines and Web sites worldwide.

CyberSlot

www.cyberslot.com

This is the site for hard-core slot car enthusiasts. You'll find a catalog of custom built engines and engine parts, in addition to links to model car raceways. And if you want to see some model racing in person, directions are given to their store in Cleveland, Ohio.

Hockey

NHL Open Net

www.nhl.com/

For the latest news about what is going on in the NHL, from wins and losses to trades and firings, this is the site. You can read the headlines on the main page, and follow the links to the full stories. If you are interested in hockey gear, stop by The Store, where you can purchase gear online over a secure connection. You can also find links to every NHL team, where you can locate that individual team's statistics and records. There is also a link to the official team's site outside of the NHL Web site. Want to see that great shot that won the game? Take a look at the Cool Shots Video page. When does your team play? You can see that as well, including if the game will be televised. No site has more to offer about the big league of hockey.

Le Coq Sportif: Guide to Hockey
www.canadas.net/sports/Sportif/

This magazine's official online site is packed full of information. You can read some of the featured articles from the current issue as well as investigate back issues. Here, you can find pages for injured players, box scores, player salaries, schedules, and game odds. You name it, it is here.

Joe Tremblay's WWW Hockey Guide
www.hockeyguide.com/

This site provides over 1,000 links to other hockey-related Web sites. You can find links to the NHL, IHL, ECHL, and other hockey leagues. Additionally, worldwide hockey, amateur hockey, goal tender, and trivia sites are easily found. If you don't know where to go to find WWW hockey sites, start here.

The Exploratorium's Science of Hockey
www.exploratorium.edu/hockey/

The Exploratorium is a science museum in San Francisco. If you have ever had questions about what the announcers and players are talking about, this site probably has your answer. Find answers to such questions as, "Why is ice slippery?," "What is the difference between good and bad ice?," and "Just what does the Zamboni do?" This offers real science with some great information.

The Hockey News Online
www.thn.com/

This is the official site for *The Hockey News*, one of the premier hockey rags around. Ask the writers about the upcoming draft as well as read some of the featured articles in the current issue of the newspaper. Also, you can find out where the nearest hockey summer camp or school is located.

Holidays

Kaplan's Holiday Fun and Games

www.kaplan.com/holiday

Procrastinators' Anonymous should put a warning label on this site. Kaplan test preparation center built this "Festive Study Break" site which is a creative and humorous, yet educational, site for anyone taking a break from life. Visit this site and send mom a Mother's Day card, or learn how to untangle those Christmas Tree Lights. You can even learn a new prank to play on Halloween. This is not only a place with links to interesting places, but where those links are leading you is half the fun! By clicking "Trick or Treat," you will go to the government's site on Extortion.

World Wide Holidays and Events

www.classnet.com/holidays/

This searchable site helps you find holidays happening all over the world. Search for holidays by name, date, or country. A different holiday is highlighted each day with explanations of its purpose, place of celebration, and history. This site will also link you to many different holiday sites of your choice.

Christmas 'Round the World (Wide Web)

www.auburn.edu/~vestmon/christmas.html

This site will point you to anything that you want to know about Christmas. It covers not only the serious side of Christmas, but traditions and humor of the season as well. You can even do your Christmas shopping here while you are in the Christmas mood.

Happy Birthday America

citylink.neosoft.com/citylink/usa/

Experience Independence Day through USA Citylink's site devoted to the sounds, history, and events surrounding the Fourth of July. Find local fireworks displays throughout the U.S., read a copy of the Declaration of Independence, or just get in the spirit by reading quotes from famous Americans.

Groundhog Day
www.groundhog.org

This award-winning site brings you to the town of Punxsutawney where Groundhog Day isn't just another holiday—it's a way of life. This well-designed site tells you everything from Groundhog Day history, to upcoming events. Find out which years "Punxsutawney Phil" (the groundhog) predicted the coming of spring correctly, or play groundhog games during your virtual visit.

Home Improvement

Better Homes and Gardens Home Improvement Encyclopedia
www.bhglive.com/homeimp/docs/index.htm

Whether you are a home improvement wanna-be or an old pro looking to brush up on a long forgotten skill, Better Homes and Gardens is a great starting place online. Their encyclopedia is organized into categories by the types of repairs offered. There's a basics section for those just getting started and plenty of in-depth information about specific types of repairs, procedures, and tools for do-it-yourself types of any skill level.

Home Ideas
www.homeideas.com

Here's a great place to help you decide what home improvements you want to make and what supplies to make them with. The site will send you any of the hundreds of product brochures they have, and they offer applications for estimating the materials and costs for your projects.

Remodeling Online
www.remodeling.hw.net

This is a great site for ideas used in remodeling your house. Or, if you aren't a do-it-yourselfer, but would like to find a good remodeler, search their online database of over 1,000 remodeling contractors.

HouseNet

www.housenet.com

In addition to a good selection of "how to" material to help you with your home improvements. This site has a couple of nice unique features. The family fun area shows some simple projects that the whole family can get involved with. And there's a section devoted to new products.

Builder's 411

www.builders411.com

This is a large online directory of builders and contractors. If you need to find a professional to do the job, here's a great place to start your search.

Humor and Jokes

Funny Town

www.funnytown.com

Funny Town satisfies even the hardest to please funny bone. This site not only serves jokes but also funny stories, satire, quotations, and real-life humorous happenings. You can read the featured funny articles, pick one of several joke categories, or even access the joke archives of past years. If you would rather receive your jokes automatically, sign up on the mailing list for jokes to be sent to you via e-mail. Have you ever heard a really good joke and couldn't remember exactly what the punchline was? Funny Town comes to your rescue by making the site searchable. You can also post new jokes to the message board and read postings from other Funny Town visitors. This vast collection includes jokes about the most teased people, such as John Tesh and Bill Clinton.

Mefco's Random Joke Server

www.randomjoke.com/topiclist.html

If your friends have heard all of your jokes, visit the Random Joke Server. You can browse through 6,000 jokes from seventeen categories such as one-liners ("Help Wanted: Telepath. You know where to apply."), jokes for nerds ("'Ethernet' is what you use to catch the Ether Bunny."), politics, lightbulb jokes, and quotations.

Laugh Web

world.std.com/~joeshmoe/laughweb/lweb_ns.html

No matter what you find humorous, you will find a laugh at Laugh Web. This site not only has the usual political and computer humor, its jokes also cover popular topics like Redneck humor, Windows 95, Star Trek, and Barney. You can even subscribe to "Laugh of the Day" to have a joke e-mailed to you daily.

The Late Show with David Letterman

www.cbs.com/lateshow

If you missed Letterman last night, you can catch up on everything from Dave's crazy quotes to the Top Ten List at CBS' Late Show home page. This site has a complete archive of every Top Ten List since the show aired on CBS in 1993. You can also order tickets, browse the photos of Dave with visiting celebrities, or find out who is scheduled to appear on future episodes.

The Daily Muse

www.cais.net/aschnedr//muse.htm

Get a fresh look at the news through the eyes of a hilarious cynic at The Daily Muse. This site is updated daily with the latest news, pictures, and the laugh-out-loud commentary to go with it.

Insurance

Insure Market

www.insuremarket.com

The insurance industry has caught on to one of the big features of the Web that people really like: timely and easy information. The Insure Market Web site is an example of many insurance sites that can provide you with real-time quotes on a variety of insurance needs. There's no need to talk with an agent, and the companies that provide quotes through this are all nationwide and easily recognized firms including AllState, MetLife, and State Farm. The "risk evaluator" is a neat way to find out how likely your model of car is to be stolen, or how your area ranks for hit-and-run or drunk driving accidents.

Insurance Information Institute

www.iii.org/consumer.htm

Buying and understanding insurance can be confusing. The Insurance Information Institute has this useful Web site that will help you find answers and information about common insurance questions and provide tips about purchasing insurance coverage.

InsWeb

www.insweb.com

InsWeb is another site that offers online insurance quotes. Their quotes include auto, life, health and other services. Some are given immediately. Other participating companies will send you a quote by e-mail or snail-mail.

Net Quote Insurance Shopper

www.netquote.com

Here's one more source for online insurance quotes. NetQuote offers quotes for auto, health, home, and life insurance. The quotes aren't provided over the Web but you will get competitive quotes from several agents via fax, phone, or mail.

Insurance New Network

www.insure.com

This is another good site for consumers to brush up on their insurance knowledge. It provides a glossary of insurance terms, information about vehicle safety, and current news that could affect your insurance coverage.

Job Searching and Employment

The Monster Board

www.monster.com

They don't call it The Monster Board for nothing. This site is bursting at the seams with more than 50,000 U.S. and International job postings. You can search the site for specific careers or just choose the Personal Job Search Agent to do the work for you. The Monster Board lists thousands of jobs in virtually every area possible including both trade and non-trade positions. You'll find listings by location, discipline, and keywords guaranteed to save you hours of digging through the classifieds or making cold calls.

The Monster Board also boasts some unique features including Online Open Houses and a complete calendar of Career Fairs coming to your area. If you are still not convinced that finding a job on the Web is possible or respectable, check out the testimonials under Success Stories. The Monster Board will also help you create a résumé online. You provide the content, and they'll take care of the rest.

CareerPath
www.careerpath.com

With almost 200,000 classified ads from across the country, CareerPath is an excellent source for helping you find the right job. Searchable by newspaper, job, or keywords this complete database of jobs not only provides you with the most recent information, but it also offers tips on how to interview and build your résumé.

e-span
www.espan.com

e-span is unique from the other career and employment sites because it provides you with jobs and helps companies find candidates for their job openings. e-span works with some of the big boys, like Microsoft, GTE, and Ameritech. And don't forget to check out the Hot Jobs list and the online Salary Calculator.

Cool Jobs
www.cooljobs.com

Forget the stuffy corporate jobs, this site is for the daring and adventurous. With an out-of-the-ordinary list of jobs that change daily, you'll find job opportunities with NASA, Walt Disney, ClubMed, MTV, and Jeopardy. You say you want to join Cirque du Soleil? Check out the very cool job description and submit your résumé online.

JobVault
www.jobvault.com

Looking for a job with a big company or just a company with a big name? The JobVault has postings with Nike, Sun Microsystems, Eastman Kodak, Ford

Motor Company, Gateway, Netscape, Proctor & Gamble, Hallmark, Phillip Morris, and many more. Submit your résumé online, get career advice, and check out the cool, exclusive interviews from celebrities about their jobs.

Languages

Berlitz World
www.berlitz.com

Over the past 115 years, Berlitz International, Inc. has taught 31 million people to speak a second language. Berlitz publishes its own books, runs its own courses, and has now started the Berlitz World Web site. The Web site contains a lot of practical information, like the 25 phrases (in four different languages) that you need when dining out. You can also find tips for how to conduct yourself in foreign countries, and how to do business. On the lighter side, there's the Faux Pas section which contains funny and true stories of people who have mixed up their foreign vocabulary and embarrassed themselves. There's also a Bulletin Board where visitors to the Web site can debate the importance of various languages and the best ways to learn them.

Foreign Languages for Travelers
www.travlang.com/languages

To use this site, you simply pick a language that you speak, and a language that you want to learn. You also get to pick the subject area that you want to focus on such as basic words, numbers, or phrases for dining out or travel. Foreign phrases and words are spelled out for you. When you want to hear the proper pronunciation, click a word or phrase and a sound file plays. C'est magnifique!

Squeal Empire Learn-a-Language
www.kaiwan.com/%7Eslayer/squeal/free.html

The Learn-a-Language site contains links to other places on the Web that have full, sophisticated tutorials for more than 40 languages. The owners of this site have checked over each link to make sure that the language tutorial is high quality.

A Web of Online Grammars
www.bucknell.edu/~rbeard/grammars.html

If you want a more academic approach to learning a language, try A Web of Online Grammars which has links to online grammar books for over 40 languages, including "dead" languages like Latin. There are also links to online dictionaries, morphologies, and other learning materials.

Animated American Sign Language
www.feist.com/~randys/index1.html

This creative and unique Web site teaches the American Sign Language (ASL) by using animated graphics that show you exactly how to move your hands to spell the words. There are also many links to other language resources and articles about the deaf community.

Legal

Lawyers On-Line International
www.global-villages.com/lawyers

All of us have legal questions that could be answered rather quickly, and therefore, we don't want to enlist the services of a lawyer who may feel compelled to charge us for his or her time. Well, given the wonderful world of technology, sites such as the Lawyers On-Line International, home of the Harvard Legal Team, are now available to you. You can e-mail this team of attorneys with your legal questions 24 hours a day. Wait, there's more. Other key features of this Web site include a segment on how to select a lawyer and how to obtain legal news. Some of the legal news topics include the latest Supreme Court decisions and major new Federal legislation. You may also want to check out the Do-it-Yourself legal forms.

West's Legal Directory
www.wld.com

You really don't have to go far to learn about lawyers, law firms, and other legal entities since the West Legal Directory is available to you at the click of a button. If you're an attorney, you can even add your contact information at this site.

Martindale-Hubbell Lawyer Locator
www.martindale.com/locator/home.html

Do you need a lawyer? Are you looking for a particular law firm? You don't know where to begin your search? The Martindale-Hubbell site is a good resource to start looking. Find comprehensive listings for 900,000 lawyers and law firms around the world.

Yahoo!
www.yahoo.com/Business_and_Economy/Companies/Law

For your convenience, the Yahoo! search engine has a comprehensive directory presented by areas of law. For an attorney to handle estate planning, try the Estate and Probate link. If you need an attorney for an International business venture, try the International Law link. This offers a wealth of legal resources at your finger tips!

USA Law Resources
www.laws.com/usgen.html

This Legal section has primarily focused on obtaining legal services. However, if you're simply wanting to do some legal research or just find out about different legal entities, then the USA Law Resources site is the place to be. Check out various law libraries, court opinions, and other legal information.

Libraries

The Library of Congress
lcweb.loc.gov

The most famous library in all of history is the ancient Library of Alexandria. The Library was built to house all the knowledge of mankind and was to be a place where scholars could freely exchange ideas. The Library contained some 400,000 scrolls when it was accidentally destroyed by Julius Caesar in 48 BC. Our modern equivalent is the Library of Congress, which contains over 17 million books stored on 532 miles of shelves. Its mission is "to sustain and preserve a universal collection of knowledge and creativity for future generations." The Library of Congress is a research library, which means you cannot wander through the book stacks, and you cannot check out books. You can, however, view any book in the Library's reading room. You can also use the Web to search their complete catalog listing for detailed information on any book the Library owns.

The New York Public Library

www.nypl.org

The New York Public Library is the largest library in the world where you can actually check out books and take them home. The research library has many fine exhibits of books and artwork which you can view online.

The Internet Public Library

www.ipl.org

The Internet Public Library has the text of over 12,000 books, magazines, newspapers, and other written material online. You can search by author, title, Dewey decimal number, or topic. They also have some permanent and rotating art and book exhibits.

Pick

www.aber.ac.uk/~tplwww/e/history.html

Pick is a Web site devoted to the history of learning, libraries, books, reading, and everything to do with the written word. They have links to library societies and associations and an active mailing list.

Carrie

www.ukans.edu/carrie/carrie_main.html

The Carrie electronic library was started in England in 1993. They now have full electronic text for thousands of books, from ancient writers to 19th century poets. The site is very easy-to-use and contains a wealth of literature.

Magazines

Pathfinder

www.pathfinder.com

This is easily one of the largest and most well-known sites on the Web. It is certainly the best starting point to explore magazines. Pathfinder is run by Time

Warner, publishers of over a dozen of the most well-known magazines. This site is a central point for access to all of the magazines online, including *People*, *Money*, *Time*, *Sports Illustrated*, *Fortune*, and *Life*. In addition to providing links to the magazine, the main site itself keeps track of news and current events in many topics. With each of the magazines, expect to find headlines and sample stories from the print edition at a minimum. With most, you'll find additional features including stories not available in print, daily (or more frequent updates), and archives of past issues.

Ziff-Davis Magazines

www.zdnet.com/findit/mags.html

If you love to read the latest news and product reviews the computer industry has to offer, look no further than ZDNet's magazine page. This is a collection of sites for Ziff-Davis' impressive collection of computer magazines including *PC Magazine*, *Computer Life*, *Computer Shopper*, and over a dozen other magazines.

The Electronic Newstand

www.enews.com

If you are looking for a magazine's Web site and can't find it here, it either doesn't exist, or it isn't worth reading. With links to over 2,000 magazines, this is one of the largest general magazine reference sites available.

Hearst Magazines

www.hearstcorp.com/mag.html

This is another publisher's "Super Site." It includes links to Hearst magazines publications, including *Cosmopolitan*, *Esquire*, *Good Housekeeping*, *Popular Mechanics*, and *Redbook*. There's enough variety here to satisfy almost any reader.

National Enquirer

www.nationalenquirer.com

With the incredible circulation that this publication has, it's impossible to leave this section without mentioning it. So, while you won't find all of the stories from this week's issue on their site, you will find enough tibdits to satisfy your craving until you can pick up a copy at the supermarket.

Movies

The Internet Movie Database
us.imdb.com

The Internet Movie Database was one of the first major sites that you could actually do something with. It's grown from a humble labor of love to a major force in the online entertainment world. So what's there? Just a completely searchable database of facts and figures for nearly every movie ever made. Are you interested in who played the T1000 character in Terminator 2? Are reviews of current theatrical releases and new videos what you are looking for? They're all here as well. And they've got movie and Hollywood news, links to local movie theater schedules, and you can even buy tickets online from participating theaters.

Cinemania
cinemania.msn.com

Microsoft's Cinemania CD-ROM is a favorite CD for many movie fans. On this Web site, they've built an online version of the movie database as well as current news and interviews. You'll also find other staples, such as local movie times, news, and gossip.

Movie Finder
www.moviefinder.com

If you find yourself constantly missing movies on TV, this site is at least part of the answer. You search their database of movies to find showing times by location. If you don't know exactly what you want to see but you need to find out when a good love story is on, you can search by genre, rating, and other criteria.

MovieLink
www.movielink.com

This site provides a useful way to check movie times for theaters in your area. You can search by city name or ZIP Code, to find the theaters and what they are showing. You can order tickets from some of the theaters. The downside is that the number of cities covered is limited. But it's still a great start.

Hollywood Online
www.hollywood.com

You would expect a site about Hollywood to be full of glitz. In addition to a movie guide, show times, and other standard fare for movie sites, be sure to check out their *Buzz* forums for online chat with other movie fans.

Movie Studios

Paramount
www.paramount.com

The major movie studios have all taken to the Web in a big way, and Paramount is no exception. Home to blockbuster hits like *Mission Impossible* and the entire series of *Star Trek* movies, this is a fun site to visit for movie fans. Look for sound clips, videos, and even interactive games relating to new releases and to blockbuster favorites. There's a whole additional offshoot of this site for fans of the Star Trek movies. Because Paramount is into television as well, be sure to look for parts of the site related to their great shows including *Duckman* and, of course, the current Star Trek series.

Fox Film
www.fox.com/movies.html

Another major studio with a first class site is Fox. Most of this site centers around current releases so the content here will certainly change by the time you see this. At least I hope *Speed 2* isn't still current several months from now! So be sure to check this site for what's new.

Disney Pictures
www.disney.com/DisneyPictures/index.html

This is one that you and your kids will enjoy. There are lots of games and downloadable snippets from many Disney favorites here. Toy Story actually has its own site and address at **www.toystory.com**. This will provide hours of family fun.

Universal Pictures

www.mca.com/universal_pictures

Universal has certainly had their run of good luck lately with *Liar, Liar* and *The Lost World*. At this site, catch up on current and coming attractions from this major Hollywood player. You can also check out the syndicated television hits offered by Universal, such as *Hercules: The Legendary Journeys* and *Xena, Warrior Princess*.

Warner Brothers

www.movies.warnerbros.com/main.html

Warner Brothers was one of the "classic" film studios of the '30s and '40s, and it is also the home of the cartoon favorite Bugs Bunny and Friends. In addition to current movies from Warner Brothers, this site offers links to sites about movies on home video and the Warner Brothers television offerings on their new network.

Museums

The Metropolitan Museum of Art

www.metmuseum.org

The Metropolitan Museum of Art in New York has over two million pieces that span over 5,000 years of human culture. The Web site has images and historical notes on thousands of pieces of art from Ancient Egyptian, Greek, Roman, Asian, African, Islamic, and Medieval Europe to more modern Italian Renaissance, Baroque, and the 19th and 20th centuries. You can also use this Web site to visit some of the museum's current special exhibits which contain detailed histories, critiques, a timeline, and a glossary of terms to go along with images of the artwork. There is also a link to the Cloisters, a medieval museum located in a beautiful park on the northern side of Manhattan. The Cloisters Web site contains a wide collection of medieval artwork, including the famous Unicorn tapestries.

The Vatican Museum

www.christusrex.org/www1/vaticano/0-Musei.html

The Vatican Museum specializes in ancient, medieval, and Renaissance artwork. The Web site contains hundreds of images of Egyptian, Greek, Roman, Etruscan, and Italian Renaissance sculpture, medieval paintings and sculpture, and tapestries, books, and maps.

The Smithsonian Institution

www.si.edu/newstart.htm

The Smithsonian Institution in Washington, D.C. owns over 140 million artifacts that are housed in 16 museums and galleries. Getting lost can be a real problem, but not on the Web site. Simply pick a tour that sounds interesting, and the Web site will guide you around the museums.

Museum of Modern Art (MoMA)

www.moma.org

The MoMA is located in New York and specializes in 19th and 20th century art. The museum has over 100,000 paintings, sculptures, and architectural models, 14,000 films, and 120,000 books.

The Rock and Roll Hall of Fame and Museum

www.rockhall.com

The Rock and Roll Hall of Fame and Museum has built a substantial Web site that shows off some of their great collections. You can listen to songs and read lyrics, view videos of your favorite rock stars, and watch the footage from when they were inducted. New exhibits arrive all the time, so check back often.

Music

MTV Online

www.mtv.com

The world's first music video network is online with all the flash and style that comes through televisions worldwide. MTV's site is the place for the latest in what's happening in the world of popular music.

Classical Net

www.classical.net

If you want to build your own Classical music library or need help in finding that perfect recording of Mahler's 4th Symphony, Classical Net is the place to go. In addition to this site's extensive resources, there are links to over 2,000 other Classical music-related pages.

House of Blues

hob.com

BB King and other blues artists live online at the House of Blues Online. This is the ideal place to get the latest Blues news and concert information. There are links that take you to LiveConcerts.com if you want to experience some music right now, or if you'd like get a job at one of the many House of Blues locations around the country.

Sony Music Online

www.music.sony.com

Most of the major record labels have Web pages, usually featuring some of their more popular offerings. Sony Music lets you sample their entire catalog from Classical to Country. Virtual Press conferences let you talk to your favorite recording artists, and afterwards you can sample their wares online with Music On Tap.

JAZZ Online

www.jazzonln.com

If you want a laid-back, cool Web page to visit, go to JAZZ Online. Here, you'll get to talk to your favorite Jazz performers, get help in distiguishing the difference between Be-Bop and Swing, and even pick up a few CDs through **JOL@Cdnow** to listen to at home after you've completed your education.

News

USA Today

www.usatoday.com

Experts predicted *USA Today* would not last long on newsstands when the paper first published in the early 1980s. Not only has it survived and thrived, but now it has a Web site that continues to break news. You'll find the familiar four-colored sections NEWS, SPORTS, MONEY, and LIFE like the morning paper but now these sections are updated 24 hours a day on the Web. Track your stocks, read up-to-the minute sports scores, and plan trips with the Travel Extra Bonus Section. Follow every known weather development in the special yellow Weather section. Teachers can enroll in the Classline feature designed to make today's headlines relevant to students. *USA Today* even reports winning lottery numbers for every state that plays to win.

The Washington Post
www.washingtonpost.com

If you want more national and international news than your local paper provides, go to *The Washington Post* for excellent in-depth coverage of the White House, Congress, and the rest of the federal government. Participate in Talk Central with *Washington Post* reporters and columnists on topics ranging from business, style, technology, and, of course, public policy.

MSNBC
www.msnbc.com

Here is the Microsoft NBC cable channel/Web site that is aiming to steal some of CNN's thunder. You'll receive up-to-the minute coverage of sports, news, politics, science, health, and the usual suspects, but you'll also hear audio clips of newsmakers and NBC's star reporters and anchors. You can also join MSNBC chat rooms to sound off on the issues of the day.

USNews Online
www.usnews.com

One of the more substantive news magazines, *U.S. News and World Report* brings the same quality to its Web site. You'll find in-depth coverage of topical national and international news as well as business and technology developments. Don't forget to check out the college and career center which stores information such as college rankings, financial aid, and career guidance.

Drudge Report
www.drudgereport.com

If you want screaming tabloid headlines, bookmark The Drudge Report. Matt Drudge won't dazzle you with Java applets and animated plug-ins, but he is a "grassroots reporter" who has the New York-Washington, D.C. chattering class talking. Based out of Los Angeles, the Drudge Report scoops the national press sometimes with stories that usually fall into the following categories: politics, Hollywood gossip, technology, and earthquakes. You can even sign up for his free e-mail updates which are a hoot. He supplies hotlinks to nearly every major news organization and columnist on the Web today.

Olympics and Amateur Sports

The Olympic Movement
www.olympic.org

The International Olympic Committee has done a top-notch job of presenting their efforts on the Web. This site describes the purpose and mission of the Olympics as well as how they are organized and managed. Sections about the organizing committee's activities and news related to the Olympics are worth a look. And be sure to check out the pages for each of the upcoming game sites for both Winter and Summer games in the next few years.

NCAA Online
www.ncaa.org

Whether you are a sports fan looking for information about any NCAA sanctioned sports, or a college-bound student-athlete looking for eligibility and enrollment guidelines, you'll want to check this site out.

NJCAA
www.njcaa.org

The NCAA isn't the only collegiate sports governing body. The NJCAA administers the activities of junior college sports. This is a great site that does a nice job providing information about the events and sports sanctioned at its member schools.

International Amateur Athletic Federation
www.iaaf.org

Track and field is one of the highest profile amateur sports around. The IAAF is the governing body for this sport and their Web site is the best place to get the latest news from the sport. For each event, the site includes descriptions and significant milestones and records.

Team USA
www.olympic-usa.org

The best features of this site are the sport-by-sport descriptions and links to biographies of the 1996 U.S. athletes. If you are looking for Team USA merchandise, it also features an online store full of all your favorite goodies.

Online Games

Internet Gaming Zone
www.zone.com

For years, playing games online usually meant hours setting up your modem so you could play Doom with your friend across the country. It was a tedious and expensive proposition at best. Now, Microsoft has joined a half dozen other companies to bring you the thrill of playing some of your favorite games over the Internet.

Kali
www.kali.net

Kali is one of the best values on the Internet today. While most online game companies have a "pay-per-play" policy, Kali has a one-time, $20 registration fee. For $20 you get to play dozens of different games over their network and free upgrades of their software. Some of the games you'll be able to play on Kali include: Diablo, Quake, Duke Nukem 3d, Command and Conquer, and X Wing vs. Tie Fighter.

Total Entertainment Network

www.ten.net

One of the largest online game providers, *Total Entertainment Network* provides a safe haven where you and your closest friends can blow one another away in games such as Blood. For the less violent among you, NASCAR Racing Online give you the chance to be the next Jeff Gordon. *TEN* has varying rate plans ranging from five hours per month at $9.95 to unlimited time per month at $19.95.

Engage Games Online

www.engage.net

Engage already provides games to online services such as *CompuServe, Prodigy,* and *America Online*. Their selection on the Net is very extensive, ranging from trivia games to strategy games like *Castles II.* Engage has a no monthly subscription fee, and you pay only for the time you spend playing a game.

Parenting

ParentSoup

www.parentsoup.com

We all grow up with chicken noodle soup, vegetable soup, and alphabet soup. Did you ever imagine such a thing as "parent soup"? Well, neither did I, but this site, Parent Soup, truly leaves a warm feeling in your heart just as the above-mentioned favorites left a warm feeling in your tummy. Join this group of parents over a cup of coffee to share joy and laughter, words of wisdom, and love at "the neighborhood's favorite kitchen table." You're sure to have peace of mind about your parenting woes after spending time chatting with some of the other members of this popular site. In addition to taking the opportunity to ask questions of other parents, you can also share your perspective on parenting. It's a great way to learn what others, like yourself, are doing in the world of parenting, and to meet people and make friends.

Parenthood Web

www.parenthoodweb.com

Find out information on a variety of topics at the Parenthood Web site's pick of the week topics. To name a few, there may be topics on children's health or behavioral issues, early childhood mental and physical development, or even family-related matters. Be adventurous.

babyonline

www.babyonline.com/

Check out comprehensive information on pregnancy, parenting, prenatal, postnatal, and other related issues. Take the virtual tour of the site to discover the various offerings you could have access to as a member of the site. Also, take advantage of such information as updates on the best baby products currently available to consumers.

ParentsPlace.com

www.parentsplace.com

Welcome to a place you can call your own. Well, sort of. This site offers information on topics like children's health, pregnancy, and family activities. You can't go wrong with a pit stop to ParentsPlace.com. You're sure to learn something or teach something to someone else during a chat session with other parents.

Disney's FAMILY.COM

www.family.com/Categories/Parenting

Everybody loves Disney! Check out this site which provides information on topics of interest to old parents and new parents alike. So what exactly do you do to prevent spoiling your child(ren)? If you "spare the rod," does that impact your child's disposition? Find the answers to this and other current parenting topics.

Personal Finance

Money Online

www.pathfinder.com/money

Looking for information on personal finance? Click **Money** under Prime Clicks of the Pathfinder site to check out the Money Magazine Web site (as shown previously) to get everything you need to enhance and improve your personal finances. If you're into the stock market, Money can tell you about the status of the Dow Jones Index and other financial markets. Learn to establish a personal investment portfolio. Also, get some help with setting financial goals for college savings, home purchasing, retirement planning, savings and borrowing, and managing your taxes. Other great features of this Web site include a wealth of information on various companies, savings and investment opportunities, and financial news. In addition to learning about some of the best places to live in America, you can also obtain advice from Money's editors.

Consumer Credit Counseling

www.pe.net/market/cccs

It may be difficult to budget your money. You can get help through the Consumer Credit Counseling Service. Manage your debt by consolidating your bills in a single monthly payment with lower interest rates. The best part is that you can learn to use cash, instead of credit, and balance your personal budget effectively.

The Personal Finance Mailing List

www.bcs.org/Groups/cad/personal_finance.html

If you're having difficulty managing your finances, the Personal Finance Mailing List is a good networking tool for you. Get online with experts, such as financial planners, accountants, and attorneys to get solid, applicable advice. Credit card usage, debt management, and estate planning are a few topics you can learn about.

BizWeb Personal Finance

www.bizweb.com/keylists/finance.personal.html

This is a great tool for finding financial information resources to meet your every need. For example, check out the Center for Financial Independence which presents financial performance ideas and tools, and provides assistance for businesses and individuals. You may also be interested in the Cyber CPA for free tax and financial planning services.

CNN Financial Network

www.cnnfn.com

Your personal finance directory is incomplete without the CNN Financial Network. Get stock quotes, and pricing and performance data on mutual funds. Visit the Reference Desk for government resource connections like the Federal

Finance Information Network and the Small Business Administration. Don't miss the Web Connection for credit and tax information, and emerging business resources.

Politics

Roll Call Online
www.rollcall.com

"Hill Rats" who can't get enough of Congress go to Roll Call's Web site to share in its insiders' reporting on Capitol Hill. Roll Call takes you behind the usual headlines to what is really going on behind closed doors of the House of Representatives and Senate. Get a ringside seat on who is fighting whom (often within the same political party) for power. You'll find news scoops, commentary, policy briefings, and other roll call files.

The Republican Party
www.republicanweb.com

If you want the party line, go to the Republican Party cyberheadquarters to get the latest in GOP strategy, issue papers, and news on GOP activities in your state. You can also join the political discussion chats and link to other conservative Web sites.

The Democratic Party
www.democrats.org

Well, it's not much different than the Republican Web site (is there any difference between the two parties?). However, you can bank on the fact that it will take the opposing point of view. You'll find press releases, news, Party information, and links to other liberal Web sites.

The Reform Party
www.reformparty.org

Got a strange feeling that the Republicans and the Democrats are just different sides of the same coin? If so, this site's for you. The Reform Party site gives you information on all the reform issues. Links are provided to State sites and you can check up on the latest issues in the news.

Free-market.com
www.free-market.com

A pro-free enterprise site containing public policy discussions such as "Privatizing Social Security" and the role of government in a free society. Download "freedom" images to add to your Web page. Follow links to other libertarian pages and sign up for the free e-mail update: "The Daily Outrage," a brief update highlighting bureaucratic follies and government corruption.

Turn Left
www.turnleft.com

Liberals should flock here to learn tactics in "fighting the right" as well as take part in interactive newsgroups. Read policy papers and follow links to other liberal magazines and pundits.

Radio

Timecast
www.timecast.com

Half a century ago, our grandparents gathered around the radio and listened to President Franklin Roosevelt's fireside chats, heard reports from WW II battlefields, and listened to shows like "The Shadow." Now you can do the same thing while using your computer. With the ingenious Real Audio Web browser plug-in (www.realaudio.com), you can listen to live sporting events, concerts, and archived shows right from your cozy computer room or laptop. For the TV Guide of radio programming, go to Timecast. This handy viewers' guide has links to live programming, news briefings from ABC, Fox, and others, as well as a directory organized by topics much like Yahoo!.

NetRadio
www.netradio.net

NetRadio specializes in over a hundred music and information links ranging from jazz, classical music, celebrity news, vintage rock, and new age music. Don't forget to whip out your wallet and go to Valuevision, which is NetRadio's version of the home shopping network.

CNET Radio

www.news.com/Radio/?ctb.radio

If you want the latest scoop on the latest Web browser beta from Netscape and Microsoft, Apple's latest operating system, and other computer industry news, then aim your browser at CNET Radio. You can listen to daily industry reports, live reports from shows like Comdex as well as seminars. Most of these reports are archived for easy access.

Atlantic Broadcasting System

www.abslive.com

An incredibly in-depth site for financial market junkies. You'll get live updates every half-hour on the NYSE, NASDAQ, and the Chicago Futures Pits. Expert analysts will also give you the inside scoop on market ups and downs. You can also sign up for the free e-mail market updates.

LiveConcerts.com

www.liveconcerts.com

Forget about listening to your favorite group's CDs or listening to tunes on an FM station, go to the liveconcerts lobby and find out which bands are playing live! Listen to interviews with your favorite performers, and if you happen to miss a live show, the site contains archives so you don't miss a thing.

Religion

The Vatican

www.vatican.va

One of the most intriguing sites on the Web in *any* category, "The Holy See" is a well-designed blending of the traditional Roman Catholic experience and modernity. This site uses a clever, hidden, three-frame layout available in English, French, German, Italian, Latin, Polish, Portuguese, and Spanish. Completely searchable, you can research papal history and documents, hear the latest news from Rome and view historic art from the Vatican in a seamless, easy-to-navigate interface. Remember, where there is love, there is hope—and where there is link, there is Pope.

Gospel Communications Network
www.gospelcom.net

The multilingual and mega-searchable Bible Gateway is just one of dozens of GCN's member ministries. Other affiliated sites range from Arab World Ministries and The Calvinist Cadets to The Fellowship Of Christian Magicians and *Christian Computing* Magazine. All these resources make this site practically omnipotent!

BuddhaNet
www2.hawkesbury.uws.edu.au/BuddhaNet

The path to enlightenment never had so many worldwide connections—and you won't have to meditate while you wait it to load. This interactive site will enable you to chat with other Buddhists, study Karma art, Buddhist art and architecture, read in-depth articles, practice meditation techniques—and there is even a page for kids. The site's graphics are clean and quick, too.

JCN (Jewish Communication Network)
www.jcn18.com

With an interactive Torah study, daily feature stories and news, an online mall, Jewish personals, and an excellent site review page to locate other Jewish Web sites, JCN is a one-stop online hub on the Web for Judaism.

Spirit-WWW
www.spiritweb.org

In addition to channeling, you can explore new and modern religious concepts in detail, including altered states of consciousness, reincarnation, yoga, and theosophy, among others. The site also includes an image gallery with fifteen different categories of images, from "animals" to "vedic deity."

Searching the Web

Yahoo!
www.yahoo.com

At some point, you'll want to find something on the Web that isn't listed in this book and that you won't find by following a link from another page. That's when you'll turn to a directory or search page to find things on the Web. Probably the best known of these is Yahoo!. Yahoo! isn't the biggest, but it is one of the best. Yahoo! has a huge directory-style list of categories with hundreds of thousands of Web sites listed. If you are looking for a Web site about a certain topic, this is a great place to start. To use Yahoo!, just click a link for one of the category topics, and this will open a page with a list of subcategories and Web pages for that topic.

Excite

www.excite.com

While Yahoo! is based mainly on a directory of sites that are handpicked and entered into categories, Excite is a huge database of sites that you can search. Excite has an automated program that visits Web pages and catalogues them into a database. When you search Excite, it may return a list of hundreds or even thousands of sites that match your topic.

Lycos

www.lycos.com

Lycos is another site that runs of a huge (tens of millions) database of Web pages that it has automatically searched and indexed. Type in what you want to look for and click **Search**. All of the sites like Lycos and Excite return long lists of possibly matching sites with the most likely matches first.

HotBot

www.hotbot.com

There are dozens of these sites that act as databases of Web sites. Everyone who uses the Web a lot has a personal favorite. HotBot is mine. I make a living knowing about the Internet and the Web, and this site is always helpful to me when I need to find something.

SuperSeek

www.mcp.com/superseek/index.cgi

With so many search sites on the Web, you may wish there were just one place you could go to search them all. In fact, there are several of them including SuperSeek. Type what you want to find at the SuperSeek site, and it searches several other search sites for you and returns results from all of them.

Shopping

America's Choice Mall

www.choicemall.com/indexnl.html

America's Choice Mall is an exciting place to shop with over 1,300 stores and services to choose from. If you're shopping for a doctor or dentist, or if you're shopping for clothes, this is a good place to start. You can begin your search by region at the 60 regional malls. For your convenience, the stores are also listed by category. Other great features of this site include customer contests, shopping sprees, and even reviews for the latest movies. If you're looking to buy or sell a home, you can even do a bit of real estate shopping at this site. This mall is America's choice because of its variety of offerings and the built-in convenience for your benefit.

World Shopping Directory

worldshopping.com/director.html

Why limit yourself to shopping at the local malls, or even to shopping in the continental United States? Shop online and you can shop the world. The World Shopping Directory can take you virtually anywhere at any time, and you never have to leave the house.

Access Market Square

www.icw.com/ams.html

Access Market Square is great place for your every shopping need from clothes, jewelry, and specialty products to audio/video, toys, and finance. This site has claimed more than nine awards as a top shopping site. Be sure to check out the World Trade Center classifieds and business opportunities while you're visiting.

The Internet Mall

www.internet-mall.com/

This is truly the world's largest shopping mall with over 27,000 stores. Choose from items such as books and media, travel, household items, personal services, professional services, and much more.

The All-Internet Shopping Directory
www.all-internet.com/

If you're shopping for something, but nothing in particular, the All-Internet Shopping Directory is a good place to begin your journey. This directory has connections to anything and everything you're looking for with its extensive database search tools.

Software

Download.com
www.download.com

The Internet is home to thousands of pieces of software than you can download and use for free. Some, you try and pay for if you keep (shareware). Others are free for as long as you use them (freeware). Download.com is one of the biggest directories of downloadable software on the Web. If you want to look for software for almost any use, this is the place to start. Software is sorted by application category and by operating system which makes it very easy to find the software you need. The site also includes reviews and ratings as well as lists of the most frequently downloaded programs.

Microsoft
www.microsoft.com

Come to this site to get the latest news about any Microsoft software product. You can download many free products including the Internet Explorer Web browser and download updates and extras for other popular programs like the Microsoft Office suite of applications and Windows.

Netscape
home.netscape.com

This is the home of the Netscape Web browser, which made this company famous in record time. Read about their other products and services here. You can buy copies of their software online or download them for a free trial.

Stroud's Consummate Winsock Apps
cws.internet.com

This is another site listing hundreds of pieces of software that you can download. This site specializes in software for use with the Internet such as browsers, plug-ins, and add-ons. Stroud has been reviewing Internet software as long as anyone and this is considered to be one of the best lists around.

Symantec
www.symantec.com

Symantec is the company that makes the popular Norton Antivirus software. Stop by their site to download monthly updates for your virus definitions to keep your PC virus-free. You'll also want to read about their Norton Secret Stuff program for keeping e-mail private and download it for free.

Space

NASA (National Aeronautics and Space Administration)
www.nasa.gov

You shouldn't be too surprised that the world's oldest and largest active space agency has not only a Web site but a comprehensive one at that, possibly the most comprehensive site on the Web. The site has almost as many links as the night sky has stars, including an immense number of downloadable movies, images, and sounds. All of NASA's latest missions are updated daily, including countdowns to shuttle launchings, and their well-honed site design will have you light-clicking your way through as you explore areas like Aeronautics, Space Science, Human Space Flight, and Education.

Hubble Space Telescope
www.stsci.edu

In addition to the latest Hubble Telescope pictures, you can track the current position of the telescope, view live video from its video components, and explore highly technical as well as more viewer-friendly research about Hubble and how it works.

The Nine Planets
seds.lpl.arizona.edu/nineplanets/nineplanets/nineplanets.html

Currently mirrored on 37 different sites in over 30 countries, The Nine Planets guides you through the history, mythology, and science behind each of the planets and moons in our solar system. Images and comprehensive technical data download quickly so you won't have to wait. Many of the pages have sounds, movies, and a complete set of links to related information.

The Planetary Society
planetary.org

Become a voluntary space explorer, read daily headlines, find out about conferences, sign up for workshops, and keep up with the Mars Pathfinder spacecraft mission. Founded in 1980 by Doctors Carl Sagan, Bruce Murray, and Louis Friedman. This site focuses on the exploration of our solar system and the search for extraterrestrial life.

The Deep Space Network
deepspace1.jpl.nasa.gov/dsn/

Managed and operated for NASA by the Jet Propulsion Laboratory, this site will take you to the heart of interplanetary spacecraft missions, such as the Galileo mission to Jupiter and its moons and the Cassini mission to Saturn and its moon Titan. The DSN page supports the international network of antennas that makes it all possible.

Sports News

ESPN SportsZone
epsn.sportszone.com

Fans of all sports will want to make "The Zone" one of their first bookmarks. If you are looking to catch up and keep up on all the scores, they've got it with a constantly updated scoreboard with all the scores of games and events in progress. You can even put it on your desktop so that you don't have to keep their Web page open. But this site is about more than just scores. All the sports news, all the inside scoop, interviews with players and coaches, it's all here. But I don't need to tell you that. If you watch ESPN on TV, you know they are the leader in television sports and their Web site is *en fuego,* too!

The Sporting News

www.sportingnews.com

The Sporting News is the definitive sports paper for serious sports fans. The site offers a lot of the same types of content as ESPN, but all with a different flavor. So if you just can't get enough sports, or prefer a different style, check out the Sporting News.

CBS SportsLine

cbs.sportsline.com

CBS Sports on both television and radio hosts some of the premier sporting events in the world, including the NCAA Men's Basketball Championships. Their Web site draws from their long-time experience with some of the Web broadcasters and reporters in the game to bring you scores, stories, fantasy sports leagues, and more.

Sports Illustrated

www.cnnsi.com/

Yes, they have some shots from the swimsuit issue here, but that's not what this site is about. When you are looking for a site that goes beyond the headlines and scores, SI Online is a great choice. The in-depth style of the magazine is preserved in this first class online site.

Audio Net Sports Guide

www.audionet.com/sports

With the right additional software installed, you can listen to almost any major sporting event on your PC from the links at this site. It no longer matters that your favorite team's games don't make it to where you live; you can bring them home live with AudioNet.

Stock Quotes

The Nasdaq Stock Market Home Page

www.nasdaq.com

Nasdaq Web site lets you research and track not only the over-the-counter stocks that are traded on the Nasdaq exchange, but also stocks traded on the

637

New York and American exchanges. You can search for up to 10 separate stocks or mutual funds to gauge their daily performance. The Nasdaq 100's performance is updated constantly during the day so you can see the market's performance at a glance.

PC Quote Online

www.pcquote.com

PC Quote is one of the few sites that displays all the major market indices at a glance and with a click of your mouse button you can watch their progress through a trading day. If you're an Office 97 user, you can use PC Quotes modules built into Excel 97 to track up to 20 different stocks.

The American Stock Exchange

www.amex.com

While not as comprehensive as some of the other stock quote sites, The American Stock Exchange offers a useful Dictionary of Financial Risk Management. This is an invaluable resource, provides essential tips for anyone trading securities whether they be a bull or a bear. The site also provides charts tracking the exchange's performance, offers up-to-the-minute financial news, and offers career options for professional traders.

NETworth Quote Server

quotes.quicken.com/investments/quotes

A service offered though Quicken FN, the NETWorth quote server works with your Quicken software to track investments and initiate trades. For those of you without a copy of Quicken, the site offers a quick look into your stocks' performance as well as some handy information about investment basics and other resources to help you make informed investment decisions.

CNNfn-Quote Search Service

cnnfn.com/markets/quotes.html

Drawing on the vast resources of CNN, the CNNfn Stock Quote service offers instant quotes of any stock, mutual, or money market fund regardless of on which exchange they're traded. After you've received your quotes, click the CNNfn logo to get the latest in business news.

Taxes

The IRS

www.irs.ustreas.gov

This is a site you have to see to believe. The same folks who give us fun literature like the 1040 and Schedule C can't be responsible for a truly great Web site, right? But they are. Here, the IRS has shed its stodgy pain-inflicting image and built a Web site that actually helps taxpayers. There are tax tips and hints from the real masters themselves, and all of the current year's forms online in a form you can download and print for use. You'll need to install the free Adobe Acrobat Plug-in for your Web browser to use any of these. But beyond that, the site is actually fun, well-presented, and has a sense of humor. This should be everyone's first stop on the Web.

SecureTax

www.securetax.com

This site takes the concept of tax software one step further by making it all Web-based and online. You fill out all of your tax forms online, check them, and then if you want to submit the return, pay a small fee and submit it. I used it this year and it was fast, accurate, and cheaper than any tax software I've seen.

1040.com

www.1040.com

You'll want to bookmark this site if for no other reason than their links to all of the state tax forms and instructions online. In addition, there is a good variety of tax help and advice.

Tax Help Online

www.taxhelponline.com

When it comes to tax tips and advice, my philosophy is that the more you can find out, the better off you are. So here's another site with a good collection of tips and advice for preparing your return, avoiding problems, and paying as little as is legal.

TaxWeb

www.taxweb.com

If you still haven't found enough tax help, TaxWeb is one more good place to look. And from there, they have a list of links to other sites with even more tax help for federal and state taxes. If the answer to your tax questions exists, you'll find it at one of these sites.

Teaching

Teachnet

www.teachnet.com

This is a site with lots of class. The lesson plans and ideas in Art, Music, Language Arts, Math, Science, Social Studies, Physical Education, and even the Internet itself are well worth the field trip. But there's much more to learn. Gain ideas on how to fill up five minutes of empty classroom time, get help with decorating your classroom, and find techniques for better class organization and management. An active forum for teachers will keep you informed.

PedagoNet

www.pedagonet.com

PedagoNet gives you instant access to learning resource materials in over fifty subjects—and you can post your own to share with other teachers. The site also has active chat and discussion areas.

Teachers.net

www.teachers.net

Like over 14,000 other teachers before you, you can create your own Web page with The Teachers.Net Home page Maker, in addition to a chatboard, lesson exchange board, and a fully functioning reference desk which has online links to dictionaries, maps, calculators, encyclopedias, and more.

NSTA (National Science Teachers Association)

www.nsta.org/scistore

The best in science education materials (over 300 products reviewed according to NSTA standards) are available to you through the Science Store for grades

K-6, 5-9, and 9-College. Titles are indexed by subject, alphabetically, and you can search for a specific product.

Math Forum Elementary Teachers' Place
forum.swarthmore.edu/teachers/elem

For grade school teachers, this site has brainteasers, math problems, and math projects to help you keep the subject exciting (and not so hard), as well as a new math problem every week. You can also browse a special career area (in case those puzzles and projects don't do the trick), which includes links to workshops, discussion groups, publications, and professional organizations.

TV Networks

NBC.com
www.nbc.com

NBC.com is a "Must-See-TV" Web site rich in graphics yet surprisingly easy to download. The site contains direct links to MSNBC Online News and NBC Sports sites, a home page layout similar to a magazine cover with featured links, and a directory of important links within the site, such as online programs with information about the show and excerpts. You can shop, search, send e-mail, check out a site map, and even chat. NBC.com is effective in using their brand recognition to attract your attention by using recognizable marketing slogans (such as "must-see TV"), the network mascot—the NBC peacock— and music also used in their television network promos.

ABC
www.abc.com

The ABC site provides more comprehensive coverage of their programming, focusing on the prime-time lineup, spotlighting individual programs, and providing new season previews. The home page changes daily, featuring a specific show which airs that particular day. The site also includes a gallery of candid photos of network celebrities.

FOX
www.fox.com

Fox site gives you instant access to updates of special programming, new video releases, movies, television listings, and history. The most impressive part of the site is Fox Interactive, which uses Shockwave to take you on an interactive adventure and show you excerpts of your favorite episodes.

CBS
www.cbs.com

CBS presents an eye-catching directory on its home page, which makes it easy for you to find updates of CBS News, CBS Sports, The CBS Store, Daytime, CBS Kids, Specials, Primetime, and the popular program, *The Lateshow with David Letterman*, and a featured in-depth news report (*The Class of 2000*). You can use the RealAudio Player to hear the CBS theme, catch movie reviews, and go to the David Letterman link to see famous Top Ten Lists.

PBS
www.pbs.com

The PBS site will take you on electronic field trips and help you find teacher connections. You can also find instructional television, adult learning, and a business channel. Since PBS is well-known for its excellent children's programming, you won't be surprised to see the several links dedicated to its most popular children's shows, such as Sesame Street, Mr. Rogers, and Shining Time Station.

UFOs

SETI Institute
www.seti-inst.edu

Are we alone in the universe? The SETI (Search for Extraterrestrial Intelligence) Institute's Web site wants to help you answer that question with in-depth articles and details on the existence (or lack thereof) of extraterrestrial life, up-to-the-minute reports of signals from Pioneer 6, Pioneer 10, and Voyager 2 spacecraft, and an online version of the SETI Newsletter.

Ufomind
www.ufomind.com

Greatly evolved from its beginnings a couple of years ago as the *The Desert Rat*, this site is one of the most comprehensive and critical sources of UFO information on the Web, including definitive coverage of Area 51 that won't leave you stranded in the New Mexico desert. You'll click for days just to get through the site's Master UFO Index, an exhaustive link structure leading to practically every UFO site on the Web with over 1,896 links and 322 people.

The Enterprise Mission
www.enterprisemission.com

UFO researcher Richard Hoagland's brainchild, The Enterprise Mission, contains a wealth of information into NASA's official (and unofficial) investigations (and denials) of the UFO phenomenon. You can study the face on Mars, the mystery of Europa, and moon artifacts, as well as the latest NASA and UFO conspiracy theory in detail.

Sightings
www.scifi.com/sightings/

Post your own paranormal experiences (and read others), listen to Sightings on the Radio six nights a week via RealAudio, and follow the show itself (from the SciFi Channel) with weekly news about UFO's, ghosts, reincarnation, and everything eerie.

Weather

Intellicast
www.intellicast.com

The Web is a great place to get all kinds of weather and meteorological information, and one of the best sites around is Intellicast. Intellicast is easy to navigate and has clear maps that are updated frequently from a variety of satellites, seismographs, and Doppler radar data. More adventuresome, scientific types looking for hard-core meteorological data should check out the Space Science and Engineering Center listed on the following page. Intellicast enables you to zoom in on any part of the world to get detailed current weather conditions and anticipated low and high temperatures. Want more? Check out where the jetstream is, get a surface analysis, or get a 24- to 48-hour forecast. If you're a real weather buff, check out the Dr. Dewpoint section, which has articles on a variety of topics from summaries of past weather patterns to the effects of sunspots on global temperatures.

The Weather Channel
www.weather.com

The Weather Channel (cable television channel) sponsors this Web site. It also has clear, accessible weather maps and forecasts, but the thing that separates it from the rest is that travelers can check to see if their flights are delayed anywhere due to weather.

Space Science and Engineering Center
www.ssec.wisc.edu

The University of Wisconsin at Madison sponsors this site, and it's not for the weak of heart. If you're tired of pretty pictures and want preciptable water vapor levels, lifting indexes, cloud top pressure, and need to distinguish among temperature and dewpoint temperature, and sea surface temperature, look here.

Weather Imagery and Data
urbanite.com/web/imagery/home.htm

Like many of the weather Web sites, Weather Imagery and Data gives you a quick and easy snapshot of temperatures and weather around the world. What sets this site apart is that it enables you to check current tornado and severe thunderstorm warnings, and view recent seismological data.

The Weather Shops
www.intellicast.com/wxshops

Want to understand more about weather or try your hand at forecasting? The Weather Shops has everything you need, from books and videos, to all kinds of instruments and gauges for measuring weather.

Weddings

Island Weddings
www.rsabbs.com/islandweddings

Paradise Island, Disney World, Barbados, and Puerto Rico are a few places that make your mouth water and your heart melt when you think of beginning your happy wedding bliss there. Take a trip with *In the Mood to Cruise* and check out the beautiful locations you could have your special day. Your every wish could come true if you just believe and dare to venture into the unknown and never-before imaginable. Don't be afraid to leap into adventure, romance, and ever-lasting memories for your wedding endeavor. You should enjoy your day and be able to cherish it for a lifetime. *In the Mood to Cruise* can help you get there with careful planning and consulting expertise. Give them a try and you could be one of the couples you see in these pictures.

Wedding Tips
www.weddingtips.com/wttips.html

If you need assistance with your wedding plans, Wedding Tips Online is a great place to start your search. They provide a wealth of resources from photography, to entertainment, to wedding and reception sites, to beauty tips. Don't miss out.

Wedding Experts
www.weddingexperts.com

The Wedding Experts National Bridal Service can provide for your every need. Don't waste any time getting to them for bridal fashions, jewelry, accessories, and more. While you're there, take time to listen to the music you'll soon be marching to down the aisle.

Bride's Do-It-Yourself Wedding Planners
www.horncreek.com/winmark

You can plan your own wedding and save yourself a great deal of money. I planned my own wedding and established my own budget for what I wanted to spend and how to spend it. I came out $7,000.00 cheaper than many of my friends. Don't be shy; see what this site has to offer.

Nationwide Services

www.bridalnet.com/states/nation_wide.htm

Don't feel limited in any way when you can take advantage of these Nationwide wedding services. Your wedding plans are at your fingertips at the click of a button.

Wine

Wine Spectator

www.winespectator.com

Wine Spectator magazine sponsors this extensive Web site devoted to all aspects making and enjoying wine. The Web site is updated daily—in the Daily Report section you'll find a featured wine, news of the wine industry, a thought-provoking question or short editorial, and current stock updates. The Wine Library contains articles from *Wine Spectator* dating back to the beginning of 1994, and an excellent introduction to buying, storing, serving, and enjoying all types of wine. In the Wine Forums, you can participate in scheduled chats with industry experts and post topics for discussion. Traveling soon or looking for a restaurant near you that serves good wine? Check out the Travel and Dining sections. The Events section lists wine tastings, exhibits, and auctions around the world.

UC Davis Department of Viticulture and Enology

wineserver.ucdavis.edu/VEN5b.HTML

The University of California-Davis has the best program in the U.S. for learning the art of making wine. The information on this Web site will give you a great start down the road toward making your own drinkable table wine.

World Wine Web

www.winevin.com

The World Wine Web site is a comprehensive wine encyclopedia that contains information about all the areas around the world that make wine. You get maps of the countries, lists of the varieties or appellations they produce, the types of grapes they use, and links to wineries in the area.

Winebid.com
www.winebid.com

If you can't travel to New York, California, or France at the drop of a hat but still want to have a shot at obtaining a premium wine, then check out Winebid.com. They have monthly auctions featuring a variety of fine wines.

Virtual Vineyards
www.virtualvineyard.com

Virtual Vineyards was one of the first wine stores on the Web, and it has grown substantially in the last few years. Not only do they carry a wide selection of wines, but they also have books, glasses, bottle openers, and every other accessory you need.

Video Games

VideoGameSpot
www.videogamespot.com

If there's one place on the Web to get the latest scoop on the latest video game releases it's VideoGameSpot. An offshoot of the Ziff-Davis' popular GameSpot site, VideoGameSpot offers the diehard platform gamer with news, tips, tricks, and previews for games available on the popular video game platforms including Sony PlayStation and Nintendo64.

BradyGAMES Strategy Guides
www.bradygames.com

The home page of one of the leading publishers of video and computer game strategy guides offers more than just an advertisement for their books. At the *BradyGAMES* Web site, gamers can find an extensive library of cheat codes for all video game platforms. Oh, and if you see something you like, you can even buy one of their books at their online bookstore.

Next Generation
www.next-generation.com

If you still crave more video game news after visiting VideoGameSpot, point your browser to the online version of *Next Generation* Magazine. Each day, Next

Generation has the latest game industry news, plenty of videoclips to see what's coming up, and links to *Next Generation*'s sister magazines. There's plenty here to keep the most ardent gamer happy.

Playstation Home Page
www.playstation.com

Sony's page in support of their popular PlayStation video game system is more than just a billboard for their product. Here, you can get information about existing and upcoming games and get codes to help you past some of those rough spots. There's also detailed information about their NetYaroze program that will let you create your own PlayStation games.

Nintendo Power Source
www.nintendo.com

Named for their magazine, Nintendo's home page is home to Mario, Luigi, Donkey Kong, and everything you want to know about games for the classic Super Nintendo Entertainment System and the increasingly popular Nintendo64. You'll find tips to popular games, like Super Mario 64 and preview of upcoming Nintendo offerings.

Index

Q

Que Web site, 581
Question dialog box, 106
Quick Link dialog box
(Internet Explorer 3), 166
Quick Links bar, 161, 279
hiding/displaying, 277
Web pages' buttons,
adding, 166-167, 279
Quit command (File menu),
41

R

RADIO attribute, 512-514
radio buttons, 511-514
RE: box, 338
Read Mail icon, 332
Read New Mail command
(Mail menu), 335
Read Outgoing FlashMail
command (Mail menu), 323
Read tab, 305
reading
messages, 372
with America Online,
387-388
offline, 393-394, 423
in Netscape Collabra,
427-428
in Outlook Express
News, 423-427
postings offline,
391-394
newsgroups Messages in
Netscape Collabra,
402-406
newsgroups Messages in
Outlook Express News,
406-409
receiving files in
newsgroups, 415
Receiving tab, 169-170
Refresh button, 138
Register me now! button, 263
registration number
(America Online), 58

relative URLS, 473
Reload button, 112, 138
reloading Web browsers
pages, 138
Remodeling Online Web
site, 607
Remove button, 409
removing
ActiveX controls, 218-219
columns, 409
newsgroups, 429-430
Netscape Collabra, 398
Outlook Express News,
400-401
Rename button, 279
renaming shortcuts, 166
replies, posting, 372-373
Reply button,
292, 328, 337, 411-412
Reply to All button, 337
Reply to Author button,
333, 412
Reply to Group button, 411
replying
Messages, 410-412
with e-mail, 411-412
newsgroups Messages,
410-411
to messages in America
Online, 389
resource information
My Computer, 186
Windows Explorer, 186
Restart command (Special
menu), 37-38
Restarting Windows dialog
box, 106
Restore button, 243, 276
Review dialog box, 51
Rich Text Format, *see* RTF,
536
Roll button, 242
Room Name text box, 267
ROWSPAN attribute,
483-484
RTF (Rich Text Format), 536
converting to HTML, 536

RTFTOHTML shareware,
536
Run command (File menu),
248
Run command (Start menu),
51, 248
Run dialog box, 50-51, 248
running
Internet Explorer 4
applications, 100
Netscape Communicator
the first time, 106-107

S

sampling ISPs, 20
sarcasm, 74
Sausage Software (HotDog),
540
Save As command (File
menu), 196
Save As command (shortcut
menu), 257
Save As dialog box,
118, 196, 222, 257, 416
Save As Type drop-down
list, 196
Save Attachment As dialog
box, 364
Save Attachments command
(File menu), 364
Save button, 118, 196, 222
Save dialog box, 339
Save Frame command (File
menu), 127
Save Link As command
(context menu), 196
saving
attached files, 363-365
in Outlook Express, 364
documents' links, 196
files, 133
Web pages, 195-197
Schedule FlashSessions
dialog box, 393
Schedule tab, 170

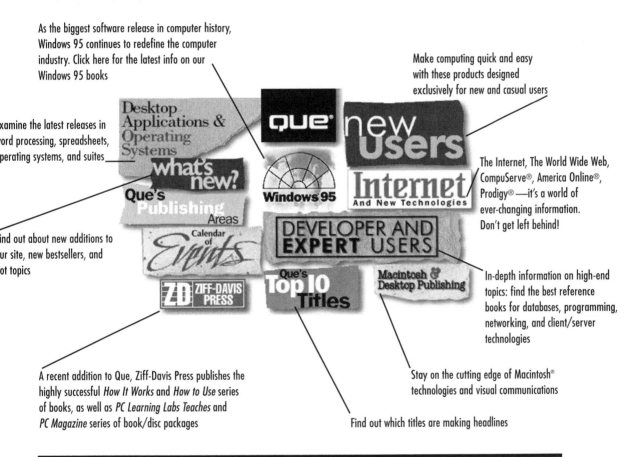

Complete and Return This Card
for a *FREE* Computer Book Catalog

Thank you for purchasing this book! You have purchased a superior computer book written expressly for your needs. To continue to provide the kind of up-to-date, pertinent coverage you've come to expect from us, we need to hear from you. Please take a minute to complete and return this self-addressed, postage-paid form. In return, we'll send you a free catalog of all our computer books on topics ranging from word processing to programming and the Internet.

Mr. ☐   Mrs. ☐   Ms. ☐   Dr. ☐

Name (first) [   ]   (M.I.) [ ]   (last) [   ]

Address [   ]

[   ]

City [   ]   State [ ]   Zip [   ]

Phone [   ]   Fax [   ]

Company Name [   ]

E-mail address [   ]

1. Please check at least three (3) influencing factors for purchasing this book.

Front or back cover information on book .... ☐
Special approach to the content .... ☐
Completeness of content .... ☐
Author's reputation .... ☐
Publisher's reputation .... ☐
Book cover design or layout .... ☐
Index or table of contents of book .... ☐
Price of book .... ☐
Special effects, graphics, illustrations .... ☐
Other (Please specify): _____ ☐

2. How did you first learn about this book?

Saw in Macmillan Computer Publishing catalog .... ☐
Recommended by store personnel .... ☐
Saw the book on bookshelf at store .... ☐
Recommended by a friend .... ☐
Received advertisement in the mail .... ☐
Saw an advertisement in: _____ ☐
Read book review in: _____ ☐
Other (Please specify): _____ ☐

3. How many computer books have you purchased in the last six months?

This book only .... ☐   3 to 5 books .... ☐
2 books .... ☐   More than 5 .... ☐

4. Where did you purchase this book?

Bookstore .... ☐
Computer Store .... ☐
Consumer Electronics Store .... ☐
Department Store .... ☐
Office Club .... ☐
Warehouse Club .... ☐
Mail Order .... ☐
Direct from Publisher .... ☐
Internet site .... ☐
Other (Please specify): _____ ☐

5. How long have you been using a computer?

☐ Less than 6 months   ☐ 6 months to a year
☐ 1 to 3 years   ☐ More than 3 years

6. What is your level of experience with personal computers and with the subject of this book?

	With PCs	With subject of book
New	☐	☐
Casual	☐	☐
Accomplished	☐	☐
Expert	☐	☐

Source Code ISBN: 0-7897-1338-1

7. Which of the following best describes your job title?

Administrative Assistant .... ☐
Coordinator .... ☐
Manager/Supervisor .... ☐
Director .... ☐
Vice President .... ☐
President/CEO/COO .... ☐
Lawyer/Doctor/Medical Professional .... ☐
Teacher/Educator/Trainer .... ☐
Engineer/Technician .... ☐
Consultant .... ☐
Not employed/Student/Retired .... ☐
Other (Please specify): _____ ☐

8. Which of the following best describes the area of the company your job title falls under?

Accounting .... ☐
Engineering .... ☐
Manufacturing .... ☐
Operations .... ☐
Marketing .... ☐
Sales .... ☐
Other (Please specify): _____ ☐

Comments: _____
_____
_____

9. What is your age?

Under 20 .... ☐
21-29 .... ☐
30-39 .... ☐
40-49 .... ☐
50-59 .... ☐
60-over .... ☐

10. Are you:

Male .... ☐
Female .... ☐

11. Which computer publications do you read regularly? (Please list)

_____
_____
_____
_____
_____
_____
_____
_____
_____

Fold here and scotch-tape to mail

MACMILLAN COMPUTER PUBLISHING USA
A VIACOM COMPANY

Technical **Support:**

If you need assistance with the information in this book or with a CD/Disk accompanying the book, please access the Knowledge Base on our Web site at **http://www.superlibrary.com/general/support**. Our most Frequently Asked Questions are answered there. If you do not find the answer to your questions on our Web site, you may contact Macmillan Technical Support **(317) 581-3833** or e-mail us at **support@mcp.com**.